MW00534002

HIMALAYAN SOUND REVELATIONS

'Frank Perry's HIMALAYAN SOUND REVELATIONS
is a masterpiece of writing about the nature and power of pure
sound as encoded into the consciously constructed instruments
of the East. No other book in the field of working with sound for
healing and spiritual development is as knowledgable, penetrating
and comprehensive as this great tome. Contained within these
pages is far, far more than an exploration of every aspect of
singing bowls, instruments that Perry literally knows inside out
through his enormous collection and varied use over many years
of practice. Each chapter is an in-depth study of what the bowls
have to offer in relation to ancient symbolism, *yin/yang* shapes,
astrology, chakras, mantra, *nada yoga*, overtones. cymatics (wave
fields), planets and musical temperament.
Along the way we are given much knowledge of these topics in
and of themselves – for example, the use of the voice. The book
balances perfectly the historical, theoretical, spiritual and practical
sides of these profound instruments and their metals. Very
helpful in absorbing Perry's wisdom are the many illustrations,
photographs, tables and diagrams. What especially sets it apart is
how Perry places them into a spiritual, historical context such as
no other text has done and thus makes the bowls (and bells) living,
breathing entities.
The tome is scholarly but not in an academic sense. It is simply
thorough and the writing is clear, direct and substantial without
unnecessary digressions. Thus HIMALAYAN SOUND REVELATIONS
will appeal both to those who wish to make practical use of
singing bowls (choosing them, playing them properly and even
caring for them) and those who would like to understand the
historical context of the bowls and their role in healing and
spirituality. HIMALAYAN SOUND REVELATIONS is truly a universal
work of a music master. It is bound to become a classic and
belongs on the shelf of every serious student of Eastern music,
meditation and spirituality.

*James D'Angelo, author of THE HEALING POWER OF THE HUMAN
VOICE and SEED SOUNDS FOR TUNING THE CHAKRAS*

Himalayan
Sound Revelations

FRANK PERRY

Including Cymatic Photography by John Stuart Reid

Polair
Publishing

Polair Publishing : London
www.polairpublishing.co.uk

First published January 2014

British Library Cataloguing-in-Publication Data
A catalogue record of this book is
available from the British Library

ISBN 978-1-905398-31-7

Text © Frank Perry, 2013
Pictures are copyright the photographer, where shown beside the
photograph; that on the title page is by Grant David Read. For
acknowledgment of quotations, see pp. 8-10
Main cover picture: Elizabeth Jardine

Text set in 11.5 on 14.5 pt Monotype Sabon
Printed and bound by the Halstan Printing Group,
Amersham, Buckinghamshire

Contents

ACKNOWLEDGMENTS

My immediate thanks to Colum Hayward at Polair Publishing (and most especially for his infinite patience) and to 'Frontiers' (Albi & David), to 'World on Wheels' (Hazel & Mike), and to John Mead, Alain Presencer, and Peter Bearacroft, Ryan Sarnataro, Adam Rankin, Rose Perry, Elizabeth Jardine, Lawrence Ball, and John Stuart Reid.

Thanks too to the many who have assisted and supported me along my path: Frank E. Perry II, Christine Perry, Joan Hodgson, Minesta & Brother Faithful, Jeremy Hayward, Ylana Hayward, Melodicium, Werner & Elsi Achermann, Joan Fraser, Oliver Nares, Richard Elen, 'Jack' Samuels, Misha Norland, Ian Dale, Chippewa & Poplar, Teresa Mooney, David Devenney, Alan Bannister, James D'Angelo, David & Jenny Kossoff, David & Fred Murrell, Jean & Emilio Perni, Velta Snikere Wilson, Michael Deason-Barrow ... and to all my family of spirit friends, especially Whitefeather, Golden Hawk, White Eagle, Brother Francis, Dr Jacques, Bozambo, Golden Bear, Lom Phook Trenglam, Ben Aschid, Chang Loo, White Bear, White Cloud, Swagigli, Kalimba, Chibiabos, Swami Saraswatyananda, Gun Luo Chi, and Zhiangu.

Grateful thanks to the photographers whose copyright work appears in this volume by permission: Jill Furmanovsky, Grant David Read, Rose Perry, Oliver Nares, Elizabeth Jardine, Vlasta Merk, John Stuart Reid, Raphael Perry and Esther James.

PERMISSIONS AND CREDITS

The author is grateful to the following for the use of copyright material.
– to Norma Levine for permission to use the quotation on pp. 59-60, from BLESSING POWER OF THE BUDDHAS: SACRED OBJECTS, SECRET LANDS, published by Vajra Publications (2nd edn, 2008, pp. 100-1), © copyright, Norma Levine
– to the Divine Life Trust Society, Uttarakhand, India, for quotations from KUNDALINI YOGA by Swami Sivananda, © 1935, 2011 and from MUSIC AS YOGA, © Divine Life Trust Society, 1956, 2007
– to the Yog Niketan Trust for quotation from SCIENCE OF DIVINE SOUND by Swami Yogeshwarand Saraswati ji Maharaj, © copyright, Yog Niketan Trust, 1984

– to John Stuart Reid, for quotation of two paragraphs, one abbreviated, from EGYPTIAN SONICS, copyright © Sonic Age, Ltd., © copyright, J. S. Reid, Ltd., 2001

– to Dharma Publishing, for quotation from p. 38 of PSYCHO-COSMIC SYMBOLISM OF THE BUDDHIST STUPA, by Lama Angarika Govinda, copyright © 1976

– to Shambhala Publications for permission to quote from TANTRA: THE PATH OF ECSTASY, by Georg Feuerstein, © copyright 1998 Georg Feuerstein. Reprinted by arrangement with The Permissions Company, Inc., on behalf of Shambhala Publications, Inc., Boston, www.shambhala.com

– to the Austrian Academy of Sciences, for permission to quote from John Vincent Bellezza, ZHANG ZHUNG: FOUNDATIONS OF CIVILIZATION IN TIBET: A HISTORICAL AND ETHNOARCHAEOLOGICAL STUDY OF THE MONUMENTS, ROCK ART, TEXTS AND ORAL TRADITION OF THE ANCIENT TIBETAN UPLAND. Beiträge zur Kultur- und Geistesgeschichte Asien 61, Denkschriften der philosophisch-historischen Klasse 368. Band, Wien, 2008

– to Indiana University Press for permission to quote from WHERE RIVERS AND MOUNTAINS SING: SOUND, MUSIC, AND NOMADISM IN TUVA AND BEYOND, Theodore Levine with Valentina Suzukei, copyright © 2006 Indiana University Press

– to Orchid Press, Hong Kong, for permission to quote the extract from TIBET'S ANCIENT RELIGION: BON by Christoph Baumer; © 2002 Orchid Press, Bangkok, and © copyright, Christoph Baumer, 2002

– to Daphne McCree, daughter of the author, for permission to quote from BELLS AND MAN, by Percival Price, published by Oxford University Press, 1983, and © copyright, the estate of Percival Price.

– to the Philosophical Research Society, for permission to quote from the article 'Ritual Instruments of Northern Buddhism' by Manly P. Hall, in volume 30, no. 4 of the *Philosophical Research Society Journal* (Spring 1971), and © copyright, Philosophical Research Society, 1971

– to Dirk Gillabel, for permission to quote from his translation of the book JOSKA SOOS, IK GENEES NIET, IK HERSTEL DE HARMONIE, by Robert Hartzman, published by Karnak, Amsterdam, and © copyright 1985, available on his website, http://www.soulguidance.com/houseofthesun

– to Rain Gray and Bodhisattva Trading Co., 10573 W Pico Blvd PMB 135 Los Angeles C.A. 90064, for permission to quote from the booklet TIBETAN SINGING BOWL HISTORY: AN INTERVIEW WITH LAMA LOBSANG LECHE, now available only at www.Bodhisattva.com/singing_bowl_history.htm and © copyright, Rain Gray

– to Mitch Nur, for permission to use information gained in conversation and in the interview granted with *Dimensions Magazine* in 1999

– to Pauline Oliveros, for quotation from DEEP LISTENING: A COMPOSER'S SOUND PRACTICE, published by Deep Listening Publications, 2005, and copyright, Pauline Oliveros, 2005

– to the Nicholas Roerich Museum in New York, for permission to quote from various writings by Nicholas Roerich including THE TEACHINGS OF AGNI YOGA, and to reproduce the Roerich painting in the colour supplement and the black and white one on p. 351.

- to Baba Bhagavandas Publication Trust, available via contact@babatrust.org (email), http://www.ashramstore.com/ (outlet) and www.anandaashram.org/ (link), for permision to quote from NADA YOGA: THE SCIENCE, PSYCHOLOGY AND PHILOSOPHY OF ANAHATA NADA YOGA, by Shri Brahmananda Sarasvati (Ramamurti S. Mishra, M.D.). Copyright © 2007 by Baba Bhagavandas Publication Trust, 13 Sapphire Road, Monroe, NY 10950 USA. Originally published 1984, Second Edition 1989, revised & enlarged

- to White Eagle Publishing Trust, for permission to quote from the published books of White Eagle and talks reprinted in the White Eagle magazine, *Stella Polaris*, © Copyright, the White Eagle Publishing Trust. White Eagle books are listed in Recommended Reading

- Prosveta U.K. The Doves Nest, Duddleswell, Uckfield, East Sussex. TN22 3JJ, for permission to quote from the works of Omraam Mikhail Aïvanhov © Editions Prosveta

– to World Scientific Publishing Co. Pte Ltd, for permission to reproduce the article 'Chinese Qing on p. 307 and a short extract on p. 186 from SCIENCE OF PERCUSSION INSTRUMENTS by Thomas D. Rossing, © copyright, World Scientific, 2001

- Soundworld Publishers, 10 Baddow Road, Chelmsford CM2 0DG, for permission to reproduce a diagram from LES SCULPTURES SONORES: THE SOUND SCULPTURES OF BERNARD AND FRANCOIS BASCHET

METRICAL CONVERSIONS

Measurements for bowls are given in the text in inches. 1 inch is 2.54 centimetres, so as a general guide, a 6-inch bowl is appproximately 15 cm, an 8-inch bowl is 20 cm, and a 10-inch bowl is 25 cm.

1. Himalayan Singing Bowls: their History and Traditions

THIS BOOK is intended to be a comprehensive study of the 'singing bowls' that have become so popular in the West. A singing bowl is a kind of bell, only one that is not suspended but sits instead upon the earth. As a result they look more like a bowl than a bell. But each is a bowl with a resonant sound, and thus a 'singing bowl'. You will see such bowls in the photograph on the title page. Also included are chapters on the *drilbu* (Tibetan handbell) and *ting-sha* (Tibetan cymbals) as these are regular ritual percussion instruments in Tibetan Buddhism and often appear alongside singing bowls in performance or recordings by Westerners.

From their lofty and magical homeland, Tibetan singing bowls and bowls from other lands have travelled across the mountains of the Himalaya, through valleys, and along ancient trade routes. The hippie culture of the 1960s led many people to seek spirituality in India. Eventually some travellers would visit Dharamsala in India, where H. H. the Dalai Lama is based, and there they would discover the *drilbu* and the *ting-sha* used in the Tibetan Buddhist rituals. Nearby stores would supply these ritual items, and the singing bowls too, and from the early 1970s on some travellers would purchase these. A few of those travellers were moved to enter enthusiastically into the sounds and so bring back these mysterious objects to the West. The story of the singing bowls, however, like the mysterious Himalaya, has lain hidden, obscured by clouds.

Of course, bowls from other regions have entered into Tibet and *vice versa*. Only a categorization of the specific designs of certain areas, or regions, or of certain bowl makers, can reliably inform us as to the origin of any one bowl while its owner could likewise abide anywhere – as indeed now many bowls have found their home in Western countries.

As far as I am aware, practically nothing has been written about the bowls from the academic point of view. There are no writings handed down to us and no courses or teachings from the ancient past from Tibet, or from the various branches of Tibetan Buddhism, that concern them specifically. However, this is true of any of their ritual instruments – although a book on the *drilbu* (by the teacher Vessantara) exists and one on the *ting-sha* (Robert Beer) has recently been published. More about these instruments can be found in Chapters 4 and 5 respectively.

With the bowls, the silence upon the subject has to do both with their being associated with the pre-Buddhist shamanic spiritual tradition of Tibet (Bon) and their traditional use as aids in meditation and inner contemplation (that is, not as part of monastic tradition but to be practised alone). Information suggesting traditions for the bowls is found from the Tibetologist Dr Alain Presencer (1981) and the booklet by Rain Gray entitled TIBETAN SINGING BOWLS: A HISTORICAL PERSPECTIVE (1989; it features an interview with a Tibetan Lama credited with having information about the bowls, while Eva Rudy Jansen in a book states that Joska Soos was the only person known to her who was actually told some of the secrets of singing bowls by Tibetan monks, and that everything she thus knew regarding the use of bowls in ritual meditation and prayer was confirmed by Mr Phuntsog Wangyal of the Tibet Foundation in London or otherwise by an interview dating from 1999 between *Dimensions* magazine and Mitch Nur (this is featured on the latter's website, www.9ways.com).

Henry Wolff and Nancy Hennings have been credited with the introduction of the Tibetan singing bowls to the West with their 1972 LP, 'Tibetan Bells'. They went on to produce a further three albums (plus another, 'Yamantaka', which is not strictly part of their trilogy) plus a final release, 'The Bells of Sh'ang Sh'ung'. Sad to say, absolutely no information regarding the bells or bowls is found with any of these releases.[1]

The first time that any kind of information regarding the bowls appeared was in the liner notes for the album 'The Singing Bowls of Tibet' by Alain Presencer (1981).[2] These notes state that he has travelled extensively in Ladakh, Sikkim, Bhutan, Nepal and, illegally, Tibet (during the 1970s and 1980s) and in the course of his travels has acquired a number of these rare bowls and has received instruction as to their use and significance by Lamas of the Bon-po sect. According to Presencer, the Bon-po made singing bowls both as aids to meditation and for other religious purposes, such as exorcism. He states that while some of the sounds from the bowls and other instruments were for the removal of demon spirits, most were intended as aids to meditation and inward contemplation.

The fact that many tons of antique singing bowls have been shipped out to the West since 1970 argues against them being items for the few. Some of them possess an exceptional sound quality that belies any belief that they were merely household utensils. Being made essentially of 'bell metal' (see Chapter 9), many do possess sonic qualities that are suited to meditation and healing, whatever our beliefs for or against. Subjectively speaking, some of these ancient singing bowls have been found to have spiritual energies present, which shows them to have been consecrated to spiritual purposes. My own experiences, and that of some others, convince me that there is a tradition that may have waxed and waned down the centuries. Arguments for and against this tradition are included in this book.

All that I can do otherwise is to share with the reader some of the information that my own sacred instruments have revealed to me during the more than forty years I have been familiar with them. This information itself constitutes the sources utilized in the writing of this book, but it goes alongside my researches (spiritual and terrestrial) and my efforts to discover what information exists.

It is generally considered more accurate to refer to singing bowls as Himalayan bowls, for such bowls are not restricted to Tibet but are found in Assam, Sikkim, Bhutan, India, China, Burma, Nepal, and further afield in Thailand, Cambodia, Korea, and Japan. In an interview Mitch Nur states,

> The bowl culture extends from the Stans (Afghanistan, Uzbekistan, Tajikistan, etc.) to Burma. The Primary countries are Nepal, Tibet, Bhutan, Sikkim, Mongolia, China, and India.... Most people believe that the bowls are Buddhist in origin, this

couldn't be farther from the truth. The bowls date back to before Buddhism and were most likely introduced to the Asian continent by the Uighurs. The Tang Dynasty annals speak of Gongs being used during the Shang Dynasty.... The original culture of Tibet is Bon, and the Bonpo were the original alchemists of Asia dating back about 18,000 years ago according to their cultural records. We know that bowl making communities existed within the Ch'iang tribes of Northeastern Tibet, as well as with the Naxi and other groups along eastern Tibet and western China. Nepal produced many of the early bowls and Bhutan has produced many also. There hasn't been a real authentic bowl made in about 100 years. The majority of what you see today are fakes.

Later in the interview he states,

Sound and Vibration was a science that was studied widely in Egypt, Babylon, Persia, and other early civilizations. Empires and Kingdoms throughout Asia had specific practices, rituals, and ceremonies that involved vibration and sound. The empire that was Tazig, as well as the Kingdoms of Li, Bru-sha, Sumpa, Trom, and ZhangZhung all were involved with sound and vibration in the sense that they developed certain structures within their cultures that used sound and vibration for shamanic healing, sonic anti-gravity, and more. The Bonpo of the Himalayan region has a rich history immersed in sacred sound practices. In fact the Indian sanskrit word Shambala is used to describe the ancient kingdom of ZhangZhung which was the spiritual home of the Bonpo.

And a final quote:

Bonpos were the first to use reciting mantras widely throughout their practices. We also know that they were the alchemists of Asia, and used Bowls as part of their Shamanic Healing. Bowls were used in a shamanic practice that utilized this formula, vibration + visualization = Manifestation.[3]

My Own Connections with Singing Bowls

I received my first singing bowls in 1971 when, as a freelance improvising percussionist, I already had a collection that included bells, gongs, drums, woodblocks and cymbals. I had begun playing drums in the spring of 1964, playing in rhythm and blues bands, and in 1966 I joined the Chicago Blues band, Black Cat Bones, with the legendary Paul Kossoff (of FREE fame) on lead guitar. When I left that band in the spring of 1968, I turned to total free-form group improvization within the field of avant-garde jazz. I got my first gong the same year. My photographer friend Jak Kilby turned up one day in 1971 with some antique instruments from Peter Bearacroft, who used to play with them at his grandmother's house. They are on permanent loan to me. His grandmother received them at the turn of the twentieth century so they are over a hundred years old. They show no signs of age, but I've not cleaned them in any way whatsoever.

In 1970, I joined the spiritual organization known as the White Eagle Lodge, and immediately worked in an 'absent healing' group. A little later I trained in meditation, and in the spring of 1974 I joined in the White Eagle brotherhood work. In the furtherance of my desire to serve spirit through my musical work, from 1971 I began to study more deeply the spiritual effects of my ancient temple instruments, using the psychic and spiritual gifts I was born with, plus help from my 'spirit' friends and my own past-life memories. I come from a family with several generations of psychics on both sides.

My interest in world music went back to 1964, when I had first listened to recordings of North Indian classical ragas. LPs of the sacred religious music of Japan, China, and Tibet were released during the 1960s and 1970s. Thus I was familiar with the *drilbu* and *ting-sha* when in Dobell's folk music shop in London's Soho area during 1972, I saw on the wall an LP called 'Tibetan Bells' with a Tibetan Buddhist mandala on the cover. I asked to hear it. I didn't listen to much of the LP because I immediately noticed electronic studio effects upon the sounds that were discomforting to me and, being a bit of a purist at the time, I concluded that the conscious

awareness of sound present was not that of Tibetan lamas, such as I'd previously experienced on LPs of their sacred sounds. There was precious little information with this LP but I eventually did discover that it was indeed the Westerners Wolff and Hennings who had made this album.

I cannot say for certain just how much awareness I had at the time that singing bowls were also part of these sounds, as *drilbu* and *ting-sha* featured in the music.

Although I had begun collecting and listening to recordings of the religious music of Tibet the previous year, the Tibetan singing bowls had never appeared on them before. Chanting and the Tibetan ritual orchestra did feature on disks I'd heard, as well as single yogis or lamas playing *ting-sha* or *drilbu*.

In 1972 or 1973 I was engaged as a percussionist by the London Yeats Theatre Company to provide music for their performance of *At the Hawk's Well* by W. B. Yeats. Working alongside me was Drew Gladstone, who contributed to the aforementioned albums, 'Tibetan Bells I' (1972), and 'Tibetan Bells II' (1978), and he was using only Tibetan singing bowls. He showed me one of them, working with water. I was not very impressed at that time because I had chosen to work with unadulterated, pure, and simple sounds. I had an antique Chinese horizontal gong, a Ming Dynasty temple bell, and a set of three four-hundred-year-old Japanese Zen Buddhist temple bells (*densho*) and wanted to use them in the manner to which they were accustomed. This was quite simply to be struck with no extended techniques.

My desire was to work with all of my antique sacred Eastern ritual percussion instruments in a pure and ego-less way by trying not to interfere with their sound process – and so the water bowls passed me by. Many of the sounds I had rang on for a long time (in comparison to the sounds of very short duration I had been used to as a percussionist), using drums, woodblocks, and suchlike. So, working in my simple way, this was a good foundation for extending my musical vocabulary, and it enabled me to add more extended techniques as these unfolded and the years rolled by.

I heard my first 'live' *drilbu* while standing in for my friend Chippewa on her stall in 'Antiquarius,' the Chelsea antique market, in 1973. I heard it sounding and tracked it down to a stall where the owner was playing it. It was for sale, and so I bought it. I returned often to that stall buying antique *ting-sha* and a *gshang* (Bonpo cymbal) from there.

In this way, the manner by which I came to work with singing bowls was a natural progression from when I'd begun to play drums in 1964 at the age of fifteen. At that age, I'd shown an immediate facility for advanced co-ordinated hand independence after just over one hour. In 1966, I remember posing myself the question 'What would the music be like on other planets?' – and upon hearing my first gong in 1968 I felt I had found my answer. I then began my lifelong pursuit, improvising as a percussionist while simultaneously incorporating exotic Far Eastern percussion instruments into my music. In this way I developed an ear for the peculiar sound qualities found within the sonic realms of metallic percussion, especially gongs, cymbals and bells.

The manufacture of such instruments usually involves a high level of chance. For instance, cymbals were traditionally hammered and beaten by hand, and the number of hammer strokes and the degree of force released upon each creates differences within the total piece of metal – thereby making each cymbal an individual-sounding item. Like any other drummer at the time, I would choose cymbals according to the sound I was looking for, or by those cymbal sounds that I was attracted to while sampling through an entire range in a shop. Sometimes, I would prefer very old cymbals to the newer variety, either because they had more character or because in some other way they had the sound that I was looking for to develop my cymbal sound 'set', for certain types of music-making. This ear training later provided me with a good basis for selecting Tibetan singing bowls and other metallic percussion instruments. Today, cymbals are more likely to be factory-made, with an emphasis upon duplicating certain cymbal characteristics, with the result that far less variation now exists.

My approach to bowls is also a performance one, since I have appeared on 105 albums to date (including fourteen volumes of Tibetan singing bowl music) to consistent critical acclaim. I have been privileged to work with some of the very finest musicians in the world – although since 1974 I have worked mostly alone, for it was then that I chose to dedicate myself entirely to my meditation/ new-consciousness music. That concentration gives me some sort of qualification for writing this book, while any real significance in my more subjective insights may derive some reliability from my supersensible hearing abilities, outlined below.

I have always felt a liking for Tibet's great yogi Milarepa who was said to hear colour and see sound. This was not an example of synaesthesia, but something else, I believe. Both composers and improvisers are involved in organizing sound. Mostly, they do this via contrasts such as loud to soft sounds, complex to simple sounds, short to long sounds, opening to closing sounds, fast to slow, and so on. Just how obvious or subtle these contrasts are varies. So we look for differences. When sorting through several hundred singing bowls it is easier to make comparisons. If we find some Manipuri Lingam bowls, for instance, we can compare their quality with each other. We may find that one bowl has a far more complex sound, is more beautiful in its effects, or rings on far longer than all the others. From hundreds of bowls we find that some show signs of great age while others look brand new. Machine-made bowls sound very similar. Merchants come into a shop, listen to one and then confidently order a boxfull, but most discerning importers of bowls might find that they actually select around 2% of hand-hammered bowls (old or new). Presented with a wide selection of bowls, we can instantly become more discerning.

Uniqueness

Differences exist as part of the pattern of life. When we visit the greengrocers we can see that in one box of apricots many have gone off, while another box is full of good apricots. Some fruits are underripe, some overripe and others just fine. We select what we are going to put into our body.

In this book we shall look into the various differences. From a philosophical point of view we can never have absolute unity, for it always breaks into variations. We can have multi-unity – perhaps represented by the union of male and female. As the Zen saying goes, 'The one is in the many and the many are in the one'.

For all that, we need to keep a balance and not get over-involved with differences. There are distinct types of bowl, and important guidelines that can assist us in a greater understanding of our bowl as well as giving indications as how best to work with it. Always follow your own truth in your own time.

Listening to the singing bowls of Tibet is like taking a 'sound-massage'. There are so many discordant noises in our modern world, compared with which the harmonious sounds of a good singing bowl are a real tonic! The ancient art of manu-facturing one of them centres upon creating a sweet sound that resounds for several minutes, with rich overtones so arranged as to create a long-drawn-out oscillation in the note. Some of my bowls have a very slow oscillation of over one second. The sound, swelling and ebbing away again as it oscillates, resembles the great rhythm of the ocean, conveying the feeling that it is massaging or washing clean our soul – or as if the sound is encir-cling the room and enfolding us. The pulsations from the sound of the singing bowls are also reminiscent of our own heartbeat, thereby providing us with a link both to human affection and to the realm of love – both human and divine. Moving our ob-servation to more inner dimensions, there is also the sense of a profound spiritual presence here, living within the sonic richness in a world of ringing harmonic overtones. The very slow dying away of the sound, to the indefinable border of silence, takes the listener beyond the actual sound itself to the limit of what is audible, and ultimately awakens us to the inaudible sound, of which I shall have much to say. This inaudible sound exists within a silence of rare depth that can at the same time be pro-foundly felt.

It is this ability of the bowls to permeate and 'hang in the air' with their spiritual vibration, long after their actual sound had ceased, that led to them being called 'singing' bowls. Also, in com-parison with other bowls made of wood or clay, they could be

said to sing, or possess a more musical quality – a resonant tone
– something akin to a voice could be heard within their sound. As
well as being struck like a bell, the bowls can also be stroked with
a wooden wand, thus conveying the experience of an eternal *Om*
sound gradually emerging from emptiness, enfolding and enrich-
ing our auric field.

Every singing bowl has its own individual sonic personality, which means that it can never really be pressed into an exact conventional musical scale together with other bowls. Each
bowl contains a set of partials unique unto itself. This, alongside
of a large number of partials present in their sound, makes it
quite problematical to hear a single pitch, which is something
that is needed if we are to apply the bowls to conventional musical scales. Being ritual instruments, they were never intended
to be used in this way, although, Tom Kenyon (on his CD, The
Ghandarva Experience, 1996[4]), describes how he purchased a
'set' of bowls from a lamaist sect of bowlmakers in Nepal who
only produce six sets a year. Certain others (e.g., Karma Moffett,
Benjamin Iobst, and Joseph Feinstein) might gather a collection
of bowls over time to create a 'set' that work well together – be
that twelve, twenty, thirty, or more bowls. I have several 'sets'
such as a spiral of seventy-five *yin* bowls, a spiral of twenty-eight
yang bowls, another spiral of twenty-six High bowls, a 'Sound
Bath' set of seven, a set of five overtone bowls, a set of *Air Spirit* bowls and then a set of Jumping bowls too. I'll explain the
names I have given them presently.

Merchants might sell so-called 'sets', and these can be a combination of singing bowls that sound well together, but the set
can also consist of bowls whose sound is close to the pitches of
our C major musical scale (mostly in the middle octave region).
These are often sold as a so-called 'chakra set'. Some sellers identify two 'notes' in a bowl, and they are not particular as to which of
these two notes is needed to provide the next 'note' in the 'chakra
set' sequence. This system is loosely and indirectly adopted from
Sir Isaac Newton, who in the seventeenth century related the sev-
en colours of light to the seven notes of our major scale and, as
far as I know, was not intending to link these notes to any other

system. Additionally, the scale used then was Just Intonation and not Equal Temperament, which is what we use today. The pitch standard was also different, meaning that the designated notes had frequencies different from what we have now. This system of correspondences plainly has nothing to do with what lives in a specific frequency, for these have undergone many changes since Newton's time.

People who apply correspondences to our Western C major scale often pay little attention to octaves, believing that the right note of the C major scale affects the specified chakra regardless of the octave it is in. For example, the pitch C is denoted for the root chakra – but we might find a bowl that is one or two octaves above middle C and meet a statement that this bowl is still for the root chakra – which is the lowest chakra. Listening to pitches in the different octaves it is usual to find that lower tones affect the lower parts of our bodies while higher tones affect the head area, and so on. Within this perspective, a C from a lower octave would be more fitting for the 'base' (or root) chakra. Through the use of intentionality a certain effect might be created, but I consider it more powerful if the note is also in the correct octave. However, I prefer to work with what I find lives within any one particular singing bowl regardless of any system.

One lady visited me after purchasing what were advertized as a 'set of chakra singing bowls', but I was unable to find a single bowl from this set that affected any chakra of mine – or even anywhere near one! I divined that two antique *Manipuri* bowls from this set (which was otherwise from Orissa) had previously been used for meditation, and was able to advise her to this effect. It must also be added that in Rain Gray's interview with Lama Thupten Lobsang Leche in 1986, the then seventy-year-old Lama states that the secret technique of making these bowls was lost a very long time ago. Furthermore, it was also stated that the finest quality bowls were produced in eastern Tibet in an area known as Megu Kutsa between 450 and 350 BCE. Production of authentic consecrated bowls stopped over eighty years ago.

Subtle Awareness

My own ability as a trance medium was something I discovered in 1965, having spontaneously gone into trance with my own spirit guide speaking through me. I instinctively felt that I should speak to my father about this experience. Remarkably, it was at this same time that I was informed by my father that he had previously trained as a trance medium. My parents had become involved with Spiritualism around 1947, and my father was told by many top mediums that he had a very high spirit guide and that he would have his own 'lodge'. Both my parents were psychic, however, and psychic gifts existed in the previous generation on both sides of my family tree. My parents attended Spiritualist development circles, and then my father was advised to run his own circle. They ran séances at the family home in Hampstead, North London, during the mid-1950s (with another couple) while my younger sister and I slept innocently in the adjacent room. My father also revealed to me that I'd demonstrated clairvoyant abilities as a young child, although my attention was never any way drawn to this fact until the conversation in 1965. I was left free and not brought up with any beliefs, or conditioning, and discovered this psychic or Spiritualist activity only after leaving home and having found myself going into trance.

After I went into trance, I remembered a portrait of an American Indian on the wall of my parents' bedroom, whose eyes seemed to follow me around the room. This led me to believe that my father might be able to advise me regarding this new-found trance ability of mine. And so it was that I spoke to him.

My father then informed me that the leader of the spirit circle (Whitefeather) had once told him that (owing to certain actions on my mother's part – I later discovered) there would be no activity for seven years, and that this time cycle had just ended (1957–64). It was later arranged that I should return home on Sundays to attend the family séances, in which either my father or I were used as a medium/channel for the spirit guides – my father by then having instructed me in the technique of safely operating as a vehicle for these higher beings. The form of trance was then termed 'light trance' (also known as 'overshadowing') in distinction to 'deep trance'. I was also commissioned by Whitefeather (my father's own spirit guide) to make (pastel) portraits of all seventeen members of the spirit circle – including six members of what is known as the Great White Brotherhood. My father had suffered from leukaemia and hence was not always available to be used by the guides, and so I was offered the opportunity to be of such service. This period lasted from 1965 until my move back to London in 1970.

Trance work was not encouraged at the White Eagle Lodge, meaning that since 1970 I have only gone into trance six times, when necessity arose, and between 1977 and 1988.

My father first gave me training in spiritual healing in 1965, and I have described how I received further training in 1970 at the White Eagle Lodge (which included contact healing) and in the White Eagle meditation. The healing helped my clairvoyant faculties to develop further and then clairaudient gifts were unfolded while I meditated at home – upon and with my increasing collection of antique sacred ritual instruments from the Far East. This is not to say that the form of meditation taught and practised within the White Eagle Lodge is specifically designed to develop these faculties. There have been a few occasions when I met others similarly gifted and their observations of my instruments confirmed my own, while my clairvoyant observations, while attending group meditations, were unwittingly fully substantiated by the facilitators during the sharing afterwards. In the early 1970s, as I travelled on the underground to attend these group meditations, I would see an angel above 'the Lodge', and from the colours and forms of this being I would know what form the meditation was going to take.

I have also practised spiritual astrology since 1975 (also as taught in The White Eagle Lodge). The training allows some clairvoyant seeing into the past lives of the client, so long as this is done with total confidentiality and sensitivity. This reading of the akashic records (for that is effectively what it is), has been regularly substantiated. Similar experiences have been observed during my sound healing sessions when I have needed to look clairvoyantly at the client's chakras to determine the appropriate treatment. Afterwards, I share my observations and explain the course of treatment. Needless to say, I make every attempt to be objective about what are regarded as subjective observations. I am primarily interested in reality and truth – regardless of whether that flies in the face of reason, logic, or expectation – even if truth is infinite and all-encompassing.

I have spelt out these matters because my lifetime's dedication to following the spiritual path, which has included more than four decades of work with sacred sound as a path of spiritual service, is the only qualification I can have for writing this book apart from the specific studies of sound I mention in the course of this book. Those equip me to share the insights gained, some of which have so far not found expression from any other source known to myself – certainly not from all the several world experts upon the subject of 'Tibetan Singing Bowls'. Otherwise, I am simply obeying an ancient law, which is to 'give as you have received'. Through this law, I am somewhat obliged to pass on my wisdom, learning, and experience and, while it is a joy for me to be supplied such an avenue of service, doubtless, there will also be those who find it helpful. I am simply sharing the sound revelations afforded me through following the way of the bowl as unfolded in my life.

I have chosen to follow my sound-related path with more of a *yin* (feminine) approach; one of following where the bowl sounds lead. Our Western society is largely *yang*-dominated (masculine), but I had long been interested in playing *through* my instruments (from *within* them rather than *upon* them) at the time I was play-ing 'freeform group improvised music' in the late 1960s. I found that this 'playing within' approach was one for which bowls were specially suitable. It is for you to decide if the resulting revelations, which are set out in this book, reverberate with your own experi-ence and have meaning or useful significance for you.

The involvement with freeform group improvisation began in 1968. I found such ancient antique instruments here and there, but also found that they didn't come with the implements with which to play them – and certainly the sellers had nothing to say about them. It might even be not too far-fetched to state that the dealers didn't even know what they were for! There was the bowl for sale, plain and simple. This complete lack of even the remotest information or advice was very wonderful indeed, for it provided me with a wide open space – one totally free for me to explore, and without the constraints of any established or fixed intellectual, ethical, or religious constructs.

Although I may have worked out the most appropriate way for me to act with the bowls myself, and arrived at various personal certainties, or otherwise unveiled the deeper significances of working with divine sound in this manner, I would never dream of making such findings a law for others. There are plenty of so-called 'rules' around which mean very little. For instance, I have encountered people who have been (mis-) informed that to play a bowl in the anti-clockwise direction is to call upon the AntiChrist! Again I have met people who have been told never to strike a bowl – and this despite the fact that bells all around the world have been struck since their inception thousands of years ago! Others have been instructed upon the one and only right way of working with bowls according  to some self-appointed teacher. While at times I may discover the deepest meaning of a single bowl within seconds I have heard tell that a certain teacher prescribes working with a single bowl for at least fifteen hours until its meaning gradually arises within. I have no desire to rob you of the freedom that I enjoyed. Rather, perhaps I can provide you with some pointers to assist you along your journey.

Aside from having a literature around them, acupuncture, Sanskrit and the various branches of yoga have traditional schools or institutions where one can go to learn and receive qualifications even. Yes, there are traditions to learn *nada yoga*, or train in *dhrupad* (sacred singing) in India and elsewhere, or learn *mantra*, although there are no university courses so far as I know and no certificates afterwards. Nothing remotely of the sort really exists for bowls! As I've said, to the best of my knowledge there is nothing in the way of written records regarding the history of the singing bowls. The most that exist are records regarding the history of bells in general, accounts that to some extent may be adopted loosely in assisting us in filling in some of the gaps to our knowledge.

Suren Shrestha writes, 'Only in a handful of the healers' homes were singing bowls commonly found. The great teacher Master Dorje Tingo of Kimanthanka is one of the healers I know who is actually using singing bowls for sound vibration healing in the traditional way. Another is Jejen Lama, who lives a two-day walk from my village.' (He was born in Nepal).[5]

He also informs us that the Shakyamuni clan are still making healing bowls according to an oral tradition dating back to the time of Buddha, one that entered Tibet from India at the same time as the great Buddhist master Padmasambhava in the eighth century CE.

Mitchell L. Gaynor, M.D. relates a conversation with the Venerable Tenzin Shyalpa Rinpoche who spoke of having been with fellow monks playing the bowls and also chanting for periods of fourteen hours.[6]

In 1971, in the absence of information, books, or courses upon the subject, there was plenty of room for originality. Just as with the free-form improvisation I used, I had no preconceived ideas, or set path, or process; no 'road map' to follow. This was good, for it meant that I had to be patient in allowing my understanding to unfold naturally in following the inner dimensions of sacred sound from mostly ritual instruments. I had no rush to reach the 'top' or the next stage.

What *was* the next stage? I advocate using plenty of patience in allowing your own understanding to unfold, and to treat what I write here as hints for your own study. Of course, you need to keep your feet upon the ground even as your head soars into the sky above. The purer we are the truer will be our experience.

In some ways this is rather magnificent, bringing, as it does, an element of the mystical path into this way. You will find that that continues throughout the book. The bowls can act as guides and teachers along our path, unfolding in a unique way for each individual who works with them. All bowls can be an instrument of such teaching, although the older ones (and especially those bowls that are more sacred in their nature) can bring more profound teaching or unfoldment. This is also a path of following sound, and therefore silence, and it is in the deep stillness and silence that teachings which will never be forgotten by the recipient can come. In the stillness of the heart chakra we find immanent divinity.

The closest I ever came to receiving traditional or inherited wisdom and instruction came from beyond the grave in 1971, in the form of a 'spirit helper' apparently drawn to work with me because of the colours I create as I perform, as Whitefeather explained to me through my father at that time. His name, he said, was Lom Phook Trenglam (portrait right by Frank E. Perry III – that is, myself) and he had been on earth in Tibet thousands of years ago, long before Buddhism entered Tibet. He would simply help me focus my concentration on observing what effects the sounds of mine were producing upon the several planes of existence: the etheric, astral, mental planes, plus, when appropriate, the Buddhic and nirvanic ones. Somehow he was able to influence my awareness so that we shared mind(s) in direct perception regarding these sounds and what was  correspondingly formed upon the several planes of co-existence above and beyond the merely physical sense-organ of the ear. I have been reliably informed that the names Lom and Phook are still in use today in Tibet.

Three other spirit guides have worked with me in the spiritualization of my musical unfoldment and these are an ancient Chinese named Gun Luo Chi (orchestral and court music), an Indian named Swami Saraswatyananda (voice – *raga*) and a Mongolian named Zhiangu (voice – *xhoomei*).

Apart from the spirit help, having made a friend of Alain Presencer in 1982 during a shared concert (which included David Hykes – Founder and Director of the Harmonic Choir of New York) I had someone to show me the technique of what he called *ululating* the bowls, which he claimed to have been shown by Bonpo lamas during his illegal visits to Tibet. At his suggestion, Alain and I swapped instruments and I also bought a few from him during the early 1980s. It was he who informed me that the bowls are made of eight metals. Alain also introduced me to the 'Panic Bowl' and 'Talking Bowl' from his collection and, completely of his own volition, later very generously and kindly facilitated in bringing examples of these very rare bowls into my own assortment of instruments. At his invitation, we often presented together, with Alain giving a talk and both of us performing – sometimes together.

What I write in this book is intended as guidelines and in no way to be the definitive course in this study of sacred sound.

Bowls in their own Context

Whilst we cannot state anything on the subject of bowls with absolute certainty, we can work within what is known regarding the cultural and philosophical consciousness of that truly ancient time when the bowls were first made and used – over two and a half thousand years ago. I am mindful to avoid the projection of modern Western thinking onto this ancient world of sound magic. I'd prefer to restrict myself to what can be reasonably assumed about the past and to make a clear demarcation around applying ideas or facts that would not have been known at that far-distant time and most probably from within remote regions cut off from the outside world. I believe that those who first used the bowls were individuals whose sole purpose in using them was ritual, meditation, healing, or their own spiritual unfoldment – individuals who may thus have been little interested to know anything more concerning their instruments (such as what 'note' they were, and other modern concerns).

It must also be stated that the vast majority of bowls currently on the market are not ancient at all. Many are probably less than five years old; the bulk are maybe ten, twenty, thirty or forty years old. Since the Chinese invasion of Tibet in 1949, which is over sixty years ago now, and the destruction of around six thousand monasteries at various times since then, it is highly doubtful that any bowls younger than sixty years old will be Tibetan (that is, made in Tibet – China now). Again, even with the centuries-old bowls, by no means all of them possess particular spiritual energies – what some might refer to as a 'power' behind their sound – and these qualities could be derived either from the lifetime of a devotee working with the sound effects of that one bowl, or else the bowls themselves could have been charged with psycho-spiritual power at their creation, or prior to their first use, by appropriately gifted spiritual persons, and so designed to assist their disciples, or else the individual in pursuit of enlightenment or spiritual service. Either way, an amount of time is involved that is often painfully missing in our modern world, so that it is unreasonable to expect that every bowl imported into your country is some ancient sacred sound tool resonant with spiritual vibrations and energies! Nothing is impossible but, painful as it might be to our egos, the likelihood of a bowl bought today being spiritually charged is small. None of this rules out that it cannot now be turned to dedicated spiritual use, or the exceptions that will occur.

In the context mentioned previously, the bowl would be charged by the initiate of sacred sound for the use of the individual who would work with it rather as a *thanka* (a painting of Tibetan Buddhist deities with embroidery or otherwise painted on cloth) might likewise be commissioned from an artist by a disciple under specific instructions from their teacher. Mass-produced bowls and machine-made bowls will have no such predestined path. Meanwhile it would also be an unwise use of spiritual power to release such spiritually potent tools out into the unknown. My understanding is that despite this there may be situations where such an initiate may desire to remain unknown, but knows the intended recipient of the bowl precisely; divine law then carries it safely to its mark. Again, there may be trust in the spiritual hierarchy that any such potentized bowl will reach its destined home.

The dating of bowls is equally problematic, even for experts, but the discernment of spiritual energies present in any one bowl is very rare indeed. It's nonetheless, and regrettably, a great sales pitch for unscrupulous merchants (or practitioners) aping such gifts.

Some people dedicate their life to the service of spirit and others are not so inclined. So it is with singing bowls and, put quite simply, some have been consecrated to spiritual purposes and others not so. We cannot point to a large army of saints upon our earth: they are few and far between. Likewise with sacred singing bowls. Bowls charged with spiritual power are as rare as saints. Some people dedicate their life to financial success, some to sporting success, others to the arts and humanities and yet others to criminal activity or the world of gangs. So it is that some people are totally involved with their outer life while others are equally committed to their inner life. Even the lord Buddha was born a prince enjoying the outer world and then became an ascetic, totally dedicated to the inner world, before settling upon the middle way. Of course, others may well have found a happy balance between the opposites.

Great spiritual masters have been likened to mountain peaks. These are not all that numerous. So don't expect every singing bowl to be sacred, or highly potentized, for the truth is that such are few on the ground. I don't have any such expectations when seeking bowls but remain open to such occurrences.

As it says in the Bible, 'Try the spirits whether they are of God' (1 John 4 : 1). Don't believe anything I say or that anybody else says. Always use your own intuition and allow that intuition to grow naturally to the point where you can trust it. In the meantime, you may need to rely on those persons alone who have been proved to be trustworthy, genuine, sincere, with great integrity and highly ethical – and not motivated by personal gain of any kind; a desire neither to impress, nor to wield power over another. Also it is no bad thing to see whether certain gifted individuals can confirm your own intuitions. For instance, in ancient American Indian tribes, if an individual had a vision and shared it with the chief it would not be acted upon unless some others had a similar vision. It can prove difficult to remove ego from our perception of truth – and 'there is no religion higher than Truth', as Madame H. P. Blavatsky succinctly put it (she was co-founder with Henry Olcott of the Theosophical Society in 1875).

We need to be somewhat on our guard when seeking to enter into the inner portal of sound. The mind is adept at rationalizing and seemingly substantiating our desires. I have plenty of stories that back this up. As an example, I received an email from a lady abroad who had bought an expensive singing bowl. Getting it home, she found that neither she nor any of her friends could get a sound from it. She asked my advice. I replied that this bowl might be cracked or otherwise unsuited to playing, and that she should take it back and ask for another. The following day came another email to say that she now found that the bowl had its own lama and so she'd be keeping it, despite it being mute!

Another lady had contacted me asking for a 'Panic Bowl'. I was not overly convinced that I could find one for her but nevertheless some weeks later one appeared! She contacted me afterwards to say that a psychic friend had told her that someone seated on an elephant last used it and that it was stolen from a monastery and that it could only be played on a Friday! A shame really: anyone suffering from demonic possession seeking help had better wait until the next Friday!

Alain Presencer mentioned an elderly gentleman who lived near Newmarket in Suffolk who had some bowls. When I first visited this gentleman I'd taken along some of my bowls in a suitcase. He asked me if there were any other people with a large collection of bowls. I told him that both Joska Soos and Alain Presencer each had around fifty bowls in their collections. He then informed me that he'd visited a psychic (or medium) some years earlier who had told him, 'You are the keeper of the bowls in the West'. He had four bowls at the time and so I had inadvertently disillusioned him.

So we must be very careful regarding such wild assertions from un-informed, highly impressionable and somewhat imaginative 'psy-chics' regardless of how sincere and helpful they intend to be.

It is always advisable, though keeping an open mind, to keep our feet firmly on the ground. We need to maintain a healthy bal-ance between our higher and lower mind. As with saints and sa-cred bowls, high-functioning psychics are also rare.

Some bowl players take the view that one bowl can work on all the chakras. Others, like myself, generally experience a single bowl affecting a particular chakra. Ancient Taoists found that fric-tion was the main thing preventing the long life they sought. Ac-cordingly, they sought to reduce friction by decreasing resistance – adopting the famous 'going with the flow' approach. Applying this principle to my work with bowls and chakras I seek bowls that I experience to have a direct effect upon the chakra in ques-tion. If I buy a kite it has the potential to fly at any time. However, it will work best if I take it out on a windy day. Likewise, I can decide to launch a boat at any moment but it may be far easier to work in harmony with nature and do this at high tide. I can wish to celebrate the birth of the spiritual light into my life at any time but I would be most supported in this by the environment were I to choose the dawn of day, or upon waking, or at the winter solstice. Going with the energy of nature in such ways is friction-less. For instance, nomadic peoples in Tuva need to be aware of changes in their environment. When they hear the singing of the bird they call *baa-saryg* they know that it is safe to plant grain; likewise, the sowing must occur before the song of the cuckoo as this indicates the end of the moist winds.

As an example of what lives in a particular note (or bowl) and the intentionality of the player, an American sound healer once stayed at my house for a few days. He brought his gong and a bag full of seven singing bowls. Seeing seven bowls laid out I asked if he had any for the chakras. He replied that he had all seven. From what I saw I concluded that there was no bowl large (low) enough to affect the root chakra and none small (high) enough to reach the crown chakra. I asked him to play the bowl for the crown chakra. He did so but, while I could see that he was thinking very hard, and intending it to reach my crown chakra, I disregarded his 'intention' and observed my actual experience of the bowl's effect, which was a resonance around my chin. I requested he play a root (first) chakra bowl. Listening, I found it was closer to my solar plexus (third chakra). I mentioned this afterwards and he said, 'Yes, that's funny, I found it was working on my solar plexus too! What's gone wrong?' We can send energy to the chakra of another regardless (as with certain forms of spiritual healing), but if we are choosing to accompany this intention with sound then I feel it best to work with the energy by finding a singing bowl that has an undeviating effect upon the chakra concerned. Thereby the intention and the sound work together synchronously. Similarly, were green to the throat chakra to be required in healing, I would select a throat chakra bowl that also produces the colour green upon the astral plane.

A couple visited me with the intention of buying some bowls. They'd just been on a singing bowl workshop where the leader had played one bowl for all seven chakras. I explained that I am very lazy, preferring to use a bowl that I found to work upon one chakra. I gave the solar plexus as an example and they asked if I had such a bowl. I played one and they immediately exclaimed 'Wow! It goes straight there! Do you have any for sale?' They bought all the three solar plexus bowls I had for sale.

And so it is that I send these words out into the world – for those curious about such findings treading an unbeaten path, or for individuals who have begun their journey and are seeking signposts to proceed on their chosen way, and in some cases for reassurance.

When I first heard a singing bowl, in 1971, I knew nothing about them. There was simply the Sound. And what a sound! Meditating and being with singing bowls for over forty years now, I offer something of what I've learnt in the words that follow. I seek to share here what the bowls that have come to live with me have taught me intuitively by way of unfoldment and during contemplative self-discipline. I say this by way of explaining the individual nature of what is revealed in some of these pages con-cerning the singing bowls. May what I say serve to inspire each reader to open up to the inner teaching of their own bowls and, perhaps, also serve to be something of an echo for those who may feel somewhat out on a limb in following 'the road less travelled'.

Teachers beyond Ourselves

There are persons with little sympathy for the mystical path, or the spiritual path, that may yet be attracted to working with either sound or the singing bowls. This book may or may not be for them. Nevertheless, the elements of self-sacrifice that attend any genuine spiritual path (even if unconscious and unsought) may well prepare such adherents to receive levels of understanding of life and sound denied those of a different persuasion. It is said by Djwhal Khul that the fifth ray (of science) is as much a part of the seven-ray spiritual path as the others.

Notwithstanding, truth is truth and often has scant regard for our beliefs or feelings or desires. It simply *is*. Spontaneously hearing the 'absolute sound' of *nada yoga* is another example of an experience of sacred sound open to all, although some institutions or groups suggest specific preparations or insist that only by being initiated into their school will the experience be bestowed. In fact, I would like to suggest, along with others, that life can initiate any individual into this awareness at any time, with no preparations at all. Nonetheless, specific traditions can point us in a safe direction for unfolding this gift. Nobody holds the monopoly on experiencing the inner sound of *nada yoga*, as it is an experience open to all.

I am sincere when I state that I was visited by a discarnate being who had lived in a country called Tibet many thousands of years ago who was certainly an initiate of sound, if not a master of it, even though it may be difficult for some readers to hear that. This being worked with me for some time in the early 1970s (infrequently, not every day, and not for very long periods of time either) and aided in expanding and awakening my own understanding of the nature of sound upon the several dimensions of being. The knowledge imparted is something I have never read in any books on music or sound, and I am certain that it did not come from my own imagination. I am aware of the difference. The insights into sound vouchsafed to me could have come from no-where else – at that time I was not aware of any schools teaching anything to do with the inner nature of sound and I believe there were very few books treating of the subject. Those that there were were extremely hard to come by and very far from the beaten path of most musicians. The sacred ritual instruments I was working with, and with them the relevant approach to sounding, were very far away from what the vast majority (if not all) the musicians who were working at that time and known to me were working with.

The gifts that Lom Phook Trenglam imparted to me during our precious partnership are ones I shall ever be truly grateful for, and I feel immensely privileged to have been visited by him and to have been afforded the opportunity to share in such sacred work. For me it was certainly an initiation into the profound mysteries of the di-vine nature of sound and it came in the only form that I could have accessed. The experience instituted an entirely new way of working with sound, one that I have followed for many decades now, and I can only pray that I might have achieved some kind of success in actualizing the directives so graciously and generously given.

I am likewise deeply grateful for the support and guidance from Whitefeather and his spirit circle, my own spirit guide and also the beautiful teaching and spirit of White Eagle and the path of service he affords us. Lest what I say appear lop-sided, I would express gratitude towards incarnated teachers such as Manly Palmer Hall, Dane Rudhyar, Joseph Campbell, Master Omraam Mikhael Aïvanhov and Joan Hodgson – to mention but a few.

As I've already indicated, there are traditions for working with the bowls. On a YouTube video, for instance, the popular Viet-namese Zen Buddhist master Thich Nhat Hanh gives a traditional practice for sounding the singing bowl. He shares with us a poem that he recommends that we use to accompany our invitation for the bowl to sound. Furthermore, he tells us that in Buddhist tra-dition the bell is seen as a friend to help us to be mindful and concentrated. I hope he will forgive me quoting the very beautiful practice he suggests.

First, before we invite the bowl to sound we bow to the bowl. We can place a small bowl upon our open upturned palm and visualize it as a lotus flower with the jewel (bowl) in the centre.

The poem is used in the following manner:

'Body, speech and mind in perfect oneness.' This is said silently while we breathe in with the sounding of the bowl. 'I send my heart along with the sound of this bowl' is said as we breathe out. When we strike the bowl for a second time we breathe in and silently say, 'May all who listen to me awaken...'

'And transcend the path of anxiety and sorrow.' This comes as we breathe out again.

When the bowl is used in a communal act, it is first struck with a half sound. The stick after striking touches the rim to silence the sound. This serves to announce to all that the sound of the bowl is coming and to prepare by stopping all talking and thinking. In his tradition it is considered that the sound of the bowl is the voice of the Buddha from within calling us back to ourselves. At this point the community just breathes in and out.

Then the full sound is offered. As it sounds we breathe in deeply three times slowly during the sounding. We say to ourselves silently, 'I listen', and every cell in our bodies listens to the sound. As we breathe out we say silently, 'This wonderful sound brings me back to my true home. My true home is in the here and now.' This happens three times, filling us with peace and joy and is repeated during the following two strikes.

To practice the entire ritual at home would be to perform the poem over two breaths and two strikes of the bowl. Then, placing the bowl upon our upturned palm, a half strike with one slow breath in and out would be followed by a full strike and three breaths (with the 'I listen' and 'This wonderful sound...', etc.) performed three times. When the final sound has died away, we place the bowl back onto its cushion and bow once more to the bowl. Thich Nhat Hanh recommends that we commence and finish our day in this manner. He also suggests that we have a room set aside for such a practice and call it a 'Breathing Room'.

Buddhism based its ritual on one of the oldest forms of worship, the *caityas* or sacred spots. It retained wind-bells at these sites and recognized that their ringing drove away demons. In addition to this, it maintained that their sounds were a manifestation of the music of the heavenly spheres transmuted into a form that could be heard by human ears. We find an allusion to this heavenly music in one of the most poetic descriptions of bell sounds ever given. Gautama Buddha related it to his disciple, Ananda, when his life on earth was reaching its close. Describing the heavenly city of Kasavati, he said:

> The Palace of Righteousness, Ananda, was hung round with two networks of bells. One network of bells was of gold, and one was of silver. The golden network had bells of silver and the silver network had bells of gold.
>
> And when those networks of bells, Ananda, were shaken by the wind there arose a sound sweet, and pleasant, and charming, and intoxicating.
>
> Just, Ananda, as when the seven kinds of instruments yield, when well played upon, to the skilful man a sound sweet, and pleasant, and charming, and intoxicating – just even so, Ananda, when those networks of bells were shaken by the wind there arose a sound sweet, and pleasant, and charming, and intoxicating.[7]

We are told by Xuanzang, an early Chinese Buddhist pilgrim to India, that when he was at Nalanda monastery in 637 CE, the director of duties there beat upon a bell to announce to the assembled monks that the pilgrim was to live with them. This seems to substantiate the tradition that Ananda, known as 'Guardian of the Dharma', struck on a bell to assemble the first Buddhist monks.[8]

What was discovered to live within one tone to the ancient Chinese was of the utmost importance. In ancient China the bell dictated everything. The emperor would be responsible for the tone of the bell. All weights and measures arose from this bell. The amount of grain it held, its length, the amount of fluid contained within the bell, and its weight: all these were the origin and pattern of weights and measures in use. Of such great importance was the tone of the bell that it was considered calamitous were it to change or be lost. Needless to say the pitch of this bell governed all music under the emperor's dominion. Bells were linked to rituals performed for the spiritual worlds in these ancient times, and still are in certain cultures today.

2. The Development of Bells in Ancient China

ALTHOUGH I have said that bowls are a sort of bell, it could be argued that strictly, the Tibetan Bowls are not bells for they are not suspended. Yet they share with bells activity at their rim and stillness at the centre, and I believe that on acoustical grounds we can include them as part of the wider bell family. We can then let them share in the same traditional sacro-magical significance that bells and other metal instruments enjoy in ancient folklore.

If we seek to discover how long bells have been around, we shall find that their earliest development takes us to China. The Chinese have used bells since their remotest civilizations for purposes both profane and sacred. Wind-bells were hung from trees, homes and temples, and their sound was considered effective in driving away evil spirits. Their divine sound mirrored to humans the celestial music surrounding paradise and the supernal harmony of nature. Great and ancient temple bells are found throughout China, Thailand and Japan. It was considered that bells had supernatural powers and helped crops to grow, and they were greatly prized. They were rung to call the ancestral shades to the offerings laid out for them and sounded in ceremonies designed to control the weather. As bronze technology progressed, different shapes evolved and the goal of bellmakers became less the volume of the bell than its pitch and tone – its ability to produce a sound sweet, lingering and mysterious. The ancient Chinese extolled bronze above all other materials in their own Bronze Age.

In Asia, the use of sounding objects as a whole is very old. For example, the Chinese Emperors had the right to the most beautiful 'ringing stones', which are hard stones, such as jade, that produce a ringing sound when they are struck. Although the first great Emperors reigned from about 221 BCE, there are records of a Bronze Age culture in China around 2,205 BCE. Such finds show only that bronze articles were made that long ago, but until even older objects are found, it is impossible to say how much farther back in history bronze was being worked. The technology of bronze was first developed in the Middle East. It is in use in Sumer, at Ur, in around 2,800 BCE, and in Anatolia shortly thereafter. Spreading spasmodically, it then appears in the Indus Valley in about 2,500 BCE, and progresses westwards through Europe from about 2,000. Around this time it is found in crude form in China, where it later achieves an unprecedented level of sophistication. From about 1,500 BCE the Shang dynasty produces bronze objects of exceptional brilliance. It is the rulers in all these regions who use bronze, as a luxury for themselves or as weapons for their armies.

The oldest tuned bells so far excavated in China date from around 2,000 BCE. It is clear that by the sixth century BCE the Chinese were far advanced in the manufacture of metal alloys and in the working of metals, from which they made perfectly tuned bells. It is difficult to say how many such bells were made before that time, but certainly a bell-like object was excavated in 1983 from 2,000 BCE at Taosi (Shanxi province). This allows some sixteen hundred years of development to pass before the creation of the astonishing set of sixty-five bells of the Marquis Yi (of Zeng, a petty ruler during the Warring States Period (482–221 BCE), but important to us). This is the famous set of orchestral bells excavated in Hubei Province in 1978 that we'll come to shortly. To produce a tuned bell that weighs more than one hundred pounds, and can produce two different pure tones according to where it is struck, demonstrates acoustical knowledge superior even to ours today. The only way that we could reproduce such bells today is by studying these ancient bells. When first uncovered it was thought that metal protrusions on the bells were merely decorative. Later, via interferometric photography, it was discovered that these protrusions were in exactly the right place on the nodal lines of the musical notes of the bell to allow the pure sounding of two tones on each single bell.

The ancient Chinese experienced a spiritual power within the

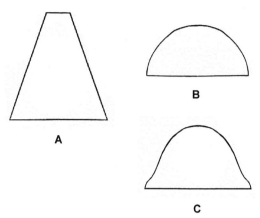

Variations on the cone (above) and the cylinder (below). Based on drawings in Percival Price's book, BELLS AND MAN.

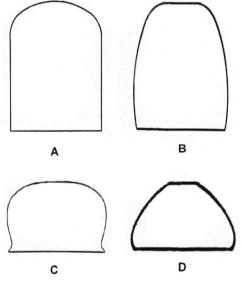

sound of their ritual bells. Their belief that the sound of these bells came from the heavenly realms most probably led to Chinese culture using the bells to bring universal harmony to earth and also to affect the heavenly regions.

With their imposing shapes and deep and prolonged sound, large round bells were widely used in Buddhism and Taoism. They also entered the imperial court and became a symbol of imperial power. During the Ming and Qing dynasties, ancient Chinese bells were divided into musical bells, Buddhist bells, Taoist bells, imperial court bells and bells for sounding the night watches.

The actual shape of singing bowls closely resembles that of traditional Chinese and Japanese large resting bells used in Buddhist and Taoist temples in these same countries for many centuries. Variously called 'Cup Gong', 'Buddha Bowl', or 'Bowl Gong', the singing bowl is, in fact, a resting bell – in contradistinction to other bells that usually have a handle or other means of suspending them. If we prefer, we can think of them as being inverted bells. Hanging bells are usually shaken (with the clapper striking the rim of the bell) or struck by an external beater (with very large Temple Bells this is often a pole made from a tree) or by a rope that moves the internal tongue – as with carillons. While bells must be raised up from the ground to ring, singing bowls and resting bells are placed upon the ground (or the hand, or a cushion); otherwise, they conform to the basic cup-like design of a bell that rings at its rim and is silent at its centre. This cup-like form is one of two fundamental circular bell shapes (variations either on a cone or on a cylinder, see over) and such bells are called open-mouth bells.

Chinese sets of great orchestral bells would not be played for mere entertainment but rather for ritual and ceremonial uses. Centuries before the time of Marquis Yi, poems describe ceremonial feasts held by noble families for their ancestors.

> Bells and drums sound magnificently. Music on stones and flutes chime in. The dead kings send down their blessings for our abundance. They are drunk. They are full. Blessings and happiness come again and again.[1]

For the ancient Chinese, then, the music of bells reaches out across the great divide into the realm of the so-called dead. Bells even now are used to summon people (albeit by calling our attention to the time of day) while in these ancient times the call of the bell reached beyond this material world to the beings of the higher realms.

Here is a quotation from the 'Golden Legend' by Jacobus de Voragine, in the thirteenth century, in the version of Wynken de Worde, a printer from the end of the fifteenth century:

> It is said, the evil spirytes, that ben in the region of thayre, doubt moche when they here the bells rongen: and this is the same why the bells rongen when it thondreth and when grete tempeste and outrages of wether happen, to the end that feinds and wicked spirytes should be abashed and flee, and cease the movynge of tempest.[2]

> [It is said that evil spirits that live in the region of the air are troubled when they hear bells rung, and that this is the reason bells ring when there is thunder and when great tempests and extraordinary weather occur – so as to make sure that fiends and wicked spirits are discomfited and flee, and cease causing the tempests.]

There are even accounts of bells that purport to ring of themselves. Often their ringing is a sign of where to establish a spiritual centre. The sacred bell so treasured in St Kinan's Convent has a story giving us an instance regarding the magic of bells. St Kinan was an Irish disciple of St Gildas the Welsh abbot. One night, when he was staying in Gildas' abbey, he had a dream in which he heard a voice that bade him depart to an unnamed land in another county to found a house of monks of his own – and that a bell would guide him to the spot. The monks of St Gildas' were unwilling to part with any of their bells, and so Gildas himself made one out of a piece of old iron and blessed it and gave it to his parting guest. They travelled for a long, long time, throughout all of which the bell was silent. Finally, in a Cornish valley near Falmouth the bell sounded the long-hoped-for signal and the group stopped by the River Fal to build St Kinan's Chapel, where the bell has been preserved and honoured ever since.

Percival Price, in his book BELLS AND MAN (1983), informs us that when we search to find the earliest bell known our attempts prove futile. He tells us that there are legendary records from China's remote antiquity before the Shang period (1600–1050 BCE) and if we give credence to these, then it would seem that the initial development of large musical bells originates in China. Fortunately, the legends, history, and artefacts all unite to support such claims. These legends take us back to the twenty-eighth and -ninth centuries BCE. It is told that twelve bells were ordered by the Yellow Emperor, Huan T'i, in the twenty-seventh century, to be made for use as pitch standards. The emperor Chuan Hao, in the twenty-sixth century, reportedly used a bell for making announcements and also in religious rites. It is said that the emperor Yu (the Great), in the twenty-third century, had two bells placed outside his palace, a larger one to be rung by persons complaining of injustice, and a smaller to be sounded by those on private or confidential business.[4] All of this is legend. Historically, the first emperor is mythical, the next two are legendary, leaving only Yu to be dated approximately to the twentieth century BCE. Although we have no hard evidence supporting these accounts, there is a general inference that the Chinese had used bells since a remote period in their civilization. If we try to get some idea of when this could have been, using evidence of when they began casting metal into the form of hollow objects, in contradistinction to flatware, then one authority places this at 1,700 BCE and another says it could have been before 2,000 BCE. Any person wishing to place the development of singing bowls back to any time prior to this is making claims that are beyond proof and unsupported by evidence.

Cast in Bronze

From a global perspective, the first development of bronze takes us back to around 3,500 BCE. Despite the claims just cited, present evidence regarding the history of bell casting proper points to it beginning about 1500 BCE, with tiny clapper bells. These were not musical instruments but rather were worn – in the manner of cowbells today – by dogs and horses. We can thus be fairly confident in stating that nobody on earth within recorded history was producing anything resembling a bronze bell before this time, at least from the standpoint of archaeological evidence. Certainly many ancient Chinese bells remain, some more than 3,000 years old, from the time of the Shang and Zhou dynasties.

Within China, bell music existed mostly in Southern China between 1500 and 1000 BCE. Bells were regarded as essential to the performance of Confucian ritual in later Chinese history. The ringing which sets the most lasting tradition was the Confucian practice of striking a large bell to mark the periods of worship. The creation of such instruments has been evolving in China for over three millennia. Studies of these three-thousand-year-old bells have provided us with much knowledge concerning the musical culture of Bronze Age China.

Once, we might have used imagination to picture the results of such lengthy experimentation but not so long ago the level of Chinese bell development was suddenly concretized. In Hubei Province in the winter of 1977, members of the People's Liberation Army were removing a small hill in Leigudun in the town of Suizhou in order to build a factory. Suizhou is around 155 km north

of Wuhan, in the same province that the famous Chinese gongs and cymbals of today are manufactured. They unearthed an ancient burial tomb consisting of several chambers. First they found unusual clay, and beneath it large stone slabs. Finally, there were enormous wooden beams that provided the roof to the tomb. At this point the archaeologists were brought in. By May of 1978 the entire tomb was exposed. Among the seven thousand objects excavated from this tomb within the larger central chamber there was found a set of sixty-five tuned bells with ninety discrete strike tones. One of these bells was markedly different in design from all of the others and only produced one tone. It also had the inscriptions that inform us that the set was created in 433 BCE according to our calendar, and was a gift dedicated to Zeng Hou Yi, or Marquis Yi of Zeng, from his more powerful neighbour the King of Chu. Zeng was a small state in the Yangtze valley.

This set of bells was hung upon an L-shaped wooden rack three tiers high. Those bells upon the highest tier are too high to play and have another purpose – mostly related to tuning, pitch standards, and scales. This set of ancient tuned bells weighed two and a half metric tons. Of course, among the archaeologists very little attention was initially paid to their musical qualities.

Dr Sin-yan Shen wrote an article for *Scientific American* and was also interviewed by the BBC for a Radio 3 programme on the acoustics of ancient Chinese bells. According to an anecdote supplied by Sin-yan Shen, during the 1950s – that is, two decades before the Marquis Yi find and in contrast to bells scattered throughout numerous collections and treated as one-off items – complete sets began to be discovered. In 1957 the Music Research Institute in China played a set of these bells in concert. Scientists and musicians were asked by politicians to find a set of bells upon which to play 'The East is Red' – a very popular piece of music in China at that time. During rehearsal the E-bell was missing in one octave. But then a player found he could get that sound by striking the C-bell on its side. He found that the bell played two tones, a third apart. If we take the example of another metal percussion instrument, for instance the cowbell, striking it at any point around its edge would produce its sound – unlike these two-toned bells. It had been assumed that these Chinese bells would be similar to a cowbell in making the same sound wherever struck. The fact that the musician had managed to get a different note from the one bell was first considered to be mere coincidence.

Some twenty years later people associated with the Music Research Institute at Beijing asked themselves whether the fact that this one bell produced the required tone was a complete accident. Was it indeed possible to produce another pitch from a single bell? Everybody in the scientific community thought not and that it was simply that this musician got lucky in finding a pitch that was usable in playing 'The East is Red'. Thereafter, musicians and scientists investigated hundreds of bells and found that all of the musical bells produced two well-defined pitches. This produced consternation amongst the musical and scientific community, for they had been proved wrong in stating that it was complete nonsense that bells could produce two distinct pitches. A debate then started around the question of whether these bells actually were designed to produce two tones or whether it was an accident or by-product of their design. This debate was finally settled in 1978, when the incredible set of bells from the tomb of Marquis Yi was unearthed.

Closer inspection revealed that the bells of Marquis Yi already had markings for indicating the two striking positions – the so-called *sui* and *go* positions. Not only this, but also these markings gave the Chinese characters for the exact musical note to be excited from the indicated position on each bell – making it an impossibility that the two-tone bells were simply an accident. It could only be concluded that these bells were actually designed to be two bells in one! The *sui* position is located in the central belly of the bell – the most natural position to strike the bell – while the *go* position is found between this central position and the outside edge of the almond-shaped bell (the oval-shaped cross-section seen when the bell is viewed vertically from above). This latter position on the bell renders a higher note than that produced from the centre of the bell. Viewed face on, there is an arch between the outside edges of the bell and at its peak is the *sui* point.

In sum, these wonderful bells produce the twelve notes of the chromatic scale (as found on the twelve notes of our Western piano keyboard – the seven white and five black keys in each octave) for over a range of three octaves (there is a less dense scale for two more octaves). The bells can play or mirror the entire melody of tunes played in medium tempos, but because of their comparatively long sustain, faster speeds could not be executed. In fact, the positional order in which the bells are laid out (there are instructions inlaid with gold on both the frames and the bells indicating where they are to be hung) could well signify that two melodies could be accommodated for pieces of music seeking to exploit such techniques. It is thought that the larger, lower-toned bells were used mainly for the punctuation of melodies. The sound of these larger bells is far more gong-like: deep and resonant, and possessing a long sustain, and so unsuited to playing fast melodies. In modern performances upon a replica set the deeper bells are indeed used to punctuate the melody.

From the implements found in the Marquis' tomb, two large poles were retained for playing the deeper bells and executed by two players, while a set of six hammers was used to play the medium- to high-pitched bells, this time by three performers each armed with two hammers. All the bells that are played during performances are hung at a slanting angle.

The musical span of this remarkable and exceptional set of bells extends, as we've noted, over five octaves. The forty-five bells residing upon the middle and lower tiers of the rack were those actually played – the upper tier being those not being played in performance. Of the forty-five bells found in the melody section of this set, thirty-one possess a *sui-go* interval of a minor third, and fourteen produce the interval of a major third. When each of these tones is struck correctly upon the bell, they produce independent tones with separate fundamental and harmonics. In fact, each single bell sounds as if it were two separate bells. The protuberances upon the bells (severally termed bosses, knobs or nipples, but *mei* in Chinese), which had initially seemed merely decorative, were proven to be in exactly the right position to enable the sets of nodes for each tone to operate successfully and to produce these two seemingly individual tones.

This game-changing discovery displayed the extraordinarily sophisticated acoustical knowledge these ancient peoples had. It vastly exceeded what we had previously understood. Obviously, the incorporation of two notes in a single bell was deliberate. As to why such people would even seek to create two-toned bells, one suggestion is that the desire stems from Chinese love of symmetry and balance, embraced within the philosophy of the two opposing yet harmonious forces of *yin* and *yang* (often depicted enclosed within a circle). I speculate that within this context the basic tone could well symbolize the Sun (being the greater light) while the higher tone produced close to the edge could then represent the Moon (the lesser light in the sky) or *yang* and *yin* respectively. Each bell would then contain these two forces at once, interacting in a state of unity (or multi-unity) and symbolizing the union of heaven and earth. It would likewise be a manifestation of the non-dual philosophy where male and female principles exist in unity. Taoism and Confucianism were dominant in China at this time, but this idea also embodies spiritual teaching regarding the interrelationship between the two opposite principles in the words: form is emptiness, emptiness is form.

I also see depicted within these unique two-toned bells the philosophy of a Father, Mother, and Child trinity (the one bell and its two tones). In quite another society, Pythagoras taught that the first two tones in the musical overtone series relate to the Father and Mother Principles. Since ancient times the sun has been linked to the number one and the Moon linked with number two. Through symbolism we might extend our analogy further, seeing that the Father Principle would then relate to Emptiness while that of the Mother is all to do with Form. Just as father and mother, being interconnected, interact and work together and are inseparable and interdependent, so each bell may embody this philosophy in its two tones. Interestingly, father and mother produce a child, creating for Pythagoras the third tone of the harmonic series, this being the interval of a fifth (or the ratio 3:2). Chinese music has been based upon this musical interval for thousands of years (and well before we adopted such a system).

Five thousand pounds of bronze was used to create this set. Producing two-toned bells necessitated far less bronze for the number of musical notes produced than separate bells, and also required far less space for their erection and less players. We now know that such two-tone bells were common in China between 1,200 and 200 BCE. Sets of such bells were called *bianzhong* (pien-chung) and early sets have been dated to 500 BCE. Price, in his book on bells, states that at this time in China the artistic use could not be separated from the magico-sacred import of bell sounds.

A question that naturally arises is how much work was needed after the casting of these bells to tune them to the scale. According to Sin-yan Shen, there were only a few bells exhibiting signs of subsequent fine-tuning. But according to other authors, many of the bells displayed signs of some slight work in the fine-tuning process. All agree, however, that from the moment of casting these bells were very close to their prefigured pitches. What we don't know is how the ancient Chinese craftsmen managed to cast a bell that would correctly produce two tones of pre-determined pitch. We know that they did it, because the markings were already impressed upon the bell prior to casting to indicate the precisely intended musical pitches at the *sui* and *go* positions.

In short, this was a tremendous feat of engineering and manipulation of acoustics for such ancient Chinese to have accomplished in 433 BCE. Indeed, our modern-day engineers had much to learn about acoustics from these ancient Chinese bells. Lothar von Falkenhausen (author of SUSPENDED MUSIC, 1993, a book entirely about the bells of Marquis Yi) was interviewed on the programme, 'Bells of the Bronze Age' (Discovery Channel: 'Time Travelers' Series, 1994). There, he stated (after testing with modern electronic equipment) that, 'whilst the tuning of these bells is not absolutely exact, yet the degree of exactitude achieved by these ancient craftsmen is quite astounding, and the creators of these instruments, in their time, would have signified the most advanced technicians of their age enjoying the comparative high esteem extended to the nuclear physicists of today!'Because of the conditions in which these ancient artefacts were kept (submerged under water), when excavated the bells sounded as they did 2,436 years ago.

The *bianzhong* found in Marquis Yi's tomb are musical bells to be used in orchestral music. Recordings and programmes featuring a modern replica set of these ancient bells do exist.[5] Sadly, modern copies cannot match the sound of these ancient bells of Zeng. If we compare them with singing bowls, it must also be said that these ancient Chinese bells are cast from bronze whereas the bowls are hand-hammered and generally speaking not cast.

We have seen evidence of a lengthy evolution of sets of bells for ceremonial music. This process would extend all of the way from putting together an assortment of bells forming a set that could then play something resembling a scale to manufacturing a complete generic set more perfectly in tune and providing a larger range of musical tones, such as those of Marquis Yi. The aim thus arose of creating a bell with a higher pitch but as sonorous as the previous bell. The ancient Chinese bellmakers found that the way to achieve this lay in reducing its size, increasing wall thickness, or to change shape – or all three. A cohesive set of orchestral bells could then be made in a somewhat more organic way than previously.

Price considers that the time of the manufacturing of the Marquis's outstanding set of bells (433 BCE) would have been the climactic period of a thousand years of bellmaking. What this set of sixty-five Zeng bells proves to us today is that about 2,500 years ago the Chinese had scales generated from the interval of the fifth (fifth temperament, a twelve-tone system in musical practice, and not just musical theory); a norm tone for an orchestral ensemble, and integration of fifths and thirds in tuning, and a preference of pure thirds over pure fifths. At this point in history China was over two thousand years ahead of Europe, not only in bell casting, but also in musical acoustics.

Buddhism in China

The era of the 'warring states' came to an end when the first of China's emperors finally unified the country in 221 BCE. The struggle for supremacy was over and so it was that the great ceremonial orchestras, associated with competitive power, disappeared. The ritual and politics of musical feasts became obsolete, as beliefs and power structures shifted. Music for entertainment took over and had already begun to appear during the time of Marquis Yi. As the fourth gave way to the third century BCE, small informal instrumental groups replaced the great bell orchestras. Music lost much of its political and religious function and became entertainment for the nobility. Royal feasts changed from pompous occasions for the dead to mere indulgences for the living. Confucianism is one of the great religions of China and its more puritanical followers railed against the new music with the spirit of debauchery and lewdness that came with it. The great ringing tones of the Bronze Age bells never again echoed in the royal courts of China.

In China from 220 BCE and during the next four hundred years the use of bells from Indian Buddhist immigrants took over from the abandoned *bianzhong*. Throughout China, wherever Buddhism became established, bells were needed. In each Buddhist temple large bells were rung to mark the times during the day when the spiritual offices were held, and also to ward off evil spirits, which is the meaning of 'apotropaic' in the following information from Percival Price's book.

> Buddhism went so far as to give verbal meanings to the sound of its bells. Wind-bells proclaimed the holy Word of Buddha with every passing breeze. Temple bells periodically diffused the greeting, '*Na-o-mi-to-fah*!' 'O Buddha, hail!' The sound of the bell was in this case apotropaic because the holy Word was apotropaic.[6]

Names were given by the ancient Chinese to some of their very large temple bells – names such as 'Yellow Bell', 'Forest Bell', 'Pressed Bell', and 'Echoing Bell' (actually, these first two terms refer to the fundamental bell and to the next bell one fifth higher).

Quite unaware of this ancient practice at first, since 1974 and in just the same way I've given names to my significant bowls: 'Bright Eyes Bowl', 'Song of Shambhala – Vision of the Plan Bowl', 'Whispering Flame of a Humble Heart Bowl', 'Ocean of Great Bliss Bowl', 'Peace Rose Bowl' and many, many more. The large temple bells tend to be more circular or tubular in their body and thus a different shape from either the *bianzhong* or the resting bells. Inside the Buddhist or Taoist temples we find the resting bell most commonly used to accompany the chanting of sutras or for group meditation. These are usually large in order for their tone to carry throughout the *sangha* (or community) of monks. Of another region, Y. H. Yum says,

> Large temple bells have been cast in Korea for more than 1,200 years. The most famous bell in Korea is the magnificent King Sung Dock ('Emille') bell cast during the Silla Dynasty (771 CE). Standing 3.66 metres high, it has a mass of 20,000 Kgs. The body has a flat circular protuberance called *dang jwa*, and a chimney called the *eumtong* opens through the top.[7]

J. S. Gale informs us that the Sung Dock bell has the following inscription for the merit of King Hyegong's grandfather:

> True religion lies beyond the realm of visible things; its source is nowhere seen. As a sound is heard through the air without any clue to its whereabouts, so is religion. Thus we hang up this great bell that it may awaken the Call of the Buddha. So ponderous is it that it can never be moved – a fitting place on which to inscribe the virtues of a king. Great Sondok was his name, his deeds eternal as the gills and streams, his glory as the sun and moon. He called the true and noble to aid him in his rule. Fitting ceremonies and music accompanied all his ways. He encouraged the farmer to a joy in his work and the merchant to the exercise of honesty. Gold and jewels were accounted as nothing in his sight, while useful knowledge and skill of hand were treasures above compare. His great aim was the right-ordered life. For this reason people came from afar to seek his counsel, and all revered him for his worth.[8]

Percival Price, in the large book which we have now many

times quoted, records the entire gamut of different bells and yet the nearest we can find to the singing bowls is the following, which is nonetheless revealing. (The *rei* is a Japanese form of handbell, derived from the Indian *ghanta*).

> There is another instrument used in Buddhist worship which, although not exactly a bell, cannot be ignored in a survey of campanology. This is the *kin*, a plain brass bowl hemispheric in shape, 20 to 40 cm in diameter, and very thin. It lacks any protrusion for suspending it such as a bell would have, and instead, rests mouth upward on a soft cushion. It is struck with a short stick, and because of its homogenous form and virtual lack of damping by the cushion it emits a clear, long-lasting note even when given a slight tap. Its origin is said to be a container made of hard resonant brass with an admixture of gold to heighten its colour which was used in temples and palaces in Korea. It is used in rituals in alternation with the rei and two percussion instruments not bells, the *orugoru*, a set of small gongs related to the Chinese *yung-lo*, and the *kei*. The *kei*, which we shall find in connection with wind-bells, is a stone or metal plate with a particular outline, derived from the Chinese ch'ing. The kin is used in both temple and household worship.[9]

The *bianzhong* possess a comparatively short sustain, as befits the playing of melodies – remembering that the larger bells are mostly for punctuation as their sound lingers longer. Alongside the development of these orchestral bells, the Chinese also asked of their bellmakers that they produce another type of bell that rang on for a long time and possessed a sweet sound. These were called *shung* (*qing* or *da qing* is the commoner form) and are properly termed 'resting bells' (the dictionary definition). These latter types of bells are struck from the outside and do not have a tongue, or clapper, to strike them from inside, as do regular bells. The *qing* bells are not suspended like the *bianzhong* but are inverted and rest upon the earth. I have yet to find a source that provides a reliable date for the beginning of their manufacture. One reference states 526 BCE. A large one is mentioned coming from the Han dynasty of China around 206–210 CE.

These circular resting bells have a sound that is less focused upon a single note and do not lend themselves to musical uses but (used singly) do find an application in ritual and spiritual uses. It is these that are, I believe, the precursors of our Himalayan singing bowls.

Thus the lengthy process of development of bells, outlined above, for musical purposes (even though in the early stages this would have evolved out of ceremonial and shamanic streams) may very well also have occurred in the parallel development of the *da qing* or resting bowl (there is one pictured on p. 308, below). If we allow that a similar degree of experimentation was applied to the resting bowl (albeit in countries outside of China, such as India – where the practice of *nada yoga* and a culture of meditation abounded) then it need not be fairytale to suggest that extra-musical intentions (alongside experimentation) led to a wide range of designs, and that these led further towards a range of applications of such sounds, embodying various spiritual or meditative purposes. The large variety in the design of singing bowls supplies us with an array of differing sound qualities suitable for a range of spiritual uses. (One hundred different forms are listed in Appendix B.)

It is my contention that a similarly lengthy period of time has pertained in the evolution of the resting bell or singing bowl. As we have seen, a very high degree of engineering ability and acoustical knowledge was displayed in the world of the cast bronze bells, and so, too, it is not unthinkable that a similar degree of expertise would also be brought to bear upon the more important world of the meditation bells (or resting bells – what we call singing bowls). The use of such sounds in the pursuit of the inner spiritual worlds would have occupied the concerns of these ancient communities at least as much as that of fulfilling the requirements of the more noble and wealthy members of society. A degree of curiosity or experimentation on the part of the bellmakers could have likewise led to the large range of singing bowls available to us today. When we include the shifts in society, already mentioned above, around 200 BCE, we can imagine that all these changes would have left the bellmakers freer to explore the possibilities of the resting bell.

3. Tibet

Himalayas! Here is the Abode of Rishis. Here resounded the sacred Flute of Krishna. Here thundered the Blessed Gautama Buddha. Here originated all Vedas. Here lived Pandavas. Here – Gessar Khan. Here – Aryavata. Here is Shambhala. Himalayas – Jewel of India. Himalayas – Treasure of the World. Himalayas – the sacred Symbol of Ascent.

Oh, Bharata the Beautiful! Let me send Thee my heartfelt admiration for all the greatness and inspiration which fill Thy ancient Wisdom, for glorious Cities and Temples, Thy Meadows, Thy Deobans, Thy sacred Rivers and Majestic Himalayas![1]

ALL RELIGIONS use sound, even if only that of the sound of the human voice. Bells, conch shells, trumpets, oboes, cymbals and drums are used in the Tibetan Buddhist rituals and in Hindu temples – where they serve as a way of expressing the power of God and as an echo of *anahata nada*. Indian Philosophers speak of the importance of sound – *nada* – as one of the controlling forces of the universe. The sound we hear in the material world – *ahata nada*, struck sound, which is the product of vibrating objects – is only an echo of an ethereal unstruck sound – *anahata nada* – which suffuses the universe and charges it with esoteric power. The inaudible sound is that which is uttered by the great spiritual teachers and avatars of the race. It is the Sound produced by the rhythm of the perfect lives embodying the will of master souls, by incarnations of the spiritual Sun. Most of the instruments used in Indian shrines have a richly resonant or penetrating quality, which calls to mind this unseen power of sound. Such primal sounds link us to our Primary Nature, to the pure essence of our divine Primordial Nature.

The primeval-sounding music of Tibetan Buddhism can be best understood in the context of Tibetan Buddhist esotericism. Unlike most music we hear, not a note of it is rooted in human feelings. It cannot be considered to be self-expression or entertainment such as we usually associate with music-making. Rather, it stems from the shamanic and animistic aspects of the earlier Bon religion of the Himalaya – beliefs that were integrated into the Tantric form of Mahayana Buddhism. Some scholars prefer to see Bon as inseparable from early Buddhism, but without entering into that debate it will be clearer if in the present context we see Bon as distinct.

In Tibet certain spiritual practitioners undertake retreats on which the senses are blocked. When the ears, particularly, are so blocked it is possible to hear the inner sounds of the body: the sound of the blood moving around the body, along with the deep pounding of our heart, and so on. Such noises from the body could also be the origin of the unusual sounds of the Tibetan ritual orchestra. The yoga of sound in India (*nada yoga*) has teachings that relate to a number of inner sounds heard during its practice. A certain sound practice from a silent retreat (as related by the Bon lama Tenzin Wangyal Rinpoche) displays certain similarities to *nada yoga*. It is also possible that some of these inner sounds he mentions are the inspiration for the sounds of the Tibetan ritual orchestra. In 'Teaching the Master-Singer' (from the book TILOPA by the Twelfth Khentin Tai Situpa) we read – from his commentary on this story – about the 'soundless sound', with its connection to the concepts of *prana, nadi* and *bindu* strongly pointing to a form of *nada yoga* tradition within the Kargyu stream of Tibetan Buddhism. The Kargyu tradition stems from Tilopa.

The mountainous inaccessibility of Tibet is one reason why the ancient power of this old tradition has been preserved. Here, where loneliness and stillness reign as on the highest mountain peaks, where conscious thinking has not covered up all deeper experience of the invisible world, a form of music could develop that is the perfect expression of elemental natural phenomena, and that builds a bridge over into the world of the spirits and the demons. One cannot fail to be impressed by the elemental power of a Tibetan Buddhist orchestra sounding forth – even if it is only to believe that one is listening to the primordial chaos before creation. The main deities of the Bonpo were originally those of the sky, the embodiments of space and light, and the embodiment of infinity and purity.

If the bowls are associated with the pre-Buddhist Bon faith, they can then have more of an association with 'psychic' practices common to such shamanistic cultures. In this case, we could say that the 'psychic content' of the antique bowls is more significant than the earthly sounds they produce, incredible as these are. Living in an age of materialistic thinking, we can be fascinated purely by the unique sounds produced by these remarkable bowls and so ignore their capacity for altering our inner, psychic nature. This is not to say that the Bon religion is exclusively preoccupied with shamanistic procedures (most shamans practise alone), for many contemporary Bonpo monks distance themselves from such associations. Bon in its monastic institutions nowadays is more closely linked to Buddhist philosophy and cosmology. The old forms of Bon have all but vanished and today it is fairly indistinguishable from Buddhism. For instance, of the four major schools of Tibetan Buddhism the Nyingma (the first Tibetan Buddhist sect in Tibet) has 'the nine ways', closely related to the nine ways of Bon. The Lopon recognizes three forms of Bon: the old Bon (entirely shamanistic); the new or Reformed Bon (which arose out of competition with the Buddhist schools); and the Yungdrung or Eternal Bon. There are many forms of Bon, but broadly speaking three main groupings – southern, northern and central. Yet another categorization sees five high clans or families of people. These are the Dru, Zhu, Pa, Me and Shen clans, each one having its own tradition and strict rules.

The act of playing a bowl requires the utmost concentration if we are to avoid unpleasant noises and if we are to surrender ourselves fully and enter into a state of at-one-ment with the bowl. A proportion of singing bowls available will range from ordinary metal bowls with no additional significance up to those with a perceivable power behind the sound. Listening to certain singing bowls (such as the 'Panic Bowl') will produce a noticeable effect within the brain to which everyone who hears it can attest.

Tom Kenyon, in the CD mentioned in Chapter 1 (p. 20), re-counts a meeting with a two-year-old child he recognizes as a reincarnation of his Tantric master from the fourteenth century. The child is holding a *dorje* and is sending *chi* energy into Tom's bowls. He recounts that when the child reached the largest (most highly prized) singing bowl, Tom heard a crack. Sure enough the bowl was broken, and he believes that his reincarnated master was teaching him the lesson of non-attachment and of transcending the ego. From this account we can presume that there is a tradition within the ancient Tantric stream of working with the bowls as instruments for subtle energies.

Dirk Gillabel in his book, SINGING BOWLS: A GUIDE TO HEALING THROUGH SOUND, relates the following:

> The Tibetan lamas told Joska Soos that certain bowls had been filled for some time with the bones of dead lamas to transfer the high energy of spiritually evolved lamas into the bowls. These charged up bowls would then be much more powerful when played.[2]

In a like manner, when wishing to consecrate a bowl to a spe-cific deity (let's say White Tara) it may have been the practice to place a sacred statue of White Tara (consecrated by a high lama) inside the bowl for some time and place the bowl upon the altar, or some such suitable place, during a White Tara empowerment ceremony. Such a practice might be the reason why certain bowls are especially blessed with this presence of a deity. However, I'd also like to add that I believe the sound of the bowl would have to be in tune with the energies of the chosen being.

By way of substantiating those rare instances where bowls possess a spiritual or psychic energy I should like to present two accounts regarding the charging of sacred objects, showing that such is not entirely unheard-of within Tibetan Buddhism or cer-tain forms of yoga practised in Tibet. Investigating a little further into the probability of certain ancient singing bowls possessing particular spiritual energies let us read from the French oriental-ist and explorer, Alexandra David-Neel, who travelled in Tibetan regions for many years at the beginning of the twentieth century:

So, when concentration of thoughts is mentioned here below as the direct cause of a phenomenon, one must remember: first that, according to Tibetan mystics, this concentration is not spontaneous, but determined; and secondly, that besides this direct apparent cause, there exist, in the background, a number of secondary causes which are equally necessary to bring about the phenomenon.

The secret of the psychic training, as Tibetans conceive it, consists in developing a power of concentration of mind greatly surpassing even that of men who are, by nature, the most gifted in this respect.

Mystic masters affirm that by means of such concentration of mind, waves of energy are produced which can be used in different ways. The term 'wave' is mine. I use it for clearness' sake and also because, as the reader will see, Tibetan mystics really mean some 'currents' or 'waves' of force. However, they merely say shugs or tsal; that is to say, 'energy.' That energy, they believe, is produced every time that a physical or mental action takes place. – Action of the mind, of the speech and of the body, according to the Buddhist classification. – The production of psychic phenomena depends upon the strength of that energy and the direction in which it is pointed.

An object can be *charged* by these waves. It then becomes something resembling our electric accumulators and may give back, in one way or another, the energy stored in it. For instance, it will increase the vitality of one who touches it, infuse him with courage, etc....

3. Without the help of any material object, the energy generated by the concentration of thought can be carried to more or less distant points. There this energy may manifest itself in various manners. For instance: It can bring about psychic phenomena. It can penetrate the goal ascribed to it and thus transfer the power generated elsewhere.

Mystic masters are said to use this process during *angkur* rites.

Lamaist *angkur*, literally 'empowerment,' is not an 'initiation' though, for lack of other words, I have sometimes used that term in the course of the present book. The various *ang-*

kurs are not meant to reveal esoteric doctrines, as initiations were, among the Greeks and other peoples. They have a decidedly psychic character. The theory about them is that 'energy' may be transmitted from the master – or from some more occult store of forces – to the disciple who is able to 'tap' the psychic waves in transmission.

According to lamaist mystics, during the performance of the *angkur* rite a force is placed within the disciple's reach. The seizing and assimilating of that force is left to his ability.

In the course of talks I had on this subject with mystic initiates, they have defined *angkur* as a 'special opportunity' offered to a disciple of 'empowering himself.'

By the same method mystic masters are said to be able to dispatch waves of energy which, in case of need, cheer, refresh and invigorate, physically and mentally, their distant disciples.[3]

For further substantiation of such indigenous occult aspects or subtle energies linked to objects we can turn to Norma Levine:

So, getting back to ritual, sacred objects, and Buddha activity, when prosperity ritual is performed, the *yang* may be stored in a special object, which then contains *yang* energy. Beru Khyntse Rinpoche revealed how a very special *dakini's kapala* or skullcap came to him. 'A few hundred-years ago, there was a family living in the area round Tsari Mountain, a famous sacred place in Tibet, who came by a *dakini's kapala*. These are very thin, like eggshell, and when you look through them, you can see the light – which is a very good sign. They are usually small, light, and a pleasing shape, with all the signs inside. Sometimes they are found open, rather than upside down, and filled with flowers. Another good sign is that there is some kind of light coming from it at night. Even if you try to find one, you cannot get it, it just has to come your way.

'There was a family feud and the head of the family, who was very attached to this *kapala*, feared that one day it would be stolen. So he offered it to me, and I kept it. Because he'd asked different lamas to perform *yangdrup* – *yang*-increasing prayers, or merit – with it, the *kapala* contained his *yang*. I've found that since I've had this *kapala*, everything is just coming to me without having to look for it.

'One of my monks also found a special *kapala*.' He added. 'He was very happy about it and kept it carefully. One day he looked for it and it was gone. Who had taken it, he didn't know; but it was lost, gone.'

No one can possess and keep a sacred object unless it belongs to him inherently. In the true sense of ownership, nothing that belongs can really be lost. It is this kind of inherent wealth that resides within our Buddha nature. It is the ultimate yang in a sense, and when that vast natural resource is opened, developed, the outer forms of wealth manifest.

I was intrigued by the implications. 'When a master obtains a sacred object,' I asked Tai Situpa, 'is it possible it can contain his *yang*?'

'Sometimes. Yes, sometimes.'

'And if he loses it, then his personal power might diminish?'

'Possibly.'

'So in that sense, the more sacred objects a master has, the greater his power and ability to perform Buddha activity?'

'Yes.' He agreed. 'I think so.' He paused a moment. 'Rather materialistic, isn't it?' he said laughing.

I shook my head. The profound meaning of Buddha activity seemed awesome suddenly. I felt a kind of stillness going deeper and deeper, like an anchor dropping into the ocean. 'I think it's very special, really quite wonderful.'

So wonderful, it may be forgotten what these messengers of the buddhas are really for. Sacred objects – whether they are *rangjung* or created, whether they are *terma* or from another realm – the basic principle is the same. As Jamgon Kongtrul said 'They're all skilful means for liberating beings.' The blessing power of the buddhas.[4]

In addition to the above there is the following, from a book by Philip Rawson.

Tibetan Buddhists took over from the old shaman-magicians of both India and Tibet the custom of using their own power-charged implements in their rituals. All newly-made implements have to be initially charged-up with power by rituals and mantras performed by specially qualified monks, but old implements, which have belonged to distinguished magicians or saints and been used by them, have an extra potency.[5]

And finally, no lesser figure than H. H. the Dalai Lama has written:

> Based on their inner achievement, the yogis can unfold energies which can serve the benefit of the entire country, such as in ceremonies which consecrate images and icons, exorcise negative forces, prevent natural disasters and epidemics, and uplift the spirit of the times.[6]

The vibrations created by how we live and behave will tune us to the wavelengths of certain invisible entities. This is the secret of magic. The priests of ancient Egypt knew this and so recited set formulas or wore masks or put on certain vestments so as to identify with the gods Horus or Osiris. In this way the god was able to speak or act through the priest that had managed to vibrate upon the same wavelength as the sublime entity. In Tibet, masks worn in certain Bonpo rituals depicting saints are kept locked away in private rooms to maintain their powers.

If we can manage to vibrate in unison with such a heavenly entity and then find a bowl that also vibrates in sympathy to such an entity then it can be used to serve in a similar way as a focal point for the release of radiant energy from that being.

Tibetan Buddhism preserved its own characteristic forms of worship and ritual partly based on ancient Indian practices including the use of musical instruments both to call the monks to worship and as an integral part of the ceremony itself. Buddhism in India, prior to entering Tibet, had already assimilated the ancient Shaivism with its magic ritual. The Mahayana Buddhism found in Tibet is a transposed Shaivism with the various buddhas and their female consorts being the exact equivalents of the Tantric deities of India and ancient Tibet. In Tibetan Mahayana Buddhism there are two types of deity – those of the one type being merely the fearful aspects of the others, who are represented as full of goodness and mercy. In any case, the aggressive gods are in no way malicious beings, but rather the protectors of faith against the demons. The *ting-sha* corresponds to the fearful deities. The Tibetan Buddhist ritual music has a major independent Asian style and has its spiritual basis in Buddhist cosmology and is concerned with supernatural levels of being and, as such, is far removed from Western concepts of entertainment, technical display, and pleasurable or organized sounds. Rather the sounds used are designed to serve the Buddhist aim of awakening to enlightenment.

The Problem of Authentic Records

Beyond what I have outlined, we know extremely little about the history of the singing bowls of Tibet. In books dealing with the ritual music of Tibet (or any Tibetan books) we find absolutely nothing that concerns these instruments specifically, even though they have been found in monasteries as well as private homes. Although 'Begging Bowls' are mentioned as being part of the practitioner's belongings, those are invariably made of iron or steel. Sacrificial Bowls adorning the Buddhist altars, while often possessing a pleasing sound, are likewise of a different shape from the 'singing bowls' and neither are they made of the same alloy. The recordings previously referred to, of Westerners playing the ritual percussion instruments of Tibetan Buddhism along with singing bowls, are not matched in the many examples of authentic sacred Tibetan Buddhist Ritual Music performed by monks appearing on many recordings that have become increasingly available since the early 1960s. In the main, we do not find local recordings featuring 'singing bowls.' The one exception, and it is relatively recent, is a CD by Buddhist Monks of Maitri Vihar Monastery entitled 'Tibetan Mantras and Chants' (1999). This has ten tracks, three of which feature chanting alongside singing bowls, plus *ting-sha*, and *drilbu* in various combinations. Unfortunately, there is no information regarding how long bowls have been included alongside chants in this monastery. There have been two other recordings of singing bowls in the last twenty years: one from 1996 by the Ven. Karma Tashi and entitled 'Tibetan Singing Bowls', followed by the CD 'The Medicine of Sound: Tibetan Healing with Singing Bowls and Chants' (2006), by the Ven. Choesang.[7] But in neither case is it stated that these recordings are representative of a tradition.

Furthermore, travellers in the Himalayas find few, or no answers, to their questions about the origin, history, or the traditional uses of the bowls within the context of spiritual discipline. The questioning of lamas or people from Tibet who visit the West very seldom improves upon this situation. We can only conclude either that knowledge regarding the uses of these bowls has been lost, or that they have never been a part of monastic Tibetan Buddhism and may only be now becoming incorporated into monastic practices as Western popularization encourages a reconsideration of their significance. Otherwise, we might conclude that other writers are correct in affirming that the work with sound, being considered very powerful, was most secret and that certain lamas did use them mostly for themselves but sometimes with others, for instance Gillabel in the book previously mentioned.[8]

From Rain Gray's booklet of 1989 we learn that the third Buddha Wasong changed the practice by the Arhats of using the bowls for begging, designating that iron bowls be used instead. According to Lama Thupten Lobsang Leche in Tibet (see below) there are three 'relic' bowls, one in Drepung, one in Narthary, and one at Sakya, all bowls were made from the pattern of the three original relic bowls. Drepung Monastery was built by the fifth Dalai Lama and behind the palace of Drepung there is a room called Kungar Awa, known as 'the throne of the singing bowl'. This bowl is a relic of the third Buddha, Buddha Wasong (2,500 BCE).

Tibetan Musical Culture

A very original civilization and musical culture developed in Tibet over many centuries, owing to its isolation by high altitudes, severe climate and formidable mountain ranges. Going back to the first millennium BCE, we find that Tibetans were herders of Central Asian Ch'iang tribes. The ancient way of life was that of nomadic pastoralism requiring alertness to the changes in nature – the passing seasons and variable weather conditions. The uncontrollable environment was thus seen to be possessed

of spirits and this led to shamanism of a kind recognized as
the Northern and Central Asian type. Spirits were individually
respected and the need to involve and relate to them may well
be the reason that the name of Tibet's indigenous ensemble
of beliefs (Bon) means, 'To make offerings', or 'conjuring the
gods by magical formulas'. We might also see a reflection of
addressing this need in Buddhism where the monks make music
for the Buddha and their divinities.

The term 'magical formulas' places a close link between Bon
and sound and, perhaps more exactly, to mantra linking with the
Hindu metaphysics of sound – something we'll explore in detail in
a later chapter.

> *In the spring, when the ice cracks and melts, we say
> the sounds are the mountain spirits performing sacred
> ceremonies.*

The borders of Tibet have moved greatly, over many centuries, meaning that many neighbouring regions would have been
Tibetan in the past. Such regions have included, to the East, parts
of the Chinese provinces of Szechuan, Kansu and Yunnan; to the
West, the now-Indian regions of Ladakh, Lahul and Spiti; and to
the South, Bhutan, Sikkim, parts of northern Nepal, the Sherpa
and Tamang regions of eastern Nepal and the extreme north-west
of Assam. Therefore, antique bowls coming from these regions,
and during those periods of history, can be considered Tibetan.
Despite this, it is probably best to speak of them as Himalayan
singing bowls.

We may think of Tibet as being a Buddhist country, although
prior to Buddhism entering Tibet, there existed Bon. Adherents
of this faith (Bonpo) still survive, especially in the east of Tibet.
Bon embodies a vast mass of ritual practices bearing on exorcism,
divination and the appeasement of wrathful divinities and also
includes elaborate teaching to guide the individual to full self-
realization.

The Bonpo do not recognize the authority of the Buddha
Shakyamuni, the historical figure who lived two and a half thousand years ago and to whom we owe the teachings of Buddhism.

They trace the source of their doctrine to Lord Tonpa Shenrab Miwoche, who for them is the real 'Buddha', the enlightened one. According to some Bon traditions this Lord visited Tibet over eighteen thousand years ago. He taught the Tibetans to reinforce their relationships with the guardian spirits and the natural environment, exorcising demons, and eliminating negativities. He also taught practices of purification by fire and by water and by the air element, introducing prayer flags as a way of reinforcing fortune and positive energy.

Tradition states that he came from a country to the west of Tibet called Tazig (sTag-gzig) – a place identified with the ancient Persian Empire – and brought Bon to Zhang-zhung (which has been called Shambhala by some), a culture in the Ngari region of north-west of Tibet in one of the highest, loneliest and most desolate places on the planet. Except for a few small bands of nomadic herders the empty plains are crossed only by the wind. The soul-mountain of Zhang-zhung was the ice-capped pyramid called Kang Tise – later known in the West by its Hindi name, Kailas. Another title was Yungdruk Gu Tseg, the 'Nine-Storey Swastika Mountain'. To Bonpo, as to Hindus, the swastika was an ancient symbol of power. The name Bon derives from Pannya, meaning one who worships the mystic cross (or swastika). From Zhang-zhung the shamanistic doctrine of Bon was introduced to Tibet and the sacred texts were translated from the language of Zhang-zhung into Tibetan. In Zhang-zhung the first form of the Tibetan written language was created. One view of Bonpo, held by John Vincent Bellezza, is to see them as a priestly caste more than as a religion:

> In my opinion, the use of *bon-po* for a type of archaic religious functionary is a more appropriate rendering, avoiding any intimation of a monolithic religion in prehistoric and early historic times. There are no definite historical indications that an organized religion with a unified ecclesiastic structure and doctrinal system existed until the end of the tenth century CE. To the contrary, it appears likely that there were a variety of popular cults based at least in part on localized clan and ritual traditions. These cults may have varied substantially from region to region.

There were also elite or royal forms of religion with a wider purview. This 'higher' religion seems to have been dominated by priests (*bon-po* and *gshen*) who protected the well-being of the kings who carried out their funerary rites after death.[9]

Nowadays, with Bon largely indistinguishable from Buddhism, we find the concepts of 'impermanence' and of the 'empty nature' of the phenomenal world and in addition the awareness of a transcendental state, 'enlightenment', this being attained through scholastic study, ritual practices and meditational experience. Bon teaches the 'nine ways', as also found in Nyingma (the Red Hat Sect – the 'Ancient Ones'), the first form of Tibetan Buddhism, which did not entirely abandon the indigenous faith but instead formed an amalgamation. Subsequent Tibetan sects tended to look to India, thus abandoning their indigenous beliefs. Bon came to be considered 'pagan' in Tibet and it is only recently that the situation has improved, which advance is partly due to H. H. the Dalai Lama's encouragement.

Nevertheless, Bonpo conserve a strong sense of independence and it may be their insistence upon maintaining a clearly separate identity – accepting new influences without rejecting old traditions – that has allowed them to build a syncretic religion.

In the earliest form of Bon there were no chapels or monasteries but, rather, crude stone altars, or stone monuments, in the form of menhirs and stone circles. Sometimes the stone altars are situated on the summits of mountains and sometimes in secluded caves amid rocks and towering cliffs. Each of these places is considered to have its own countryside god – as, too, is each mountain pass. These sacred places were used for primitive nature worship by the Bonpo in order to interact with their gods of heaven and earth, of sun and moon, of stars and of the four spatial directions.

From among their rituals, therefore, the propitiation of various divinities, protectors of Bon doctrine, is considered most important. These divinities were usually old mountain gods or forces of nature that have been symbolically subdued and put to the service of religion. Often the origin of the chant used for such rituals has its roots in legend, where a venerated spiritual figure from the lineage of transmission has received a visitation from one of the important guardian spirits – whereby the chant was revealed.

Confronted with the space and silence of the Himalaya man feels insignificant. The awareness of something greater than himself fills him with a sense of awe and of unseen powers and forces. And so ancient Tibetans knew their country was inhabited by invisible legions of gods, demons and spirits. These ruled earth, water and air, guarded mountain passes and river fords, dwelt in the hearth of every home and the ridgepole of every tent.

Over and above all of them were the mountain gods, with mountains the centres of Tibet's ancient folk religion. A holy peak was as a mighty lord: it embodied a region's 'soul' and protected those dwelling in its shadow. It is said that Tibet's first king descended from heaven onto a mountaintop in response to the prayers of the people, and when their reign was over it was from a mountaintop that the early kings returned into the sky.

Nowadays the Bon seek to restore ceremonial practices almost forgotten in their country. They intend to make better known the musical aspects of a ritual tradition that has remained largely unknown to the western world and ignored by the Tibetans themselves. It is a tradition which is nevertheless representative of the native elements of Tibetan religion, and contributed to the formation of the first school of Tibetan Buddhism.

Tibetan Ritual Music

In Tibetan ritual music, both instrumental music and chanting are employed. The large instrumental orchestra of Tibetan Tantric Buddhism, with its complex texture, provides the greatest contrast to the comparatively soft, restrained, unison-chanted sections, and the contrast creates the sense of passing from time to the timeless, from melody to sounds-in-one, from sound to silence. What lives in the magic of tone provides expression for going beyond the world of names and forms to the Formless, which Buddhists hold to be the nature of the ultimate reality. Drums, handbells, and large cymbals can accompany the chanting, whereas the entire orchestra (with the horns) features more as an interlude between sections of the chant.

In the course of their long history, Bonpo seem to have used flutes of animal horns and trumpets made of human thighbones. However, there are two chief instruments, both of Tibetan origin, and these are the *phyed-rnga* (single-headed drum) and the *gshang* (the 'flat bell' – with its rim turned inwards and its separate beater [horn] – used in both Bon and Buddhist religions). According to legend, the Bon priest playing his drum is considered to be riding a flying steed, carrying him up into the heights of spiritual ecstasy in communion with the celestial spirits.

Buddhism in Tibet is a form of Mahayana, syncretized through an early blend with Tantrism in India and with Bon in Tibet. Its monastic system, with Tibetan everywhere the liturgical language, has existed not only throughout the whole region of ethnic Tibet, but also in Mongolia, Buryat Siberia, the Caucasus, Manchuria, and parts of China and Turkestan (Xinjiang). With this religion, sound has always been an important way to spiritual enlightenment, such sacred sounds being used to assist the practice of meditation, devotional communication, and the cultivation of special insights and powers.

In the temple gigantic trumpets are roaring. The Lama asks:

'Do you know why the trumpets of our temples have so resonant a tone?'

And he explains: 'The ruler of Tibet decided to summon from India from the places where dwelt the Blessed One a learned lama, in order to purify the fundamentals of teaching. How to meet the guest? The High Lama of Tibet, having a vision, gave the design of a new trumpet so that the guest should be received with unprecedented sound; and the meeting was a wonderful one – not by the wealth of gold, but by the grandeur of sound!'

'And do you know why the gongs in the temple ring out with such great volume, and as silver resound the gongs and bells at dawn and evening, when the high currents are tense? Their sound reminds one of the beautiful legend of the Chinese emperor and the great lama. In order to test the knowledge and clairvoyance of the lama, the emperor made for him a seat from sacred books and covering them with fabrics, invited the guest to sit down. The lama made certain prayers and then sat down. The emperor demanded of him: "If your knowledge is so universal, how could you sit down on the sacred books?" "There are no sacred volumes", answered the lama. And the astonished emperor instead of his sacred volumes found only empty paper. The emperor thereupon gave to the lama many gifts and bells of liquid chine. But the lama ordered them to be thrown into river, saying "I will not be able to carry these. If they are necessary to me the river will bring these gifts to my monastery." And indeed the waters carried to him the bells, with their crystal chines, clear as the waters of the river.'[10]

At the time these words were written, the bowls were often mistakenly called gongs here in the West, or 'Bowl Gong', so that references to 'gongs' used by the Buddhist monks may well have referred to the singing bowls. I also find it easier to relate a 'silvery sound' to a bowl than to a gong. Mitch Nur in the interview already quoted on pp. 13-14 states, 'Singing Bowls are a type of resting Gong, and the Mongolian word for a singing bowl is *mon* which means gong'.[11]

The author of the sacred books story, Nicholas Roerich (Nikolai Rerikh in Russian) was an artist, archaeologist, peacemaker, writer, poet, philosopher, and traveller born in 1874 in St Petersburg. With his wife Helena he brought the Agni Yoga Teaching to humanity. Their Master was Mahatma Morya, head of the first ray, and one of the Dhyani Chohans in what Blavatsky referred to as the Trans-Himalayan Occult Brotherhood or the Great White Brotherhood. The Roerich family (with two sons, George and Svetoslav) travelled for five years throughout the Himalayan region, also taking in Tibet, during the 1920s. Roerich was also a Buddhist and a member of the Theosophical Society for a period, and his paintings (of which there are reputedly around seven thousand), in his final 'Himalayan' period, are deeply spiritual in nature.

The nomadic Tibetans, in their migrations, would experience the sound of wind passing through certain mountainous regions. It resulted in strange eerie sounds, suggestive of voices – especially to a nature-worshipping peoples rooted in the shamanic awareness of the proliferation of spirits. Such experiences contributed

to the development of their wind instruments (thighbone trumpets, *kang-dung, dun chen* and *gya-ling* [oboe]), with the largest
horns producing a thunderous roar audible for miles. These are
used in pairs to welcome a visiting high lama and otherwise to
call on and warn the spirits of ceremonials. This phenomenon of
the wind in the mountains can also arise within our bodies. Some
exercises in sound can lead to us experiencing bodily sounds, including a low-pitched roaring: one that we easily see reflected in
the deep resonant roar of the *dun chen* and within the very deep
vocal register achieved through undertone chanting in the Gyuto
and Gyume schools of Tantric chanting. In producing the lowest
possible sound from a human voice, there is association to the
fundamental root foundation of existence – the spiritual source
of being. In actuality, overtone singing is also combined with the
undertone technique to produce a chord within a single voice.

Chanting, trumpets, drumming and bells all focus sound and
varied patterns of sound are focused in the form of the ritual orchestral sounds. The aim is to experience the Whole via sonic unity, identified (in Kashmiri Shaivite doctrines that were transmitted
to Tibet) as *nadabindu*, sound-seed, or *spanda*, primal vibration.

Sound in the great desert.
Ring out the conch shell. Do you hear it?
The long, lingering, wistful call vibrates, quivers, melts in
the chasms.
Is there perhaps a monastery or a hermit?
Here we have reached the most deserted spot. Not within
six days from here is there one dwelling. Where, in these desolate mountains is there one lama, thus sounding his evocation?
But it is not a lama. We are in the mountains of Dunbure,
and from times beyond memory this signified: 'The Call of the
Conch Shell.'
Far off, the mountain call fades away. Is it reechoing among
the rocks? Is it the call of the Memnon of Asia? Is it the wind
furling through the corridored crevices? Or is the mountain
stream somewhere gurgling? Somewhere was born this enticing, lingering call. And he who named these mountains by
their caressing title, 'The Call of the Conch Shell,' heard the
summons of the sacred desert.[11]

One of the ancient Indian symbols of the Primal Sound, the conch shell trumpet, finds a place in the monastic music – as it does in the spiritual ceremonies of many cultures. The conch produces a very loud sound and in Buddhism is only used for *dharma* (the Law), calling monks, or for making *puja* (ritual offerings), and for this reason the sound of the conch is called *dharmachakra* (for that means the Wheel of the Law). The double-sided skull drum (*damaru*), another old Indian emblem of cosmic vibration (associated with Shiva), is played by a rotary flipping movement whereby the tethered bead strikes each side alternately. The two heads symbolize the dual nature of reality: the conventional reality and the ultimate. The Tibetan handbell (*drilbu*) is yet another symbol of the Primal Sound, and can also be used as a sonic focus for meditation by rubbing its rim gently and continuously with a stick (with this technique exclusively used by individual shamans and some Bonpo), so producing a sustained hum – similar to the stroked singing bowl (another symbol of Primal Sound). As used in Tibetan Buddhism the bell is always accompanied by a *vajra* (thunderbolt – see more in Chapter 5). The bell represents both the doctrine beyond hearing, and emptiness (due to its hollow form), the *vajra* the compassionate means to benefit others. In particular rituals every monk has the *drilbu* to sound at certain points during the ceremony.

The *drilbu* is basically of one design and is recognized anywhere, whereas the singing bowls have a greater diversity of shapes and forms. Variations in the design of these produce different sounds and combinations of these several designs produce yet further variances. Yet other bowls (from countries such as Japan, China, Thailand, and Korea) may bear similar appearances in form and yet produce different acoustical phenomena. I have identified a hundred such basic differences (see Appendix B) in bowl designs compared to the one type of Tibetan handbell.

A Firsthand Account

The Communist Chinese military occupation of Tibet in the 1950s, and the subsequent, almost total, destruction of its monasteries, has contributed towards the esoteric knowledge of

the Tibetan singing bowls all but disappearing. And although it
has been over forty years since Tibetan singing bowls and their
incredible sounds were first introduced to the Western world,
that destruction cannot have assisted in the survival of traditional
sources of information. It is also highly probable that during the
time of Tsong-Khapa (1357–1419 CE), a period of reformation,
any activities associated with shamanism or Tantric practices
were discouraged, so that owners of bowls who used them in
such a manner would have taken trouble to disguise their usage,
possibly by using the bowls for storage purposes, or as vessels
for food and drink. Thus, in time, such knowledge would have
gone underground and eventually disappeared.

Tantra was best suited to the teacher-student relationship plus
years of seclusion and therefore, judged by Tsong-Khapa to be
unsuited to monastic life. Certain Tantras were kept and allowed
in his reformed Gelugpa sect. It is also the case that the Tantrism
practised at his time had become distorted and emphasis was
placed upon more selfish aims. Tsong-Khapa kept those Tantras
geared towards selflessness or spiritual purification.

There is the story of the guru who had a cat. While he meditated, the cat proved a distraction and so he tied the cat to his bedpost. His disciples then interpreted this to mean that you cannot
meditate without a cat tied to a bedpost! By similar misinterpreta-
tion, singing bowls could quite quickly be considered as an expensive household vessel, pot, or bowl. Bowlmakers could have used
the bowls for domestic purposes between sales. It could also be the
case that bowlmakers sometimes used reject bowls as household
implements, perhaps even as signs of prestige, instead of recycling
them. Any such irregular use could contribute towards their being
seen as household items, and indeed there are stories that today's
bowlmakers lend them to villagers to be used, in order to age their
appearance!

Many people have deliberately travelled through the Himalaya
in an endeavour to discover something about the bowls, only to
return no wiser than when they left. In a booklet I shall quote
very shortly, we find that Rain Gray travelled and lived in the
Himalayan region for ten years, and it was eight years before he

could find any single individual, either monk or lay person, who could tell him anything at all concerning these instruments. He then turned to his Tibetan brother-in-law, Lama Lobsang Molam, and asked him for his help.

Lama Lobsang Molam, a Tibetan monk born in Lhasa, was at that time living at a small monastery in Swyambunath, in Kathmandu, Nepal. He assured Rain that he would try his best to find someone who could provide him with some information. After several months of enquiries the lama arrived at Gray's door one morning with exciting news. He had found an old monk who had the information Gray had been searching for. That monk was Lama Thupten Lobsang Leche who was around seventy years old at the time of Gray's interview in October 1986. Lama Thupten Lobsang Leche came from Drepung Losel Ling Monastery, the largest *gompa* (Monastery) in Tibet, having moved from Tibet to Nepal before 1959. Drepung is one of the four great monasteries of the Gelugpa Sect of Tibetan Buddhism and was said to have housed over forty thousand monks.

Here are short extracts from his interview which, it will be seen, is the source of some of our information earlier in this chapter. They are from his booklet, 'Tibetan Singing Bowls: A Historical Perspective. Lama Thupten Lobsang Leche as interviewed by Rain Gray' (1989).

> Lama Lobsang Leche: '...Fifth Dalai Lama he built it in Drepung, his first palace is in Drepung Monastery. So that singing bowl lives behind this palace, we call Kungar Awa, his throne, like a "singing bowl House", you know.'
>
> Lama Lobsang Molam: 'Someone says, one older than him, (a) monk, he said "This singing bowl comes from India side and before this previous Buddha", we call Sange Wasong, "is for begging bowl this is". That time this singing bowl is used for begging bowl of that previous Buddha.' [*According to the Tibetan Mahayana tradition, there have been many Buddhas in the past, and many more to come in the future. The next coming Buddha is known as 'Maitreya'. It is interesting to note that one translation of the name Maitreya is 'harmonic resonance'!* (footnote by Rain Gray)]

LLM: 'Yea. So, he said that that bowl is in Drepung Monastery, Tibet. July fifteenth time many Tibetans visit that singing bowl, also whole Drepung Monastery, all people coming, visiting and offering....'

RG: 'Three of these relic singing bowls?'

LLL: 'Yea, relics. One is (in) Drepung Monastery, one (in) Narthang. Narthang is big printing place.'

RG: 'Where their (sic) publishing and printing the books, the sutras. Kanjur?' '...And that the enlightened beings will then gather in this place Shambhala. I think there's kind of a connection to this sound and Shambhala. That's my feeling, I don't know, I think that somehow the ringing of these bells, of this sound, will somehow gather that positive energy, that force, you see, in order to fight back against those people who are trying to destroy the world.'

LLM: 'Yea.'

RG: 'If this is the sound of the Void, and the sound of the *dharma*, then in ringing these bells this is bringing the force of the *dharma*....'

LLM: 'If somebody has seeds of dharma, Westerner or Easterner, doesn't matter, you know....'

RG: 'Then this will awaken that seed, this sound?'

LLM: 'Yea, if so dharma goes to (the) West, Guru Padmasambhava said that 'dharma goes to West' means that definitely they have seeds. Of course, you know, all sentient beings have enlightened beings seeds, nature of dharma, of Buddha, you know, really. So, before all teaching is Asia, most teachings in Asia. So, actually, yea, yea. Also, Buddha is not in the world now, this world. So many other world(s) his presentation now, he's giving teaching. So, singing bowl can give teaching to (someone) who has the seeds of dharma. Each sentient has many different natures, many different 'ears.' That's why, yea of course, singing bowl can give you dharma. Really ... have that connection of that Buddha or Shambhala, same you know, really connection of singing bowl or those sounds connection to the Shambhala. Means singing bowl sound gives you yeaching (sic) then you can go to Shambhala. That is really (the) connection. Now Buddha is not here but singing bowl (is). Someone who can play the singing bowl, really, immediately you can get Buddha's teaching. Then you can meditate on this teaching, or sound, with bell you can become enlightenment. Singing bowl sound, and bell sound, and tingshaw sound is incredible really, Not like those ordinary sounds.'

Before the interview, Lama Leche stated that he had seen over four thousand monks playing Tibetan singing bowls during a religious ceremony at Drepung. He also said that when he was a child the monks had a set of seven singing bowls that were considered very rare, valuable, and difficult to replace (that is, no longer made). You can find the entire article published on Rain Gray's site: http://www.bodhisattva.com/history_singing_bowl.htm.

It is understood that bowls were made at Derge on the far eastern border with China and also (this from Rain's publication again) at Megu Kutsa where there were two factories. One is in Jang and one is in Hor. Those made at Hor can be distinguished by their heavier hammering marks and those from Jang have the nine heads. Lama Leche stated that the technique for making them was lost a long time ago. From the viewpoint that the bowls have more to do with the Bonpo, it is also interesting to note that Bon is prominent in the region of western Hor and holds undisputed sway over all the Hor tribes, while most of the Bonpo colonies are found between Derge and Golok in easternmost Kham and many Bonpo monasteries are found on the Nepalese border (many bowls are made in Nepal).

At source, depending upon who one asks, it is reputed that the singing bowls are made from an alloy consisting of anything from two, three, five, seven, nine, to even twelve different metals. Legends state that one of these metals is meteorite iron (see Chapter 9 for a longer discussion). It has been hypothesized that this use of meteorite iron may be one of the reasons why Tibetan bowls have such amazing sounds. However, I understand that meteorite is used sparingly and only for special bowls. I own a few bowls I believe to contain meteorite and my observations are that these bowls are invariably connected to spiritual initiation. Such bowls as these I observe carry an extra-terrestrial spirituality (somewhat distinct from the 'human' race), while bowls associat-ed with spiritual initiations are most rare. Also, as the meteorites found in Tibet have travelled through a thinner layer of oxygen than at lower levels, there may have been less burn-up of the me-teorite iron. Hence the meteorites found there may have a quality different from other meteorites found in other parts of the world.

Given that so much may have become lost concerning the bowls, all that we can now do is to sit peacefully and allow our intuitive feelings and our Higher Self to unfold the Divine Truth of the Void (the Buddhist conception of the ultimate nature of re-ality, referring specifically to the lack of an inherently existent self in all phenomena and beings) while listening to this unique and ancient sound world of the Himalayan singing bowls. Up amongst these lofty peaks, far removed from the hustle and bustle of the world below, in the stillness; in the Great Silence, the ancient seek-er found connection to Source. The Sound of Silence – a Sound that never leaves that silence, or stillness, that lives within the One Sound (*nada*) of the void – within the sacred singing bowl.

> Let us make this quite clear. The cultivation of silence in the breast, the cultivation of response to the inner voice, will lead the aspirant to the reception of the clear Voice of the Master, whose command he awaits.
>
> White Eagle[12]

More Testimonies about the Bowls in Tibet

I'd like to close this chapter with an assortment of stories about the bowls, all of them to do with their ritual and sometimes magical use in Tibet.

Speaking over the phone around 1985, Alain Presencer in-formed me that the spiritual adviser to H. H. the Dalai Lama re-searched the singing bowls and supplied the following informa-tion. 'The bowls have been found to be linked with "Fire Wor-ship". They are very old and come from a very early period of Tibetan History. They were kept in lamaseries. They would wor-ship the tones but didn't know what they were for. They seem to have originated from a very remote sect close to Bon – a primitive and animistic sect dedicated to fire and fire worship believed to be related or connected to the indigenous peoples of Nepal called the Newars. They were then used in meditation and also for astral travelling. The sound was experienced as moving from the bowl right around the world and then returning back into the bowl. Meditation with this, if possible, meant that one could likewise travel around the world. The bowls came across the silk route into Tibet and were then used for food and begging. Some Tibetans got into the sounds.'

In Alain's online book DISCOVERING TIBETAN ART (www.discovertibetanart.com) we read:

> Although these bowls are found in Tibet and recently a colleague (Ref. D. Aschencaen) discovered a giant bowl being currently used to induce states of altered consciousness in a remote part of Tibet, there is some controversy as to their authenticity as a Tibetan musical instrument.
>
> However, the author, who plays and has studied the bowls over many decades, has also researched thoroughly these amazing and mysterious instruments to discover via a communication from His Holiness the Dalai Lama's Library of Tibetan Works and Archives in Dharamsala, India, that, and 'It seems that Singing Bowls, although known in Tibet, are of Nepalese origin used by the Newaris of Nepal in the religious rites of Fire puja (burnt offerings) rites, now lost in the mist of antiquity.' (Sonam Choephell, private letter 10 May 1985, Office of the Dalai Lama, Library of Tibetan Works and Archives).

This link to Fire is interesting given the link to Tazig and Persia – seat of Zoroastrian fire worship – previously mentioned.

In a letter of December 1968 to another friend of mine (the late Mr Hector Benson, who owned four Tibetan Bowls), John Blofeld (author of MANTRAS and THE TANTRIC MYSTICISM OF TIBET) states that

> Metal objects of high quality were made for the Lhasa people in Nepal, in Derge (a place in the Tibetan part of China proper) and, above all, Peking. It seems clear enough that the bowl really came from Tibet, although China and Japan are

the place where musical bowls are commonly used in rites. It follows that the bowl (of a kind not usually used in Tibetan rites) could perhaps be a Chinese one sent to Tibet with a lot of specially designed Tibetan-style objects. I have a very cheap Bangkok made Chinese-style brass musical bowl which produces several notes and several kinds of vibrations according to how and where it is struck. I should say that most of them, even the cheap, ordinary ones, do produce an effect that is conducive to entering certain holy states of mind – that is what they are for.

In a letter from Tom Dummer of 'Urgyenpa Chos Ling' to Ralph White (1980s), a friend of mine, we find:

Lama Yeshe Dorje from Dharamsala is a Ngag-pa, otherwise known as a tantric yogi. I asked him about the 'singing-bowls' and their significance in Tibetan Buddhism. He was rather inclined to dismiss the importance of them saying that yes, people do have them, but he had come across them very little even when he was in Tibet. Moreover, he thought they were rather of Chinese origin, rather than purely Tibetan.... he obviously thought that the music of the 'singing-bowls' was not integral to our spiritual practice.

I have myself received several ancient and very sacred Tibetan ritual instruments directly from Tibet, demonstrating that there is a degree of familiarity with these powerful tools of transformation and magical ritual. This is not to deny that it may have been a path for the few. To give just two examples of those I have received: a twelfth-century meditation cymbal passed on by a visiting yogi from Tibet (Nyingma tradition); another was an extremely rare and very old 'Talking Bowl' from the Tibetan Master H. H. Dilgo Kyenste Rinpoche (head of the Nyingma School, a root teacher of H. H. the Dalai Lama and since reincarnated – who is considered to be one of the greatest spiritual masters from Tibet in the twentieth century).

Again, in support of the argument for a singing bowl tradition within Tibetan Buddhism is the story of Hungarian shaman Joska Soos, whom I met at the time of the story in the summer of 1981 at the Festival of Mind, Body and Spirit in London's Olympia – where I had all of my equipment permanently set up for daily performances of my music. Joska wanted to buy my recently released LP 'Deep Peace',[13] and he greeted me by saying, 'Me shaman. You shaman too'. I am referring to the story that appears in Jansen's book[14] published some ten years after, in which we read about his stay in the UK the year we met. He visited a Tibetan Buddhist monastery and during his time there the monks studied his horoscope and advised him that he could speed up his evolution if he worked with sound. Taking him to a small room, which had some singing bowls inside, they left him alone there and he spent time listening to the sounds. Later they presented him with some bowls. He took these bowls and listened to them more intently and so entered into a mystical experience. In the account he tells us that the bowls are used by the lamas but only in secret rituals and only by those acknowledged as being masters of sound. Joska informs us that it is strictly forbidden to share this knowledge of the secret rituals or even to mention the bowls because this secret knowledge regarding sound is very powerful. The sound masters working with the bowls are able to connect to the planets and the spirits residing therein and even to visit the abode of the higher beings. They live either in Shambhala or the subterranean kingdom of Agartha – a place that Roerich heard of on his Himalayan travels and depicted in several of his paintings, for instance, 'Command of Rigden Djapo' (1927) and 'Chud. The Subterraneans' (1929–30). You can view these on the Roerich website, http://www.roerich.org.

Another account of Joska and the bowls is to be found on Dirk Gillabel's website:

In the spring of 1981 he went to London for two months, but in the end stayed for five. One day when he strolled around on Portobello Road, he saw some Tibetan ritual objects. A strange feeling of familiarity with those objects came over him. He felt that he in some past life not only had owned similar objects but had also used them. Desiring to know more he went to the Victoria and Albert Museum, where he met a man who gave him an address of a Tibetan antiquary. The antiquary was in contact with a group of lamas who sold him all kinds of personal objects they had taken with them when they fled Tibet. Joska was invited to their informal meetings. Aside from a few spiritually interested non-Tibetans, they all belonged to the red cap monks of the Karmapa Order. So, Joska attended their meetings on a regular basis and talked about many aspects of lamaism, and about his own experiences. They made a Tibetan horoscope for him, from which they concluded that he had been a Tibetan lama in a past incarnation, and before that a Chinese mandarin and Taoist. They organized a special ritual to bring him, and a couple of others, in contact with their genetic past.[15]

So the monks from Samye-Ling (the monastery in England here referred to) steered Joska towards the singing bowls. After one of my concerts in London a woman who was studying Tibetan medicine at Samye Ling approached me saying she'd asked the lamas about the bowls but was simply told that it was something that the Nepalese did to make money. There is the saying that 'when the pupil is ready the Master appears'. I felt that this was what was behind the response the lamas gave, putting her off the trail. There is the right time for things in our lives. If and when it is the right time to work with singing bowls it will happen. Some people might have to wait until a future lifetime. It is said that Joska Soos bought bowls from Tibetan lamas while he was in London and was told by them that bowls were produced at four Tibetan monasteries. Some lamas deny any knowledge of singing bowls whatsoever, while it seems that others are willing even to sell them to certain people, including Joska and myself.

Alexandra David-Neel, some of whose story we read earlier, wrote in her book, TIBETAN JOURNEY, about a wonderful experience with sound. Alexandra had entered a Bon monastery at Tesmon when one of her bearers wandered into the temple becoming very abusive. The Bonpo priest eventually made a sound upon a *shang* (a kind of cymbal) and the man ran out terrified, convinced that he was being chased by a 'snake of fire'. Even the other bearers saw 'flashes of light'. Alexandra spoke with the Bonpo about this and wrote:

Such is the power of the *zungs* (magic word) that I uttered,'

declared the lama, with a slight emphasis. And he continued
in a low voice:

'Sound produces forms and beings, sound animates
them…. As to me I am a master of sound. By sound, I can kill
that which lives and restore to life that which is dead.'[16]

The next day, before parting, he said to her:

'All beings, all things, even those things that appear to be inanimate, emit sounds. Every being, every thing gives out a sound
peculiar to itself; but this sound, itself, becomes modified, according to the different states through which the being or thing
that emits it passes. How is this? – It is because these beings
and things are aggregates of atoms (*rdul phra*) that dance and
by their movements produce sounds. When the rhythm of the
dance changes, the sound it produces also changes.

'It is said that, in the beginning, the wind, in whirling,
formed the *gyatams*, the base of our world. This whirling
wind was sonorous and it was sound that aggregated matter
(*rgyu*) in the form of *gyatams*. The primordial *gyatams* sang
and forms arose, which, in their turn, generated other forms
by the power of the sounds that they gave out. All this does
not only relate to a past time, it is always thus. Each atom (*rdul
phra*) perpetually sings its song, and the sound, at every moment, creates dense or subtle forms. Just as there exist creative
sounds, which construct, there exist destructive sounds, which
separate, which disintegrate. He who is capable of producing
both can, at will, construct or destroy. There is one sound that
is called by our masters: 'the sound that destroys the base'.
This sound is itself the foundation of all destructive sounds.
The dubthob who could cause it to sound would be capable
of annihilating this world and all the worlds of the gods up to
that of the great 'Thirty-three', of which the Buddhists speak.'

*(The priest was a 'White Bon'. Dubthob is a Sage who pos-
sesses supernatural powers.)*[17]

In TIBET'S ANCIENT RELIGION: BON, Christoph Baumer tells us:

Even though today we are still not able to date the beginning
of metallurgy in Tibet, the bronze figures found by Tucci in
western Tibet are highly informative. They show that Tibetan

metal smiths had reached a high degree of skill long before the
dawning of the Buddhist era. They had obviously used as a
model imported patterns drawn from ancient Iranian art and
that of the Central Asian steppe cultures. These finds include
small figures of khyung birds, and among these a particularly
rare one is composed of two joined bodies and four heads. In
all likelihood, this was an amulet.

These examples of ancient metal-working art are not surprising in view of the fact that in Tibet there were rich deposits
of raw materials such as copper, iron, lead, zinc, silver and
gold. The exploitation of the gold resources of western Tibet
must have begun at the latest in the middle of the last millennium BCE, since Herodotus (485–420 BCE) already speaks of
'gold grubbing ants' busy at work in the regions to the north
of India. Other accounts, notably that of the famous Buddhist
pilgrim Xuanzang (603–664), permit us to conclude that these
marvellous gold fields were located in the western Tibetan region of Shang-shung.[18]

Again, Gillabel, in SINGING BOWLS: A GUIDE TO HEALING THROUGH
SOUND, sets out evidence for bowls existing for over 4,000 years
through an excavation (1938) of an old Bon temple dated at 2,400
BCE, where two singing bowls were found. I asked him where he
got this information and he told me that it came from Joska Soos.
With a view to verifying this account I then contacted scholar, explorer, writer, and pilgrim John Vincent Bellezza, who is widely recognized as one of the foremost specialists in the archaeology and
cultural history of Upper Tibet. He has lived in the high Himalaya
for over a quarter of a century. A pioneer in his field, he is credited with the discovery of hundreds of pre-Buddhist archaeological
sites, describing the monuments and the people that built them in
great detail. However, regretfully he was unequivocal in stating
that no such finding existed regarding this Bon temple and bowls.

The letter by John Blofeld reproduced above presents the likelihood that some bowls have been gifted to Tibetans or brought
into Tibet, and are therefore not indigenous, so that certain bowl
forms are not Tibetan. Further complications arise if we consider
that certain yogis practising Tibetan methods of empowerment

(mentioned above) – be they indigenous Tibetans or not – may have applied such magical practices to bowls they owned and used that may have been manufactured outside of Tibet. If we also allow that wandering metalsmiths made some bowls, then the design of such bowls may well not have originated in Tibet even if that was where they were commissioned and produced. As I stated in the opening chapter, the more accurate term will always be 'Himalayan bowls', as they exist throughout the region and can neither be said to be specific to Tibet nor even to have originated there.

Lastly, and on the side who reject the authenticity of singing bowls, it remains an incontrovertible fact that many of the travellers who visited pre-Communist Tibet and wrote about their experiences make no mention of ever having witnessed anybody playing a singing bowl. Such an experience would have been worthy of comment if they'd seen it. However, it is also possible that those working with profound sound would not have advertized their activities – especially to rather academic Westerners. One exception of course is the case of Alexandra David-Neel accidentally witnessing a Bon working with the power of sound. That, at least, hints at such realms. If it were the case that working with bowls went underground during the reforms of Tsong-Khapa, this would be another causative factor.

Against this, the study of sound and the effects of vibrations was so advanced that in China so-called 'spouting bowls' were made from the fifth century BCE. These are bronze bowls with very specific shapes and dimensions. When one is filled with the indicated amount of water and the handles (attached to the two sides on the flat rim of the bowl) are rubbed in a special way with the moistened palms of the hands, a humming sound is produced. A fountain of water rises up. Inscribed on the inside bottom of the bowl are often four fishes with open mouths and from above these four mouths small fountains of water arise eventually forming a fountain which experts can raise to a metre high!

Knowing of these, I went on to discover a rare type of singing bowl designed to create similar effects and for these, decades ago now, I originated the term 'Fountain Bowls'. They have very specific markings to indicate their intended purpose. To be exact,

*Fountain
Bowl*

there is a line engraved upon the inside of the bowl in an unusual position, and when the bowl is filled with water to that exact mark, it then works as a Fountain Bowl. Other water bowls are sometimes referred to as 'Star Bowls' (because of the star shapes that form upon the surface of the water when played). Although it may be possible to reproduce the fountain effect with many bowls, few have a demarcation line for the specific amount of water required.

The singing sound of various metal alloys has been extensively used in the many different gongs found in Asia. The discovery that metal objects produce sounds was made all over the world, and (according to Jansen) small, metal, skull-shaped bowls were known around 1,100 BCE.

In the mid 1980s I first met a Shamanic friend, Ngakpa Chogyam. He then owned three Tibetan singing bowls, which he had received from one of his Tibetan 'Root Teachers' of the White lineage of Ngakpas, who had used them in connection with healing. This would seem to indicate that the bowls sometimes do appear in such little-known lineages within Tibetan Tantric Buddhism. When he played one of these bowls during his workshop I saw episodes from the life of Padmasambhava pass before my inner vision.

What is known as the Direct Path flourished in Tibet among the hermits, wandering *chodpas, dzogchenpas, ritodpas* and within nomadic encampments of practitioners in isolated valleys and in mountain caves where *naljorpas* such as Milarepa spent years in isolation. We may be astonished to learn that there are many different lineages, little known outside Tibet, of which the Ngakpa tradition is but one. Most of us when thinking of spiritual life in Tibet would immediately bring to mind monks and nuns in the monasteries. However, there were other practitioners living in different ways and one of these is the Ngakpa lineage of householders: family men and women, although it is to be admitted that some lived in isolation or as wanderers.

We can recognize a Ngakpa male by his uncut hair, which symbolizes the way of transformation rather than renunciation, the latter usually identifiable by the shaven head. The former denotes the Tantric path and the latter the Sutric, which is one of renunciation at the external level and has a strict code of behaviour to govern our internal spiritual pathway. In the Tantric way, one works with the Dhyani Buddhas to transform the distorted energy of any one or more of the five elements in wisdom (there is more on this and how it relates to the bowls in Chapter 14).

The ancient tradition of the Ngakpa has had many realized women – which again may not be something that we immediately think of in connection with Tibetan Buddhism. This inclusion of the feminine is personified in the mother essence-lineage of Kuntazangpo. Since we are possessed of free will it is possible for us to go against the laws of nature. However, it is always possible to live in harmony with them and, like the rest of nature, we will then move away from any idea of escaping the earthly side of our life – realizing the interrelatedness of everything through this path of integration (not hedonism). When we have harmony with our essential nature but remember that life on earth is about growth, providing us with endless opportunities to evolve, everything is perfect exactly as it is.

The meditation technique known as *shi-ne* (silent sitting) is designed to assist us in harmonizing the five elements. If one of them manifests in our lives in a distorted manner, then this meditation can help us raise our energy to a more refined manner of expression. The Nyingma have maintained this tradition, although it can also be found in all Schools of Tibetan Buddhism and with the Cherokee Indians (who call it 'listening'). The Japanese call it *za-zen* but no matter what it is called it refers to the stilling of our continual internal dialogue and thereby entering into the great silence. The sound energy of a good singing bowl arises from this silence in a way that very little of that silence is lost – so encouraging our mind to contemplate the silence and enjoy direct perception of anything through a form of entrainment.

In essence, the practice of *shi-ne* merges us with the space element and so loosens our attachment to the logical thought processes. Entering into the realm of space we encounter awareness or being and insights can come in a flash, circumnavigating the everyday rational process of thinking and providing direct perception of the ultimate reality to which we are all related. This quite spontaneously awakens compassion towards the great human family and for all life in the universe that shares the vast space of essential being.

Certain singing bowls have a sound that is in harmony with such an expanded sense of Self, while being consecrated to serve such a purpose. They afford us the opportunity of being a focal point for the compassionate and selfless release of this awareness out into the world and universe.

Hopefully, we have observed from reading much of the above that the use of sound in this spiritual culture of Tibet is identified with inner-world spiritual activities including magical dimensions. At the very least we can say that working with Tibetan singing bowls from within such contexts is somewhat in keeping with these sound traditions, and neither a foreign nor a modern projection.

4. Ting-Sha

THE PERCUSSIVE metallic ritual artefacts usually found in Tibetan Buddhism are the *rolmo* and *silnyen* (pairs of large orchestral cymbals), *ting-sha* (otherwise known as *ting-shags*, *ting-shaws*, *ding-sha* and Nagani Bells, a pair of small cymbals), and the *drilbu* (or handbell). The *drilbu* are always covered with specific Buddhist symbols and nowadays the *ting-sha* are likewise adorned. *Ting-sha* are most often sold as a pair joined by a piece of leather (or a metal chain) to be struck together but are sometimes made to be sounded alone. However, I have always found such single cymbals to be plain without any symbolic markings. These are not so commonly made nowadays and thus most likely to be antique when found. The more usual matched pair of *ting-sha* has the correct difference in pitch between the two cymbals in order to produce the characteristic rapid beat frequencies that occur when they are struck together – this sound phenomenon (beats) also exists in the single cymbals that I own. Nowadays this matching of pairs is not always carried out, meaning that only dedicated merchants, prepared to spend time sorting through cymbals, pair them together properly and achieve this uniquely traditional acoustical effect. Some modern bowls are being produced with Buddhist symbols upon them, while others are also engraved with a deity and others even have a three-dimensional Buddha at the inside centre! These features are almost always more recent additions.

The most common marking on *ting-sha* is that of the Tibetan Buddhist mantra, 'Om a hung' (*om ah hum* in Sanskrit), usually found on the underside, or otherwise the eight 'auspicious' Buddhist symbols (*ashtamangala*), the Tibetan mantra 'Om Mani Peme Hung' (the *om mani padme hum* of Sanskrit), while *dorjes* or dragons adorn the upper side and may be either engraved or embossed. The three syllables inscribed on the underside in an anti-clockwise direction represent the enlightened body (*om*), speech (*a*) and mind (*hung*) – that is to say, purity in deed (body), word (speech) and thought (mind). Traditionally these are also symbolized in colour at their respective chakra positions of the crown (white *om*), the throat (red *a*) and the heart (blue *hung*) on the reverse surface of a *thanka* (deity painting), where they serve to consecrate or 'empower' the main central figure/deity.

These syllables also symbolize the transmutation of the three 'poisons' of ignorance (white *om*), desire (red *a*) and aggression (blue *hung*) into the three enlightened qualities of wisdom, compassion and power. Additionally, they represent the three 'divine bodies of a Buddha': the physical 'form or emanation body' (*nirmanakaya* – white *om*), the visionary 'enjoyment body' (*sambhogakaya* – red *a*) and the pure, empty, 'truth or *dharma* body' (*dharmakaya* – blue *hung*). Usually there is a fourth syllable represented by a short horizontal line with a small circle above and another below and this is known in Tibetan as a *ter-shay*. This is a full-stop symbol and it is frequently found at the close of a mantra and indicates that the mantra in question was revealed through a *terma*, or 'hidden treasure', text.

However, I own several *ting-sha* that are centuries old. One of these (estimated to be from the twelfth century) I've had since two days before my twenty-fifth birthday in 1973. There are a few others, all single *ting-sha* with bone strikers (one with a deer antler), and plain with no markings above or below. The ancient one does have an engraved circular line just in from the upper edge of the cymbal and close to the edge of the central dome. They also possess much softer, rounded edges, unlike the modern versions that are flat and angular. Finer examples have a chain linking *ting-sha* and striker.

Pictured on the next page is the ancient single *ting-sha* from the twelfth century. It was Ron Bonewitz (a geologist who was selling crystals at the time) who, at the Festival for Mind, Body, and Spirit in London's Olympia in 1981 (where I was performing daily) showed me the crystals that had formed in the metal of this cymbal. He explained to me that this deposit takes at least five hundred years to form. Hopefully, you will be able to see these flecks of crystal in the dome of the cymbal close to the leather from which it is suspended. This is one reliable method of dating metal. However, the flecks need to be of a certain type as sometimes, owing to the process of manufacture, similar-looking crystallizations appear but they don't have the colour of a crystal. They will be more golden. Such crystallized metal likewise occurs in bowls over five hundred years old, too.

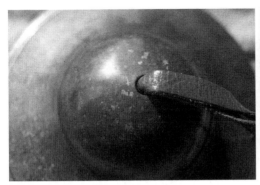

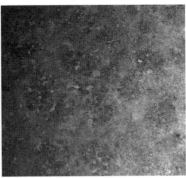

Crystallized metal in a twelfth-century ting-sha *('Silver Ray of the Great Master')*

Crystallized metal in ancient 'Great White Light Initiation Bowl' that also has meteorite.

The *ting-sha* somewhat resemble the traditional shape of UFOs, perhaps prompting speculation that they were a gift from extra-terrestrials! As we recognize that the sound of the *ting-sha* serves to recall our mindfulness practice, there is no reason that they shouldn't serve to recall our connections with interplanetary beings. Certain of those beings that we call angels are beings from other planets. The possession of a physical body is not the only form of life in the universe. Perhaps one of their uses was a ritual, in which the *ting-sha* were struck to call the attention of beings beyond the visible planet? Esoteric wisdom states that God-men walked the planet in the ancient past, while it is also taught that *dzogchen* (teachings) exists in over thirty other solar systems!

Ting-sha have a very thick rim and can be played in three basic ways: hanging down and their edges brought together, or the top one held vertically and brought down upon the other one lying horizontally, or traditionally with both cymbals held vertically with the upper one being brought down at right angles to the lower one

and struck together (as shown).
This last method produces the
most dramatic sound.

The sound of the *ting-sha*
is like a powerful summons. It
also cuts across our thinking
to bring us right into the here
and now. They seem to make
everything 'crystal clear', calling every atom of our being to
attention in the here and now,
while also cleansing our aura.
One of their traditional uses is
in meditation, marking both the
beginning and end. They can also serve to bring us back to the
centre of our meditation when our mind wanders. As we listen to
their cleansing sound, our awareness can begin to hear the silence
within all sounds, the silence of the Universal Presence which sustains our lives. It is like sending radiating throughout space the
light of primordial being: sending its love rays to all – like the sun,
but with sounding fire – purifying! They radiate forth as a clear
beam of light to awaken all beings to their own essential pure
Buddha nature! This quality of projection with their sound can be
utilized in directing this healing energy of pure spiritual fire and
divine light towards others.

Traditionally *ting-sha* are played at the level of the heart chakra.
This can serve to remind us when using the power of spiritual
sound and light to work always from the heart of compassion and
pure selfless love.

In the boxed set of *ting-sha* and small book by Robert Beer (TI-
BETAN TING-SHA: SACRED SOUND FOR SPIRITUAL GROWTH) there is information regarding traditional rituals and uses. They are used in rituals for guidance of the dead (Bardo Thodol or 'Liberation through
hearing in the between'), and to summon the Hungry Ghosts or
Pretas (also known as *yi-dag*) to collect their offerings, the Water
torma and *sur* offering for the Four Classes of Guests. Apart from
these and their use as an aid to meditation they appear in only a

few rituals, which are usually performed by single practitioners.

Otherwise they were also used to exorcise wicked spirits from a house where someone had recently died. A modern application in the West is their use in space-cleansing rituals and for healing tears or holes in the human aura. For space-cleansing purposes they are struck together in the most dramatic fashion (traditional method) and I perform this three times in each corner of the room in which space-cleansing is taking place (in every room – if an entire house is being cleansed). Personally, I prefer to use a pair having a sound that channels or resonates with the space-cleansing energy. If you are seeking to work in this way you may like to consider such aspects when choosing a pair.

As with many such instruments, each *ting-sha* is individual. In no way are pairs manufactured with such precision as to be each exactly the same and, consequently, predictable in their sound and thus application. One has to discern a certain quality within the sound in order to use them for a specific purpose.

In fact, it is the difference in pitch between each single *ting-sha* that is exploited in the beat found in properly matched pairs. Beer states in his book: 'After casting, each individual *ting-sha* is skilfully tuned by hammering around the thick outer rim to create a perfectly matching pitch for each pair'. I have never noticed any sign of this in all the hundreds of *ting-sha*, I've seen nor in the pair that accompanies his boxed set of *ting-sha* and book. The *ting-sha* being cast, subsequent hammering would be somewhat superfluous. He also states that the *ting-sha* sold with his book are 'pitched in approximately the "key" of E major' – however, my pair didn't even sound an E but rather a F# ([+46] so not a 'pitch' at all) and,

3040	F# (4) + 46		2471.5	Eb (4) – 12	
3071	**G (4) – 36**	1	2543	Eb (4) + 37	
3101.5	G (4) – 19		2577.5	E (4) – 39	2
			2649	E (4) + 7	3
			2683	**E (4) + 29**	1
			2717.5	F (4) – 47	
			2789	F (4) – 2	

Table #1

regrettable to say, it is impossible for one pair of cymbals to sound a 'key' (of seven different notes) from a Western major scale. In Table 1 these *ting-sha* from Beer (left) are compared with another pair of mine (right). The final number along the line indicates the loudest pitch. The pair on the left (Beer) had three pitches and those on the right had seven. The *ting-sha* on the left rang on for thirteen seconds while those on the right lasted for twenty-four. I'd say that fifteen seconds was about average – as a guide for when you are selecting a pair.

Ting-sha come in quite a variety of sizes created by craftsmen of differing abilities and skills from a choice of alloys. Mine range in size from 2.35 to 3.65 inches. It is said that the finest are cast from a pure bronze alloy of copper and tin with a white metal component of zinc and nickel. The relatively recent addition of raised symbols has the effect of reducing the responsiveness of the cymbal, resulting in a loss of the upper partials and shortening the duration, so that a pair sought for space-cleansing may best be chosen from pairs with no decoration (or featuring an engraved design).

Furthermore, pairs of *ting-sha* (also the single ones which are sometimes referred to as 'meditation cymbals') produce quite a variety of sound characteristics, with some pairs producing a gentle and peaceful quality, and others stilling and meditative; and while certain pairs are dull and unappealing some have a bright, sweet, and lingering sound. Particular pairs may produce a quality that heightens one's awareness and successfully cuts through our wayward thinking when trying to meditate, and yet others are very lively, with a degree of dissonance in the interaction of the upper partials around the beating phenomenon. It is from among these latter that I choose to work in a space-cleansing capacity. In such work I tend also to use one of my space-cleansing singing bowls and in situations involving serious black magic I also have recourse to my 'Panic Bowl' – traditionally used for exorcisms in Tibet.

Regarding the syllables decorating pairs of *ting-sha*, the *om mani padme hum* is usually translated as 'Om the Jewel in the Lotus'. This is the mantra of Chenrezig (Avalokitesvara in Sanskrit), the chief deity of Tibet. OM is considered to be the closest sound to the primordial tone or, otherwise, the hum of the entire universe.

When the Eight Auspicious Symbols are used, these are:

The Parasol	*Attribute of royalty, it symbolizes the protection of the Dharma.*
The Treasure Vase	*This is used as a sacred receptacle and thus symbolizes hidden treasures.*
The Pair of Golden Fishes	*These symbolize spiritual liberation. As water allows fish to swim freely, so Buddhist belief emancipates the soul.*
The Lotus	*The image of a lotus, symbolizing purity, is widely used in Buddhist iconography.*
The Victory Banner	*A unique Buddhist object, the cylindrical layered banner symbolizes victory over ignorance and death.*
The White Conch Shell	*Used in Buddhist worship as a trumpet or offertory vessel, it symbolizes the spoken word.*
The Glorious Endless Knot	*An auspicious geometric diagram, it symbolizes the unity of all things and the illusory character of time.*
The Golden Wheel	*Represents the unity of all things.*

The eight-spoked wheel symbolizes the 'Noble Eightfold Path' of Buddha Shakyamuni's precept. At the centre of the wheel is *dharmakaya* – the Buddha teaching. The spokes represent the eight stages of the path. The wheel's outer circumference shows that all the different forms are unified. In spinning the wheel, no spokes can be seen. We see only their oneness.

It is considered by some that the *ting-sha* were first used by the Bon before Buddhism entered into Tibet and that the Bon used them to call the *naga* spirits.

Varying in their quality, with *ting-sha* you get what you pay for – unless the dealer isn't too greedy and is prepared to make a more modest gain on his resale, or if the seller is unaware of the true value. Spiritual centres may sell them at a lower price but there is no guarantee that they have the best sound. The monks from Tashilhunpo monastery were selling good quality *ting-sha* and I commented on this to their most senior representative (second in rank to the Abbot). He replied that they had indeed asked the makers to improve the sound. As with any of these instruments, if you wish to work with sacred sound you really must listen for yourself. It is not advised to listen to 'sound samples' over the net or to base your purchase upon descriptions in catalogues. There is no substitute for your own ears and the 'hands-on' experience of your whole being as you interact with the sounds – regardless of any claims that may be made. Some sellers demonstrate using a pair of cymbals but sell you another. I believe it best to buy the pair you hear.

Here is a story that's perhaps of interest. I was at the home of Evan Parker, the tenor and soprano saxophonist, listening to the latest LP of his duo with percussionist Paul Lytton (1972). Paul is an improvising percussionist and, at that time, one of the highest compliments I could have paid him would have been to say what a lot of noise he created!

As was customary for me, I was listening with my eyes closed, attentive to the complex soundscape. As the music faded it dwindled down to the single sound of a pair of Tibetan *ting-sha*. I was utterly taken aback as I wouldn't have expected any of my contemporary improvising percussionists to have such a spiritually aware intention behind their played sounds. I thought to myself, meaning it only with reference to the sort of music he played, 'If this is Paul Lytton, then I must radically rethink my view of what he is doing in his playing'. I thought that I was the only contemporary percussionist ensouling my sounds with spiritual meaning. This because I had stated my intentions along these lines in several magazine articles that had been published around that period and in that I was alone. In fact, it seemed to me that I was one of the very few musicians on the entire scene living a spiritual life (abstaining from alcohol, drugs, smoking, the eating of flesh, etc.) and striving to make spiritual music – there being no shortage of agnostics or atheists. I instantly 'heard' the consciousness (the thought-awareness) behind the sound of these Tibetan cymbals. But after three strikes there came the roaring sound of the Tibetan long horns and I realized that Evan had switched records from his duo to Sacred Tibetan ritual music! What a relief! My ears hadn't deceived me.

Because of my supersensible studies into the effects of my percussive sounds, I was more involved with what these sounds did to the various bodies of the listeners. Because of this the shift, during that listening experience, from sounds without any deliberate intention to affect the inner consciousness of the listener, was starkly contrasted with that of the meditating Tibetan monk sounding his one pair of *ting-sha* in the deep intensely concentrated act of sacred sound.

5. Drilbu

THE TIBETAN handbell known as the *drilbu* is often heard in the rituals of the Tantric Tibetan Buddhist monks and also during certain passages of their orchestral music. Otherwise, it is played in isolation by yogis, *ngakpa*, wandering *chodpa*, and shamanic practitioners. Its model, the *ghanta*, comes from India – even as the models for the *ting-sha* are the small Indian cymbals, *tala*. The handbell features during certain moments of many religious services accompanied by the *dorje* (Sanskrit *vajra*, seen in front of the *drilbu* in the picture). With a large group of people it is necessary to sound a call for those moments when they are to gather. We may extend this act of invitation a little farther by sending this call to those spirits no longer in physical bodies and to the angelic brethren, and so on. And so it is used (like the *ting-sha*) to summon or attract attention. In Tantra it is frequently used in order to summon, invite, or attract deities or other figures to attend and participate in the functions of the ritual.

The English phrase 'That rings a bell' is about calling to mind something previously experienced. Thus the purpose of the bell is to remind us of our need to reconnect regularly with our essential being and purpose – hence we have the 'mindfulness bell' (singing bowl) that helps us to remain 'awake'.

The *drilbu* is always accompanied by the *dorje*, where during the rituals the *drilbu* is held in the left hand while the *dorje* is held in the right. This represents working with wisdom and compassion respectively. For ritual purposes the *dorje* is first picked up by the right hand and then the *drilbu* with the left. The *dorje* is a ritual implement that is laid upon the altar for certain ceremonies and is used in various mudras (symbolic hand and finger positions), and the half *dorje* is often attached to sacred ritual implements such as the *phurba* (ritual dagger), cutter, sword, and hammer. It is also known as the diamond sceptre and is derived from the *vajra* of India. The *dorje* is a symbol of spiritual power, and its link to the diamond indicates the indestructibility of the spiritual essence. In these two implements some see an expression of the mantra of Tibet – 'Om Mani Padme Hum', 'the jewel in the lotus', whereby the *vajra* ('diamond' jewel – masculine) is in the feminine (*padma* or lotus – bell-shape) unfolding universe.

The *drilbu* is almost completely covered with significant Tibetan Buddhist symbols so that it becomes a three-dimensional mandala when viewed from above. The mandala is as a palace for the central deity and we shall now follow this path inwards from the circumference. We can view the bell as being comprised of four parts. There is the half *dorje* at the very top (*para* sound) and beneath this is the face of Prajnaparamita (*pashyanti* sound) and then the shoulder of the bell (*madhyama* sound) and finally the main body and rim (*vaikhari* sound); for the terms, see pp. 331–2, below. This is a general statement, given that there may well be other markings in between these main parts.

From THE VAJRA AND BELL by Vessantara, 2001, we learn the meaning of the symbols that adorn the *drilbu*. Some of the following is based upon that information.

The full circumference is at the rim of the bell, symbolizing the disc of space. Immediately above this rim are three symbols. First a line of pearls, followed by a circle of *vajra*s and then another line of pearls. These form the circle of protection that guard and delimit the mandala. It is said that the *vajra*s are usually in multiples of

eight or twelve (although none of my twenty-seven *drilbu* conform to this – despite a few of them being antiques) with one at the front being crossed (the *visva-vajra*). My antique *drilbu* do not have the *visva-vajra*. This is a ring of upright *vajra*s and they represent the great *vajra* fence and canopy that surrounds the mandala within the ring of wisdom flames. The *vajra*s form an impenetrable barrier, preventing any inimical forces from entering.

The upper pearl rosary represents the third protection circle, made of lotuses. Then upon the main body of the bell (the 'lotus') we find eight *makaras* (sea-creatures from ancient Indian iconography) in the eight directions. In-between these are eight *vajra*s that represent the eight great Bodhisattvas.

Just below the shoulder of the bell is another ring of *vajra*s, this time sixteen in number and usually horizontal. These represent the walls of the mandala palace. Next come eight lotus petals interspersed with eight seed syllables (in either Sanskrit or Tibetan). The syllables are the subtle manifestation of the consciousness of eight Tantric deities. These figures represent the wise and compassionate beings that are in attendance on the central deity.

Then we find twenty-four lotuses that form the lotus throne of the deity.

Above these are four lifelong vases that are the emblem of Amitayus (Buddha of longevity). They are filled with *amrita*, the nectar whose name literally means 'the deathless'. In the case of the *vajra*-bell, these four vases are understood to represent the body of Prajnaparamita, the central deity, which is regarded as being of the nature of nectar. This symbolizes that Prajnaparamita grants all spiritual accomplishments. Again, this does not always feature and, in fact, with other designs of the *drilbu* there is a hollow ring of metal at this point. The several designs primarily coming from different periods of manufacture.

Then we reach the face of Prajnaparamita crowned with a diadem bearing five great jewels – representing the wisdoms of the five Buddhas – that merges into the eight lotuses at the top of the half *vajra*-bell's handle. In another school it is the face of Vairocana.

At the top is half a *dorje* (*vajra*) usually with four spokes (but sometimes with eight – favoured by the Nyingma tradition) that curl inwards around a central rod that runs out beyond the spokes. In the aggressive *dorje* they project outwards. The four spokes are made of the *makara*. This symbolic composite creature has the eyes of a monkey, the tusks and ears of a wild boar, the jaws of a crocodile, and so on. Once its teeth are sunk in its prey the crocodile will not let go. This serves to represent our intense dedication to the path of spirit and spiritual truth. In the main there are five prongs, which represent the five Dhyani Buddhas.

The *drilbu* can also be stroked (pictured left with wand especially designed by myself) but it is not used this way by Buddhist monks, rather by some *bonpo* and shamans.

In general, *drilbu* come in a range of sizes. Mine are in the following heights: 11.4, 14.1, 16.3, 18.3 and 21.1 centimetres. As with the *ting-sha*, you get what you pay for. Cheaper bells will usually carry an inferior sound. Some *drilbu* have areas that are gold-plated (handle and *dorje*) and these will therefore be more expensive. This is because of the gold and does not necessarily mean a superior sound quality. If the merchant isn't too greedy then you might find a decent bell for a reasonable price. There is no guarantee in purchasing a bell over the internet from a 'spiritual' source (ashram, etc.) that it will have a good sound – even if the vendor states it to be so. Unless those in the ashram have good ears, their

opinion is unlikely to be very helpful. They will not normally be
trained musicians but rather persons who have dedicated their lifetime to the pursuit of spiritual unfoldment. One might be fooled
into thinking that the lower price from a 'spiritual' source reflects
spirituality rather than the quality of the sound. If you wish to
use the *drilbu* for sound work then there is rarely a substitute for
going to the seller and listening to what is on offer.

> With the *vajra* in one hand and the *vajra*-bell in the other, the
> priest held two very strong symbols. The *vajra* represented the
> adamantine, the thunderbolt, the universal male sex principle.
> The bell, symbol of the lotus, represented the female sex prin-
> ciple. The combination formed intuition and compassion, also
> awakening and illumination, the world of appearance. The
> world of appearance is passing and deceptive, like the sounds
> of a bell.[1]

Practitioners of the highest Tantra are committed to keep a
vajra and bell with them permanently. These are viewed as sacred
objects for they symbolize and help actualize the realization of
ultimate reality. In the highest (or Anuttarayoga) Tantra the Vajra
family comes to the fore with Buddha Akshobhya, head of the
Vajra family, taking the central position in the mandala of the Five
Buddha families. We may call to mind that the Tantric path in
Tibet is called either Tantrayana or Vajrayana.

The most common of all ritual implements is the diamond
baton (Sanskrit *vajra*, Tibetan *dorje*, and Japanese *kongo*), often
referred to as the 'thunderbolt'. The implement is symbolic of the
cosmic power of the Hindu God Indra. Subsequent to Indra con-
verting to Buddhism, he used his diamond club to dispel the darkness and scatter the enemies of the Law. It is not only used alongside the *drilbu* but is combined to form several ritual implements
as aforementioned. As a ritual implement in and of itself it comes
in a range of sizes including very large. However, when supplied
with a *drilbu* its size will match that of the half *dorje* atop the bell.

> Some students of Tibetan ritualism consider the term 'thunder-
> bolt' as inappropriate for the *vajra*. They feel that while it was
> the thunderbolt symbol of Indra, it had an entirely different

meaning after it was taken over by Buddhism. They prefer that the *vajra* be considered a sceptre, or wand, representing the diamond foundation of existence.

Actually, in Japanese Buddhism there does not seem to be any question that the *vajra* is a thunderbolt. Each student can decide the term he prefers, but by any name the instrument is a symbol of final spiritual authority, and the Kongo deities retain their strange and tempestuous appearances.

In ritualism the *vajra* is carried by Tantric priests, who practice transcendental magic. There is a secret art relating to the use of the *vajra*. Broadly speaking, it may be considered as symbolizing the positive electro-magnetic current and as contributing to the victory of consciousness over the assaults of Mara, or any negative spirit bent upon embarrassing the Magus.[2]

In Tibetan the word *dorje* means the king of all stones – the diamond. There is an archetypal symbolism (with some variants) while smaller or cheaper versions may lack details.

The *dorje* is symmetrical, featuring a central sphere depicting the *dharmata* – the sphere of reality itself – and representing the seed or germ of the universe in its undifferentiated form as *bindu*.

Next outwards from this central sphere are found three rings of pearls that remind us of the three doors of liberation – or three means of entering into that central sphere of reality. These are *animitta samadhi*, *apranihita samadhi* and *shunyata samadhi*.

Now come eight lotuses standing for an archetypal set of eight great Bodhisattvas and on the complementary end another eight for their female consorts.

Then there are another three sets of rings that, together with three below the lotuses, represent the six great perfections. (See the exercises for the second partial in Chapter 16.)

Now we find the prongs each emerging from a *makara* with four being the most common. Together with the central rod that extends beyond these four we have five linking to the five Buddhas of the Vajradatu Mandala. We find the white Buddha Vairocana, the blue Akshobhya, the yellow Ratnasambhava, the red Amitabha, and the green Amogasiddhi. The opposite end symbolizes their

five female consorts of corresponding colours: Akashadhatesh-
wari, Locana, Mamaki, Pandaravasini, and Tara.

In certain rituals the *dorje* is held vertically, in which case the
upper five represent the five Buddhas, and the lower five are their
female consorts. Yet the two are formed into one piece. A diamond
is distinguished by its being able to cut other materials while nothing can cut the diamond. Perhaps here we see that the union of
male and female energies cannot be split apart. The spiritual practitioner, as he or she meditates upon the inseparability of these two
aspects of truth ('absolute' and 'relative'), can reach a moment of
self-realization – the suddenness of which can be likened to being
struck by a 'thunderbolt'.

Buddhism placed great significance on both the visual and
acoustical aspects of this small bell. In proper hands it could be
powerful; in improper ones dangerous. Its sound, a clear high
note to mortal ears, contained a mystical quality that attracted
the attention of deities. Therefore, the person who rang it, the
times when it was rung, and how loud and how long were rigidly
fixed in the liturgy. At some places there were different *ghanta* for
different deities. Taoist priests of China in the Han period rang
handbells to improve life by exorcising demons. As a matter of
fact, in days of old only lamas were allowed to touch these bells.
Eventually, shamans began using the handbells in their rituals possibly in order to be associated with the holy lamas or as symbolic
of being fit to handle such sacred and spiritually powerful objects.
Nowadays *drilbu* are freely available, being sold to tourists, and
indeed everyone.

The version of the *drilbu* used by shamans is plain with no decoration. In shamanism bells are used to summon spirits, and their
sound represents the element of air, being the realm of the spirits.
In Tantric Buddhism too there is this link to the element of the air.

© Grant David Read

6. The World of Singing Bowls

Beyond Kinchinjunga are old menhirs of the great sun cult.
Beyond Kinchinjunga is the birth-place of the sacred Swastika,
sign of fire. Now in the day of the Agni-yoga, the element of
fire is again entering the spirit and all the treasures of earth
are revered. For the legends of heroes are dedicated not so
much to the plains as to the mountains! All teachers journeyed
to the mountains. The highest knowledge, the most inspired
songs, the most superb sounds and colours are created on the
mountains. On the highest mountain there is the Supreme.
The high mountains stand as witnesses of the great reality. The
spirit of prehistoric man already enjoyed and understood the
greatness of the mountains.
Whoever beholds the Himalayas recalls the great meaning
of mountain Meru. The Blessed Buddha journeyed to the
Himalayas for enlightenment. There, near the legendary sacred
Stupa, in the presence of all the gods, the Blessed One received
his Illumination. In truth, everything connected with the
Himalayas reveals the great symbol of mount Meru, standing
at the centre of the world.[1]

IN TIBET itself knowledge of the bowls is virtually lost. Partly,
this is because of the degree to which they have been associated
with use in ritual and ceremonial magic, and used in this way by
individuals in isolation rather than groups of monks in a monastery.
The other reason is the destruction of local monasteries during and
after the Chinese takeover more than sixty years ago. However,

it is certain that the bowls were never intended as 'musical instruments' to be played for entertainment. Rather, I suggest, they were intended as aids for spiritual practices along the path of sacred sound (*nada yoga* in India) and also with other spiritual practices including healing, exorcism, meditation, trance states, certain Tantric practices, and other shamanic activities for those so inclined. For this reason, they're often charged with spiritual light. We can almost say, experientially, that they are the 'sound of light'. Some of them do create very specific, pure, 'colours' upon the astral plane of light when seen with psychic faculties.

There are some who argue that the singing bowls are merely household utensils and have nothing whatsoever to do with either sound or meditation or healing. While it is undeniably true that many in Nepal use bowls for cooking, eating, drinking tea, and similar uses, it seems rather extravagant to produce such a wide range of designs and forms which directly relate to a variety of fine sound qualities and also to include in their composition precious metals and meteorite, if they are intended for these purposes alone. I can see no practical reason for bowls to possess a thick rim, for instance, if they are merely storage or cooking bowls. Again, many singing bowls have a very thin base and this would make cooking with them very difficult. The Elephant Bowl would be quite impractical for eating, drinking, or cooking. How could the Lingam Bowl, with its central 'lingam', be useful in the kitchen? And why create a bowl that produces over twenty sounding partials simply for a household utensil – and why use 'bell metal' and not bronze or brass?

So far I have addressed the basic debate about singing bowls trying to show that the arguments are quite complex, but now I wish to turn attention to the effect the bowls have on us. This may be regarded as even more controversial, because not everyone who comes into contact with bowls will be looking to regard them with the subtle senses. In the process, though, I hope to show that acoustic and musical analysis of the bowls not only justifies some of the claims made for their effects, but also goes a long way to show that their form implies deliberate design, and that the sound they produce is no more the result of happy accident than the dual tones of the *bianzhong* bells.

Resonance and Entrainment

One of the effects users have commonly noted is that the tones from some bowls are found to balance the chakras, bring the subtle bodies into alignment or, when used in a certain application – namely what I call 'matched pairs' (see Chapter 10) create a balance between the left and right hemispheres of the brain. According to Ted Andrews, for instance:

> They resonate with every cell in the body to release blockages and restore balance. The bowls and their unique tones have been used to restore blood pressure, correct asthma and emphysema, and even to rebuild adrenal function after failure from steroid intake. They open and balance the meridians of the body and they improve the synapse response in the brain. They have been used with hyperactive children and can stimulate the immune system.[2]

Naturally, it is not the case that all bowls will do any one of these things, but it is certainly my opinion that special bowls, or else certain advanced bowl-playing techniques, can successfully accomplish these several objectives. It does not seem necessary to establish this as a traditional usage for their success arises from their actual sound properties, and that is the important point. The idea has been mooted that they might even be a type of *torma* – a hidden treasure – waiting centuries for their deeper meaning to enter into our awareness. Alternatively, they may be remnants of a forgotten age of oral culture in sound yoga. Even today there are certain yogis in Tibet who have renounced their vows of silence because their branch of yoga is in danger of dying out, as no one has come forward to learn or dedicate themselves to these practices. If the yogis featured in the film *The Yogis of Tibet* (JEHM Films, 2002)[3] hadn't agreed to being filmed, there might remain no record of their lineages. Therefore, it is not beyond the bounds of possibility that certain obscure yogic practices have disappeared, and maybe one of these is sound yoga using the bowls. The yogis of the film had just a handful of adherents, indicating that we must not necessarily believe that all spiritual traditions in Tibet had huge numbers of followers and, therefore, were well known.

How might bowls have healing or balancing effects? Resonance is one of the fundamental laws of music, and 'harmonic resonance' is one possible translation of 'Maitreya', the name of the coming Buddha, according to Rain Gray. The usual way to demonstrate this law of resonance uses two tuning forks of the same pitch. We find that when one is struck the other begins to vibrate in sympathetic resonance. This is similar to what takes place within us while a bowl is being played, I would suggest. The bowl is one tuning fork and we represent the other, attuned to the bowl! By the same token, if we are unable to resonate in complete sympathy with any one bowl we will experience some form of discomfort if we listen to it.

It is worth noting, here, the acoustical phenomenon of interference. Interference can be constructive or destructive, or a combination of both. When constructive, typically two sine waves that are almost the same speed in cycles per second (cps) or hertz (Hz) reinforce one another, their waves combine together, and this produces audible beats. There is a pulsing as they move in and out of phase. The times when their combined sound waves unite produces a raising of their amplitude (i.e., they get louder) and when their combined tones move apart this amplitude decreases. The alternation between these two states produces a beat or a pulsing (for example, if the difference is 4 Hz, then there will be four beats per second). This acoustical phenomenon relates to pure sine waves such as are produced in a physics laboratory and which, being a single frequency, are dissimilar from the waves that singing bowls (or any other musical instrument) produce.

To take a musical example, in 'Septet for Three Winds, Four Strings and Pure Wave Oscillator', by Alvin Lucier, the oscillator is tuned to Middle C, sounding continuously throughout the performance, while the players minutely vary the pitches of their tones to produce beats of different speeds. The piece is in four movements. For example, in movement one the players split into trios and, starting a semitone above and below the oscillator tones, step up and down in eighth-tone increments, crossing the tone, stopping at the opposite semitone above and below it.[4]

This effect is exploited in a sound healing application known as 'binaural beats'.

Binaural beats require the combined action of both ears. When stereophonic headphones are used and signals are sent separately to each ear – signals of 400 and 404 Hz, for example – one ear hears only the 400-Hz signal, the other hears only the 404-Hz signal; but somehow the sounds are blended *inside the brain* and set up a binaural beat frequency of 4 Hz. That is, the 4 Hz beat frequency, never an actual sound but only a frequency difference between two actual sounds, is 'heard' within the brain itself, created by both brain hemispheres working simultaneously. As a result, the entire brain becomes entrained to the internal beat and begins to resonate at 4 Hz.

Michael Hutchison, MEGA BRAIN (1987)

There are currently eight classifications of brain waves that may be duplicated with musical pulses:

Lambda (100–200 Hz) – these are very rapid waves that seem related to mystical and 'out-of-the-body' experiences and to integration and wholeness.

HyperGamma (40–100 Hz) – are waves that have been detected in Tibetan Buddhist monks doing a loving-kindness meditation. They relate to higher awareness and mystical experiences.

Gamma (40–100 Hz) – are associated with higher mental activity, greater focus and also certain shamanic or mystical states.

Beta (13–30 Hz) – are rapid waves that occur when we are in a waking and rational state. Usually the eyes are open when we are in the *beta* state. Our attention is directed externally, and we are functioning at normal mental activity. This is considered our normal waking consciousness.

Alpha (8–12 Hz) – are slower waves that occur when we relax, perhaps closing our eyes to move into a light meditation but still awake. They are active during self-hypnosis. Typical 'Zen' meditation is associated with this brainwave state.

Theta (4–8 Hz) – are very slow waves that occur when we move more deeply into meditation, or into auto-hypnosis, vivid daydreaming, or that para-conscious, highly creative state where we 'float' just before falling asleep at night or waking in the morning. The classic shamanic 'journeying' is experienced here.

Delta (0.5–4 Hz) – are the slowest waves normally encountered, and occur when we are in deep sleep or very deep states of meditation like being in the void or other timeless or formless states.

Epsilon (0.5 and lower Hz) – are even slower, and said to be those attained by yogis when in suspended animation (for instance, buried alive for days or weeks). When functioning at the level of the higher chakras in the head these frequencies will become dominant and it is said that we will be able to perceive the higher frequencies of sound and light. Ecstatic states of consciousness are likewise found within this range.

Other than this we have *High Beta* (16–32 Hz) – often linked to states of anxiety, followed by *K-complex* (32–35 Hz) – creativity and moments of sudden realization, and then *Super High Beta* (35 – 150 Hz) – 'out-of-body-experiences' and *kundalini* releases and other psycho-spiritual states.

After the identification of brain waves came the discovery that certain electronic soundwaves caused a 'frequency-following response' in the brain: this is similar to the tuning fork experiment mentioned above. The brain responds to an audio signal by reproducing it – by becoming synchronized. This is a form of entrainment that is exploited through the binaural beats products and also, by extension, as part of the sound healing work I have done with Tibetan singing bowls.

Back in the 1980s I would buy small Manipuri *yang* bowls, and when I got home I'd compare them with my existing set. Sometimes the bowls were close together in pitch and, although my first instinct was to discard these bowls as being similar, I noticed an interesting interaction between such pairs of bowls. And so I decided to keep these other bowls, until eventually I had five pairs that I've used in my sound healing work for many years now. I called these sets 'matched pairs'. If we relate this phenomenon to the singing bowls, there are generally several beats present (from such pulses existing at different pitches) arising between the partials of the two bowls (or, within one bowl, producing a '*vibrato*' effect). The speed of these beats between the fundamentals of what I have termed a 'matched pair' of bowls can be very slow (from less than 1 up to 5 Hz – within the *delta* range) while the higher partials might pulsate at between 7 to 9 Hz (*theta* and *al-*

pha range). It is this phenomenon that resonates with the different brain states that also beat at a similar rate of Hz and we might term this a form of 'entrainment.' As I've already stated, this is not the acoustical phenomenon known as 'constructive interference' (produced by using a pure sine wave – a single tone) for this features as simple a sound as can be made, in contrast to the complex combination of tones found in singing bowls. But, facing a complete lack of any suitable phrase being provided by acousticians, I have coined the term 'reinforcement' for describing this acoustical phenomenon within the world of singing bowls.

Participating in a series on the BBC World Service (in 2004, I think), I mentioned my use of matched pairs. The producer wanted to test my statement and arranged for me to visit the National Physical Laboratory. I entered the anechoic chamber there and produced my solar plexus matched pair. With the BBC's £10,000 microphone (the software used being equally expensive) they recorded the sound and we could see the pulses on the screen visible as large changes in the size of the waves. I asked the acousticians there what this phenomenon was called, but they couldn't tell me. They simply called it the 'Wow' factor. I then asked if they could record each bowl separately and analyse their frequencies. We see the results in Table #2 below.

In my sound healing work ('Spiritual Sound Healing', in which I use only singing bowls) I have an assortment of what I have named 'matched pairs' (since 1985) for the chakras below and including the heart chakra. On occasion other bowls are added to such pairs. For example, the matched pair that I use in sound healing for treating the solar plexus chakra consists of the following frequencies:

FIRST BOWL	SECOND BOWL
91	91.75
261	263
503	508/9
806	830
1,170	1,172

Table #2, *illustrating the various partials of each bowl*

The difference in cps between the fundamental of these two

bowls is less than 1 cps (0.75 Hz), producing a beating of 0.75 of a second and placing it within the *delta* range. With 'binaural beats' each sine wave is played to each ear separately, and using the singing bowls ('matched pairs') these are similarly placed on either side of the head. Were I to use the current association between chakras and musical notes (see Chapter 1) then the note E would be expected for this chakra. E in our Equal Temperament would be 82.4075 Hz and F would be 87.3075 Hz and G 98 Hz. This pair (91 Hz) are closest to an F (87.3075 Hz) and not an E.

In the table on the previous page, the two bowls were sampled separately but under identical conditions. Both are *yin* bowls, and are of a very similar size and height. According to the (whole number) ratios of normal instruments (the discovery of which is attributed to Pythagoras) the first harmonic is the octave and with the first bowl in our example this would then be expected to be 182 Hz, whilst its next overtone would then be 273 Hz. You will notice that neither of these numbers appears in the table. The octave is missed entirely, while the 261 Hz nearly approaches the (expected 273 Hz) second overtone. Neither do the partials of the bowls obey any single law, with the fourth partial in this example being the most markedly different, having 806 Hz with the first bowl and 830 Hz with the second. Then, finally, we find 1,170 Hz compared to 1,172 Hz where the two bowls are far closer than between the previous 806 and 830.

It is not possible (as it is with normal instruments and the human voice) to predict where the next partial of a singing bowl will appear. Because of this, anyone who states that singing bowls have a set sequence of overtones (such as an octave followed by an octave, or else the octave followed by a major fifth) is sadly mistaken. I have sampled over sixty of my bowls and each one follows a law uniquely its own. In fact, it is quite an occasion when I find an octave present between any of the partials in a single bowl. Normal instruments contain harmonics, appearing at every octave.

Sometimes the complex structure of partials in a bowl may mean that when it is struck similar pulses arise within the interactions of its own order of partials, without the need of another bowl to heighten this affect. This phenomenon is known as doublets (or warbles). We may well be able to discern three or more oscillating beats, or pulses, within the entire sound spectrum of such bowls, each pulsing at different pitch levels. We might also bear in mind that it could take a long time before our ears are sufficiently educated into this new level of deep listening to enable us to hear the entire spectrum of any one such bowl (see table #5 below for Blue Sunset Bowl). Nor should we expect every bowl to contribute a large number of partials. There are limits as to the smallest interval between two pitches that the human ear can discern. Then there is the matter that not every bowl is designed, or made, to create such a wide range of sounds: in some instances bowls are very focused upon producing one dominant partial, regardless of what we play them with.

Choosing Bowls

Considerable care is needed when choosing an antique bowl, and also in how we use it! Some bowls can be charged with very definite psycho-spiritual energies, possessing powerful forces that, for the uninitiated, can prove difficult to control or use. Although it's said that some Buddhist lamas do use them, the bowls are generally associated with the Bon, what we have seen as the ensemble of indigenous pre-Buddhist faiths in Tibet, and Bonpo were certainly involved with magical practices. Therefore some few bowls will have been used for either black or white magic. The primary difference between these two forms of magic hinges on the single word 'coercion'; the will of the black magician seeks, for entirely selfish purposes, to dominate the will of another individual. Needless to say I recommend avoiding that – at all costs.

Accordingly, our fundamental intention before working with these powerful instruments should be one of selfless service to the rest of creation, adopting the attitude that all beings may receive the beneficial effects of our action. Besides being the safest foundation for the spiritual path, or journey of initiation, this will also purify and protect us from harmful influences.

Certain bowls, alongside specific ways of using them, channel very powerful healing energies, and this is another one of their traditional shamanic uses. Putting egotistical desires on one side is something shamans have needed to practise throughout history: all true healers today strive to rise above their individual egos and worldly thoughts in order for the higher energies from the angels of healing to pass through them to their patient and help to restore harmony there.

You can ask your sprit guide to lead you to the right bowl. I believe that every single person has a spirit guide for his or her entire lifetime. They are by your side and will hear your call. It doesn't matter whether you are aware of them or not; they will still assist you. Ask once and trustingly leave it in their safekeeping until the right time arrives.

In selecting a bowl, you need to listen, feel, and experience thoroughly. You can begin by simply looking at the bowl and feeling its 'presence'. If there is something there for you, next hold it in your hands and relate to it more closely. Then strike it with an appropriate mallet (by size and weight). However, if you feel nothing at all, or the bowl simply doesn't sound pleasant at that moment, you can safely take this to mean that it is not the right one for you right now. Carry on looking and don't settle with 'almost', as singing bowls can be an expensive investment. Also don't panic by thinking that your choice must come from what is available. There are other shops or sources and another shipment is likely to come in the future. Be patient and don't be fooled into buying what looks like an old and aged antique – it's probably fake! And don't let yourself be talked into anything you don't want, or else you'll buy a story instead of a bowl. If you feel comfortable – possibly more relaxed, centred, or clearer in your head – then the singing bowl has touched something within you and you can work with it for a while – possibly for the rest of your lifetime.

Avoid bowls with cracks – unless in the base. If you hold the rim of the bowl at eye level, you should be able to see if it is very uneven, meaning that the height of the wall of the bowl varies considerably around the rim, producing many partials, which in turn lead to a more complex-sounding bowl, one that may prove too distracting or even inharmonious. Large variations in hammer

strokes can also produce an inferior-sounding bowl. Most seek a clean, focused and harmonious sound from a bowl for use in healing or meditation.

When checking a bowl, we must allow any impressions we receive to die away – back into the stillness between strikes. In other words, it is not always a cumulative process but also a letting go of desire, need, or expectation. We are dealing with what *is*. This is somewhat akin to 'mixing' music in a recording studio. The musician listens to the same piece of music over and over again, adjusting levels between instruments, trying to find the right balance or 'mix'. Sometimes, one has to get away from it all and return later with a fresher pair of ears. Similarly, we take a holiday from our expectations, or needs, or desires, and return to what lives in the sound of the bowl. We may find that the bowl has nothing more significant than its sound, or we may find the bowl is a doorway or gateway into a realm of energy and spiritual/mental/emotional qualities, properties and energies.

If we enjoy the sound of the bowl, we can go a bit further and, turning our attention away from listening with our ears, open up to what our body is telling us. Place the bowl at the level of your navel, striking it and feeling what your body is telling you. You can do the same at the position of the heart chakra and then throat chakra and even the third eye.

I believe that one way ahead for the spiritualization of music lies in focusing upon what lives in any one single tone. This is where the unique qualities of the singing bowls excel. Each bowl produces one total *om* sound, making it easy for us to focus our entire attention upon the soul quality we find in its individual sound-universe; the sense of presence surfing its sound-waves. We ask ourselves: 'What is the bowl "saying" to us?' In essence all bowls when stroked with a wand create a kind of 'womb of sound' (open, simple, humble, innocent, and trusting) resonating with this childlike quality. We have to learn to *follow* the sound of the bowl to where it lives. This is the *yin* approach (see the next chapter). However, it might be easier to observe the effects of a bowl while striking it, rather than stroking, because it then has more impact upon the aura. After playing the bowl of your choice for some minutes (or some other competent person playing it for you), and after the sound has faded away then study how the sounding of the bowl has changed you and your sense of your auric energy-field.

Some people prepare to select a bowl having considered either what kind of pitch they feel comfortable with (deep, medium, or high); or how they're going to use the bowl – for instance, to attune a group before working together (amplitude would then be an important consideration), or perhaps as a space-cleansing bowl/purification bowl (e.g., between clients if they're counsellors or sound healers); as a water bowl, or an ululation bowl (see Chapter 10 for the different types of bowl); how simple or complex they'd like the sound to be (if they're musicians); how large a bowl (taking into account playing or transportation considerations

– see the illustration and consider which of these two you'd rather carry around!); whether they seek a bowl for one of the chakras, or one for meditation purposes, a *yin* or *yang* bowl, a bowl for use in sound healing work, or for aiding relaxation, a bowl for one (or a set of bowls for all) of the elements, or one for use in trance work, a bowl for 'soul retrieval' work, a bowl to heighten their awareness of sound; even, considerations regarding the price range. If you are looking for a bowl for yourself, do you seek one to calm you down or one that is stimulating and uplifting or energizing? You could try singing to the bowl, in order to find one that resonates with your voice as you sing a note that is comfortable for you.

Personally, I've found that certain bowls require particular techniques – so that 'space-cleansing' bowls, for instance, are always stroked, as are bowls for the chakras including and above the heart chakra. I am looking for a particular quality in the arrangement of the partials that will stimulate the energy sought after. When choosing bowls if I see a number of a certain design present I'll have an idea as to what to expect from their sound and I will use the appropriate technique and implement to discover if any perform in the desired way. For instance, 'Broken Heart Bowls' are usually found from Thadobatis, about nine or ten inches in diameter, and played with a leather wand. Again, I'm looking for a certain quality in their sound so that from forty or fifty such bowls I might select four or five. These carry an energy that is reassuring, trusting, soothing, consoling, safe and enfolding that can prove helpful to those who have closed down their heart after enduring heartache or emotional abuse.

You may also wish to consider the speed of pulsation from the fundamental of a bowl. This is the lowest sound that the bowl makes. It generally produces a sound cycle moving between loud and soft, the speed differing with each bowl. It is something of a matter of personal preference as to whether you want this pulsation (when the bowl is struck) to be fast or slow. The pulsation can be slower than 1 beat per second, or it can reach up to 6 or 7 bps. Bowls that have a slower pulse are generally deemed more suitable for healing or meditation, as they are less excitable and assist us in slowing down our activity in order to focus our attention upon inner and deeper states of consciousness. With a basic pulse of between minus 1 and 7 bps we are in the *alphas*, as outlined above. *Theta* and *delta* areas of brain wave activity are linked with deep meditation. It has been found that most bowls (above the fundamental) possess an audible pulsation of 8 to 12 bps when struck. This is produced when certain partials of the bowl lie close together in frequency and so produce a pulsation (a kind of vibrato effect – a warble). This is also the range of the *alpha* waves (8–12 Hz), which is a happy 'coincidence', because these are the very frequencies created by people during relaxed states or in light meditation.

It is obvious from this that the bowls can be valuable aids for meditation. Meditation takes many forms, among which are concentration, contemplation, and the ancient path of *nada yoga* – the Path of the Inner Sound of which the bowls speak. Before leaving for the shop, focus on what you need, holding your intention in mind, as this can help attract the right bowl to you – or else simply trust that what you truly need will announce itself to you.

It is probably best to strike the bowls unless you are already proficient in the stroking technique, which is more difficult. As a guide, small bowls three inches in diameter after striking should ring on for thirty seconds, six inches or larger for sixty seconds, and from ten to thirteen inches for one or two minutes (exceptional bowls can ring on for over four minutes!). If selecting from a

large number of bowls, you may find it helpful to place them into
piles – those you instantly were attracted to, those you immediately disliked, and finally those you are unclear about.

For example, over a number of years I had an arrangement
with a shop close by Portobello Road market in London whereby
I'd be given first pickings from their bowl shipments. However, another person took over and when I next turned up to sort through
their latest delivery of bowls I was surprised to find a man buying
bowls. He'd come in off the street, as it were, and was just then
buying a rare bowl that was shallow and decorated with lovely
peacock designs. He could simply tell that this bowl was different
and so special in some way. The dealer told me afterwards that
this man knew nothing about bowls at all. So I asked the new
person dealing with bowls to look for any unusual bowls and, if
found, to put these aside for me. I left it at that, simply trusting to
fate. The next time he phoned to say there was new stock he mentioned that he'd found some dissimilar bowls. So off I went. With
my very first glance at the unusual design of these bowls I intuited
that they were made for working with water. I asked for some water and was delighted to find the most astounding sounds! These
proved to be exceptional water bowls and so I termed these 'water
spirit bowls'. I'm certain that other users have similar tales to tell.

It is also possible to purchase a bowl over the internet. Some
merchants provide a photograph of the bowl along with a sound
file. There are certain dangers here, and when you are using the
internet almost all of the advice up to here is redundant. It might
be well to realize that there will also be VAT, Import Duty, Cus-
toms and Post Office charges to add on to whatever the bowl is
selling for.

We would do well to remember the Buddhist begging bowl,
where the monk accepts whatever food is offered. What we might
call the Way of the Bowl requires such acceptance, openness and
complete surrender to the sound – becoming at one with the
sound. This is also similar to the way of Tao. In such emptiness we
come to inner silence, maybe even the 'sound of the void'. We may
come to discover that our entire life revolves around this central
still flame found in the silence of the heart.

Within the total silence of the year we find such a period of silence or stillness when we come to winter; it is the winter solstice. In the stillness we may hear the voice of the silence. Through becoming very still, we come in contact with a deep inner silence where the voice of truth is heard. There are two such points in our yearly cycle, the other being the opposite time of the summer solstice, but then there is such an emphasis upon outer manifest activity that it can prove more difficult to retreat inwards and find this still point at the centre of our being.

> May I give you an idea? Suppose you go to an instrument, a piano, if you will, and strike a note or many separate notes. To some you will remain indifferent. Some will make you flinch, some will almost thrill something in your being. Continue until you find the one note which seems utterly satisfying to a sympathetic vibration within your heart, not your mind or brain, and you will have found your tone-note. You may not find your particular note upon a piano. Some like best the strains of a wood instrument, as more akin to nature. Others find that which they seek in the song of birds, the breath of wind in the trees, the murmur of the waves. To hear your true note or tone, however, you must learn to find the silence. To find your note or tone sounded on any instrument will be most difficult although you may go near to it. If all souls were true to their intuition, or voice of their spirit, rapid progress would be made, but most people are too noisy themselves or too busy with others to listen-in to the silence.
>
> White Eagle[5]

Old or New Bowls

In considering the sound they make, we find a range from crude to superb bowls whether they are old or new. The older bowls have a more mellow sound and may also show a beautiful patina. A few old bowls may possess spiritual energies stemming from their creation and use within a sacred tradition steeped in the ancient wisdom. The older bowls may also feature an alloy of many metals (including gold and silver) and include meteorite intended for sacred uses. Of course, we can consecrate any bowl to a spiritual purpose.

Certain old bowls seem to have been consecrated or created at specific times in order to align them with particular energies. We can consecrate our new bowls. You may wish to create your own ceremony for this, or have them consecrated by someone skilled in such ritual. When performing such an act yourself you may wish to consult certain tables such as Planetary Hours. These are tables for the passing influence of each hour for each day of the week and there are also two other tables arising from dividing the day up into either three or four major periods, each under a different planetary ray.

> Consecration is a ritual whereby you put an object under the protection of a spiritual entity. But if you wish to consecrate an object, you must begin by exorcising it, since it has already received the influence of the people who have touched it and the events that have taken place around it, leaving behind fluidic traces, pure and not so pure. These fluidic traces prevent your thoughts from permeating the object, as they form a sort of barrier, a screen that blocks them out.
>
> Once the object has been exorcised by prayers or even incense, you can proceed to consecrate it: you place it under the influence of a heavenly power, which permeates it with light, setting it apart; it's as if there were a notice on it saying 'Evil spirits keep out', but heavenly entities can come and take possession of it and use it to help you in your spiritual work.
>
> Omraam Mikhail Aïvanhov[6]

Listening

How many sounds or notes can you hear when listening to any one bowl? In other words: just how silent are you inside? How still are you emotionally and physically? Are your thoughts gently at rest? Or are there so many thoughts buzzing around inside your head that you haven't enough silent emptiness to hear all of the sounds inside of the bowl, or to hear its gentle voice speaking to you? We can meditate and concentrate upon the sound of the bowl in order to still those busy thoughts or those unsettled feelings. Then we may be able to hear five, or seven, or more, ringing tones within the bowl – depending also upon the sound quality of the bowl being listened to. It is common for most of my bowls to have around ten different sounds while one has the sum of twenty-five present in its total sound. Be patient with yourself as it can take a while to educate your hearing to open up to the full sound of a bowl.

However, don't be too hard on yourself. It has taken me over four decades of working with singing bowls (and almost five decades listening to cymbals and other metallophones) to develop my listening abilities. I once had a visit from a musician who had perfect pitch. Her boyfriend (also a musician) informed me that she could tell by how much a note was higher or lower than it should be. She had perfect hearing, he assured me. Out of curiosity, after the sound healing session I played a bowl for her and asked how many sounds she could hear in the bowl. I kept playing the bowl until she gave me a number. Finally she told me she could hear four tones. I informed her that there were twenty-three partials within the bowl and showed her a list of the notes. As I say, it can take a very long time to develop an ear for these unfamiliar sounds. (See Table #5 on p. 123). In some ways it doesn't really matter, except that it provides us with a strong argument for the bowls not being household utensils! Nonetheless, the ability to discern several sounds within the bowl can help us choose one where these different sounds get along together.

I once decided to analyse a recording of the 'The Tamburas of Pandit Pran Nath', released by La Monte Young and Marian Zazeela.[7] The *tambura* is the drone instrument of North Indian classical music. I am sure that most people listening to the sound recording would say that it was making one sound. To be fair, it is in the background of Indian music – with the improvising musician very much to the fore. A Western musician listening might hear three sounds (octave and fifth). As I listened to the entire recording (around seventy-four minutes) I gave myself plenty of time to explore how many sounds I could hear and surprisingly found twenty-two sounds. I wondered whether I had imagined this number and so I then analysed it with software (Wavanal[8] – especially developed for analysing the partials of bells) that showed there were twenty-four sounds. So I was almost there. I imagine that very few listeners (including musicians) would hear twenty-four sounds at a first brief listening. So accept where you are and be kind, gentle, and patient with yourself. Your hearing can deepen over time to discover ever-richer sound worlds.

For instance, let us examine the notes in a few of my bowls.

GREAT STAR MOTHER		
115	Bb (-1) - 23	
338	E (1) + 43	
341	F (1) - 41	# 1
652	E (2) - 19	
655.5	E (2) - 9	# 2
1041	C (3) - 9	
1044.5	C (3) - 3	
1491	F# (3) + 12	
2010.5	B (3) + 30	
2025	B (3) + 42	

Table #3: 'Great Star Mother' Bowl

'Great Star Mother' Bowl has nine heads (these are the number of rings, or indented lines, on the outside of the bowl, under the rim), which means that it was made by the Tibetan Buddhist monks at Jang. It is a *yang* bowl around eleven inches in diameter and is of a silvery colour. The #1 in the table indicates the loudest sound from this bowl and #2 naturally is the next loudest. There are ten partials to the sound of this bowl with the third and fifth being the most prominent. This primary tone is just sharp of an E and so almost mid-way between an E and an F: not a note at all in musical terms. This is often the case with singing bowls. A note that is perfectly in tune with our Western music would show in the table as a nought rather than plus or minus. You will notice that this doesn't happen with any of the notes from the various bowls analysed. (You can see the cymatic image of this bowl in the colour section).

To read these tables we start from the left with a figure showing the cps (cycles per second) of the partial. Next is the Western note from our scale. In brackets there follows the octave that this note is in. And finally we have how near or far it is from the actual note – with the minus sign indicating that it is lower than the note. Beyond this is a number that I have added to the table every now and again to indicate the comparative strength of the partial within the overall bowl sound.

78	Eb (-1) + 4	
100	G (-1) +34	
231	Bb (0) -15	#3
458.5	Bb (1) - 28	
749	F# (2) + 20	
754	F# (2) + 32	#4
916.5	Bb (2) - 29	
1102.5	Db (3) - 9	#1
1511	F# (3) + 35	#2
1957	B (3) - 16	
1962	B (3) - 11	
2205	Db (4) - 9	
2445.5	Eb (4) - 30	
2953.5	F# (4) - 3	
3475	A (4) - 22	
4402	Db (5) - 12	

Table #4: Divine Mother Bowl

'Divine Mother' Bowl is a Bengali-type bowl. It is *yin* and very light in weight for its size – around eleven inches. Here the loudest pitch from the bowl is almost a D*b*. There are sixteen partials to the sound of this bowl. From among these the eighth, ninth, third, and sixth partials are the loudest respectively. So we should expect to be able to hear these prominent four sounds, but to discern all sixteen would require a very trained ear. (Again, you can see the cymatic image produced by this bowl in the colour section).

I discovered immediately I used the 'Silver Ray of the Great Master' *ting-sha* that my hearing was cleansed and heightened. I found after striking it three times (each time allowing it to return to the silence) that the very first sound I heard immediately afterwards sounded as if I was hearing it for the very first time. In this way I would approach any bowl the significance of which I was finding opaque.

Finally, below is the analysis of the Blue Sunset Bowl, with its twenty-three partials (yet again, see the cymatic image in the colour section). We finish with something to meditate upon.

BLUE SUNSET	
• 159	Eb (0) +37
• 460.5	Bb (1) -21
• 473	Bb (1) +25
• 879	A (2) -1
• 885	A (2) +9
• 921	Bb (2) -21
• 946	Bb (2) +25
• 1345.5	E (3) +35
• 1352	E (3) +43
• 1381	F (3) -19
• 1384	F (3) -16
• 1844.5	Bb (3) -18
• 1946.5	B (3) -25
• 2269	Db (4) +39
• 2592.5	E (4) -29
• 2614	E (4) -15
• 2831.5	F (4) +23
• 3310.5	Ab (4) -6
• 3330.5	Ab (4) +4
• 3893	B (4) -25
• 4076.5	C (5) -45
• 4560.5	Db (5) +48
• 4694.5	D (5) -1

Table #5: Blue Sunset Bowl

For me, the word OM is like the sound of a large bell. It's first of all perceptible, then imperceptible, before finally fading away into infinite space. Thus the phenomenal world fades away into the Absolute. The unrefined, subtle and causal states are lost in the Great Cause; in the Absolute. The states of waking, dreaming and deep sleep merge with the fourth state, *samadhi*.

When the bell sounds, it creates waves like those that form in the ocean when we cast a large stone into the water. The phenomena of the universe – e.g. the unrefined, subtle and causal state – seem to emerge from and return to the Absolute. The three other states of awareness are also derived from the

Absolute, which is the fourth state. The waves of the ocean again merge into the ocean. By this image of the 'dong' of the bell, I mean that the everlasting word OM symbolizes the evolution and involution of phenomena from the absolute to the Absolute.

My divine Mother has shown me that, in the infinite ocean of the Absolute, waves rise, then disappear into it. In that infinite spiritual space, millions of planets and worlds rise, then dissolve. I know not what your books say, but I have seen all that.

Ramakrishna

7. Yin–Yang

IN THEIR ESSENCE, singing bowls are a perfect symbol of non-duality – that is, of Oneness. Yet looked at from the viewpoint of the number two, we have what I define as *yang* and *yin* bowls. Viewed from the angle of three we have three parts to the bowl – rim, wall, and base. Again, viewed from the number four we have the four pulses of the fundamental of all bowls and the link to the four elements. To be non-dualistic all of this is part of the unity that is one. We cannot say, 'It is here. It isn't there'. This chapter nonetheless looks at one of the major distinctions between two basic types of bowl that is reflected not only in their shape but in the character of the sound they make and (often) the way in which they are best played.

For me, the difference is fundamental in distinguishing bowls and my division of them into the two primary categories of *yin* or *yang* dates back to the early 1980s. The two types actually look very different. *Yin* bowls have the same thickness up their walls to the rim, while *yang* bowls have a thickening at the rim, providing a lip. These represent the two great principles of female and male respectively. There are also two ways to play all bowls, which are also distinguished as masculine and feminine: that is, strOking them (feminine) or strIking them (masculine).

In the photographs overleaf we have two *yin* bowls and two *yang* bowls. You will notice that the *yang* bowl in the distance has a very pronounced thick rim whereas in the one in the foreground it is not quite so prominent. The bowls in between are *yin*.

Yang bowls are identified at the lip of the bowl, where the thickness of the metal has been increased relative to that of the wall. This indicates that such a bowl is primarily for striking, so that the sound of a *yang* bowl is equivalent, within bowls, to that of a tuned gong (also known as a dimple gong, boss gong, domed gong, or nipple gong). A tuned gong is one with a raised dome

at its centre. This serves to restrict the number of overtones produced when striking the gong and helps us to focus upon its fundamental tone or note, thereby allowing us to call it tuned. When struck it produces a note of definite pitch. Similarly, the *yang* bowl doesn't produce as many overtones as the *yin* bowl. By contrast, it often produces a very clean, clear, and focused tone – even when stroked. I am not suggesting that *yang* bowls are tuned, as tuned gongs are, however, only that the sound is more focused.

The dictionary definition of a gong tells us that it is something active at its centre and still on the rim. If we strike a gong and then touch the rim it will not stop the gong sounding, as it will do if we hold the mallet at the centre. The dictionary definition of a bell is the opposite, namely active on the rim and still at the centre. Because of this the rim is crucial in the formation of the sound of a bowl – meaning that features here (thickness – as in *yin* and *yang*) exercise most influence over a bowl's sound characteristics.

Yang is masculine. The masculine aspect of our nature correlates to the will, and accordingly we find that *yang* bowls serve to centre us and assist us in creating a powerful alignment with our spiritual will. Like the *ting-sha*, their sound cuts right across our thinking, bringing us right back to our point of focus during practices of concentration. This is in keeping with the traditionally vertical symbolism of the masculine energy of self-discipline – the application of the spiritual will to bring about change or transformation in our lives. For instance, if during meditation our concentration wavers, then by striking the *yang* bowl (or *ting-sha*) our attention can be immediately brought right back to whatever was our intended objective. This assists us in the process of self-discipline: that is to say, the act of our spiritual will to bring about a transformation within our personality, so that it might align more perfectly with our divine spiritual nature; so that the personality might become a disciple of our Self. It represents an act of Self-discipline; a mindfulness discipline.

Yang bowls, with their thick lip, repudiate the theory that the bowls are merely for cooking, storing, or begging. One doesn't require this thick lip from a bowl of hard metal for any of these activities, whereas the feature most assuredly significantly alters the sound of the bowl!

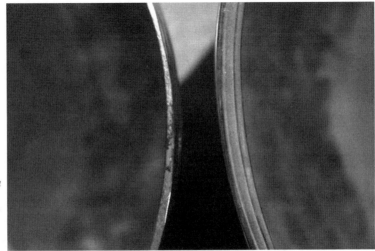

Photograph contrasting the rims of a yin (L) and a yang bowl (R)

Yin bowls do not possess a thick lip but rather maintain their thickness right up the wall of the bowl to the rim. If the wall is very thick then the sound of the bowl approaches that of a *yang* bowl. This is because the amount of matter to set into vibration is too dense to allow a large range of partials. Thick walls tend to produce a dull sound that ends comparatively quickly and the note produced will be higher due to the inflexibility of a greater mass. *Yin* bowls, carrying the feminine energy, are far richer in their structure of partials than are *yang* bowls. Listening to a group of *yin* bowls, it is as if one experiences a sense of opening out into space. This opening and expanding energy (essentially creating a more receptive quality) is thereby more feminine in nature. We feel as if we are inside a womb of space. As we listen to the sound of a singing bowl we resemble a mother during pregnancy who shares her aura with that of the soul of the child – our aura likewise becomes infiltrated by the vibrations existing in the various dimensions of the sounding bowl (in those bowls where these other dimensions are present). This aspect represents the *yin* or feminine way of listening to a bowl. The Divine Mother aspect has more to do with numerous kingdoms of beings, both beneath the human and between this human level and the Divine Father aspect – whereas the masculine approach (perhaps we can say being less 'family-oriented'), as it has manifested in past centuries, has more to do with ignoring these other beings and making a one-to-one contact with God or the Absolute Being, or Truth, Essence or Reality.

Another variety sees a *yin* bowl with an outward fluted edge, somewhat mimicking a *yang* bowl – although without the defining extra thickness at the rim.

In general, *yin* bowls appear to sing best when played in a stroking manner, which is the feminine way of playing a bowl – striking it being the more aggressive, masculine approach. Again, both are acceptable and necessary fully to appreciate the sound of any one bowl.

However, it is also true to say we can find that certain individual bowls are designed primarily for one or other of the two approaches, since they don't work well when the other technique is applied. In other words, certain bowls will sound beautiful when stroked and yet possess a very dull sound when struck. Yet other bowls possess a ringing and lively sound vibration when struck but create a rather dreary sound when stroked. Otherwise, the cause may well be more accidental, for instance if we are simply dealing with inferior singing bowls.

In Tibetan Tantra, we often see the deity depicted in sexual union with his or her consort. This may be interpreted to mean that the experience of divinity within the heart of the spiritual practitioner takes the form of father and mother. In order for a man and woman to become a father and a mother requires the birth of a child. Out of this, therefore, we have an interdependent trinity born of love. Also, the union of practice with compassion creates

the transcending of opposites and the entering into at-one-ment –
or unity – whereby the female (physical existence) experiences its
unity with the masculine (spiritual) in pure *nirvana* (liberation).
This is according to ancient symbolism and has nothing to do with
any kind of sexism.

Therefore, we may say that *yang* bowls relay the experiencing
of the divine within, whilst *yin* bowls refer more to the experiencing of the divine without. Both are absolutely necessary and
neither is superior to the other, for they are different aspects of
the one experience. In order to develop certain spiritual qualities
(or at certain stages of our spiritual development) it may be necessary to conceive of the divine as coming from outside of oneself,
while other qualities will be developed by experiencing the divine
as originating from within one's true Self. We achieve balance
within our spiritual nature by not holding rigidly to one of these
approaches alone.

Certainly, we can say that we play a bowl outside of ourselves
and yet we experience how this changes us inwardly. Does this
experience come from within ourselves or from outside of ourselves? Does it even matter which? If we meditate with the sound
of a bowl it is interesting to try to listen for when the bowl stops
sounding. Is it then still ringing inside of us or is it still sounding
outside of us? Certainly, in order to avoid the pitfalls of egotism
on the spiritual path, it is often useful to relate to a Greater Whole,
within which we live and move and have our being.

There are many typical bowl shapes, and in a sense every
bowl is unique in itself. However, I have chosen to place them in
these two fundamental families, either *yang* or *yin*. We find another more fundamental duality between the bowl and the wand.
We can see that the bowl, with its vagina-like, open and rounded
shape, is feminine, while the upright penis-like shape of the stick
is masculine. As a result of this, the somewhat aggressive act of
striking a bowl – emphasizing the masculine symbol – contrasts
with the gentler act of stroking the bowl with its more feminine
connotations – arising as they do from the circular shape of the
bowl. Striking emphasizes a single point on the circumference of
the bowl (stressing individuality) and stroking stimulates the en-

tire circle of the circumference and aligns with the more feminine holistic philosophy. It is just as within our own psycho-spiritual development both aspects need to be developed. Perhaps we can contrast this emphasis upon the circle as relating to the beginning-less infinitude of time and the emphasis upon one single point to the present moment in time.

That the bowl is created from earthly material is a way in which our physical bodily existence is represented in the metaphor. We may become quiescent and still, as the bowl is before being sounded. What arises from this inner silence? How do we act from this position of stillness? Where are we when every reference point is removed? The sounding potential of the bowl is ever-present – simply awaiting the awakening from without. The openness reflected in the emptiness of the bowl provides a space that allows the tone to manifest. When we open ourselves to our higher, spiritual nature, we can then resound with the fullness of being. We are then whole. The somewhat hemispherical shape of the bowl (as an archetype for the bell) could be seen to hint at the other half of the sphere that exists in the non-physical, realm. Uniting with, or opening up to, this other half could bring balance and equilibrium and the fullness of being whole. We open to the non-physical and so enter into the spiritual world(s) with its many 'mansions' (levels).

The act of playing the bowl places us in the process of time, and yet the past, present, and future coexist equally and can be seen as interdependent. It may also be considered that while we play the bowl its sound reaches those in the past, present and future. The bowl may have been producing its sound for centuries past and continue for centuries more to come.

While you are playing a bowl it is sometimes possible to transcend the object/subject and inside/outside divide and become absorbed in the experience of being the void. After such a precious moment of communion we return again to the time and space where we began our journey into sacred sound a little richer for the experience and strengthened in our spiritual path through such altered states of consciousness.

The stroked *yang* bowl seems to carry the significance of sound encircling a fixed point – rather like the planets encircling our sun – whereas stroking a *yin* bowl embodies a sense of moving outwards away from this centre, into ever-widening and expanding spheres. Thus taking the solar system as our model, we can say that the stroked *yang* bowl centres our focus upon the ever-present sun at the centre and sees all things as dependent upon this central sun, whereas the stroked *yin* bowl would seem to be taking us upon a journey through the solar system, moving from one planetary orbit to another, away from the centre – embracing ever wider spheres and yet no less centred for that. One could say that within this context the *yin* bowls are inclusive whereas the *yang* bowls are exclusive. In the same way the feminine planet, the Moon, involves itself in the process of manifestation (outwards into material form) and the masculine planet the Sun invites us inwards towards the Source.

Some bowls are wider at the rim (*yang*) yet there is no thickening of the metal (*yin*).

In the act of opening the lid of a jam jar our hands work against each other in opposite directions and yet work together in the one aim. So it is that the opposites are interdependent with our need to maintain balance or equilibrium between the two poles. That is not to say that we must each own a *yang* and a *yin* bowl but rather that we should avoid exclusiveness or separation.

You should understand that you are divinities. Yes, divinities, and you live on a higher plane free of limitations, shadows and darkness, sorrow and suffering, in the midst of abundance and joy. Do you know what prevents you from manifesting the splendour of those higher regions here below? The personality. Your personality is too unadaptable, too self-centred to capture the subtle messages from those regions ... like a radio that cannot pick up all the stations. The waves and vibrations released by Cosmic Intelligence in the higher spheres are swift as lightning, and the matter of the personality is too dense, too hard of hearing to vibrate in tune with them, and so it cannot seize divine messages. They flash by without making an impression and we continue to live in ignorance, far from knowing or experiencing the wonderful joy of our higher Being.

There are ways of changing this situation. If you choose to lead a pure life and become once again a child of God, then your heart will open and become generous, your mind will clear and your will become indomitable. The personality will become the willing instrument with which to express the divine life of the individuality more and more fully and correctly ... until the day comes when both the personality and the individuality become fused with each other, the personality ceases to exist and becomes one with the individuality.

Omraam Mikhail Aïvanhov[1]

8. Mallets and Wands

THERE ARE two principal ways to play the bowls. We use a 'mallet' (or striker, beater, hammer – the masculine approach) to strike the bowl and a 'wand' (also known as a 'puja stick') for stroking it, which is the feminine way. In each case it is customary for the contact to be with the outside of the bowl. We need total concentration when stroking the bowl, paying attention to the correct rhythm, pressure, grip, angle, etc, and this itself is a form of perfect meditation: of becoming 'at-one' with the bowl and its ancient sound, and losing all sense of a separate 'self' in the wonderful absorbing sound-world of the singing bowls! The sound itself seems to encircle and enfold us and to fill our several bodies with divine light.

When choosing which mallet or wand to use, the general rule is the larger the bowl then the bigger the mallet or wand. Mallets vary in width and density and in the weight of the head and we increase these dimensions when using the mallet for larger or for *yang* bowls. Again, wands of greater widths made from progressively denser woods will suit bowls as their size increases. Selecting from such ranges will also affect the sound of a single bowl, bringing out a different arrangement of its partials. Not all bowls produce the full range of partials, which is what make Himalayan bowls so unique.

Striking the Bowl

Before discussing striking, we need to look at the different mallets available. For large bowls we can use a soft gong mallet, or a hard felt beater. Coming in different sizes, these can be used with even the smallest of bowls. In Japan and China leather-covered strikers are traditionally used. Chinese bowls come with a *yang* lip and the larger Japanese bowls are similar, so that Himalayan bowls featuring a *yang* rim will sound best with such a mallet.

When using a mallet there are three main ways to strike a bowl. If the bowl is resting on a cushion, the floor, or upon our hand, then we can come from above with the mallet hanging downwards. In this case we can use the action of gravity to strike the bowl. Although we use the term 'striking', and even though the traditional term for an outside striker for bells is a 'hammer', I don't mean to suggest a violent or aggressive hitting action. That is too forceful, and it's unnecessary to move the arm or hand and hit the bowl as one would hammer in a nail. Simply try to avoid any stiffness or rigidity in the movement. If we hold the mallet as we might a pen, between our thumb and forefinger, then we can use either our first or second finger to move the mallet backwards and allow gravity to move it forwards, back into contact with the bowl.

If we are holding the bowl on our hand, then a second option is to come from below. In this case, in order to avoid 'hitting' the bowl, we can use a movement of the wrist. If it is a large bowl, and we are using a large mallet (e.g., a gong mallet), then it is advisable to use the thumb on the handle in order to steady the mallet for greater control over the force applied (when struck from below).

The third method is to strike the bowl using the mallet in a horizontal position. This action can be either a straight horizontal movement (to and from), or a glancing attack in an upward-curving arc. We can also use a thick stick covered in felt (such as would normally be used for stroking a large bowl) and fetch a gentle glancing blow in a horizontal plane sweeping in an arc towards and then away from the rim of the bowl.

Finally, as a variation on the first method, there is a *staccato* approach, in which we again use the wrist to strike the bowl but immediately the striker touches the bowl we pull it back. This technique works well with *yang* bowls and also with certain Manipuri Lingam bowls (see Chapter 10), where four or more distinct tones are present. In general, this technique tends to emphasize the upper partials of the bowl. I normally select from a range of strikers covered with leather for this effect, although for small Manipuri and Orissa bowls I sometimes use a piece of very hard Mexican

rosewood (also known as *bocote,* or *palo escrito*) that I turned in
the form of a striker, or even the metal clapper (tongue) fallen from
the inside of a *drilbu,* or the WBTST ('Chalklin Wood Ball Bamboo Handle Timpani Staccato' – available from Footes) mallet.

There are large ranges of mallets available to percussionists,
including ones intended for playing vibraphones, marimbas, timpani, glockenspiels, bell plates, or gongs. Most of these have soft
heads, thus avoiding the sharp, more discordant sounds that come
from harder mallets (such as the wooden ones made for playing
xylophones). A range of mallets with felt heads is also available
from India and some bowl sellers stock these. Being cruder, these
do not possess the balance found in custom-made professional
mallets, but they are a lot cheaper.

Pictured below is an assortment of mallets used for striking the
bowls. These generally produce harder, more strident tones from
the bowls – although not as harsh as bare wood against the bowl.
Far left is a traditional antique Chinese mallet of leather-covered
wood, then a straight half leather-covered wand from India, a
felt-covered from Nepal, next a human bone with leather tied by
string, then a piece of very hard bocote (Mexican rosewood), next
a cane with a brass ball on the end, then another mallet covered

with leather, and then five pieces of wood covered with leather with the fourth from the right being a traditional antique Chinese striker. Some of these I made myself.

Pictured on this page is another assortment of mallets and beaters used for striking the bowls. From the left is a traditional Lambswool gong mallet, next is a special mallet for Paiste Sound Plates (Paiste Mallet 12), then another traditional hard felt gong mallet, followed by an antique gong mallet, then a typical hard felt mallet from India, another antique hard felt gong mallet, a small Chinese mallet, a modern large hard felt mallet from India. Following are three manufactured by Chalklin. Paul Chalklin produces a range of percussion mallets, and in his 'Symphonic Range' we find mallets for glockenspiel, xylophone, vibraphone, marimba, and bass marimba. MS14 SOFT for Vibraphone is good for the larger bowls. These three are (from the left) MS 24 'Soft Sewn Felt' Timpani Mallet, then a WBTST, and thirdly a MS17 MED/SOFT Marimba Mallet. Finally, there is a small Chinese mallet. Another Chalklin mallet (not illustrated) with a bamboo handle and covered with felt that isn't quite so hard is the BT 22S Timpani Bamboo Sewn Felt Staccato. The WBTST will tend to bring out the top end of the bowl partials, while the BT 22S, being a little softer, is less brusque but brings out some upper partials. These are professional mallets (not cheap) but they come in pairs – so you can think of them as lasting twice as long! Paul Chalklin also makes

mallets for Paiste and aside from the one pictured above I've another in a smaller size (PAISTE TG 1) – for Paiste Sound Plates.
This is good for bowls with diameters eight inches and over. Softer
mallets like these bring out the lower partials making the sound
softer, warmer, and more full-bodied. The wooden mallets or hard
felt from the previous photograph give a brighter, more complex,
shrill sound via stimulation of the bowl's upper partials. Percussion
Plus produce a good beater (manufactured to play the Slit Drum)
that has a soft rubber ball on its head and this gets a good sound.

Stroking the Bowl

The other way to play a bowl is by rubbing a stick around the
outside rim (rather like the finger on a wineglass trick). I call this
stroking the bowl, and the stick I call a wand.

When I began working with singing bowls in the early 1970s
there was nothing to play them with at all. As I mainly found
them in antique shops, the seller would generally be unaware that
the bowls had anything to do with the production of sound! So
I learnt woodturning to make my own wands for striking and
stroking and later went on to produce these for others.

In the photograph on the following page is a small selection of
wands to illustrate the range of woods and variety of widths needed for different-sized bowls or to elicit the various partials from a
single bowl. I turned them all myself, following the original design
I developed in 1982.

And so we come to the question of choosing a wand! The bowl
really does 'sing' once the correct wand has been found. We can
use many wands to produce the basic sound of the bowl but only
the right one will produce the special singing sound, which is easily distinguished. That is to say that a particular wooden wand will
arrange the several partials within the sound of the bowl in the
most harmonious way. Using a range of wands from different sizes and densities we can also learn to bring out the several partials
of a bowl in isolation. In the photograph overleaf are a variety of
wooden wands from four inches in diameter (willow) down to
half an inch and made from woods varying in density, oiliness,

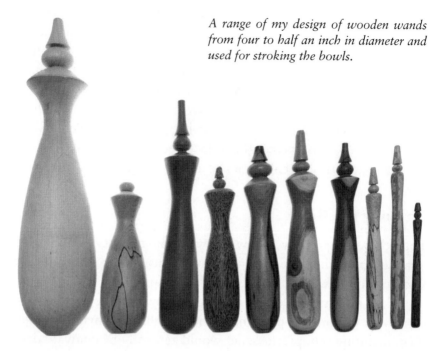

A range of my design of wooden wands from four to half an inch in diameter and used for stroking the bowls.

hardness and weight. Some of these pictured above are from spalt-ed woods (caused by a form of disease).

When using a wand I use a 'pen grip' (illustrated opposite). Often a stick is supplied with the bowl when you buy from a shop; and this is commonly of a consistent diameter with felt or leather for a proportion of the length with the remaining part bare wood. This can be used to stroke the bowl, or for striking the bowl using either end. However, the bare wood is often hard wood and will tend to give a harsh noise played in either way. Sometimes it is a softer wood, which works well when stroking but if used to strike the bowl then it might easily get dented, and so become harder to use for stroking afterwards. Another drawback with these has been that with only one size usually offered, the stick it is too thin for large bowls and too thick for small ones. It is not unusual to be listening to a totally new sound from a bowl once another wand or mallet is used. I have often witnessed the wonder upon the face of a bowl owner when a more appropriate implement has been supplied them.

To obtain the fundamental from the bowl, we ideally apply

the wand perpendicularly to the wall – holding the wand in an upright vertical position.

By adjusting the angle at the rim we can change the sound produced – with an acute angle normally bringing out the upper partials (see the two photographs over-

leaf). This also means that if we wish to produce the fundamental, we need to make sure that we are roughly holding the wand in this upright position. That can prove taxing when using a larger bowl – unless we have long arms! If we want to focus upon one of the upper partials then, usually, we'd move towards a thinner wand made of harder wood. Around 1993, I invented very thin wands (half-inch diameter or less) for the purpose of producing the upper partials. I make them from hard woods such as ebony, kingwood, blackwood, pink ivory, cherry, pear, violet rosewood, tulipwood, cocobolo, piquia amarello, laburnum, and so on. *Yang* bowls, with their thick rim, and because of the extra metal, are much harder to work with this way. With *yang* bowls it is possible to get higher partials than the fundamental, but this usually involves using a wider wand made from hard woods. As always, because of the variations involved in manufacturing a hand-hammered singing bowl, we can only apply a general rule of thumb here, as there will invariably be exceptions to any rule we may wish to establish.

Sometimes when choosing a wand another factor to consider is the amount of noise created by the act of rubbing the rim from a variety of woods. Even if we like the sound of the bowl from

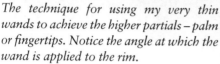

The technique for using my very thin wands to achieve the higher partials – palm or fingertips. Notice the angle at which the wand is applied to the rim.

one piece of wood, we may find that the noise of stroking is too distracting. This is often the case with hard woods such as purpleheart, whereas aspen, being a soft wood, is quieter. Using a wand covered with felt or leather (as in the picture on the next page) removes this worry. In general, such wands as these will tend to focus upon the fundamental. With larger bowls this is often the case, especially if we use one of these thicker wands.

For many people, the bowl is the thing, just as for many seeking gongs the gong is the thing. Few stop to consider what the object is going to be played with. That is of secondary importance to them. However, when they come to me to buy the wands I've designed they are extremely surprised to find that it often takes them up to three hours to choose the right one! There may be ten or twenty wands lying around the floor, all of which get a good sound from any one bowl. As the hearing grows more discerning, it is found that each wand will elicit a different arrangement of the partials singing inside the bowl. Some of these partials within the bowl will come to the fore whilst others will recede. These differing preponderances of the several partials that constitute the sound of the bowl result in an altered perception in hearing the bowl; they change its effect upon us – and this is all due to using different

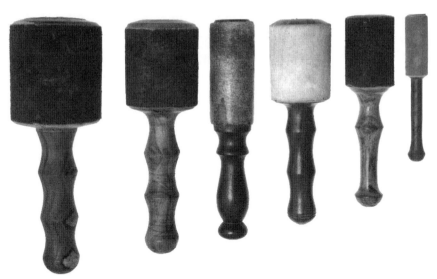

wands. When the correct wand is found (creating the best arrangement of the bowl's partials) it is then that the bowl can be heard to
really 'sing'! – it seems to be sounding its own note and to be true
to itself – which is something we can all aspire towards in our lives.

Many factors contribute towards the sound that the bowl will
produce. Some wands will stimulate several partials simultaneously and more or less equally, whereas others will elicit one partial
audibly louder than any of the others. The width of the wand, the
angle of application of the wand to the rim of the bowl, the nature
of the wood (whether it is oily, softwood, hardwood, heavy or
light, coarse or fine, and so on), plus the manner in which we hold
the bowl and how we hold and apply the wand (pen or hammer)
to the bowl, all have their effect. It is a question of determining
which variation of these factors is best for your bowl – or the
sound you prefer to get from it.

Then there is also the factor of the sounding potential of the actual bowl and its design. A bowl with a poor sound quality cannot
be improved upon, no matter what we use to produce the sound. I
find that beech is a good wood for trying bowls, as it tends to get
a sound out of any bowl, so I invariably take a piece when sorting
through bowls. Each type of wood is suitable for particular bowls
or different effects. Some bowl sellers/players have their own fa-
vourites. For instance, Aidan McIntyre favours aspen and John

Mead holly. As we've seen, aspen is a light and soft wood that produces little unwanted noise when stroking, but it is seldom good
for awakening the higher partials of a bowl. It is best at producing
the fundamental (often experienced as a warm sound). As a general rule of thumb, if a bowl rings on for more than twenty seconds
after being struck then it will usually work when stroked.

Grip and Pressure

You will find that a different grip on the wand affects some bowls,
while others may demand a different pressure. At what stage
between the extremes in operation do you tend to grip a wand or
apply pressure? A common problem is found in the rather ugly,
discomforting, rattling or clanging noise sometimes produced as
the bowl is stroked. This is most often caused by either stroking
too fast, or if your grip on the wand is too tight or too loose. It
can also result from your holding the wand incorrectly (that is,
in the wrong position), not applying enough pressure, using the
wrong angle between the wand and the rim of the bowl, or by
using a wand that may be inappropriate for the bowl through
being either too wide, too narrow, or manufactured out of a
wood that is far too hard for that bowl. It can also result from
applying an inconsistent rhythm, or speed, encircling the bowl's
rim. Otherwise, scratches or marks around the outside rim or
irregularities in its edge or shape may also be a factor.

Some persons using my design of wand hold it at the top rather than at its waist. This provides them with little control over
the pressure applied, and can be a cause of these unwanted noises. Nonetheless, there will be certain bowls that sound best using
such an extremely loose grip with gentle pressure. When the bowl
merchants of the East began making wooden wands they were
all made from hard woods and were around one inch thick, and
straight, regardless of whether one was buying a bowl of twelve-
inch or of four-inch diameter! In general, a wide wand needs to
move slowly around the rim, whereas a narrow wand will work
well when played faster. There are no hard-and-fast rules with
singing bowls so it is always advisable to experiment. However,

we will always need to use the co-ordination of both hands between the pressure from that hand holding the wand against the other hand upon which the bowl rests.

Certain unusual bowls need to be played in a position sideways to their base, making it necessary for us to hold the wand horizontally. Small Chalice Bowls (another form with an added base) can be played this way – especially if their sound is suitable for space-cleansing – but the specific ones to consider are the 'Talking Bowl' and the 'Panic Bowl'. The names for these types of bowl were given me by Alain Presencer. Alain had such bowls in his collection when I first met him in 1982, so the names originated some time prior to that. It is useful to stay with these terms in order to avoid confusion for now we have persons selling a 'Panic Bowl' or a 'Talking Bowl' that is nothing remotely similar to these types of bowl – either in design or sound. The only other categorization apart from these two labels that he made back then was a 'Star Bowl': one which, within the inside base of the bowl, has an eight-pointed star inscribed.

With both of these rare bowls the wand used is around two inches wide, with the size of the 'Panic Bowl' being around four inches in diameter and the 'Talking bowl' around three inches. In the photographs below the 'Talking Bowl' is shown on the left hand side and the 'Panic Bowl' is seen in the photograph on the right. Interestingly, the 'Talking Bowl' needs to be held very loosely and the wand also requires a very loose grip (both almost falling out of one's

Talking Bowl (left) and Panic Bowl (right: at home in London in 1982)

© Esther James, Ringwood 1995

© Jill Furmanovsky

hands) compared with the 'Panic Bowl' that requires a very tight grip on the wand (made from ebony). The bowl, being very heavy for its size, it is also necessary to grip it very tightly; the pressure between the two hands is thus most intense. The intensity actually works very well because this bowl is traditionally used for exorcisms. It produces a very intense and loud high-pitched sound that most people choose to run away from (or at least cover their ears), which is why Alain Presencer called it a 'Panic Bowl'.

When it comes to selecting the best wand for a bowl, we find that one wand might produce an arrangement of the partials where one of the prominent tones creates a cold feeling. Yet another wand produces a warmer feeling because it has brought forward a different arrangement of the tones from the bowl, and yet with this rearrangement of the partials it is found that the higher tones are missing – so that the bowl is rather dull sounding. Sometimes one can hear a tone inside the bowl and work through many, many wands, trying to bring this note forwards in the sound mix. A fellow bowl musician, Andy Thurgood, visited me once to buy bowls and wands and he brought a small bowl with him. We could hear a high tone in the background when it was struck and we tried to sound this tone with every single wand I had for sale but to no avail. Just as he was leaving I remembered that there was one wand we hadn't tried. It was in another room, resting beside a bowl used for crystal cleansing that this wand was good for. We tried this small wand, made of African blackwood, and it worked immediately – it was seemingly made for this bowl! Andy was a very happy man and left with this most precious piece of wood! I then went off to find a replacement wand that hopefully would work as well for this crystal cleansing bowl as the one Andy had taken.

I have often found that one particular piece of wood produces the very best sound from one bowl. When I lay out my bowls many of them have their allotted wand close by. There have been other occasions when I have had to release one of my wands because it is the only one that produces the right sound with somebody else's bowl. People sometimes approach me at fairs and try a wand on their bowl and it gets the right sound for their bowl. Then they turn to their partner and ask him or her to make one like it. It is hard to explain to people just how individual the wands are, and that the likelihood of another working just as well is very far from being guaranteed. Even if I produce three wands from one single piece of wood they will not all get the same sound from a single bowl.

Occasionally the bowl itself is oriented towards sounding a single prominent partial – usually the second (providing the six pulses) – and, regardless of the wand used, it will always sound that partial alone. In a similar manner some bowls sound best when stroked, and others produce a much better sound only when struck. But this situation is rather rare.

When percussionists buy Paiste gongs there will be one mallet considered to produce the correct sound from that gong. Aside from that, though, one can experiment with many other implements and discover a range of sounds hiding inside that gong. Likewise, once we have found the right wand for our bowl, we might choose to wander away from this optimal prime tool in order to achieve alternative sounds from it, using either wider or narrower wands, or ones made from softer or harder woods. In this way we can accentuate the lower sounds or the higher sounds, respectively, within that bowl.

Sometimes several of the various partials within a particular bowl might be sounding together when we are playing with a certain wand, yet as we change wands it is possible (for instance) to rearrange the focus upon the higher partials. This might be done by using progressively thinner wands made of harder woods and also by altering pressure and the angle at which these wands are being applied to the rim and varying the speed. If we apply the wand perpendicularly to the wall of the bowl we are likely to produce the deeper tones, whereas as we adjust the angle to a more acute one (sometimes to 45°) we will encourage the higher partials within the bowl to gain prominence. In such ways it is possible to focus on the partials of a bowl one at a time, with one wand achieving the fundamental then another producing the second partial, and yet another producing the third, and so on up to the fifth partial. In this manner one singing bowl can be enabled to sound like five separate bowls! (See Table #6)

I have used this technique in recordings so that a number of bowl sounds are perfectly in tune with the one from which all these sounds originate. It will sound as though five different singing bowls are playing at once and all perfectly in tune – their tones resting within each other. I can strike the bowl (hard and soft) and also stroke it with different wands and bow it with water inside. I recorded an entire section of a piece in this way using the Aldebaran Bowl ('Tibetan Singing Bowls, Volume 3: Ancient Tibetan Initiation Bowls', Track #1: 'The Light Shining through Aldebaran'; recorded in 1993 – released 2001).[1] Similarly, I used the same technique with the Great Star Mother Bowl on 'Tibetan Singing Bowls, Volume 1: The Healing Bowls of Tibet. Track #2: 'The Way of the Bowls' (1997). There have been other occasions also.[2]

If we hold the bowl upon the palm of the hand we will encourage its lower tones, whereas if we wanted to hear the higher tones within the bowl we might change to holding it upon upstretched fingers and use a thinner wand of harder wood and at the same time adjusting our angle of playing. We might also be required to apply greater pressure between the wand and the rim of the bowl, or altering to a faster speed of stroking the bowl. If we change our manner of holding the bowl by way of moving our hand and fingers up the outside, we will also prevent the lower tones from sounding and encourage the higher notes within to sound. However, there is a difference to the higher sounds in this case, as the fundamental of the bowl is then missing. Alternatively, being able to produce the higher tone without restricting the lower tones of the bowl produces a more full-bodied sound. It is analogous to the effect of a *basso profundo* singing a higher bass or baritone part. Another technique involves using a wedge-shaped wand so that we can move up or down along its shape, thus providing ourselves with a decreasing (or increasing) diameter of wood to apply to the bowl.

So, as you can see, there are many factors involved in achieving a sound from a bowl. Are we using the right size and form of mallet for the bowl? It might be useful here to think along the lines of automobile engines – a small engine for a compact car and a larger more powerful engine for a pantechnicon. A big bowl requires a larger wand or mallet, whereas a small bowl demands less effort and so a lighter wand or mallet will be used. How are we striking the bowl? How we are holding the bowl in our hand, how fast we are moving the wand, how much pressure are we applying to the rim of the bowl, how firmly or slackly we are gripping the wand? Have we considered the type of wood (thick or thin, hard or soft) of which the wand is made, even the length of the wand and its design and balance? Some practitioners use the plastic handles of particular makes of screwdriver. Karma Moffett uses a particular type of plastic. In each case it is a question of attaining the optimum performance from a bowl by experimenting with a range of wands or mallets. Below are some guidelines when using wands.

The rhythm of the stroke and thickness of the wall are both important factors when stroking.

Thin-walled bowls (and also *yin* bowls) possess a high level of responsiveness and so are very easily stimulated. Therefore we need to use a slow rhythm plus a looser grip – less pressure and a wand of softer wood.

Thick-walled bowls (or bowls with a thick rim, i.e., *yang*) are harder to excite, therefore we need a faster rhythm. We may also need a tighter grip and may want to use a wider wand and/or a harder wood.

Of course, there are not simply two types: rather it is a matter of whether the bowl is light (hence made from thin metal), if it is of medium weight (from thicker metal) or heavy (from thicker metal still). All kinds of levels of thickness exist in between the extremes, with these being general guidelines only. As ever, with bowls I can only give generalizations: the rest comes out of your own experiment and experience.

Wand Diameter

The width of the wand is also a significant factor in the playing of a bowl. Thin wands can prove more difficult in exciting the bowl, therefore play with a faster rhythm and possibly use greater pressure and a tighter grip upon the wand – also adjusting the angle. Once the wand 'bites', as it were, you can slow down the speed as if riding the sound. However, each bowl is unique and some might require a constantly higher than usual speed. In general, very thin wands will work best on small bowls and of the *yin* variety – although exceptions will occur.

Thick wands easily stimulate, therefore play in a slow rhythm and also maybe use a looser grip upon the wand and use less pressure, although this will depend upon the thickness of the bowl and its rim also. Mostly bigger wands will work best with larger bowls or bowls of the *yang* type. On average, two-inch diameter wands are for bowls of four- to nine-inch diameter, three-inch for bowls of eight- to eleven-inch diameter and four-inch for bowls in excess of that.

Thicker or heavier bowls, possessing more mass, will generally require a more oily wood (such as mopane or tambuti) or a harder wood to generate more friction.

Finally, there is another way of playing the bowl that is similar to the stroking technique and that is by bowing the bowl – either with a cello or double bass bow.

THIN wand on a THICK bowl	on a small bowl may produce the higher partials. On a large bowl a thin wand probably won't produce a sound at all!
THICK wand on a THICK bowl	will produce fundamental plus some partials providing us with a richer sound than with the leather wands. May easily 'override'. So don't go too fast.
THIN wand on a THIN bowl	tends to stimulate the upper partials. You may need to adjust the angle of the wand to assist in reaching these top notes.
THICK wand on a THIN bowl	produces the fundamental & partials. Easily 'over-rides' so avoid too much pressure and take it slow and use soft wood.

Summary: wand diameters and bowl types

9. The Metal of the Bowls

THIS CHAPTER considers not only the metals used in bowl manufacture, but also how the chosen metals may have a symbology that further distinguishes one bowl from another. This added significance enables us to link them via astrology with specific elements and soul paths. It is to be remembered that although there are traditionally four elements in the West (Earth, Air, Fire and Water), the Chinese system offers us Fire, Earth, Water, Wood and Metal and the Tibetan Fire, Earth, Water, Air and Space.

Elementally, the most obvious connection made when we first encounter a Himalayan singing bowl is the link with Metal, which relates to Fire. To obtain metal we must use fire. Fire is the element associated especially with the Hindu god Agni, and so we find a link to *agni yoga* – the yoga of fire, where the earthly personality is prepared to be the vehicle for the Divine Spirit within. From this there comes also the association of the bowls with ancient fire worship. Fire is light and heat, and in the spiritual astrology of the White Eagle Lodge, which is the form I studied, the element Fire is linked with learning the lesson of divine love. The sound of a beautiful singing bowl can open our heart to love, perhaps even to divine love. In this way Fire is linked with the heart – also because it rules the astrological sign of Leo, which (for the ancients) rules the heart.

However, the light of the Sun is also connected to another fire sign, namely Aries, which rules the head. Fire (divine love) in this way may unite head (Aries) and heart (Leo), as in wisdom and compassion. Heat seems to have a direct link with the passions of the heart, whilst light is connected to en-lighten-ment, a quality that manifests as compassion once the heart is linked to the wise mind. Several metals are brought together in the fire and made as one unified whole. In Tantra, there is a principle in which a variety of energies are 'woven' together through our practice.

Working with the archetypal number of seven in the context of metals, the seven metals said to be brought together in the bowls (which we shall look at shortly) represent the seven planets – including Sun and Moon. These can helpfully be approached as seven aspects of the one light of the Sun. As a result, we create a link to the seven chakras and the corresponding seven levels of consciousness-development, seen as branches on a tree reaching ever-further towards the source of all life. This source is the Sun; the Christ; the Golden ONE. The seven planetary metals united together may also thus encapsulate the solar system as a giant womb, in which the sun acts as entry point for the cosmic fecundation of these several worlds.

If we remove the Sun and Moon, these being not strictly planets but Principles, there would be five actual planets. These may also link with the five Jinas (Conquerors), as well as the five chakras of the Tibetans and the five parts of a Tibetan Stupa and five Tibetan elements.

Overall, the symbolism is this. The bowl metal must enter the fire in order to be formed into a new shape, and so we must enter into the spiritual fire of divine love and with the hammer of the mind forge a new form for ourselves. We must form the 'new bottles' ready for the 'new wine'.

The metal from which traditional bowls are made is said to be a fusion of seven metals. This is unproven, but offers a useful link with the seven spiritual Rays and with the 'Music of the

Spheres', the seven planetary rays. The metals are gold, silver, mercury, copper, iron, tin and antimony. Some bowls have components of meteorite added (or in place of the iron). It must not

be imagined that when these seven metals are present it is in equal measure: for thousands of years, worldwide, bells have been predominantly made of copper and tin, so that any of the other metals are in tiny proportions. Also the manner in which the metals are combined is not known, for the originals were all handmade to a specific formula known only to their masters. The order is important, though, because diverse metals melt at different temperatures. Regular bells worldwide are cast from 'bell metal' (bronze – a mixture on average of 77% copper and 23% tin). Western bellmakers know that if they add more than 1% of lead to the alloy that the sound will be ruined. Bronze is used because it emits a more sonorous tone and withstands deterioration longer than other easily available metals. Some Tibetan bowls were made at certain phases of the Moon; yet others were created under special, and different, astrological conditions.

In his book SINGING BOWLS FOR HEALTH AND INNER HARMONY (2008), the German Peter Hess informs us that he spent many years searching for the formula until:

> with the help of my long-term Indian co-worker, Sunil Sharma, I finally made a breakthrough in the beginning of 1997. Sunil had met on one of his trips to the eastern foothills of the Himalayas, a 94-year-old man who had been making traditional singing bowls in his youth. We also received support from a metallurgist of that region, who analysed the metals of many old singing bowls for us.... The twelve are the seven planetary metals and Zinc, Meteoric iron, Bismuth, Galena & Pyrite.... The molten metals are poured into a thick slice. While still hot it is forged by four to five smiths into a singing bowl. The production of a quality bowl of about 2 kilos (4.42 lbs) takes about 32 hours.

In a certain study of an old broken bowl it was found that the basic metal was indeed the usual copper and tin (uniformly used for the making of bells) but there were many trace elements including gold and silver.

It is sometimes said that the bowls are made of three metals (but also of five, eight, nine, or twelve) and it is not necessarily the case that all bowls are made of the same seven-metal alloy, or indeed by any consistent formula at all. Some are said to include carbon and nickel, although both of these arise from iron in different stages of its production. Some writers and sellers claim that the bowls contain nickel, but in such an alloy this is usually found in a form of brass used for industrial purposes. Despite the claims of numerous salespersons, the only way to verify any such statements involves destroying the bowl. There are ways of faking ancient bowls – so follow your spiritual heart and inner voice of the silence regardless of the degree of exciting information that may accompany the selling of a bowl!. Glancing at my range of antique singing bowls a large variety of colours is to be found, indicating a wide range of alloys. It is also said that some bowls are plated with a mixture of more precious metals to raise the price.

Again, we learn from Tom Kenyon's CD (see Chapter 1, p. 20), that the set he purchased takes one year to make and that they cast the gold at the full moon – and then, in the next astrological configuration, they add the silver, and so forth. Every addition is made according to the astrological changes in the heavens. The lamas believe that because it takes them an entire year to complete this process, the bowls are tuned in to the cosmic rhythms. He goes on to mention that his own experience with these bowls confirms this, with the sound of the bowls altering according to changes in the heavens.

This account would seem to be at variance with the accepted procedure of making an alloy from the admixture of the several metals. I've not seen Tom's bowls, so cannot testify to there being evidence of building the bowl up one metal at a time. Regardless of how puzzling this method seems, nonetheless it is an account to be taken along with the rest, unless there has been a misunderstanding and the lamas were speaking about the times when they gathered the separate metals over the year and smelted the individual metals into separate ingots prior to fusing them together to create a bowl.

In 1996 there was a scientific analysis at Concordia University in Canada of two bowls, which provided us with a table of constituents: aside from the regular bell metal here shown as being 77.2% copper and 22% tin you will notice that the percentages of some of the other metals present are very small (fractions of 1%;

see Appendix A, p. 455). In fact, in a recent email exchange between Mitch Nur and R. T. Patterson, the analyst who conducted
the tests, it emerges that the amounts of other metals present are
consistent with impurities but that the technology used at the time
would not have shown up small amounts of gold or mercury.

I have also found bowls where one metal can be seen to predominate. Mostly this has been either gold or silver. Interestingly,
both gold and silver are from neutron stars and thus are extra-terrestrial in origin! It can occur that a bowl will look as if it were
made entirely of silver or gold. However, that is most certainly not
the case, because gold, for one, has poor sonic qualities. Silver can
produce a lovely sound but the cost of either is prohibitive (unless
cost was not an issue at the time of the bowl's making). In such
instances it can nevertheless prove helpful for us to consider the
links to the planet of that metal. For instance, silver would link the
bowl to the Moon. Then following the astrological associations
we find that the Moon rules the astrological sign of Cancer – sign
of the mother and the cardinal water sign. Water is used mainly
for cleaning and for purification.

The Moon has always been linked with ritual and magic. It
is also symbolic of the mother; the feminine principle, whilst the
reflective qualities of the Moon can represent the alignment of our
'personality triad' to the 'triad of our individuality'; symbolically, the union of the Moon with the spiritual Sun. Similarly, when
gold has a strong presence, then we have links to the Sun and so
with the astrological sign of Leo (the father or masculine principle) ruled by the Sun and of the fire element. Fire is also a cleanser,
although more of a purging influence than water. However, the
warmth of golden fire links it to the energy of love, which could
be seen as the great healer. This energy of spiritual love can lead to
deep communion with the spiritual centre and so to a loss of ego
and the sense of abiding in the Self.

Both water and fire can be seen as cleansing or purifying. In the
Bible, John the Baptist says, 'I am the voice of one crying in the
wilderness'. 'Repent!' comes from the Greek *metanoein*, meaning
to change the direction of our thoughts – away from the outer
world towards the inner realms.

I also have some rare bowls where meteorite has a strong
presence. The meteorite tends to resonate with spiritual energies
that are beyond human spirituality. Being truly of extra-terrestrial
origin, the meteorite can then act as a cosmic, or intergalactic,
messenger. I have even come across bowls made of iron (ruled
by the fiery planet of Mars). My 'Panic Bowl' looks to have been
dipped in liquid gold after being cast. Otherwise, there is a red
copper and when this is present the bowl can be mistaken for
being a gold bowl. The patina is the key.

In reference to the more esoteric aspects of bowlmaking,
which may sound surprisingly complex, we can glean some possible hints from the practice of casting sacred statues. In the case
of statues it is customary to cast a horoscope chart for the most
auspicious day and to pray (do *puja*) before using the metal. It is
said that the craftsman should not be a hereditary blacksmith, or a
butcher, or any other occupation considered to be of low status in
Tibetan society. It is best if created by a monk or layman who has
taken the five basic vows; not to kill, steal, engage in sexual mis-
conduct, drink liquor or lie. The artisan should cultivate the attitude of a Bodhisattva (Vajrapani) who represents the concentrated
power of all Buddhas – regardless of what image he's working
on. Everything associated with the task should be considered very
sacred, even the clay or metal being worked on. Before starting
work the craftsperson should take refuge in the Buddha, *dharma*
and *sangha* (the 'Three Jewels'), and should think of the image as
being made for the benefit of all sentient beings. He should meditate and recite the mantra of the particular deity being fashioned,
and must also seek the permission of the Spirit of the Earth before
using her substance to create the deity, asking her to allow him to
create the statue for the welfare of all beings.

We find an example in an account of the making of long metal
horns for a monastery. We are told that the *rinpoche* collected
metals (jewellery, etc) to take to the blacksmith monks at Derge.
People also donated jewellery and items of gold and silver and
other precious metals, to gain credit (beneficent *karma*).

There are markings on some old bowls, even writing sometimes. For instance, one bowl of mine has written upon it, in Ti-

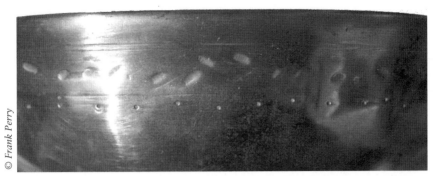

© Frank Perry

betan, words that might translate as 'On the Surface of Sound' (this is as told me by Alain Presencer). There is nearly always a circle inscribed within the centre of the bowl (almost worn away in some); there can also be certain markings on the top of the rim, around the outside, and sometimes within circles in the centre of the bowl, being made from a 'dot-within-the-circle' punch (this symbol being the astrological glyph for the Sun). Sometimes these might be worn away, leaving only marks of the central dot. But it is doubtful that bowls featuring a lot of decoration are Tibetan. These are more likely to originate from India.

The number of markings can have significance. Markings on the outside just beneath the rim can also include parallel lines around the bowl; otherwise, a kind of 'half-moon' punch is used here (see the photograph above), either as diagonal slashes in groupings of irregular numbers. Sometimes they are deliberately shaped to represent lotus petals. On other occasions single-dot punches may produce pearl-like patterns or other ornate designs. The parallel lines sometimes found running around the outside beneath the rim are most commonly the markings of the makers and most certainly not evidence of fine-tuning (as some people believe) because they are exactly the same on every bowl from the same maker. Nonetheless, according to Lama Leche, when there are nine such rings ('heads') it was made in Jang, or if with seven then at Hor. Nowadays the machine-made 'Tibetan Singing Bowls' from Nepal come with writing and designs all over them.

The actual colour of Tibetan bowls is generally a silvery grey-green (owing to the higher silver and tin content) or sometimes golden. Some persons assert that all singing bowls are made only

Whistling Bowl with the inscription 'On the Surface of Sound'

from copper and tin, but the variety of colourings of the bowls contradicts this assertion. Their basic shape resembles that of a crescent moon, although the larger sizes generally become more bell-like. Bhutanese bowls are often mistaken for Tibetan bowls, but are shaped more like a saucepan, in other words they have a much flatter broad base and a straight wall (Thadobati) and most often possess a thickening at the rim. However, they are generally far easier to play than Tibetan bowls. At one time bowls from Orissa in South India flooded the market, and these are of a similar design to Bhutanese but seldom have this thick rim. Bowls from Orissa resemble the shape of the glass (so-called 'crystal') bowls and like the glass bowls can produce a very strong and focused sound. Other bowls from India in my list (Appendix B) are the Bengali Bowl, Manipuri Bowl, Bharampur Bowl, plus Jhamkar Bowl, Asham Bowl, Chaken Bowl, Chape/Nara Bowl, Kabare Bowl, Khara Bowl, Sora Chaken Bowl, Bengali Khara … although to be honest there is precious little to distinguish some of these latter bowls from India other than weight, thickness of rim or height or contour of wall.

Cleaning Bowls

I am often asked how I clean my bowls. First I cover the inside base of the bowl with a washing-up liquid, fill the bowl with boiling hot water and then place a rod of aluminium inside the bowl. This sets up an electrolytic action. I leave this overnight and empty it the following morning and then rinse it under the tap whilst using a soft cloth to remove any traces of dirt. Then, if more cleaning is necessary, I fill the bowl with a mixture of warm water and freshly squeezed lemon juice (the number of lemons depends upon bowl size). Again I leave the bowl overnight and the following morning proceed as aforementioned; I follow this by cleaning in warm soapy water. One can also wash one's bowl in a stream or in the sea or simply in warm soapy water. Whichever procedure is followed it is best to dry the bowl immediately afterwards to avoid damage.

If necessary, as a final resort I finish off by using brass wadding. I've had some modern bowls that are coated with a diesel and old sump oil mix that I could feel on my fingers and also smell, and this sort of substance I would certainly remove! If a degree of rust is present, or other obstinate excretions (I've even had bowls with tar on them!), then I will empty some liquid brass polish and leave them a little while before working.

Sometimes the copper in the mix has risen to the surface during manufacture and there is nothing one can do to remove this. We have the choice of altering any discolouration here but that is all. If liquid has been left upon the bowl then rust will form and it may be necessary to use fine papers to remove it. My friend Hector Benson had a special technique he devized for using a liquid polish. He employed a piece of cloth and, as he polished, tiny particles of the metal from the bowl would gradually adhere to the cloth. He would then apply this part so that the bowl was being polished with its own metal! Some bowl aficionados favour a water-based silver polish. With bowls containing a lot of silver, use silver polish or 'silver dip'. For predominantly gold bowls use 'jewellers rouge'. On my budget, I may have to use brass polish, but this would be once in twenty or thirty years and so unlikely to wear away the bowl! It was used with Manipuri bowls between one and two hundred years old with no signs of patina, only dirt!

My older bowls, which carry a wonderful patina, I usually leave alone. With a large plastic bowl full of warm soapy water- or lemon juice, one can immerse the whole bowl but if there is a lovely patina on the outside of the bowl then only use the cleaning water on the inside. Sometimes I clean the inside just once if this has suffered abuse through misuse – normally with the first two methods outlined above. Stains can be removed with soaking in warm water with lemon juice for two to three hours followed with liquid brass polish such as Brasso. Leave this for a while to remove the stains. Metal polish will remove some molecules of metal but compared to the wear and tear that would accrue from cleaning after years of eating and drinking from the bowl this is minuscule.

You may also use fine papers for smoothing down around the rim of the bowl to remove file marks, scratches, dents, or other rough marks. Doing so will then serve to improve the sound of the bowl when stroking it with a wand. This may be particularly important for musicians who have to record the bowl with an undiscerning microphone that hears everything. Firstly, run cellulose tape or masking tape around the outside leaving about one eighth of an inch below the rim. In this way we limit how much metal is removed. At this point we apply the paper. I sometimes make a mark on the tape/paper to show where I began. Don't worry if the paper damages the tape – it's only a guide. The easiest fine paper to get hold of is probably Wet Silicon Carbide Paper. You could begin with a grade of 220, and then 400, finishing with 600 or up to 800 or higher if you wish to. If there is little damage, you can avoid the coarser papers. If you are of a patient disposition you might use the finer papers only, although this takes a lot of time and is expensive, as fine papers quickly clog up with metal particles. If you live in the U.S.A., you may find it easier to get hold of Crocus Paper or Cloth. An alternative would be to use a granulated metal polish.

Some bowls come with a black lacquer-like coating on the outside and it is best not to eliminate this, as it is a traditional feature. Removing it also affects the sound.

When transporting bowls, to avoid damage it is important to avoid the metal of one touching another. To do this we can place a cloth (e.g., an old tee-shirt or bed sheet – or, of course, brand new cotton if you prefer) in between bowls, or even 'bubble-wrap'. Sacred bowls that are charged with spiritual power, or those of

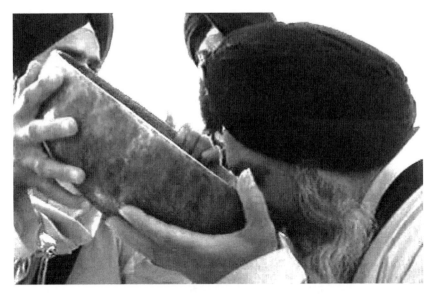

our own programming, might be best wrapped in silk to retain the energies. For playing, if we do not have a cushion then we can use a piece of leather, or else rubber non-slip cloth, upon which to rest the bowl. I sometimes use rubber dog rings as they don't affect the sound and they stop the bowl rotating – it's particularly useful when stroking several together.

For all I've said, singing bowls can get used for a variety of purposes in their home environment aside from sounding and above we see a typical singing bowl (*jambhati*) being used in taking *amrita* (a sacred drink) during a sacred Sikh ceremony.

10. Techniques: How to Use some more Exotic Bowls

NOW WE COME to the question of how to hold the bowls. If you wish to enjoy the deep note of a bowl then rest it upon the open palm of your hand. Otherwise, to encourage the higher sounds, hold it as you would a small bowl – upon the tips of your extended fingers. With a very small bowl you can either rest it upon your extended fingertips or, turning your hand as if to shake the hand of someone and forming a letter 'O', with your forefinger curled inside your thumb, rest the base of the bowl upon that circle. These basic positions can be used for either method of striking or stroking a bowl. See over for illustrations.

I generally advise stroking the bowl in a clockwise direction. In this way we play it for the benefit of all living beings. Begin by placing the wand on the bowl at the point directly in front of you. I refer to this as the new moon position, and it is always advisable to begin any project at the time of the waxing moon. You can play the bowl in an anti-clockwise direction, but you must understand that this places an emphasis upon the lefthand side, which is the receiving side, and therefore carries more of a self-centred emphasis. According to occultism the lefthand side of the body is receptive, while the righthand side is positive. In Tibetan Tantra the lefthand side is feminine and the righthand side is masculine. To play anti-clockwise places the emphasis upon this lefthand side and so the energy is coming into ourselves. In contrast, when playing the bowl clockwise the

righthand side is emphasized and therefore the result of playing the bowl is to reach out towards others and to benefit all beings.

In this way we avoid self-centredness and cultivate compassion for others. It is perhaps helpful here to remember the Buddhist practice of circumambulating a sacred building in the clockwise direction. However, if we are ill and require the benefits of the bowl it may then be justifiable to play it anti-clockwise. Otherwise, self-centredness being inadvisable, I always say it is best to stroke in a clockwise direction. I do not wish to be dogmatic about this subject but, rather, leave you to make an informed choice regarding what you may wish to encourage within yourself.

We get back what we give out in life. Therefore treat your bowls with respect and reverence as this helps to build up a good attitude for working with the ancient power of sound.

Avoid touching the sides of the bowl with your fingers unless you wish to prevent the deeper sounds of the bowl from sounding. Although it is one I never use, some practitioners use a technique of slowly moving their fingers up the outside walls during playing in order to raise the pitch (not the technique used with Flying Bowls, which, unaided, move upwards through an ascending order of tones). Try to restrict your contact to the base of the bowl only. If you are able to produce the higher tones without restricting the sides of the bowl a more full-bodied sound will result. If it is a Water Bowl, then you will need to hold it between outstretched fingers and thumb in a tilted position. 'Jumping Bowls' also require a certain technique involving a movement between the palm and the base of the bowl. (See below for Water and Jumping bowls). Not every bowl will produce this effect whilst those that do can often also be used with water. Another technique is to strike a bowl and then move one's hand towards and away from the wall of the bowl, accentuating different partials. The palm is held upright here, parallel to the wall. There is another application derived from this technique that is called 'tipping'. For more on extended techniques see the close of this chapter.

Ululation

For a number of bowls we use different techniques. Ululation is one of these. Some bowls, when stroked, can be ululated and others are excellent this way when struck. According to Alain Presencer, ululation is a traditional technique that was taught him by a Bonpo lama in Tibet. It involves placing the edge of the bowl against the open mouth (but not touching it). It is said that the lama imagines this sound entering and travelling around

© Jill Furmanovsky 1982

The author demonstrating ululation

his body, so that when it re-emerges it is considered somewhat holier. By changing the mouth cavity, we draw out one or more partials from the bowl (typically two when stroked and around seven struck). This is similar to part of the technique used in Mongolian *xhoomei* (throat singing) where the mouth cavity is adjusted to resonate with the different harmonics.

I worked with a Zulu jazz musician on occasion during the early 1970s, the late alto saxophonist Dudu Pukwana, and he used to speak sometimes in a strange way making clicking sounds. Sometimes it sounded as though he was sucking the sound of the word into his mouth. This is part of the traditional Zulu vocal repertoire. Practising this ululation technique, I went on to include this sucking into the mouth of the sound, and also to use the tongue to produce fluttering bird-like effects (as flautists do, or like the 'tonguing' of trumpeters), minus the clicks, in my repertoire. It is best to breathe through the nose with this technique. I find it works best when stroking to move the wand to and fro at the point opposite to the mouth (180°) and at this same point when striking. Often when I have used this technique in concerts or workshops people ask if I am breathing on the bowl. But that is not so. It is usually not possible to 'amplify' the lower partials with large bowls, owing to the limitations of our mouth cavity.

Placing your mouth close to the rim (as in the photo above), change the shape of your lips as if making certain sounds – only keeping silent. Experiment with different forms such as Oaa – Oaa – Oaa (a as in Father – back of throat) or Wow – Wow – Wow, or Woe – Woe – Woe (as in 'woe betide'), or two vowels O and I ('oh' and 'eye'), slowly or Wee – Wee – Wee (faster).

Water Bowls

Another technique is to add water to a bowl. Typically, water bowls produce very marked and startlingly exotic effects when an amount of water is placed inside. It is not always necessary to pay great attention to the amount of water so placed, for some bowls will produce these exotic sounds using a variety of water levels, but generally speaking it is a rather small amount. Other bowls, in order to produce the optimum dynamic effect, require very specific amounts of water. It is really a question of experimenting to find the amount of water that produces a particularly marked effect with any one bowl. With any 'fussy' bowls, once I have found the exact amount of water I place that into a glass jar and mark the level (with a hacksaw and an indelible marker). This saves time in a performing situation and guarantees the optimum sound when next I wish to hear these captivating and mysterious sounds. Modern machine-made or cast 'Tibetan Bowls' made in Nepal often have a very thick base, and this will not work with water or 'jumping', another technique I shall shortly describe. So it is not the case that every singing bowl will work with water added. Lastly, do not confuse the names: the bowl with water is wrongly called a 'Talking Bowl' by some.

As I mentioned before, water bowls must be tipped – suspended between extended thumb and fingers with little or no contact with the base of the bowl, upon which the water will resonate (see photo opposite). Typically, the lower sounds from the bowl arise from the base of the wall, with the higher tones stemming from the rim. Accordingly, tipping the bowl with the water closer to the rim will produce the higher tones. Generally, when stroking one needs to use a wand that is thinner and/or from harder wood in order to excite the higher partials of the bowl. It is seldom the case that sounding the fundamental of the bowl brings out startling water sounds. It might require time before one is able to continue stroking the bowl with the wand while also moving the bowl backwards and forwards, from side to side, and up and down, in order to move the water across the surface of the base and curve of the wall of the suspended bowl, and thus avoid unpleasant noises. An alternative technique employed by some is to move the wand backwards and forwards on a section of the rim on one part of the bowl and so avoid having to play using the entire rim of the bowl. One can also strike or bow a water bowl.

One design of water bowl is represented by very shallow-walled *yin* bowls. The walls can be either straight or curved. These have a wide base and this type of bowl very often works well with water, which has led me to conclude that this is the intention behind such a form. I also have some *yin* medium-height walls with a domed lingam that work well with water.

It is best to wipe any bowls dry after using them with water to avoid the risk of rust.

Another advanced technique I developed over twenty years ago can be employed when a bowl suited to ululation (when stroked) also works with water. We can then use both techniques simultaneously. The bowl is held up high for the mouth to perform the ululation whilst the bowl is also moved around slightly (up and down and side to side) in order to awaken the water sounds. I used this approach for track 2, 'Awakens the Five Treasures of Mt Kanchenjunga', on 'Tibetan Singing Bowls, Volume 3: Ancient Tibetan Initiation Bowls', which I recorded in 1993.[1]

Jumping Bowls

Then there are bowls we call Jumping Bowls. This technique requires a slight moving to and fro, between making contact and not, with the base of the bowl and the palm of the hand. The bowl seemingly 'jumps' or bounces upon the flat of the palm of our hand. We hold our hand out flat with the base of the bowl touching the central palm of our hand and then we change the form of our hand 'cupping' it whereby the centre of our palm moves away from the base of the bowl. This movement changes the sound of the bowl so that it seemingly 'jumps' between these two notes. (See photo below.) With certain bowls possessing a very thin base, this produces a marked change in pitch. As we do this, the sound of the bowl moves between two pitches – higher as we move away. Jumping bowls will also nearly always work with water because these bowls are more active in their base. This technique has more lately become known in the USA as the 'hand wah-wah' effect ('wah-wah' being the American term for ululation). As with other distinguished bowls, it is always the case of a highly pronounced effect that allows us to characterize such bowls. Alain has one in his collection that is the size of a teacup. He told me that the Bon-po use it in a way similar to that of the *ting-sha* – in exorcism and assisting ghosts to move onwards.

But I must stress that not all bowls can be used in these ways! Some are just not the right design to produce significant ululation results, and some will be unaffected by any amount of water placed inside. Similarly, do not expect to apply the jumping bowl technique successfully to every singing bowl that you come across. This is why I have placed such types into categories of their own.

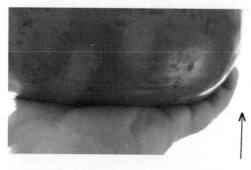
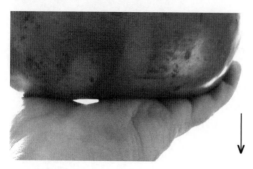

© *Frank Perry*

Flying Bowls

We now turn our attention to yet another category of bowls that derive their name from their unique acoustical properties. We may hear numerous tones within the sound of a bowl, but here one partial is louder than the others from the start. This is the first partial (or fundamental) of the bowl, which gradually fades as the next partial begins to assume a dominant volume over the other tones. This in turn gives way to the next partial and that finally gives way to the last audible tone, which continues for as long as the bowl is played. By this time the lowest tone has completely disappeared and often the next highest pitch too so that this final pitch is very dominant and often loud (almost as if 'screaming'!). I have several of these bowls and none of them go beyond this fourth partial – giving us three transitions between four pitches. Changes in playing technique can facilitate this result with these special bowls and the techniques are set out below.

During meditation or spiritual communion we oftentimes feel as if we are rising up and out of our everyday consciousness into the higher world, away from all of the problems and concerns upon our earthly level of existence. This can help us to loosen over-identification with our physical body. Furthermore, this sensation of rising upwards into higher, more refined realms seems to be reflected in the sound of these particular singing bowls. As our attention is led ever higher by virtue of the change in pitch of the bowl as it moves through higher tones, so we can easily feel the suggestion of merging with a higher, formless and void-like state. As I dwelt upon this after playing, during consideration of how to designate this type of bowl, I thought of the name 'Flying Bowl', and at that very instant I heard an aeroplane flying over my home, which I felt sealed this appellation! So it was that I originated this name for this type of singing bowl – long ago in the 1980s.

The gradual upward-moving alteration in pitch-focus of these bowls can be described as an organic progression and therefore cannot be forced to rush onwards from one stage of its sound to another. Also, it will only move in this upward direction, as it is not possible to reverse the process by beginning with the highest and then going down to the lowest tone. The course of the bowl's sound, unfolding in its own time, is a natural product of such bowls, in itself requiring no special techniques. One also uses the same wand throughout the duration of playing the bowl. Nevertheless, certain techniques can come into play and assist in the procedure of eliciting the subsequent change of emphasis within the partials of the bowl.

Generally speaking, if one alters the angle of the wand inwards this encourages a higher pitch from any bowl. The form of wand that I have designed tapers upwards, and by applying a thinner diameter of the wand to the bowl's rim a higher tone can also be encouraged. However, I find no need to apply these changes to genuine flying bowls.

The principal technique applied here lies in the degree of pressure exerted between the wand and the rim of the bowl. We begin with a soft pressure, but as the bowl of itself moves into higher partials so the amount of pressure can increase, in order to sustain the process. To a lesser degree the speed of moving around the rim from slow to fast promotes the move from low to higher tones. It is also affected by the looseness or tightness of the grip of the wand, with the lower tones coming from the looser grip and a small amount of force in application, and the final, more intense, higher tones, being helped by a tighter grip. Additionally, because we need to begin with the lowest tone, it is advisable to hold the bowl upon the open palm of the hand. In my experience flying bowls are rare and mostly are found in small and shallow dish-like bowls of the Manipuri or Assam type, although I do also have two that are in the Vase variety (see below, pp. 170-1) that have chamfered *yang* lips that aren't too pronounced.

When working with such a bowl, we may wish to choose either a meditation that moves into subtler regions of our being (physical, astral, mental, and spiritual) or to use the traditions of *nada yoga* in Chapter 17 (where you will find more on the fourfold stages of sound), and so follow the process of *vac* back to its source (*vaikhari, madhyama, pashyanti,* and *para*: see below, pp. 331-2).

Yoga Bowls

Another type of bowl with a unique sound quality is one I term 'Yoga Bowl'. The Yoga Bowls derived their name by virtue of the term *yoga*, which means 'union' and here refers to union between two. These bowls demand another technique that is less physical. I gave this kind the name 'Yoga Bowl' because of the acoustical properties that reside in the bowl – in short, its being able to sound two distinct tones or partials simultaneously – both a clean higher partial and the lower fundamental partial – when being stroked.

Listening to such a bowl it is easy to imagine the higher pitch, being less earthly, relating to the higher self (or individuality) with the lower, more encompassing sound, signifying the lower self, or personality. The two playing together in perfect harmony presents us with a wonderful model for integration of our basic natures. One can contemplate the significance of how the higher tone is seemingly enfolded by the lower – even as it is said that a spark of the divine fire resides in the heart chakra of each one of us. This category is derived from the sound properties of the bowl and does not depend upon a particular physical form.

Such bowls are comparatively rare to find, as the majority of bowls may produce a range of partials, or else there is a lower tone that disappears after a short while, or a higher note that simply won't get any louder (or may also disappear), leaving only the lower tones. But every now and again we find a bowl where there are these two pitches sounded together simultaneously for the entire duration of our playing. To a certain extent the technique here demands the correct wand to produce this effect. In my experience so far, these have been *yang* bowls – so that the wand needs to be made of a hard wood to stimulate the upper partials of the thick rim and made of a width that would stimulate the lower tone. Typically the wand is at least two inches wide for bowls between six and ten inches in diameter. As ever with bowls, I can only give guidelines, as there are no hard-and-fast rules. Some such bowls are extremely sensitive and troublesome and with these you can only experiment. In the case of one bowl I possess, I can spend hours searching for the correct wand to produce the effect, only to find on a subsequent occasion that this 'correct' wand will produce nothing at all!

The technique applied here stems from meditations using visualization. In this manner we can ponder on a suitable vision to represent the union between the higher and the lower parts of ourselves. My first encounter with the bowl mentioned above led me to find the blackest bowl I'd ever come across. Once cleaned, it was evidently strong in silver and tin and very old. It is a somewhat unique design being rather shallow with rounded sides and a *yang* rim. Whenever I play it, there comes a vision in deep blue of a lake high up in the mountains at night with a single star (representing our higher self – even as sailors used to navigate by the Pole Star) shining bright and still above and reflected perfectly upon the still waters of the lake. I call it Blue Mountain Lake Bowl. It is a beautiful peaceful bowl and the lower tone produces a gentle, soothing, comforting, enfolding, and reassuring warmth in the heart chakra. But with Yoga Bowls mainly we focus upon achieving greater harmony between our lower and higher self.

Harmonizing Bowls

With these bowls we experience a definite effect within our brain. The Panic Bowl most often finds people experiencing a rapid horizontal movement between their left and right hemispheres. I've another singing bowl that I experience as though it were entering through my left ear and passing out of my right ear, balancing the brain hemispheres.

Bowls with Unusual Forms

Many bowls of unusual design contain unique sound characteristics too. I named the Vase Bowl another category of singing bowl because I thought that it resembled the form of a vase. The name remained, as the vase is one of the eight auspicious Buddhist symbols known as 'The Treasure Vase'. Very many years after originating this term I have lately seen this type of bowl named 'Ultabhati'. The unique sound characteristic I have found with most of these bowls lies in audibly moving through the first four partials of the bowl in ascending order, as previously mentioned with Flying Bowls, providing three intervals. This recalls the *triratna* ('Three Jewels') of Buddhism, which are the Buddha (the truth), his teachings (*dharma*), and his community of followers (*sangha*). These bowls turn inwards just before reaching the rim of the bowl but then they turn back outwards again to the original diameter usually taking the form of a curve. It is as if someone had tightened a belt around these bowls just beneath their rim. There are again both *yang* and *yin* varieties of these bowls. The *yang* ones that I own have a chamfered edge (see left in photo below). The *yin* variety simply continue upwards to the rim and these can further be of two types one bending outwards (as with the *yang* form), while the other seemingly continues upwards (either straight or slightly leaning back outwards) and these I termed Waist Bowls (see right in the photo below).

I own three of the *yang* type, and two of these are flying bowls, whilst the other (Kanchenjunga Bowl) has a very much larger pronounced *yang* lip along with thicker walls. These features serve to centre the sound upon the fundamental of the bowl. The Kanchenjunga bowl is a large bowl (around fourteen inches) and so produces a slow pulse of four (the fundamental) when stroked with a leather wand. Sacred Mount Kanchenjunga is translated as 'Mountain of Five Treasures.'

The two *yang* Vase Bowls that I own are very different in their psycho-acoustic effect, with one creating a sound that seems to be screaming to break free whilst the other is far gentler. I use both of these in my sound healing work and typify them by aligning the former with the energy of the planet Pluto and the latter with that of Neptune. The planet Pluto has been characterized by some astrologers as being somewhat akin to that of a volcanic eruption. That is, there are certain elements in the subconscious seeking re-

© Frank Perry

A Vase (left) and a Waist Bowl

lease that finally burst through into the consciousness, often in a totally surprising manner – although a retrospective enquiry often shows that indications and warning hints of this eruption were previously present. This one, which I call Fiery Worlds Bowl, is used when the client has such submerged elements seeking release and it is necessary for them to make a conscious discharge. The Neptunian (Ocean of Great Bliss Bowl) I characterize as being rather similar to a meeting with a representative of Divine Mother – where we might feel as though all of our baggage, worries, and anxieties simply fall away in the spiritual loving presence. The former bowl is more 'confrontational' whereas the latter's effect is at an almost completely unconscious level.

During a sound healing where such a situation has to be dealt with, I must consider which is the correct method for working with the individual, and sometimes I am obliged to have recourse to the confrontational approach, because it has been the nature of that individual to 'sweep problems under the carpet' but now they must not take the familiar passive manner of denial, and of ignoring the problem until it goes away, but rather make a conscious effort to deal with the issues. Naturally, I always warn the client afterwards that things are likely to 'surface' for a week or two following in a manner of release and that it might be wise to mention this to those others with whom they share their home and life.

Shakti Bowls are shaped like the downward-pointing triangle that makes up half of the Z Star, which itself symbolizes the union of Shiva and Shakti. You can read more about the six-pointed Star in Jenny Dent's book, A QUIET MIND COMPANION.[2] This triangle represents the response from the whole to the individual. It is a coming down into matter; a condensation or crystallization of the idea down into actualization, and so it carries the energies of the Mother. Shakti bowls work best when stroked. They have a discordant sound when struck but when stroked they can produce an intense high-pitched clean sound.

These are *yang* bowls with a wide lip. However, this is not an accretion of extra material as is generally the case with *yang* bowls. Rather it is composed of the same thickness as the wall. It appears as though the wall has been bent inwards parallel to the

© Rose Perry

base of the bowl. See the photograph of my 'Realm of Pure Light' Bowl above. The technique once more features a tight grip of the wand (thinner than would be usual for this diameter of bowl and of hard wood) and more pressure than is usually applied to bowls.

The opposite of the Shakti bowl is what I term the Tantric Bowl. Here the walls are similar to the Elephant Bowls (an up-ward-turned triangle) and, comparable with the Shakti bowl, it also has a *yang* lip of around the same thickness as the wall. Only here it is turned in the opposite direction – that is, back outwards. As with the Shakti bowl its sound is one of the most discordant of all bowls when struck. The few that I have found can be stroked producing the fundamental. These have all had a strong vibrato when struck emerging from out of an interesting although dis-cordant sound – hinting at Tantric transformation.

Rare as the Tantric bowl is, there is yet another variant, rarer still, and that is the Tantric Lingam bowl. I've seen two of this design and the walls had a gradual curve up to the rim, missing the conical shape. The sound is similar only missing the dissonant quality present at striking of the Tantric Bowl and, of course, there is the lingam in the base.

Then there are bowls that we call Elephant Bowls – so-called due to their shape, which resembles that of an elephant's foot

(they are also known as Mani Bowls). These are from Bharampur in India. Their main feature lies in the narrowing conical wall
ending in a very thick lip. They are usually louder than the average
bowl. They have a high piercing tone usually a lot higher than
one would expect from a bowl of the size. Initially there is a low
sound, rapidly changing to a higher tone when struck. When they
are stroked it is usually very hard to produce a tone other than the
fundamental, where we have the four basic pulses to one circuit
of the rim. When stroking several of these together one can often
find rather marked heterodyning effects (two tones combining to
seemingly produce a lower tone) present from the various interactions of the several bowls. Being a rather unfamiliar sound, these

© Frank Perry

Tantric (Purple Haze Bowl, above) and Elephant Bowl

phenomena can produce a rather electrifying effect upon many listeners. One becomes aware of the 'air' coming alive with the magical presence of the being of sound. I find a two-inch diameter wand of aspen works best. When I first bought these bowls in the 1980s I found *yin* versions and I've recently seen those named as 'Remuna Bowls'. Such bowls are shaped like the complementary upward-pointing triangle. I have a number of both *yin* or *yang* types with certain ones in either category working with water.

Very similar in sound to the Elephant Bowls are the Lingam Bowls (also known as Shiva Lingam Bowls and sometimes as Mount Meru Bowls). This is because such bowls have a conical form in the inside centre of their base resembling the Shiva Lingam. This form is sharper and more pronounced than the central dome-like shape found in Manipuri Lingams, for example (see over for pictures of both bowls, and p. 177 for the central dome). Where other bowls with this feature in the base are formed from the same thickness as the base and wall of the bowl (and are more dome-shaped), in contrast the conical form here in Lingams is thicker, often simply with a hole underneath, inside the cone. Striking the base of such bowls the sound is often very pure – very few partials arise. These bowls also have a thick rim which, as stated elsewhere here, acts somewhat as a tuned gong in reducing the partials present. With the *yang* rim plus the reduced sounds from the base, we have a very focused and strong sound. These also produce only the fundamental when stroked. It is a very loud sound (as with the Elephant Bowls) and can be compared to the volume of the glass bowls that are similarly restricted in their number of partials only there that has to do with the inflexibility of their glass material. As with the Elephant Bowls, an aspen wand often works best.

Manipuri Lingams are usually made with a thick rim. This is not too pronounced, but it is there. They resemble the form of a Manipuri Bowl whilst they also have this central dome within the inside centre hence the name (see below). However, they differ from other bowls with this feature inasmuch as the outer contour of these bowls is flat right across the base, leading one to conclude that the dome here is of solid material. I have sorted through a small number of these (partly because they are rather rare – hence pricey)

© Rose Perry

Lingam Bowl

and in each case the sound has been very clear, with four distinct partials typically present. These are not large bowls: the largest I've come across is around six inches in diameter. They often feature many ornate patterns (as illustrated below). I prefer to strike them using the 'staccato' technique.

Next come what I term Chalice Bowls (others call them variously Stem Bowls, Naga Bowls and Pedestal Bowls) pictured opposite. The defining feature is the welded base upon which they rest – although in sound healing one can also suspend them from the hand by this base, using them to encircle the head of the listener/client, or for use in concert swinging from side to side, thus applying a sort of 'Doppler effect' (as listed below). The bowl itself often possesses a very curved base. With the 'stand' there is no necessity for the bowl to have a flat base. However, the 'stand' reaches up the wall of the bell and acts as a dampener upon the sounds. Because of this feature, these bowls will also often produce a tone higher than one might generally expect from a bowl of similar diameter. They come in both *yin* and *yang* varieties. With their base inhibiting the sound, these bowls tend to sound best when stroked. Leather wands can work

Manipuri Lingam Bowl

when they have thin walls, otherwise no particular wood is favoured. The walls can vary from a natural bell-like curve to the rim towards being sharply angled where they mostly bend up back inwards to the rim.

Then we have what are called Planet Bowls. This whole term most probably originated again with me. When I received my sacred twelfth-century Tibetan singing bowl in 1981 ('Golden Voice of the Sun Bowl'), which is tuned in to the Master Jesus and has the primary

Above, Manipuri Lingam Bowl; below, Chalice Bowl

colour of gold, I also noticed that it was attuned to the spiritual Sun/Son. At workshops from then onwards I would demonstrate these links using several of my bowls that I felt channelled planetary energies. When visiting the gongmaker Paiste in 1979 I likewise referred to working with planetary energies, as well as with the four elements, with some of my instruments. That led to their set of Sound Creation Gongs. Then in 1987 Hans Cousto had his book THE COSMIC OCTAVE published, giving frequencies for planets mathematically derived from the periods of their orbits. Paiste then had a mathematically-based, more scientific and less

intuitive, model with which to work and so they developed their
Planet Gongs. Now others working with, or selling, bowls seem
to have adopted this system of correspondences. For more on the
subject of Planet Bowls please see my chapter under that heading
(Chapter #19).

I began compiling my set of singing bowls in 1971 and overall
I have sorted through more than 9,500 bowls in order to assemble
my own unique collection of around three hundred and fifty. So
far I have found 101 basic types of Singing Bowl, plus thirty-four
sound characteristics, and some 124 supplementary types. Here
are some examples:

> *Yin* Bowls, *yang* Bowls, Shakti Bowls, Tantric Bowls, Elephant
> Bowls, Lingam Bowls, Manipuri Bowls, Assam Bowls, Oris-
> sa Bowls, Ululation Bowls, Jumping Bowls, Whistling Bowls,
> Water Bowls, Yoga Bowls, Fountain Bowls, Pulse Bowls, and
> Purification or Cleansing Bowls (that's to say: space-cleansing
> or inner psychic cleansing – in Tibetan Tantric healing there
> are three types of 'ghosts'; inner, secret, and outer), and so on.

See Appendix B, for my full list of 271 categories. You may also
wish to view my videos on YouTube (under Frank Perry) where
you will find the series 'Comparing Singing Bowl Shapes and
Sounds', parts 1 to 6.

Otherwise, I consider that bowls fall into one of three basic
categories of bowls: loosely linking with the three Buddha bodies
(Body of Buddha, Voice of Buddha, and Mind of Buddha) – and
the three basic 'categories' of 'vehicles' in Tibetan Buddhism, those
of Hinayana, Mahayana and Vajrayana (otherwise Tantrayana).
That's to say physical bowls – bowls which simply make a sound;
soul virtue bowls (peace, joy, etc.); and bowls dedicated to, or that
can be useful for, specific practices for the higher Tantric path including Chakra Bowls, Deity Bowls, and bowls helpful for certain
dzogchen practices (e.g., Sky Gazing, *shi-ne*, etc).

Other Techniques, for Non-Musical Settings

There are other extended techniques and many of these have
a more musical application where our focus is upon the sound

produced – as listed in the section after this. I do not apply the non-musical techniques in this section to sacred bowls myself, but rather to bowls of the first category – sounding instruments.

Aura Bowl. Here I use a very large bowl (eighteen inches in diameter) that is basically shaped rather like a frying pan. It has such a wide base it is possible to stand inside such a bowl. The basic effect of standing inside a ringing bowl serves to align us with our Higher Self and also to attune the aura to its fundamental energy when unaffected by outside influences. It provides an opportunity for one's spiritual guide to draw close.

Hat Bowl (or Umbrella Bowl). The technique involves placing a large singing bowl upside down on top of one's head. One practitioner contacted me on one occasion to ask if I had any large singing bowls that were also light in weight. He was treating someone for a neck injury and chose to place a large bowl on top of his or her head. Unfortunately, the heavy weight of the bowl had made the neck condition worse! So be careful with this technique. It is useful for getting inside the sound of the bowl, as we feel surrounded by the sound. Again, use a soft mallet and play gently as the sounding rim of the bowl will be close to the ears – unless it is very large or high-walled (but then also heavy!). Place a piece of cloth between your head (or the head of the person with whom you are working) and the inside of the bowl.

Matched Pairs **in Mind/Body Attunement.** Here we take a 'matched pair' (see pp. 108–10) that is rather large in size: large enough, in fact, to place one over our head. The other we will hold directly in front of either our heart centre or throat centre. With 'matched pairs', one bowl is slightly higher in pitch than its companion. Place the bowl that is lower in pitch over your head. You may want to place a piece of cloth between your head and the inside of the bowl. Use a felt gong mallet for this. I find it easiest to strike the 'head' bowl directly from the position between the eyes and the 'lower' bowl from the side.

Suspended Inversion. Similarly, we can place an upturned bowl on our hand. Hereby we place a singing bowl upside down on top of an upstretched hand, resting it either upon the fingertips or the fist. Here the bowl sound is somewhat modified through being upside down and also due to the effect of the hand and arm inside the bowl. This technique is dissimilar to that of Gamelan (see p. 180) as we play the rim of the bowl as normal and not the base of the bowl as is more usual when applying the 'Gamelan' technique.

Underwater Bowls. These we listen to at the same time as taking a bath. The bowl floats upon the water and we sink our ears beneath the water and listen to the sound through the water. The Orissa-type bowls work best here, with their flat bottoms, and the lighter *yin* version is less likely to sink. Unless you have a large bath, or you yourself are very small (or a child), you would require a small bowl of six inches in diameter or so. You may like an intimate friend to play for you to avoid the bowl from hitting the side of the bath and to prevent the mallet from getting wet. Mostly the fundamental travels through the water.

Touching Bowls. Taking a bowl with a three-dimensional Buddha figure (or some such form) inside, we can hold the bowl by this figure and then place it upon the hand, or stroke it across body parts, of a listener (particularly a handicapped person) or swing past their head bringing the bowl sound into the sense of touch for the client.

Encircling. Taking a Chalice Bowl, we strike it and then move the bowl forward to behind a person's head. Next we circle it around their head in a clockwise direction, striving to bring the rim of the bowl as close to the level of their ears as is practicable. I prefer to use a rather hard leather-covered striker rather than a softer type to bring out a broader sound. Moving fairly slowly allows the listener to experience the sound moving between the two ears. If we are using a so-called 'Dummy Head' microphone, or suchlike, we can encircle it with the Chalice Bowl. The dummy of a human head has microphones inside the ears thereby replicating what is actually heard in the human (dummy) ears and also the direction in the three-dimensional space from where the sound is coming. Played back on the right equipment the listener would hear the recording as if experiencing this technique of encircling the head.

Sizzling. Here we place some grains (lentils or rice, for instance) inside the bowl that produce a sizzling effect when stroked or struck. I find that Water and Jumping bowls, being more responsive in the base and walls, work best when this effect is desired. Hold the bowl on the fingers not the palm.

Spinning is done with two bowls of contrasting sizes. We spin the small bowl and then strike it, or else we stroke the smaller bowl and it then 'spins' of itself upon the flat base of the lower, upturned larger bowl, and makes a special sound. A small *yin* bowl from Orissa, made of thin metal, would be good to use for the smaller bowl: one possessed of a flat base and of light weight. It's best to look for a larger bowl with less of a curved base upon which to place it. Not too much friction though! This tends to be more similar to a spinning coin, getting faster as it approaches its end. We strike or stroke the small bowl with a thin wand.

Advanced Techniques in a Musical Context

Drumming (or playing with fingers). This is a technique adapted from hand drumming – particularly drumming with the *darabuka* (Turkish hand drum). One can play rhythms with the fingertips or finger nails upon the rim, wall, or base of the bowl. Although I have created this name for the technique I am not its originator. It's featured on 'Tibetan Bells II', track 4: 'Shadow and Distances', featuring guest musician Hamza El Din 'drumming' the bowl.

Tapping, where a further variation involves tapping the base of the bowl with the holding hand using one or more fingers (mostly the middle two) either alone or alongside the drumming technique.

Doubling, which involves placing a single beater between two bowls and rapidly moving it between the two, thereby producing a single-stroke roll between two bowls (left then right, LRLRLR, etc.). This would involve a pair of bowls similar in height and oscillating the beater close to the rim of both bowls. This technique uses the wrist. A longer mallet is useful here such as a vibraphone mallet. The other hand is free to play additional bowls if required. The technique is briefly used on the CD, 'Ancient Tibetan Initiation Bowls', track 2: 'Awakens the Five Treasures of Mt. Kanchenjunga', which I recorded in 1993.[3]

Brushed Bowls. Here I use wire brushes. They feature mostly in jazz music with acoustic piano trios. Again, they are used upon the upturned base of the bowl and work best with flatter bowls (shallow walls), providing a larger playing field. This is a soft approach, resting upon the silence. We can also suspend vertically downwards such flat-based bowls from the rim and wall in one hand and move the wire brush up and down rapidly. An adaptation here involves using special homemade wire brushes (constructed from ladies' hair grips tied onto an outworn conductor's baton): the tiny metal globules on the ends excite high partials from the base of the bowl.

Rocking Bowl. Usually best performed with a smallish bowl of the Orissa type (wide flat bottom) where we 'rock' the bowl between the base of the palm and the mounds just beneath the fingers. This produces a kind of 'wah-wah' effect similar to ululation although not as pronounced. While I have created this name for this technique I am not its originator.

Matched Pairs. As previously mentioned, the basic technique here is to find two bowls that have fundamentals very close in pitch, so that when played together they beat or pulse at a speed that relates to the difference in frequency between their fundamentals. This technique features on various tracks of my own, the first being on the CD 'The Healing Bowls of Tibet', track 1: 'Treasure of the Mountain.' (1997/98).[4] I have applied this technique regularly in my sound healing work since the mid 1980s. When using it, the timing of the strikes is important, in order not to distract from the effect.

Uluwater. As I mentioned previously, this is when we have a bowl that works well with the ululation technique and also with water. The technique involves doing both at once while stroking.

Because of stroked ululation we move the wand back and forth at a point opposite to our mouth at the same time as moving the bowl up and down and to and fro to excite the water. Two examples where this can be heard are the CD, 'Ancient Tibetan Initiation Bowls', track 2: 'Awakens the Five Treasures of Mt Kanchenjunga' (see previous page) and also singly at the very beginning of the CD, 'Tibetan Peace', track 1: 'Fiery Space' (2007).[5]

Spirit Voices. This involves using a special bowl that is rather shallow in height – thus possessed of a wide base that works well with water. However, the technique here is to grip the bowl by its rim and base, tipping it downwards to strike the underside of the bowl and to produce strange sounds through the water. One can also produce glissandos here by a rapid raising or lowering of the outside edge while striking once. This appears on my CD, 'Path to Shambhala', part 2: 'Olmo Lung Ring', track 5, 'Into the Unknown,' and track 6, 'All-Victorious Ones of Space' (1999).[6]

Gamelan. Here we turn the bowls upside-down and play upon their bases. This produces a sound similar to Gamelan music. The base of many bowls is very thin so that we need to exercise caution here with regard to how hard we strike the bowls as cracks can and will appear if we are too heavy-handed. You will need to use drumsticks to pay faster rhythms or rolls – again choosing lighter drumsticks with finer acorns. I use a long pair of chopsticks made from thin wood. To apply the technique of 'rim shots' one strikes the surface of the bowl flat with the stick. Playing in different areas of the bowl produces differences in pitch, as will different angles of attack. This is found on my CD, 'The Overtone Choir: Sound and Light', track 3, 'Jalan, Jalan' (1998).[7]

Harmonizing Choir. Here I take a prominent partial from a 'matched pair' and use this pitch to select another matched pair (or trio) of bowls the fundamental of which is very close to the selected partial. This is used, featuring a range of bowls, on the CD, 'Path to Shambhala', part 2: 'Olmo Lung Ring', track 7: 'All-Victorious Ones of Space'.[8]

Crossing. Again we use a 'matched pair' and place them on

a drumhead with one in the centre and the other on the edge. A 'Tambour' works best for this, as there is no metal rim. A larger drum is needed (fourteen to eighteen inches in diameter) here. Using a thin hardwood wand we strike the bowl on the edge and then that one in the centre while depressing this central bowl, thus bending its pitch. The sounds of the bowls cross over each other contrasting the static bowl with the changing bowl, again creating beats between one or more of their partials.

Resonant Bending. Similar to the above but only using one bowl. This is a technique I have used since the late 1970s. Back in the late Eighties I was providing percussion for a Rudolf Steiner Mystery Initiation drama with 'The Rose Theatre' and for parts of this I placed a bowl on the skin of one of the pedal tympani. With this drum we can change its pitch using a pedal, and this alters the sound of the bowl – similar to a guitarist or sitarist bending the note of a string.

Stroked Bending. Here we play the bowl resting upon the drumhead by using a bow. Usually, this would mean using small bowls – depending upon the size of the drum. Using a stick or our finger we depress the bowl, thus bending its pitch.

Organic Harmony. This technique has been mentioned elsewhere in this book and involves taking one bowl and playing it in three or more ways. This is mostly for recording purposes where 'multi-tracking' can be used. I used it with my Aldebaran Bowl on the opening track of the CD, 'Ancient Tibetan Initiation Bowls': 'The Light Shining through Aldebaran' (see the section, 'Doubling', above). The bowl is struck and it is also stroked, first with a leather-covered wand and then with a wooden wand (bringing out some of the higher partials) and finally bowed with water inside. On the CD, each was recorded separately and played back simultaneously. This sounds as if four bowls are being played. However, all of the four sounds recorded are fully harmonious, being derived organically from one single bowl.

Escalator. Chapter #11 fully explores this technique, which I discovered during the 1980s. By the application of numerous wands we isolate any of the first five partials. Flying bowls move through these partials in an ascending sequence and in their own time. But in this instance we are free to focus on one of five partials. This function can be used in a bowl recording featuring the studio facility of multi-tracking as outlined in 'organic harmony'. Used thus we hear a kind of 'choir' of bowls (although one bowl) and no striking is involved.

Spirit Presence. This involves applying 'single stroke' rolls upon a 'matched pair' with the two sticks (Vibraphone mallets) one on each bowl. It's most easily performed using the 'matched grip' (as opposed to 'orthodox grip'), similar to that used by a timpanist or most rock drummers where each hand has a matching grip as if holding hammers. The rolls continue for as long as you wish. Single-stroke rolls are played left then right, LRLR, etc. (or you can begin with the right hand, if you prefer). This is used in a few places: my CD, 'Tibetan Singing Bowls, volume 7 (Himalayan Studies, #2), track 9, 'Shambhala Protects' (2005).[9] and also on the CD, 'Ancient Tibetan Initiation Bowls', track 3 (1999), 'Within the Space of Silence.'[10] This is a *yin* and *yang* pair. Rolling on a 'matched pair' reinforces the partials and we can vary these via the mode of attack (force, angle, and speed). It is possible to stimulate very high partials that simulate the experience of listening to a harmonic choir where certain overtones seemingly float on the air in a rather ghostlike manner.

Spirit Whispers. Here we take a 'matched pair', and while stroking one we strike the other. There is a mysterious interaction between the upper partials arising through this technique. It's to be found on my CD, 'The Healing Bowls of Tibet', track 2: 'Way of the Bowls' (1997).[11]

Spirits Whispering. Here we again take a 'matched pair' as above, stroking one of them and after striking its companion we next add another two or three bowls ascending in pitch to strike. The matched pair can be a combination of both a *yin* and *yang* bowl or else be both *yin* and *yang* but the added bowls should be of the *yang* type.

Floating Spirits features the 'matched pair' again, but this time we add a drone bowl (stroked to produce a continuous drone-like sound) and this can be of a higher or lower pitch than that of the 'matched pair.' In this instance the drone is most easily performed upon a Chalice Bowl, as that requires only one hand.

Windhorse. Named after the Tibetan prayer flags that carry their printed prayers on the wind to all corners of the earth. For this I typically use the spiral of Manipuri Bowls (in microtonal tuning) and simultaneously play a Jumping Bowl. One can link together the speed of the jumps and that of the struck Manipuri Bowls. The Jumping Bowl takes two hands so one must be very established in the stroking technique in order to move seamlessly between striking the Manipuri Bowls and stroking the Jumping Bowl. Care is needed when coming back to the Jumping Bowl that we don't press too hard and thus stop its sounding neither press to loosely and create those unwanted clanging noises. Using a soft wand helps too – such as aspen wood. I use this technique on the CD, 'Tibetan Peace', track 10: 'The Spirit of H. H. the Panchen Lama Shines Brightly through the Darkness.' (2007).[12]

Whispering Presence features the above technique, only minus the Manipuri Bowls and instead working with a 'matched pair' – or any number of Bowls that reinforce the fundamental of (or one or other of the prominent partials within) the Jumping Bowl. The sound of Jumping Bowls can be reminiscent of receiving oral teachings whispered in one's ear by the teacher. The resonant 'matched pairs' add the sense of spiritual presence. Again take care when moving between striking and stroking.

Singing River involves a set of Bowls (a *yin* and *yang* set or whatever 'set' you have created), to be struck as you perform a drone upon a Chalice Bowl. The Chalice Bowl, with its own base, can be played with one hand leaving the other free to strike a range of Bowls. A slight refinement occurs when we choose a Chalice Bowl that carries the subtle energy quality of the set being struck, e.g. opening or all-pervasive for a *yin* set, or stilling or centring for a *yang* set.

Reinforcement. This appears during a struck sequence using 'overtone bowls'. Here I choose a set of five bowls that are very close in frequency with regard to their most pronounced partial (usually the fundamental). The effect of playing several together creates a resonant sonic cloud, and when one or more of their other partials are also close we have a few layers of such resonant clouds. When this features in a musical context I can vary the sounds by using different mallets to emphasize higher partials of certain selected bowls from the set. A recording of this technique appears on my CD, 'Path to Shambhala', track 7, 'Fiery Worlds' (1999).[13]

Rain Bowls. In the 1970s I invented the technique of resting a very fine and lightweight metal necklace against the surface of a gong that I called a Rain Gong. This produces a sizzling effect similar to a 'sizzle cymbal' (which usually has rivets). I then adapted this to singing bowls. I dangled the chain against the upper rim of a *yin* bowl to produce this effect. It brings out very fine upper partials unobtainable any other way. I use this technique on the CD, 'Tibetan Singing Bowls, volume 7 (Himalayan Studies, #2), track 4: 'Pentecostal Visitation'.[14]

Dancing Bowls is another variation of the previous technique. This time, I dangle a conductor's baton (either with a cork top or of solid wood with a ball-like finish) against the rim of a *yin* bowl. Striking with a soft mallet awakens the deeper sounds of the bowl (yet quietly) and helps to bring to the foreground the rapid strikes (with their accompanying enhanced upper partials) from the bouncing baton into focus. It sounds as if we are playing the bowl with tiny sticks with rolls and accents that stimulate very high partials. It's very busy but the very high upper partials compensate.

Silver Rain Bowls. This is a further adaptation of mine where I use an old snare from a snare drum against the rim of a tilted bowl. This is similar to the rain bowl but more constant and faster. I first used this technique back in the early 1970s on the edge of large traditional Chinese cymbals.

Gamelan Damping. In the Gamelan ensemble is an instrument called a *saron*, which usually has seven thick keys. The technique to play this instrument involves damping the key that has just been struck at the moment when the next key is struck. Here we strike the bowl and the instant that we strike the next bowl we stop the previous one. This works best playing a sequence of small Orissa bowls – especially those that are possessed with pronounced upper partials. This technique enhances our hearing of them. I use this technique on the CD, 'Tibetan Singing Bowls', volume 7 (Himalayan Studies, #2), track 8: 'Invocation to the God of Eternal Sound'.[15]

Hi-Lo. This derives from a technique used in drumming called a 'Flam.' Typically, this involves two sticks striking close together, with the first one quieter than the second main stroke. To do this we use two mallets – one light and the other heavy placed on opposite sides of the bowl 180° apart. A felt gong mallet and a vibraphone mallet make a possible pair. The idea is to sound the higher tones (vibraphone mallet) alongside of the deeper notes of the bowl (felt mallet). It is a matter of choice which mallet you prefer to use for the first strike.

Broadband Spectrum is similar to Hi-Lo except that here we strike the bowl with both mallets at once. Some bowls are 'bottom heavy' and others 'toppy', but a bowl can be made to emphasize the lower end with a soft large mallet or the upper end with a small hard mallet. By applying both types of mallet at once we can bring out a wider spectrum of the bowl's sound, both low and high. The sound is comparable to the one just mentioned except that we don't hear two strikes, only one. Here the two strikes are similar in strength, although you may wish to experiment to find your preferred sound from the bowl.

Chords. Above, we strike one bowl with two beaters, but in this technique we hold two mallets in each hand and strike four separate bowls (any combination of *yin* or *yang*) thus producing a complex chord. This works best with the 'staccato' sticks (WBTST, see Chapter 8) that accentuate the upper partials of the bowls and provide us with a broad range of tones from the bowls.

Communal Travel involves stroking two bowls at once. I use this technique especially with Elephant Bowls (a.k.a. Mani). Of course, one must be firmly established in this stroking technique in order to be able to concentrate on two bowls at once – as they can sometimes require different speeds of circling. I also use longer wands that I have produced for this – to avoid backache! The sounds of the bowls interact.

Spiralling Layers is the same as Communal Travel, only working with a larger array of bowls and moving between them. We can begin with the lowest pitched bowl and play this constantly as we move upwards through the other bowls or, avoiding a stable bowl, move between any two out of however many we have. I have a set of six Elephant Bowls that I play this way and astounding interactions arise between pairs of these, electrifying the air!

Mala. This technique involves a rapid movement along a range of bowls. They can be in a straight line or a semicircle, and we move the striking mallet rapidly, touching all the bowls. They are laid out rather like the beads on a *mala*. This has a powerful awakening effect, leaving a rich bouquet of shimmering tones hanging in the air. You can hear this on the 'Ancient Tibetan Initiation Bowls', track 2: 'Awakens the Five Treasures of Mt. Kanchenjunga'.[16]

Harp features a technique mimicking the harp when playing arpeggios. You may have heard a harpist stroking the strings rhythmically. Here we place a sequence of bowls in a circle and run the stick at a speed of your choice around the inside – similar to *mala* above. We can either continue to go round and round or pause between cycles.

Unstruck Bowls. Here I apply the technique, used with gongs, of stroking the bowls with a rubber ball on the end of a flexible cane skewer. My percussionist friend Alex Cline from Los Angeles had a friend give him a pair of these sticks back in the 1980s and he kindly passed a pair on to me. Here we avoid the sound of the attack found when striking a bowl. The sound emerges as when using a bow. We also get a more vocal sound arising from bent notes. Again, it is best to use a bowl with a wide flat base and shallow walls (suspending vertically from the rim, by hand – or else by laying inversed upon lines of strings [as in traditional Javanese Gamelan]). There is a bouquet of the sounds of the bowl similar to an echo as an after-effect of stroking. This technique can enhance our listening powers and attune us to greater silence and stillness.

Staccato. Repeated in this section in the interests of comprehensiveness, this involves striking the bowl with a wrist action. We strike the bowl with a thin and hard leather-covered beater (or the WBTST mallet) but the very instant it touches the bowl we withdraw the stick very quickly. This is good for *yang* bowls and for bowls that feature prominent upper partials as it brings these to the fore.

Tipping. Here we have two bowls with one upon the hand and the other resting on the floor or cushion. After striking the second bowl we move this towards the wall or rim of the stationary bowl. We get an interaction between the two, resulting in a modification of their sounds. This is similar to an old technique I used back in the 1970s whereby I would apply my open hand to the top of a cymbal (particularly small Chinese cymbals with a large dome) or side of a bowl to affect its sound, bringing out the partials. It also has similarities to playing a pair of *rolmo* (large Tibetan orchestral cymbals) where we notice changes in sound as we move the dome of the central bells across one another (horizontally) and also up and down (vertically) after striking the cymbals together.

Rotated Tipping. This is an adaptation of mine based on the above technique. Here I apply the moving bowl to the rim of the standing bowl while rotating it in a vertical circle against the side of the resting bowl. Alongside the different partials from the interaction of the moving wall going upwards and downwards there is also the so-called 'Doppler effect' produced. The sound appears to move forwards and backwards getting louder then softer with the rhythm dictated by the speed we are moving the bowl. Again, this works best with *yin* bowls due to their larger range of partials. I use a thin pair of the Bengali type, around ten inches in diameter. This sound suggests the cycles that we find in life, bringing us into tune with the rhythms of life.

Water Rotated Tipping. This is a further adaptation of mine where, applying the previous technique, water is placed inside the moving bowl. Here we have the most complex sound from this technique with the combined effects of the 'Doppler' and the water sounds. The raising and lowering of the bowl during its circular movement stimulate the water sounds. Naturally, we need a bowl that works well with water.

Doppler Effect is where we take a Chalice Bowl and, suspending it from the attached base, strike it and then swing it at arms length from side to side. Moving it through the air to the listener, the sound seems to come and go rather as the sound of a car passing us by.

Dipping Over involves the suspended Chalice Bowl once more but dipping it over and enfolding a smaller bowl. We raise the Chalice Bowl up and down, which creates a kind of 'Doppler effect' but with more pitch-bending. Striking both bowls adds to the complexity of the tones involved. Most Chalice Bowls are not large, meaning that a smaller bowl of around four inches in diameter or less and of the *yang* variety works best. The higher partials of the enveloped bowl re-emerge once the Chalice Bowl has risen above its rim. Paying attention to the harmonic musical relationship between the two bowls can enhance the experience.

Dipping Into is the alternative to the above, wherein the Chalice Bowl dips inside and so penetrates a larger bowl. Again, we are looking for a bowl that is around an inch (give or take) wider in radius than the Chalice Bowl. Once more, striking both bowls produces the maximum effect – as does featuring a *yang* bowl as partner. You may wish to pay attention to the musical relationship between the sounds of the two bowls (as above). The sound begins to change around twelve inches above the second resting bowl (leading one to suspect that sound is spherical) and we can make rapid movements here or descend right into the resting bowl and back up. There are various stages in the journey up and down where marked changes occur in the sound of the bowls. It has similarities to the 'Doppler effect' but with a curious 'whooping' sound.

Moving In is where we again take the Chalice Bowl, suspended upside down, and having struck a selection of small bowls, move it suspended (unstruck) just above the row of bowls. As we move it along, it acts like a resonator – so making louder the bowl over which it hovers, bringing its sound into the sonic foreground. This is far less dramatic than other techniques using such a bowl. This is possibly because of the large array of partials sounding a complex chord when using *yin* bowls – rendering such a technique somewhat superfluous. Therefore, this technique works best using small *yang* bowls and following some few seconds after striking. Striking the Chalice Bowl before moving across a row of struck bowls also works quite well. If there are matched pairs in the *yang* assortment then this brings out the upper pulse when held stationary above a pair. Variations exist, such as partially covering the lower bowl to emphasize certain partials – often the fundamental. Moving to and fro across the lower bowl produces interesting sounds. Over *yin* bowls it works best when covering two at once for some time.

Matched Pair Echo involves the above technique, simply applied to a matched pair of small bowls amplifying and emphasizing their pulsing activity. The matched pair must be small enough to be embraced by the cavity of the Chalice Bowl, which is best left unstruck.

Rotated Matched Pair, Echo #1, is the same as above, only here we rotate the Chalice Bowl in horizontal circles above the singing matched pair.

Rotated Matched Pair, Echo #2, is the same as above, only here we also strike the Chalice Bowl before rotating it in circles above the singing matched pair. With more sounds going on this is more complex and lively. It has a 'brighter' character, as the sounding Chalice Bowl interacts with the partials and beats of the matched pair.

Echoing. Here we take a fairly large bowl (around eleven inches in diameter), and after striking it we sing against the rim. Our mouth is in a similar position to what it is when we are ululating the bowl but here, instead of silent mouthing, we actually sing one or more of those sounds described under 'Ululation' (pp. 162-3). We can choose a bowl that has a sound similar to one or more of the overtones of our voice, or we can adjust our voice to pitch to one of the partials of the bowl. This technique was used by Alain Presencer on his album, 'The Singing Bowls of Tibet' (1981) on Side B, track 1: 'Bon-Po Chant'. He didn't call it echoing. In fact, he didn't name it (see note 2, in Chapter 1).

Nataraja. This is similar to Echoing, except that we perform overtone singing and accompany this with a Water Bowl, adjusting our overtones to resonate with one or other of the sounds from the Water Bowl. There is a dance between the harmonics of our voice and those of the Water Bowl as we move in and out between the two. This features on the CD, 'Ancient Tibetan Initiation Bowls', track 2: 'Awakens the Five Treasures of Mt. Kanchenjunga', during the transition from the solo overtone singing back to the instrumental passage. Here it occurs between the harmonics of the Whistling Bowl and the vocal harmonics.[17]

Bowl Ruffs is another technique taken from the drum rudiments, where this one is known as a Four-Stroke Ruff (but also as a Single Stroke Four; see 'Doubling', above, for single stroke rolls). Here we take two pairs of similar mallets (one pair in each hand) and play a sequence of four medium-sized bowls. You can play in ascending or descending order of pitch. This means that you play either left then right of left hand followed by left then right of the right hand, or, alternatively, right then left of right hand followed by right then left of left hand. The important thing here is to keep all four strikes at the same speed and the same distance apart – playing in a rhythm of five and six but keeping the five and six silent. In drumming ruffs are played fast but find a speed that suits your ability or musical taste.

Ululated Pairs – as opposed to 'matched pairs.' Sharing events with Alain during 1982–3 he became excited over an inspiration to ululate two bowls together. Naturally, the rims need to be at a similar height and the two bowls a suitable distance apart, so that placing one's mouth and lips between the pair will work. It is difficult to use ululation with large bowls simply because the cavity of the mouth is insufficient to amplify the lower partials of a large bowl. Working in this way works best with a pair of smaller-sized Manipuri *yin* bowls around six inches in diameter.

Rapid Response. Taking a wand, we rapidly move it to and fro at a point on the rim so that the bowl rapidly sounds forth its tone. Ryan Sarnataro (see his 'Best Singing Bowls' website) likes to use this technique. It is a useful technique when sorting through hundreds of bowls to quickly find their stroked sound.

Finally, a word concerning 'musical' harmony with the bowls. Many players seek out bowls that have a sound close to a Western note and gradually build up a scale, and then play them using the familiar harmonic intervals (fifths, thirds, etc). Among another couple of methods that I have developed for some decades past, one involves working with the partials of a bowl and choosing other bowls that have one or more partials very close to the source bowl. This works best when the partial related to is audibly pronounced within the initial bowl. A further method is to work energetically. Here I relate co-existing or subsequent bowls according to energetic harmony. For instance,. if the originating bowl carries the energy of peace and tranquillity, then this becomes like a keynote, dictating that all other subsequent or co-existing bowls likewise possess this same energetic quality. Of course, in each instance we can choose either to sustain the 'harmony' or to move away from the established position, perhaps into 'dissonant harmony'.

11. Subtleties of Struck and Stroked Bowls

THE TWO BASIC ways in which we can play the bowls, as Chapters #8 made clear, are firstly, we can str-I-ke them (I have highlighted the 'I' to indicate how the vertical line of this vowel in the language of symbolism inclines towards the masculine/vertical axis and the head/thinking; Fire and Will are also accentuated). Secondly, we can str-O-ke them (here I've highlighted the 'O', since, through the circular shape of this vowel, the complementary feminine/circular and the body-torso/feeling, along with the Water and Love energies, are brought into play). In general, these two fundamental ways of playing the bowls are experienced by the listener as producing a masculine or a feminine effect, respectively. The masculine pole produces the effect of being centred within, while the feminine pole creates the sensation of being enfolded in a womblike space. That is to say that the masculine, or vertical axis, is concerned with aligning ourselves along the vertical axis that exists between higher or lower levels of consciousness and being. In contrast to this activity the feminine, or horizontal, axis is more preoccupied with sharing and relating to other fellow beings that exist upon a similar or shared level. Actually, there exists a third way and that is found in bowing the bowl – but it is really a variant on stroking it.

To demonstrate how the strIking and strOking complement each other, and to explore the symbolism further, consider the tongue (traditionally male) and the lips (female). Together they form words. These two are interrelated, for the bowl (lips, and the vowel 'O') and the wand (tongue, and the vowel 'I') working together create sound (or words). In Hindu or Vedic symbolism the union of Shiva and Shakti is denoted by the symbol of the dot

within the circle. There we find the dot representing Shiva and
the circle of space around this dot representing his female consort
Shakti. Extending our symbolism on the same lines, the wand can
be seen to represent the male genitalia whilst the open space of the
circular bowl would symbolize the female genitals. We can also
see here a correspondence to the two Tantric principles in Tibetan
Mahayana Buddhism, found in union between the principles of
wisdom and compassion.

> Just as moonbeams cannot be separated from the moon nor the
> rays from the sun so Shakti cannot be distinguished from Shiva.
> *From the Saiva Puranas (4, 4)*

When a *yang* bowl is struck, it serves to bring our consciousness in towards a focus. Striking a *yin* bowl conversely expands
our consciousness outwards. Stroking a *yang* bowl also embodies
the more focussed energies related to concentration (the dot within the circle) whereas stroking a *yin* bowl carries the sensation of
being enfolded within the sound (the circle). A stroked *yin* bowl
allows us to feel an expansion of ourselves. If you like, it is the
experience of the God Without ourselves whilst a stroked *yang*
bowl aligns us more strongly with the sense of the God Within
ourselves. Both of these views are helpful and complementary –
they are not mutually exclusive, nor is one superior to the other.

At another level, sounding a bowl draws our attention to three
main phases of activity: silence, sound, and then again silence,
whether we are striking or stroking the bowl. Herein is another
trinity: the one found in the three modes used in astrology that
define for us the cardinal, fixed, and mutable signs. The cardinal
signs each initiate one of the four seasons, and so their mode generates power. The fixed signs then organize this energy into rhythmical activity (they provide substance to the impulse generated
through the cardinal signs) and supply more concentrated focus
upon the energy released by the cardinal signs. Finally, we have the
mutable signs: these serve to distribute the energy generated from
the fixed signs and then to disrupt the established rhythm and so
prepare the way for the release of the different energy produced
by the next cardinal sign. They provide flexibility and adaptability.

For example, the three signs of the Spring season in the Northern hemisphere are Aries, followed by Taurus and ending with Gemini.

I have found it helpful to correlate the two main ways of playing the bowls with the cardinal and fixed modes found in astrology. When a bowl is struck there is this threefold pattern of activity, with emphasis upon the cardinal or initiating energy, arising with the moment of striking, whereas when it is stroked we have far more stress upon the fixed mode; upon rhythmical, repetitive, or cyclic activity. This could link stroked bowls with the four fixed signs symbolized by the Bull, the Lion, the Eagle, and the Angel-Man: that is also to say they have a link with the four elements of earth, fire, water, or air respectively. So, too, do they have a focus upon resonating with any one of these elements in their established phase. Each element is at its height during this fixed phase.

We shall look shortly at another aspect of the elements to use when striking the bowls. First, though, to enter into the elements through the act of stroking a bowl we find that for Earth (Taurus) we could stroke a bowl the sound of which suggests the qualities of solidity, security, stability, or steadfastness, and this could be accomplished by emphasizing the fundamental of the bowl (four beats) – particularly from the larger bowls of ten inches' diameter or bigger. By contrast, with Fire (Leo) we would work with a bowl that conveys the energies of fire – warmth, creativity, inspiration, enthusiasm, joy, or love (a quality often found in a loud third partial – eight beats); and then with Water (Scorpio) a bowl with the quality of comfort, contentment, reflection, acceptance, going-with-the-flow, peace, insightfulness, or compassion (sometimes conveyed through a prominent second partial – six beats) and, finally, with Air (Aquarius) we could work with a bowl the sound of which conveys flying, uplifting, awakening of intuition or the quality of sharing or of community or otherwise of working with the power of creative thought attuned to goodwill.

The bowl has a powerful higher partial (what I term a 'Messenger'), seemingly drowning out all other sounds from the bowl, that appears to float through the air so that it is easy to imagine a thought or intention being carried upon this sound similar to the practice of windhorses or prayer flags sending their message upon

the air to all beings. Stroked Elephant or Lingam Bowls often produce a powerful sound that we can think of as a beam of light to
direct healing energies upon. Various techniques of sounding the
bowls can add to this – for instance, ululation can be used for the
air element and adding water for the water element.

The table overleaf illustrates how using a different mallet (or
striker) can bring out another sound from the one bowl. The bowl
in question, from my own collection, I call 'Voices from Beyond'
Bowl and it is about ten inches in diameter and very thin. It could
be called a Bengali Bowl (originating from Bengal) or a 'Jambhati' bowl (having a curved wall). In the diagram you will find the
frequency of each partial in cycles per second (cps), and following
along the line we find which note it is in our scale. In brackets is
the octave the note is in, and next on from that is how far from
that note it is, minus or plus. The dominant partial in the sound
(using the particular mallet) is shown – with that entire line set
in bold – and the final number in brackets further shows us (as
before) how prominent in the sound it is, relatively, with (1) the
most dominant. As an example, reading the second line on the top
left of the chart, we have the frequency of 235 cps (Bb (0) + 14
[1]) meaning that this loudest sound from the bowl is a Bb in the
0 octave only sharper (higher) by + 14 cents.

Using a soft mallet we can awaken nine partials from this bowl.
Using a medium mallet we only awaken three partials, while a
hard mallet brings out fifteen ; finally, a very hard mallet provides
us with a total of eighteen. Some of the partials remain consistent throughout (235 & 460.5 for instance), but their prominence
within the total sound of the bowl varies, with the second loudest
sound being 460.5 with the soft mallet, 77.5 with the medium
one, 1106.5 using our hard mallet and finally 235 using the hard-
est one of all. Of course, our ears hear the difference between the
use of these several mallets in the singing bowl sound. But I hope
that you find it helpful to be able to see how using a particular
mallet or beater will give us another bowl sound. This diagram
demonstrates the importance of our choice of mallet (or beater/
awakener/striker/inviter/hammer) in obtaining the sound we hope
for from our bowl. The recordings analysed for this demonstra-

Voices from Beyond Bowl

Soft Mallet

77	Eb (-1) – 17	(3)
235	Bb (0) + 14	(1)
460.5	Bb (1) – 21	(2)
694	F (2) – 11	
755	F# (2) + 34	
921	Bb (2) – 21	
1106.5	Db (3) – 3	
1215.5	Eb (3) – 40	
1512.5	F# (3) + 37	

Hard Mallet

77	Eb (-1) – 17	
235	Bb (0) + 14	(1)
460.5	Bb (1) – 21	(3)
755	F# (2) + 34	
917.5	Bb (2) – 27	
1106.5	Db (3) – 3	(2)
1215	Eb (3) – 41	
1512.5	F# (3) + 37	
1861.5	Bb (3) – 2	
1964	B (3) – 10	
2213	Db (4) – 3	
2267.5	Db (4) + 38	
2448	Eb (4) – 28	
2619	E (4) – 11	
2956.5	F# (4) - 2	

Medium Mallet

77.5	Eb (-1) – 16	(2)
235	Bb (0) + 14	(1)
460.5	Bb (1) – 21	

Very Hard Mallet

78	Eb (-1) + 4	
235	Bb (0) + 14	(2)
460.5	Bb (1) – 21	
755	F# (2) + 34	
920.5	Bb (2) – 22	
1103.5	Db (3) – 8	(4)
1215	Eb (3) – 41	
1509	F# (3) + 33	(3)
1861	Bb (3) – 3	
1959.5	B (3) – 14	(1)
2448	Eb (4) – 28	
2612.5	E (4) - 16	
2713.5	E (4) + 49	
2956.5	F# (4) – 2	
3478	A (4) – 20	
3917	B (4) – 14	
4063	B (4) + 48	
4406.5	Db (5) - 11	

Table #6

tion were all done under similar conditions – using the same microphone in the same room and microphone and bowl in the same position relative to each other – all in one single recording session.

Symbolism of the Struck Bowl

Let us now turn our focus to the symbolic significance of striking the singing bowl in contrast to stroking it. These two basic approaches provide us with what I have termed the masculine and the feminine approaches to playing a bowl respectively.

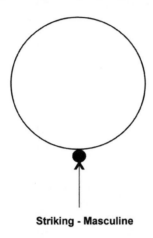

Striking - Masculine

Diagram #1

From the above diagram you will see how striking the bowl places an emphasis upon one single, individual, part of the circumference of the bowl. Although here it is external, symbolically it corresponds to the dot in the centre of the circle, used as the astrological symbol for the sun as well as for the union of Shiva and Shakti. This correlates with the more masculine energy of individuality – or of emphasis upon separation and isolation.

The striking of a bowl provides us with the experience of a point in time – an occurrence. This makes an impression upon our consciousness; it resonates with those episodes in our lives when an event happens that forces us to attune to spirit. When someone close to us dies we may be forced to reconsider and realign to a truer standard of values. At such a time nothing seems very important to us anymore. That visit to the hairdressers, or to service the car, loses its significance. This is like the impact of a struck bowl. As another example, we might suddenly find that we have a serious illness – very possibly experienced as a kind of 'wake-up' call. Such impacts can be found during those points in our lives when we are hit, or indeed struck, by the energy of an event – moments that constitute the trials, tests, and initiations met on the spiritual path. They constitute a release of power and yet have the effect of making us turn within, towards the Source/the Power/the Father aspect. There is a real need here that calls upon the essence of our own soul and spirit (in other words, one that resonates with the universal being). A release of spiritual power floods our own being and we receive the strength and the means to continue along our chosen pathway.

There is such power in this moment! The past has gone and the future not yet in sight – and all we have is this moment! When we strike the bowl what Note do we wish to strike? What forces do we wish to set in motion? What is the Way ahead for us? 'I AM the WAY', the Christ said through Jesus. The way to Act is revealed from that source of the universal Christ spirit within. The desire to Act for the benefit of all humanity – for the Universal Good – for the coming Brotherhood of Humankind!

> Kailasa, Manasarowa, Badrinath, Kedarnath, Triloknath, Ravalsar – these glorious gems of the Highest always fill the heart with special blissful tremor. When we were within a day's journey from Manasarowar the entire caravan already became uplifted – thus far around does the aura of a holy ashram act.
>
> Another vivid recollection arises from the path to Triloknath. A long line of Sadhus and Lamas stretches along this road – the old sanctuary, the site of pilgrimage and prayer. These pilgrims have met here from many different roads. Some already completing their spiritual journeyings, are walking alone with a trident; some carry bamboo staffs; others are without anything, even without clothing. And the snow of the Rotang Pass is no impediment for them.
>
> The pilgrims proceed, knowing that the Rishis and the Pandavas dwelt here. Here is the Beas or Vyas; here is Vyasa-kund – the place of the fulfilment of all wishes. Here, Vyasa Rishi compiled the *Mahabharata*.
>
> Not in legend alone; but in reality, did the great Rishis live here. Their presence breathes life into the cliffs which are crowned with glaciers, into the emerald pastures where the

yaks graze and into the caves and the roaring torrents. From here were sent forth those spiritual calls of which humanity has heard through all ages. These calls are taught in schools; they have been translated into many languages – and this crystal of acquisitions has been stratified on the cliffs of the Himalayas....

Before us is the road to Kailas. There rises one of the fifteen wonders described in Tibetan books: the Mount of the Bell! Along sharp ridges one climbs to its summit. It stands higher than the last junipers, higher than the last yellow and white mountain ranges. There Padma Sambhava once walked – this is recorded in the ancient monastery Gando-La. It is exactly here that the caves of Milaraspa are situated. And not one but many have been sanctified with the name of the hermit, who hearkened before dawn to the voices of the Devas. Here, also are the spiritual strongholds of Gautama Rishi. Not far away are also legends which surround Pahari Baba. Many Rishis walked here. And he who gave the mountain its enticing name 'Mount of the Bell' also thought of the call of the Bell for all, of helping all, of the Universal Good!

Here Rishis lived for Universal Good![1]

When we are playing a *yang* bowl through which a quite specific spiritual power flows, that power is released during the act of striking it. In a crude way, we might consider its initial sound the doorbell of an angelic being. However, we must not be like silly children who ring the bell and then run away. No, we must welcome that being and provide the resonant atmosphere and form for it to feel at home. We must prepare ourselves beforehand to use that energy and spiritual power. We need to be responsible when working with such rare and powerful instruments. I find a similarity here to the Tibetan Buddhist *mandala*, whereby a form resembling the palace of the being concerned is created just so that the being may find a resonant home here on earth. Interestingly, the original meaning of the word 'temple' was more like 'home' or 'abode'. In a sense it was the body of the god, and so it was that in Egypt the Luxor Temple, or abode, had a geometry teaching us about the being – one that is explored in the work of R. A.

Schwaller de Lubicz and others.

In the same way that a singing bowl can be considered to be the temple, sound *mandala,* or body of a particular (sound) spirit, so we can consider also that our lives (physical behaviour, emotions and thoughts) can be structured to create a temple for the Divine Light to manifest upon earth and to shine forth. This is one possible meditation or contemplation to explore while we play our bowl.

When we strike a bowl, the sound starts to die from the very moment of impact. Having emerged from silence, the sound moves always to a future silence. The energy draws inwards, rather like the autumn part of the yearly cycle where the sap in the trees begins a return to the source – a returning towards essence.

Were we able to view the act with inner vision, when we strike the bowl we would see rings of light radiating outwards from it. This pattern may even remind us of the music of the spheres, as we would be observing spheres ever increasing outwards from the centre. If we take the basic symbol of the point of activity and a single ring of sound vibration around it, then we again find the astrological symbol for the sun, the dot within the circle. We can then use this vision to enter into the body of the spiritual sun and to sound our own note – where we ourselves are the dot at the centre of the circle. We sound the sacred OM – that sound representing all that is, all that ever has been, and all that ever will be.

If we own just one bowl with which we are truly in tune, we can use it in helping us to sound our own note in life. We may come to add other bowls as time passes. Similarly, in the world of *mantra* certain practitioners will have one main or root mantra but in addition to this they will, on occasion, use the vast reservoir of mantras from which to find one that can best help them meet the particular challenge life has placed before them. The greatest challenges are those revolving around the path of spiritual initiation, and the mantric sounds can assist us in developing or unfolding certain soul qualities that help us to sound the right note to pass the particular initiation placed before us. Here initiation is taken to signify an expansion of consciousness or an awakening into deeper levels of spiritual understanding. Even as we all experience the change of teeth around seven years of age and then

HIMALAYAN SOUND REVELATIONS

puberty around the age of fourteen, so, if we stay alert to the pulse of life, we may ever expand into other dimensions of the fullness of our being as we respond to the subtler, less physical, changes along the path of the spiritual life.

I consider certain sacred bowls to be an incarnation of a particular mantra. That is to say that in the same manner in which language serves to share what is in the mind of one individual with the mind of others, so, too, may inanimate sound perform such a service. The sound of *om* was considered to be the sound of the great hum of the universe by the ancient sages of India. Speaking generally, every bowl produces an *om* sound, especially when it is stroked, giving a constant sound. Over and above this *om*-like sound, certain rare antique sacred bowls produce a sound quality that I find resonate with the vibration of the *bija* (seed) mantra of a god or goddess. For example, repeating the *bija mantra 'shrim'* for the goddess Lakshmi serves to bring us *en rapport* with her being. Lakshmi is associated with the planet Venus. Through her *bija mantra* we become attuned to Venusian energies – that is, to the spiritual vibrations of those beings that reside on Venus. Being with the sound of a singing bowl so attuned may likewise assist us to reach a similar experience of communion with these beings, for instance my Chintamani bowl, which I find is attuned to Venus.

The several qualities that unfold from this process of the initiations of life can be linked to one of the spiritual Rays (or the planetary rays or spheres). There are seven rays of spiritual unfoldment and, at a certain stage of our evolution, our soul will choose to 'specialize' on one of these for several lifetimes in order to unfold the qualities of that ray. The form that each initiation takes varies according to the ray that one has chosen. The main thing is to be true always to our inner self (the voice of the spiritual heart, deep within), to that spiritual spark within. It is to sound our own note; to reach that vibration at the very core of our being and to be faithful to its calling. In this way we attain the highest within us.

It is not simply a question of being true to the voice of either our physical body and its needs, or to our emotional body and its desires, or to our mental body and its judgments, ideas, or opinions, but rather to enter into the 'mind of the heart'. As with our rings of light, we need to find the right balance or relationship between these several areas of our being. It is necessary to find the correct arrangement, or hierarchy, in the intervals between these several bodies that constitute our total being. We need to establish where to place our main emphasis, even as the sounds that constitute the total sound of the singing bowl arrange its partials and they then resonate with certain states of consciousness, or beings – creating a chord, which in turn assists in the actualization of these selfsame qualities.

In all of our relationships this is found to be the case. We might ask whether, in our relationship to life, our emphasis is upon the physical, the emotional, the mental, or the spiritual. Of course, we have all four aspects active in varying degrees of significance in our relationships. It is simply a matter of arranging the emphasis given to any single one, or combination, of these elements. For instance, the main focus of our attention with a partner may lie in the physical activities, or it may be attachment to the emotional area of engagement, or again we may relate principally on the mental level through shared interests in philosophy or ideologies. Lastly, the main purpose behind the relationship could be spiritual, with the relationship serving our spiritual needs and, perhaps, bringing spiritual initiation with its concomitant tests, challenges, and trials – matched by its promise of spiritual growth.

We all can find this ability to ring true by entering the world of silence and stillness – that virgin space of re-potentialization in which we are born anew. Here we are born of the spirit and to the sound of our spiritual name or note. When we are initiated into a spiritual school or stream (sisterhood/brotherhood) it is often customary to be given a new name, symbolic of our life along the path and indicative of the particular qualities we may bring to that brotherhood when we can fully resonate to the spiritual nature of our given name.

One way in which we can work with our bowl (or the one that we intuit as being close to our own spiritual note – which is not the 'musical' note) is to help us turn to this still, small, quiet voice of pure spirit in the silence within ourselves. We let go of all our busy-ness and turn to this one simple sound. We enter into that simplicity and relax into the quiet within. Our physical body has withdrawn from engagement with outer activity and our breathing has become gentle and slow. Our emotions have stilled, and perhaps our mind has stopped or slowed its endless chattering. Thus we are left in stillness and silence and we may then enter the Virgin Space of Repotentialization. We are born again of the Virgin (Isis) – even as Jesus raised Lazarus from the dead.

Isis, and rebirth, relate to the astrological sign of Virgo, which the sun enters around harvest time in the northern hemisphere. This period somewhat resembles a compost heap, where the old forms that we identified with as being ourselves are decomposing and returning to the source. At the same time as we follow into that world beyond and behind the physical form (leaving our old accustomed sense of inherited self-identity behind), we may experience a sense of nothingness or emptiness. From out of this vacant space we sound our own note, the I AM. As a sun we find that space illumined with spiritual sound and light. We find that the various planes of our being are vibrating anew, like planetary spheres in their new arrangement around the central Note of our true name. And even as the sun gives life to our earth, so, too, this vibration we sound rings out to affect all of those around us and even beyond them. The process requires us to make absolutely sure that this sound is rooted in the deepest levels of truth, from pure spirit, whereby our individual note makes its own unique contribution toward the one great Chord or Note of God. That Chord is composed of the entire universe harmoniously sounding as one grand brotherhood/sisterhood of all Life. Notwithstanding, we each have a freewill choice to abstain from sounding that One Chord. Undergoing such a process, we imitate the forming of this entire universe where in the beginning was the Word and the first-born of that Word was the light.

We then come forth as an 'arisen one', raised up from the earth and united with our pure spirit, experiencing greater alignment with our true spiritual self, the One Self. We then must bring into action this pure spirit and become ever more mindful of how we integrate the new energies into our daily living and work upon earth. The great Note is ever that of love, of Christ love, or the infinite compassion of the Lord Buddha: by whatever name we choose to call it, that pure vibration of spiritual love is always found in the note of a great spiritual Master. It is itself the divine I AM.

Both loud and sharp sounds tend to penetrate our aura. Striking the bowl works best for reaching the chakras and achieves optimum effectiveness when the bowl being struck resonates with the chakra concerned – either physically affecting the area of the chakra or resonating to the subtler levels of the chakra.

Mention has already been made of the four elements and how to find these when stroking the bowl. Now we turn to look at how we might determine the presence of one of these elements within our bowl whilst striking it. As previously stated, this relates to the cardinal signs that each initiate one of the four seasons. Something of the difference shows itself if we take the example of fire – the first element in Western astrology. Aries I symbolize by the beginning stage of a fire where it isn't yet established (as it will be in the fixed fire sign of Leo). Flames leap from log to log and appear here and there and fade and perhaps we are uncertain as to whether our fire will get going at all.

Aries – bowls with a warmth or beauty about their sound that touch the centre of love – the heart – that inspire us towards compassionate ways of being.

Cancer – bowls that possess a quality of contemplation, reflection or relaxing peacefulness in their sound.

Libra – bowls that engender a high ideal or that turn our mind towards new ways of thinking or that otherwise inspire greater self-awareness.

Capricorn – bowls that suggest qualities of stability, solidity, or inspire positive changes in our daily living habits bringing greater self-discipline, or that have a profound majesty in their sound.

Although I might term this 'striking' the bowl, I do not mean to imply that force must be used. I strike bowls by a tilting action of the striker. I tilt it backwards, away from the bowl and allow gravity to come into play as I release the striker, so that it moves by its own natural momentum. I prefer this method to that of actually hitting the bowl (where a degree of force is used) by applying the arm, hand, or wrist. Perhaps it is unnecessary to state it, but, once struck, we need to remove the striker from the rim of the bowl. It may also be helpful to think of the mallet as an 'Awakener' and thereby avoid the more aggressive approach that is suggested by the word 'striker'. Going further, we could use the term 'inviter' – with the mallet used to invite the bowl to sound.

Actually, and in general, percussionists find that 'touch' is most important. Touch affects the sound enormously, for instance in the tympani, so that the difference between 'hitting' the instrument and the preferred method of attack is really distinct. A timpanist who strikes the tympani like a hammer (using the arm and with a tight grip) produces a dull sounding thud. Allowing the mallet to bounce off of the drum skin produces a warm, full-bodied sound. This means that the manner by which the mallet is taken off the object has the greatest effect over the quality of sound produced. Compare this with your own bowl practice, and compare the sound of someone 'hitting' (bashing or thrashing) a gong to the sound of a gong that is played properly, and you will begin to see a huge difference in the sound you make.

Symbolism of the Stroked Bowl

The diagram below shows how stroking the bowl emphasizes the whole circuit of the rim of the bowl. This symbol of the circle stands for Shakti – the female counterpart for Shiva.

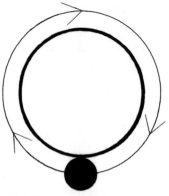

Stroking – Feminine

Diagram #2

When we stroke a bowl the sound emerges slowly (and indeed softly – unlike the struck bowl's sound). Once the sound has reached its maximum amplitude it continues for as long as we wish. The brain of the listener relaxes, as it perceives steadiness and safety in the environment. The most primitive part of our brain encourages us to be always on the alert for new sounds in our environment, thus alerting us to possible dangers. When the sound environment is consistent, this primitive area of the brain can relax, feeling safe from threat, and other areas of the brain can then function. Via a form of entrainment between the steady and slow pulse produced with wands we can enter *alpha* or *theta* brainwave states, with their associated altered states of consciousness. With this stroking action there is a steady and unchanging rhythm and the sound is organized. When we stop stroking, the sound slowly dies away. In Chapter #8 we saw a photograph of leather-covered wands mainly designed to offer focus upon the fundamental of the bowl – producing a warm and soft sound alongside the four main pulses of a bowl, their several sizes being for various bowl widths. As you play with these wands the brain can experience a pleasurable and simple sound continuously.

When we are stroking the bowl, once the sound is established, there is this steadiness about its rhythmical, cyclic sound, suggesting infinity. There are exceptions to this rule, with the sound of some bowls changing through the period of stroking. Nevertheless, having established the correct rhythm and the required effect, we can also relax attention upon the playing and, from this position of being grounded in our centre, radiate the energy outwards. One way of doing this is to visualize the centre of the bowl and to see the world there and direct the loving energies of the bowl into world conditions. Alternatively, we can visualize an individual, whom we know to be in need of healing energy, in that central spot. The individual, or the world, is then bathed and encircled in the healing energies of the sounding bowl. Naturally, this is far easier if the sound produced by the bowl is harmonious with healing energy.

StrOking the bowl is a far more feminine approach, creating a kind of womb of space through the sound created. It resembles the experience of being enfolded. A real womb creates a 'sacred space' for creation to take place. As with a magic circle, we define a 'space', or we define a boundary, and inside it something is built which then manifests. The note of the bowl attracts beings with a similar resonance/vibration to manifest within that space, just as we sound a note upon the inner planes with what we create with our thoughts, feelings, and actions. When these are dedicated to a higher purpose through visualization, meditation, or prayer, or worship, then what is created is beneficial to all. 'Like attracts like.' The action of playing the bowl awakens certain thoughts and feelings and we can see this as a union of our three bodies of thinking, feeling, and willing; or wisdom, love and power – or, again, mental body, astral body and physical body with their higher octaves.

Just as Divine Mother does, we create a space for the Child (the Seed) to enter in. It's really the seed of our own being that accompanied us into incarnation. As the fully-grown tree is present in the acorn, so, too, the seed of the trinity of omniscience, omnipresence, and omnipotence is likewise present within us. Stroking the bowl creates a circle for this inner spiritual Child to appear and unfold within this love-filled space. This bowl sound assists us in becoming childlike, and therefore receptive to the spiritual worlds: most especially to the vibration of spiritual love. We can work with the bowl in this way so that the universal spirit of Divine Love may grow within our heart and direct our life into ways of being ever more inspired by this spiritual seed.

> The pupil must regain *the child state he hath lost* ere the first sound can fall upon his ears.[2]

Professor Thomas D. Rossing provides us with the following account of the stroking method, but applying it to a wine glass:

> A moving finger excites vibrations in the glass through a 'stick-slip' action, much as a moving bow excites a violin string. During a part of a vibration cycle, the rim of the glass at the point of contact moves with the finger; during the balance of the cycle it loses contact and 'slips' back toward its equilibrium position.... The location of the maximum motion follows the moving finger around the glass.[3]

As I showed in Table #6 above (p. 199, the sound analysis of the 'Voices from Beyond' Bowl), various mallets will awaken different arrangements of the partials within the body of sound of the bowl. Just as variations in the mallet used produced a different sound from the singing bowl, so it is with the choice of wand. When struck, most of the several tones will sound together; if there are higher tones that you wish to emphasize, then either a thinner mallet will need to be used, or one that is harder, or else a staccato attack. To achieve these distinctions while we stroke the bowl we need to try wands of changing widths, or else select from a diverse range of woods, and this will arrange the various partials that constitute the sound of the bowl into a different hierarchy, with each wand producing from the one bowl a sound dissimilar to the others – even if very subtly. From out of the several partials within the bowl, the use of one wand will arrange these into a particular order (as was also found with mallets). For the same type of analysis, see overleaf, Table #7: 'Song of the Mountain Waterfall' Bowl. Because of the difference that wands make it would depend upon finding the right wand that really allows the bowl to 'sing' its own true note before it can have the full intended effect upon the listener. Certain wands will stimulate two or more partials and in that instance a somewhat irregular rhythm might be set up, owing to the polyrhythmic interactions of the several pulses (e.g., three against two).

I have previously mentioned using one bowl for a demonstration of its several partials. I have used this practice for over twenty-five years now and I sometimes demonstrate this during my workshops. In Table #7 I again use the singing bowl that features as the first of my solar plexus 'matched pair'. This bowl I call 'Song of the Mountain Waterfall' Bowl. It is nine and three quarter inches in diameter, is antique, and is of the *yin* type. It has a curved wall. For its cymatic image, see the colour section.

In the table, I have used five different wands, in order to produce singly each one of the first five partials of this bowl. It is easy to tell which partial is being produced because of the beats, or pulsations, produced during the playing of the bowl – moving through the even numbers from four up to twelve pulses. As I've

Song of the Mountain Waterfall Bowl

Using Five different wands to isolate the first five Partials

Stroked for First Partial

89.5	**F (-1) + 42**	**# 1**
271	Db (1) – 39	# 2

Stroked for Second Partial

263.5	**C (1) + 12**	**# 1**
528.5	C (2) + 17	# 2
768.5	G (2) – 34	
810.5	Ab (2) – 42	

Stroked for Third Partial

262.5	C (1) + 5	
507.5	**B (1) + 47**	**# 1**
811	Ab (2) – 41	# 2
1016.5	B (2) + 49	
1316	E (3) – 3	
1619.5	Ab (3) – 44	
2005.5	B (3) + 26	

Stroked for Fourth Partial

811	**Ab (2) – 41**	**# 1**
1163	D (3) – 17	
1619.5	Ab (3) – 44	# 2

Stroked for Fifth Partial

1163	**D (3) – 17**	**# 1**
2329.5	D (4) – 14	# 2

Table #7

stated elsewhere, I have not been able to produce a higher partial above the fifth (twelve pulses). Once the bowl has settled into the specific partial that is the focus of our attention I have then analysed the sound. All the wands are of wood except for the first one, which I made from leather decades ago now, as this one is intended to bring out the fundamental of singing bowls by reducing the upper partials. All samples were recorded at the same session and in the same conditions. Again, in each case the line in bold and marked as #1 is by far the loudest in the frequency analysis – sometimes markedly so, and at other times maybe twice as loud as any of the others.

As I've already mentioned, the method of playing that I term stroking is feminine in nature. I should like to share how this affects the listener, when we are using either a male (*yang*) or female (*yin*) bowl. The stroked *yang* bowl seems to carry the significance of sound encircling a fixed point – rather like the planets encircling our sun – whereas stroking a *yin* bowl embodies a sense of moving outwards, away from this centre, into ever-widening and expanding spheres. Taking the solar system as my model, I should like to say that the stroked *yang* bowl centres our focus upon the ever-present sun at the centre and sees all things as being dependent upon this central sun. By contrast, the stroked *yin* bowl would seem to be taking us on a journey through the solar system, moving from one planetary orbit to another, expanding away from the centre, embracing ever-wider spheres and yet no less centred for that. This way of working emphasizes that our sun is also a star.

One could say that within this context the *yin* bowls are inclusive, and the *yang* bowls are exclusive. This would mirror the astrological symbolism whereby the Moon, a feminine planet, involves itself in the process of manifestation (outwards into material form) and the masculine planet, the Sun, invites us inwards towards the central source. In this sense the awareness of being a separate individual is more *yang*, whilst the female *yin* energy is found in expansiveness, moving away from the immediate sphere and opening into ever-widening spheres. An analogy would be when we maybe feel a link to our family, which then expands outwards, linking with our street, and then out into our country, then including the entire planet – then further outwards still to embrace our whole solar system, and then further extending to enclose our Milky Way galaxy. Finally, it enfolds the entire known universe. It is as if we were moving through a sequence of wombs, where we outgrow one, and then expand into a larger one, and so forth.

Using another metaphor, we could see this as being invited to go upon a spontaneous journey of adventure, as contrasted to leaving on a journey with very specific goals (e.g., going to town shopping, or to the cinema, or going to visit a particular friend), demonstrating again the *yin* and *yang* stroked bowls respectively.

Mention must also be made of those bowls that combine these two forms (e.g., Bengali bowls) where there is a thickening at the rim but this is far less exaggerated than with *yang* bowls proper. Their sound likewise is restricted by the influence of the thickened rim, but there is less emphasis upon a higher partial being equal to, or louder in volume than, the fundamental pitch of the bowl.

The thickening of the rim present with a *yang* bowl has the effect of producing a higher note, one that is very clear, over and above the lower note produced by the large body of the bowl. It is this combination of a clear high tone combined with a low tone that suggests a relationship along the vertical axis of below and above. There are also fewer partials with the *yang* bowl, bringing a sharper focus upon this higher harmonic and its relationship with the fundamental lower note of the bowl. *Yin* bowls produce a wider range of partials, often with no discernible emphasis upon any one single partial. In certain cases some of these partials can be close together in pitch. When this is the case a certain oscillation (warble) is brought about, one we experience as a kind of vibrato effect. It produces a shimmering sensation and a vibrancy that suggests excitement and intensity.

I find the quality of the energy contained within any one bowl can often be correlated with those approximate intervallic relationships that predominate in the sound of the bowl. In other words, the dominant partials of the bowl can come close to one of our western diatonic intervals. The meaning of these has been delineated, for instance by Rudolf Steiner (See his THE INNER NATURE OF MUSIC AND THE EXPERIENCE OF TONE, 1983). To give an example, and allowing much wider orbs than would be tolerated in music: a singing bowl with two dominant partials that are approximately sounding the musical interval of a sixth can also bring something of the characteristic quality of that interval (longing for something that has gone away) while we listen to that bowl. We can envisage the several partials within any one bowl as constituting a kind of orchestra of several bowls. Are they all serving the same purpose ('playing from the same score' or 'singing the same tune') or is there disharmony? United purpose represents a 'good bowl' whilst the disharmonious sounding bowl might often produce interesting effects, perhaps helpful in assisting us to integrate or transmute any disharmonious or chaotic elements within ourselves (a kind of sound alchemy), or else be so out-of-tune with itself as to invite negative energies, or vibrations, into our lives.

Padmasambhava Bowl					
Struck			**Stroked**		
165	**E (0) + 1**	**#1**	**470**	**Bb (1) + 14**	**#1**
469.5	Bb (1) + 12	#2	942.5	Bb (2) + 18	
883	A (2) + 5	#3			
1406	F (3) + 11				

Table #8

In the table above we can compare the two methods of playing a bowl by the sounds produced. This is a *yang* bowl, one I use for the throat chakra, producing the colour green and linked to the planet Saturn. In the following table (#9) is another throat chakra bowl, but in that instance it is one that produces the colour Blue. When the Padmasambhava bowl is stroked it produces two strong pitches (B*b*), a little over an octave apart.

However, the Padmasambhava Bowl is usually stroked during healing sessions, so that the prominent tone from this bowl is then 470 (B*b*), more than an octave higher than the other throat chakra bowl ('Song of the Crystal' Bowl), another that is mostly struck for healing purposes. This is a *yang* bowl too. So, you can see, I have no regard for 'systems' of notes based upon a musical scale of any sort. You can see, too that I do not use a mechanistic method along the lines of 'the throat chakra should be vibrating at a certain frequency and to heal it I must realign it by playing a bowl of the prescribed frequency'. The fundamental of each here is very different, with Padmasambhbava Bowl being 165 cps (E) and 'Song of the Crystal' Bowl 201.5 (almost a G#). Notice also that in each case the sounds of the bowl differ according to whether it is struck or stroked. Again the line in bold and the number on the far right of each table of frequencies represents the place of the partial within the hierarchy of sound for the bowl in question. You can see the cymatic images for these two bowls in the colour section.

Song of the Crystal Bowl					
Struck			**Stroked**		
201.5	**G (0) + 47**	**#1**	201	G (0) + 43	
583.5	D (2) − 11	#2	**586**	**D (2) − 3**	**#1**
1106	Db (3) − 4	#3			
1751	A (3) - 8				

Table #9

Finally, within this context there is a further chart opposite, Table #10, showing a bowl we have seen before as part of the solar plexus 'matched pair' that I use in healing. When I play the 'Song of the Mountain Waterfall' Bowl to people they immediately tend to feel a relaxing in the solar plexus chakra. As mentioned, this bowl is close to an F#, whereas using the system currently in vogue it should be an E for this chakra and the colour yellow. Rather, this bowl produces a beautiful blue – although it can produce a gold when played with a different mallet. It is a *yin* bowl, and again we can compare the partials found from striking or stroking it. I have also given an additional sample from stroking this bowl: it demonstrates to us the different partials that are heard in the opening six seconds of playing it, before the sound settles down to simply two

Song of the Mountain Waterfall Bowl

Struck		Stroked	
91			
261		**263.5**	**C (1) + 12**
503		**528.5**	**C (2) + 17**
806		768.5	G (2) − 34
1,170		810.5	Ab (2) − 42

Stroked - First 6 seconds

90.5	F# (-1) − 37	#3
262.5	**C (1) + 5**	**#1**
374	F# (1) + 18	
507	**B (1) + 45**	**#2**
598	D (2) + 31	
810.5	Ab (2) − 42	
886.5	A (2) + 12	
1162.5	D (3) − 18	
1563	G (3) − 5	
2052	C (4) − 34	
2483.5	Eb (4) − 3	
2522.5	Eb (4) + 23	
3580	A (4) + 29	
4119.5	C (5) − 27	
4518.5	Db (5) + 32	
4618.5	D (5) − 29	
4766.5	D (5) + 24	

Table #10

partials. A wooden wand was used here, which is why there are so many partials sounding initially. You will see that in each case this single bowl produces a different array of partials which, were we to hear these three recordings separately, could almost be misconstrued as coming from three different bowls!

Bowls that Sound Best either Struck or Stroked only

It is also sometimes important, when appropriate, to ascertain the purpose of a bowl, and in order to do this we need to play it in the correct manner to bring out its best features. A case in point is a very small bowl that I bought from Alain Presencer around 1983, one that he told me he had procured from a wandering yogi from Nepal. He said that it didn't sing (produce a sound when stroked). Now that I have a far larger range of wands available to me I know it can be made to sing. I prefer to ascertain whether a bowl has a 'message', and this is best accomplished once we have established that we are producing the sound from the bowl that it was created to produce or otherwise best represents its potential. The bowl in point sounds best when struck. It is a *yang* bowl and is very centring. It has deep indentations created by the bowlmaker on the outside, the pattern depicting the petals of a lotus flower, and it is precisely this feature that makes it hard to get this bowl to sing. For me a wonderful presence of the Dhyani Buddha Amitabha (see Appendix C) arrives when this bowl is struck, one that I have both seen and felt during its time with me. It serves to bring one right back into the now. For this reason I use the energy of this bowl to close each sound healing session or occasionally to return to centre during improvisations.

I have also come across other singing bowls that either sound very good when struck, but produce a disappointing, discordant, or miserable sound when stroked, or even none at all, or else are not impressive when struck, and yet can be made to produce an altogether more significant sound when they are stroked. While most singing bowls can produce good effects played either way, certain can't – whether it was intended to be the case or otherwise. But this situation is fairly rare.

The meaning of the sound of a bowl enters another dimension, once the true purpose has been discovered and one is listening to the intended sound behind its design and form (when applicable). As a further example, my 'Christ Light' Bowl (which I use for space cleansing) when played with a softwood wand (an inch-thick aspen) produces a soft, warm and gentle sound that is very heart-warming and lasts for as long as we play it. Approach this very same bowl with a thin wand (such as the three-eights-of-an-inch-thick porcupine-wood [coconut tree] or laburnum-wood wand, invented by myself back in the early 1990s), and we bring its third partial into prominence, giving us eight pulsations. Then, we have a very intense high-pitched screaming sound that is very powerful and focussed. It's one that decidedly cleans the space with Christ Light. How the type of wand used can very dramatically dictate the sound we hear: in workshops, demonstrating this never fails to astound people. If you couldn't see, only listen, you could easily believe that you were hearing two very different bowls!

Just as there are bowls that sound best struck or stroked, so too there are some bowls that always produce a certain partial no matter how they are played, or with whatever wand. This tends to be the second partial, with six pulses. A thicker wand may bring out the fundamental for a short period of time but the bowl will always gravitate towards what we can only conclude is the partial it was intended to sound. Or we may play it with a thinner wand, or one of harder wood, and the higher tones sound briefly but then die away.

In both cases we must accept that this is the sound that the bowl wants to produce. Of course, there is nothing wrong with this situation. I am simply stating that while some bowls can be made to produce a range of isolated partials (first up to fifth) other bowls are unable to be used in this way and will always sound the same partial regardless of how they are played or the wand that is used.

Another example presents itself with Water Bowls. With the addition of the element of water certain bowls are dramatically transformed and they sing a very different tune! I think of a bowl as a Water Bowl when the sound effect is very dramatic, leaving little or no ambiguity as to whether or not it was intended to work with water. Other bowls might be slightly altered with water in them, but then I tend to discard the effect as being somewhat accidental. In order to try and ascertain the potential significance of a true Water Bowl, water is integral to its meaning and so should be present when divining its purpose.

Studying a painting by the Russian master Nicholas Roerich (see p. 224), one can often perceive that the canvas has been primed with one colour (constituting a kind of keynote or Wagnerian *leitmotiv*) and every single item depicted in the painting serves the one fundamental purpose within that root colour. There is a wonderful music in such a painting; a music that sounds in our soul as we contemplate the symbolism of the subject matter of the painting and the colour harmony and synthesis of details (shape, line, or depiction of specific details – such as a particular personage, e.g. 'Oirot, Messenger of the White Burkhan', in the colour supplement) – which all work together and serve the invisible spiritual purpose that inspired Roerich's vision for the painting.[4]

The sound of a good bowl is rather akin to such an experience. All of its partials, we can feel, are serving a single purpose. Another analogy is an ashram where we feel that all of the people living therein are seeking to follow the one Master. They each live within the spiritual vibration of their Master (living or dead). All of the devotees are at different levels ('partials'), yet they are united in their dedication to the spiritual path taught through their Master. This harmony resonates with spiritual beings from the inner worlds and serves as a focus for a release of their blessings.

In general, a harmonious-sounding bowl (where all of its partials work together and support one another) is termed good. In a 'bad' bowl the sounds fight against each other. The former creates a healthy vibration and the latter an unhealthier situation – although the dissonance so created may call forth a response within the listener to resolve the conflict, thereby producing a healing effect within them. Noticing our instinctive response to the sound of a bowl is helpful if we are not schooled in hearing its many sounds.

12. Bowl Stories and Subtle Dimensions

THE MAGICAL sound of a good singing bowl fills us with a sense of presence. Striking a stationary bell causes the sound to radiate equally in all directions, and this enriches the sound with a magical presence filling the space. Listening to a stroked singing bowl has us enveloped in sound. There is no sense of direction in the sound, such as there is when we are listening to a trumpet player. Yet there can also be an extra factor: accumulated, or consecrated, spiritual power. Our aura is comprised of the qualities found in our several subtle bodies. Our ability to resonate with the subtle qualities that may, or may not, abide within a singing bowl depends upon the presence of these same qualities within our total being, itself comprised of all these bodies. Ancient teachings inform us that we each have a physical body, an etheric body, an astral body, a mental body, and three higher bodies still. The point of entry into our consciousness for these several bodies comes through the chakra system. It is interesting to note that the throat chakra is associated with hearing and inner listening. Therefore, simply playing any bowl will automatically help to unfold our throat chakra to some extent. This chakra is associated with our purification, creativity, simplicity, humility, and also with spiritual union. In unfolding it we learn to 'be ourselves' and to play our 'part' within the 'great symphony of life'. White Eagle teaches that this chakra becomes active in a person passing the Air initiation. He also tells us that breathing is another important factor at such times alongside sound. In India this chakra is also associated with the fifth element of space or ether, to be found at the very centre of the Tibetan *mandala*.

Taurus is the astrological Sign that rules the throat. The planet

Venus rules Taurus and of all the planets Venus has the orbit around the sun that most closely resembles a perfect circle. Copper is the metal of Venus and comprises almost 80% of most bowl materials. The glyph for Venus (the circle above the cross, see p. 433) represents the ascendancy of spirit over matter. It is associated with values and also with harmony. To sound our own note also means to be true to the spirit within us. By being absolutely true to the highest within, we cannot avoid being in tune with the cosmos and therefore come to contribute our own unique energy to the universal symphony of life. Taurus is also known as the Builder, perhaps alluding to the power of harmonious sound to build. In St John's defining phrase, 'In the beginning was the Word'.

I have found that some bowls are especially designed to help us unfold a specific chakra and so assist us in our spiritual evolution. Because we each follow different spiritual paths, and are also at different stages, there is in Tibet no rigid system linking simply one tone, colour or whatever to one chakra. It is far subtler than that. *Not all bowls are intended for use with chakras, however:* for example, I have found just two sacral chakra bowls from sorting through over 9,500 bowls since 1973!

Chakras, Deity and Master Bowls

In 1974 a percussionist friend, Trevor Taylor, told me that there was a shop in Poland Street ('Tony Bingham's'), on the edge of London's Soho area, selling renaissance instruments, and, more importantly, Chinese and Japanese Resting Bells. I went down there and bought two antique singing bowls. There were around nine bowls in this shop. Most of them were highly polished and were in various degrees of abuse as they had been used as plant pot holders – which was a common custom at that period. However, there were three that were musical – they had a good sound and had not been abused. They had retained their dark lacquered finish. The two largest had their own original stand while the largest of all had its original striker or mallet. One was sixteen inches in diameter, the next fourteen inches and the smallest of the three was ten inches. The situation was that for one hundred guineas I could take the largest or I could take the other two (separately eighty and forty-five guineas). Being a musician, two singing bowls were better than one so I went for the latter deal! It took me around one year to save up the other one hundred guineas and purchase the largest bowl. I trusted that it would still be there and so it was – and this gave me the feeling that we were destined to be together, as all of the other bowls had been replaced with similarly battered stock. I was amazed that nobody wanted this beautiful-sounding bowl. I could only conclude that the sound was of no significance whatsoever to most buyers – luckily for me! But then, I suppose if you wanted to use them for plant pot holders then nice shiny ones would be preferable and the sound quality irrelevant.

While performing and presenting at the Mind, Body, Spirit festival in London's Olympia in the summer of 1981, I often passed a stall ('Himalayan Arts' was the name, I think) selling a few Tibetan singing bowls. My thirty-third birthday fell during that week and I decided that on the day I would treat myself to one. I visited the stall only to discover that they had sold out of bowls. The owner very kindly offered me his own personal singing bowl, stating that I was the only person in the world that he would do this for. I can only assume that he had seen me perform at the festival over the days that it had been running and held me in high enough esteem to part with his own bowl. It was an absolutely wonderful bowl with which to begin my collection of around 350. It is a beautiful-sounding bowl resonating with the heart chakra and the master of the spiritual path of healing and love that I follow and also produces definite colours upon the inner planes. This went far beyond any expectations of a lovely birthday present!

I got the bowl home and meditated with it, as had been my custom since 1973 with all of my instruments. It was immediately apparent to me that it worked upon the heart chakra and the Master Jesus appeared each time I played it. The heart chakra concerns itself with the love principle, and it is always such a supreme joy for me to engage with this ancient twelfth-century singing bowl, which I call the 'Golden Voice of the Sun' Bowl. I had joined the White Eagle Lodge in 1970 and behind this Lodge are two spiritual Masters – the Master Jesus and the Master R. Jesus is known in the White Eagle brotherhood as being head of the sixth ray – the healing ray. I have been told that in the early days of White Eagle Lodge the connection with the Master Koot Hoomi (head of the second, the music ray – who had a previous incarnation as Pythagoras) had been particularly strong. Both the second and sixth rays are linked with the quality of Love. So, in a sense, one could say that Jesus is my master and this probably made it easier for me to identify his loving spiritual presence through the sound vibrations of this singing bowl. Also I recall an incarnation with Jesus at that time, and also one with Pythagoras.

As an antiquarian, Alain Presencer estimated the bowl to be around eight hundred years old. I noticed that it had a higher degree of gold in it than was usual. Meditating upon the effect of its sound, I noticed that it created the colour gold on the astral plane. This is the colour of the spiritual Sun or Son. The next colour to appear, and secondary to this, was a soft pink rose, carrying the energies of selfless love and spiritual compassion, while the final colour was a mid-blue, signifying the spiritual quality of loving devotion. Interestingly, I recently found out that these astral colours I see with the bowl are the very same colours for the Medicine Buddha.

I had wondered why a Tibetan bowl should be in tune with the Master Jesus but in the Trans-Himalayan occult brotherhood, also known as the White Lodge (first spoken of in the West by Madame Blavatsky – co-founder in 1875 of the Theosophical Society) the master Jesus is the head of the sixth ray, that of devotion and healing, while records of the time spent by Jesus in the Himalayas (during the 'missing years') were held at Hemis Monastery in Ladakh. Known under the name of Issa, Jesus is thought of as a very great Bodhisattva in Himalayan regions. So, finding a link between a Tibetan singing bowl and the Master Jesus was not so impossible after all. Several persons discovered these records – the Russian traveller Nicholas Notovitch (with his book THE UNKNOWN LIFE OF JESUS CHRIST, published in 1895), Swami Abhedananda (who visited Hemis in 1922 to verify the story), and Nicholas Roerich and his eldest son George in 1925. George Roerich could speak many languages including twenty-eight Tibetan dialects, and thus was able to translate the text himself whereas the other two writers were dependent upon translators. Others have visited Hemis and attested to these records of Jesus, such as Henrietta Merrick (1921), Swami Trigunatilananda (1895), Mrs Gasque (1939), E. Caspari (1939), Edward Noack and his wife (in the 1970s), Dr R. Rawicz (1973) and U. Eichstadt (1974).[1]

During workshops, when I have shared experiences of working with the bowls placed into my care, I have mentioned my collection of bowls for the seven major chakras. I would demonstrate with this ancient bowl to show the link to the heart chakra; to the Master Jesus, to the extra amount of the metal gold in its alloy and to the astral colours produced by this exceptional bowl. This means that through my workshops, since the time of this very first Tibetan bowl (1981), I would have therefore, unwittingly, originated the terms Chakra Bowl and Master Bowl. I am quite satisfied that certain bowls are intended to assist in the unfoldment of a specific chakra and its related consciousness levels (these are mostly ancient bowls) whilst other bowls (not pre-conditioned, as it were) might happen to strike the right note to enable one to work with an exact chakra. The former carry spiritual energies whereas the latter are simply bowls, albeit ones whose sound can be used and developed to work with the chakra in question. This could also be the case with the older bowls, but my intuition tells me that some of these were intentionally made to work with a specific chakra from the outset.

In determining whether a singing bowl works with any one chakra, in some cases I can feel the tone of the singing bowl vibrating in a certain chakra, while in others the sound of the bowl may resonate with certain psycho-spiritual qualities related to a precise chakra. The terms that I originated are now bandied about without the faintest relevance to these initial attributions I made. When such terms are used for commercial gain they are almost bound to be debased.

Centuries ago, and in the Far East particularly, time was not so tangled up with money as it is today. A spiritual practitioner could spend hours, days, weeks, months, or even years looking for a bowl that had the right sound for their spiritual work. Simply listening to all the bowls for sale or on offer until finding one that awakened the response, which would assist them in their practice – especially along the path of sound – is likely to have been an intuitive process.

Returning to my somewhat unintentional origination of several of the terms in use today, during workshops I would share how certain of my sacred bowls were attuned to specific spiritual Masters, certain merchants/practitioners present went on to sell so-called 'Master bowls'. When I asked the proud new owner why their bowl was called a 'Master bowl' there was no answer. I suggested that possibly they were a 'Master bowl' because their sound was superior to other bowls, or they had been made by a master bowl maker, or that they were master quality for so-called master practitioners or, as I had used this term, they were attuned to a spiritual master. In each case there was nothing but dumb silence in reply to such queries. But if this latter reason were the one, then why not know whom that Master is? For the Master connected to the bowl might be on a spiritual Ray different from the purchaser's. For instance, perhaps the Master is of the first ray whilst the purchaser is on the fifth ray? But I think that would be taking a commercial claim far too seriously. Of course the same is true of chakra bowls. The easiest way for a non-intuitive person to associate bowls with chakras would be through a system such as that which ascribes a certain note of the Western musical scale to a particular chakra. Then it is simply a question of just how accurately one identifies that Western note!

I am not giving these ideas to confuse the purchaser further by arming the seller (who may read this book) with even more ammunition with which to mislead him or her. I am informing the purchaser of some of the disingenuous information that accompanies the selling of bowls by some unscrupulous (or, at best, confused) or unethical merchants and dealers!

When my youngest son Gabriel was christened at the White Eagle Lodge in London in November 1982, I had arranged for Mrs Joan Hodgson to dedicate my collection of sacred ritual instruments to the service of the Great White Brotherhood. Joan was one of the original four founding members of the Lodge, alongside her parents, Grace and Ivan Cooke, and her younger sister Ylana Hayward. Joan and Ylana at this time were jointly Lodge Mother. Both have now passed on. Subsequently, after the ceremony of dedication, she commented that I had owned them in a previous lifetime – nearly all of them. I was thankful to receive such unsolicited confirmation of my own intuitions from such an eminent spiritual figure.

Among those that were present were the priceless heart chakra bowl ('Golden Voice of the Sun' Bowl) and the extremely rare and powerful Tibetan meditation cymbal ('Silver Ray of the Great Master'), which I received from Tibet in 1973 and is estimated to be around the same age, also the two rare bowls – Talking Bowl and Panic Bowl, plus the set of three four-hundred-year-old Japanese Zen Buddhist Densho bells, a Ming Dynasty Chinese Temple Bell and the set of three antique Burmese resting bells. I understand that my last Tibetan incarnation was in this, the twelfth, century. I have another bowl that I bought from Jane Werner in 1983 from a sale at Sotheby's and from the Younghusband expedition. Her husband was Tibetan and he and his Tibetan teacher (a Geshe) and Alain Presencer all estimated this bowl ('Blue Sunset' Bowl) to be around eight hundred years old.

In the early 1980s, I had a visit from a Tibetan with the unlikely name of Joseph. He came to my home in Hornsey, North London, and gave me a bronze incense burner and a bottle of orange juice. He told me his story, which was that he had some trunks of his possessions in storage in Liverpool and that he needed some money to retrieve these trunks and that inside one of them were some singing bowls and he wanted me to have them. I offered to travel up to Liverpool with him to help but my offer was declined. I gave him what money I had but never heard from him again. I was a little sad, as I would have given him the money anyway without the need for any such promises. I also found out that he had done the same thing to a friend of mine involved with the antique business. Contemplating the meaning of this during a morning meditation I received a vision showing me that I would receive two large singing bowls in compensation (at this point in my collecting, I would have expected large bowls to be around nine to eleven inches in diameter). I thought no more about it. Further on in this chapter (under the heading 'Examples of some singing bowl encounters' and on pp. 240-1) you may read more about the Chintamani and Padmasambhava bowls.

A few years later (1984 and 1985), I bought two exceptional bowls that fulfilled this vision. Both of them are of a rare design (in fact, they're the only ones I've ever seen like it) and just as rarely, I found both to be attuned to specific chakras, visualizations, colours, thoughts, planets, and Masters. If these were compensation for the abuse of my trust, then I was more than fairly recompensed! When I was first meditating with one of these bowls (Chintamani Bowl) to discover its significance, my father's spirit guide Whitefeather drew close and told me that it worked on the third eye chakra. He also told me that he used singing bowls when he was in Tibet. After deeply profound spiritual experiences as I listened to an LP recording of the spirit teacher White Eagle in 1971 I had gone to his London Lodge to offer myself in service, having recalled from my previous visit in 1965 that members of the founding family were up on Tuesdays. It happened to be Ylana (Mrs Hayward) who was up on this occasion, and upon the first instant of her seeing me she immediately invited me into the little office. During this one and only time that we met together she 'relayed' to me that White Eagle, my father and his guide Whitefeather, along with my guide Golden Hawk and myself, had all been in Tibet together. Whitefeather is a member of the Great White Brotherhood, one who specializes in healing the mind. He was a Comanche.

There is another Whitefeather of the Great White Brotherhood but he is of the Blackfoot tribe and he works through another medium with no connections to my family. There may be any number of guides named Whitefeather but the one I know and work with has not yet informed me that he is working through, or is the guide of, anybody else currently in incarnation. It is also true that such guides are not limited merely to one past earthly personality. Golden Hawk is likewise a member of the Great White Brotherhood and was also a Comanche and he specializes in aura healing.

As I previously mentioned, the form of mediumship practised

by my father and I was called 'light trance' or overshadowing (to-day this type can be called channelling – although that is a non-ex-clusive term and one used to describe the practice of light trance). In this practice, we move aside from our body and allow a spirit to take over and speak through it. Of course, we have means of assuring ourselves that the spirit present is the being they claim to be. The other traditional form of mediumship is called deep trance and in that instance the medium's active consciousness is taken away while the spirit being uses the body, so that the medium knows absolutely nothing of what is said during the séance. The difficulty with light trance is that one is always consciously aware of what is being said so that the medium has to be sure not to in-terfere by using their own mind or wishes but, remaining 'outside', instead allows the communicating spirit to say what they want to say. It is highly probable that this training assisted me later to 'stand to one side', as it were, in order to hear what those bowls with stories and their own special energies had to say.

When the Mahatmas overshadow an Adept or you as an indi-vidual, it's as if you are the pencil and the Hierarchy is the lead. This is where your Straight Knowledge comes from. It's part of your development.

Any person who is leading an (Agni yoga) group can be overshadowed if they so desire. It will never be inflicted by the Guru or the Mahatma, but if you desire it, you will be com-pletely linked in. Many times the personality of the individual changes while he is being overshadowed and then goes back to his own personality afterwards. When this happens, the ego must be completely removed.

In the Bible it says, '… few saw the Christ that overshad-owed Jesus.' This is like the overshadowing of the Hierarchy over various individuals in the Teaching. Many people feel this is an imposition and their personality is being taken away. This is not a possession or anything like that, but to be overshad-owed by a higher spiritual force is the most wonderful thing that could happen because it brings absolute cosmic wisdom, and this is the only way it can be brought about. It cannot be taught in schools or learned from books. It comes through a development of striving, and as you strive and work through meditation and living ethics you will change yourself, because the Hierarchy never changes anyone. Even the Guru does not have the right to impose good on the disciple. You protect them and pray for them and you hope, but they must do it themselves.

Guru R. H. H. (the painter Ralph Harris Houston)[1]

I find that the Chintamani bowl is attuned to a spiritual master – namely the Master Koot Hoomi. So the two complementary rays, the second and sixth (both concerned with the quality of love), are represented for myself in the Chintamani and Golden Voice of the Sun bowls, attuned to the masters of these two rays (K. H. and Jesus). Of these two bowls that came to me as compensation, the other (Padmasambhava Bowl) works on the throat chakra and again is old. It contains a higher degree of gold and has a strong connection to Padmasambhava. This Padmasambhava bowl I find is also attuned to the master at the head of the fourth ray, which is that of 'Harmony through Conflict' – namely Serapis Bey.

So far I have provided some examples above of one way in which the connection between a singing bowl and a chakra has been found by myself, and with the other of these two significant bowls I can provide another example. The first instant that I heard the sound of what I have named the Padmasambhava bowl, with my inner vision I saw the still surface of a lake of water. I was impressed that the surface of the water was absolutely still with no ripples. I felt the vibration of the bowl resonating a certain bone along my spine (the second thoracic vertebra – the ancients related this bone to the astrological sign of Taurus), and it resonated with my actual throat chakra too (Taurus rules the throat), bringing increased awareness of the magical and creative power of sound vibration – particularly as this relates to manifestation. I was also aware of the presence of a very strong and pure spring green colour.

I use this singing bowl in my sound healing on those occasions when it is required to bring the colour green to the throat chakra (I have another three bowls for the throat chakra and these provide me with the colours blue, gold, and white, thus offering any combination of these four). I intuitively knew that this bowl was attuned to a meditation with which I was familiar, from the White

Eagle Lodge, namely a meditation featuring the Lotus Pool. Later I became aware that this bowl had previously been used to visualize a large lake with the child Padmasambhava (also known as Guru Rinpoche and by eight other names – or perhaps titles is a better term) resting upon a huge lotus flower with the sun and moon in the sky. When stroked, the bowl produces a strong second partial that in two cycles can conveniently fit with the Tibetan mantra for Padmasambhava, *Om a hung ben dza gu ru pad ma sid dhi hum*, so that often I will inwardly and silently chant this as I play the bowl. It is very rare in my experience with bowls that there are specific visualizations accompanying them, but each one of these two special antique Chakra Bowls (which I believe came to me as divine compensation for the experience with 'Joseph') do have such an attribute.

So sometimes I am aware of a resonating vibration in a specific area or bone of my body and at other times I am able to enter into the deeper levels of relevant bowls by virtue of my clairaudient and clairvoyant unfoldment. On other occasions, as I mentioned previously, the area of resonating vibration proved to be that of a particular chakra. There are occasions when the energies of a singing bowl are found to resonate with more than one chakra. Otherwise, they can bring different energy to the same chakra. For instance, my pair of solar plexus chakra bowls, through applying a different way of playing, can bring either blue or gold to this chakra.

I hope that I have conveyed something of the manner in which what I term a Chakra Bowl is arrived at and how they work. In contrast to certain schools of thought that seek correspondences between chakras and musical notes, the method of working I use has absolutely nothing to do with musical notes – let alone those of our Western scale. As unlikely as it may seem, my two Chakra Bowls for the sacral centre are higher in pitch than my solar plexus chakra bowls, even though the sacral centre is conventionally listed before the solar plexus and might therefore be expected to be connected with a lower and not a higher pitch. Practising a kind of direct perception with no preconceptions, I am content to accept the wisdom of my body, or subtle bodies, or intuition, when striving to penetrate the mysteries of any one significant bowl. Nonetheless, I also strive to be objective and I am always blessed with confirmation and reassurance from trusted sources. Interestingly, the Theosophist Charles W. Leadbeater, in his monograph on the chakras, actually recommends using an alternative location for the sacral centre, which is at the spleen centre (higher up the body, so that a higher pitch might then be expected).

There are also many systems of working with sound and the chakras from the East by using the voice. Nonetheless, the majority of these that I have encountered use word-sounds for the chakras and pay little attention to the pitch. In the main, they are all chanted upon the same pitch and do not even go up a scale of notes. The mantra used and its sound would seem to be of far more importance than the 'musical' pitch in many instances.

The form of yoga that works with sound and the voice, is *nada yoga*. I shall deal with this more fully in chapter seventeen. For the moment, I want to point out that there seems to have arisen some confusion between the practices of *nada yoga* for non-musicians and its practice among musicians. Musicians play instruments, or sing, according to strict rules, whereas the various musical scales of diverse cultures are derived from different roots. The yogi who is not a musician may well chant or recite *bija mantras* (including the traditional seven sounds for each of the chakras) in order to unfold his or her own chakras, whilst a musician who wishes to study *nada yoga* (being used to playing a larger range of notes) may well find that certain pitches stimulate specific chakras more than others, or that the different musical intervals carry the significance of certain chakras. Again, it may simply be that they have adapted their practice of singing scales to apply to the chakras also. Working with a seven-note scale, it is not unreasonable to find an association with each of the seven chakras. These pitches, scales or intervals are the tools used by the musician, and the practice of *nada yoga* can help to awaken the musician to yet deeper layers or realms of sound. The non-musician relies more upon the pronunciation of the word and combination of letters while the musician is more swayed by the energy within a particular musical note.

The essence of *nada yoga* is that of *anahata* (or the unstruck sound): in that respect we can say that it has nothing whatsoever to do with audible sounds. Therefore, many teachers pay no heed to scales and focus far more upon the words used, so that each *bija mantra* may well be chanted upon the same note. However, and understandably, many of those attracted to this form of yoga are those working with sound – and thus musicians. It remains that the essence of *nada yoga* is the inner inaudible sound as a means of uniting with the Supreme Being. There are always present with *nada yoga* the inner and outer aspect to sound, but the greater emphasis in *nada yoga* is upon the inner inaudible sound. One does not need to be a musician or to practise any kind of musical discipline in order to follow *nada yoga* – listening to the inner sound. One does not even have to pronounce mantras or any audible sound whatsoever. Many teachers of *nada yoga* were not musicians and did not teach music, signifying that musical discipline hasn't always been attached to *nada yoga*.

In the process of sorting through several thousands of bowls since 1971, I have noticed some that work upon the chakras not so far mentioned, until I now have bowls for each one of the seven main chakras and four minor chakras too, providing me with a total of eleven chakras. However, it is not so simple that I have a bowl for each of the chakras. The whole subject is very complex – and some practitioners go so far as to state that everyone has an individual note for their own chakras. I have eleven bowls for the heart chakra, but this is not according to their so-called musical note but rather it concerns their capacity to affect the chakra. In this instance they are not even the same musical note, or pitch, but rather cover an interval span of an augmented major fifth.

Pictured overleaf is my basic set for the seven major chakras and illustrates their varying sizes. Some of the thirty bowls I use with the chakras have been used by one of their previous owners (or even all of them) for working upon the chakra in question. As far as I know the other, newer bowls have never been used this way, nor intentionally made to affect the chakra concerned; nevertheless I have found them to possess qualities that resonate with a certain chakra and so use them.

This is a way of listening that is not solely focused upon what the physical ears tell us but is also open to other dimensions of activity of the sounds of each bowl. It involves discerning what these

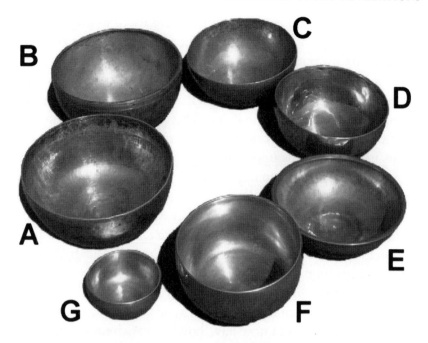

multiple phenomena awak-
en upon the different levels
of our whole being (or not,
as the case may be). It has
been found that the ear is
not the only entrance for
sound vibrations to enter

Letter	Name of Bowl	Chakra
A	Aldebaran Bowl	Root
B	Singing with Solar Winds Bowl	Sacral
C	Song of the Mountain Waterfall Bowl	Solar Plexus
D	Golden Voice of the Sun Bowl	Heart
E	Song of the Crystal Bowl	Throat
F	Chintamani Bowl	Third Eye
G	Celestial Spring Bowl	Crown

our consciousness, but rather that our entire body can receive the
messages of sound. If I may extend this further, why not include
our 'subtle bodies' also! An analogy for this method would be
listening to the sound of wind moving through the leaves of trees,
or of silent communion with a tree. We might ask, what does this
tree have to teach me? What does the leaf of this flower have to
tell me? Obviously, no actual audible sound is involved in this process; rather, what we might term the 'third ear' comes into play.
During such silent communion with the 'nature' spirit it is possible
to receive beautiful teaching. In such a way we can open ourselves
to the story of each bowl. We follow the sound of the bowl, and
having arrived at its home we can then pay attention to how it has
changed us.

If we consider the heart chakra for the moment, we can already discern two levels on which the energy might work. It may unfold the quality of human love, or it may engender divine love. With human love we are working to unfold the quality of compassion for all of our fellow human beings, while with divine love we are aiming to transcend this human – all too human – level and reach the spiritual dimension of unconditional love. The path of human love (relating to others on the same level) is in a horizontal direction and with the path of divine love we relate to (divine) beings above our level to assist in our upward journey – which is therefore more vertical in nature. Naturally, both are necessary with the two creating a cross, and with the heart chakra at the centre we can easily see our Rose upon the Cross, which was so beloved by the Rosicrucians.

Similarly, we can again notice that some heart chakra bowls possess a very strong love energy – very positive and outgoing – while others convey more of a gentle, kind, caring, nurturing, comforting, and reassuring note that helps those with a closed heart chakra slowly to begin trusting again, and reopening to loving energy. This is just one example of the variety of experiences around this chakra and its relationship to musical notes or sounds.

As I've said, Rudolf Steiner, the great Hungarian mystic and occultist (1861–1925, of Austrian parents) stated that the heart chakra has twelve petals but that all of humanity during its evolution (he was a great advocate of reincarnation) has unfolded six of these with six thus remaining.[3] I therefore find it difficult to think of one note for this chakra, with its six petals (or soul qualities). I would imagine at least six different notes designed to unfold one of each of the six virtues of the heart chakra (or twelve if you don't agree with Steiner). Steiner says something similar of the throat chakra with its sixteen petals (eight of these having been already unfolded during our past evolution).[4] However, it is also true that each chakra is said to possess a single *bija mantra*. For the heart chakra, for instance, this is *yam*. With our heart chakra, then, this would be a question of one, seven, or thirteen different sounds.

One of my heart chakra bowls is also attuned to the coming Buddha, Maitreya. I believe that the spiritual quality of this being can be heard in the sound of the bowl. Another ancient heart chakra bowl is attuned to Neptune, and carries the energy of mystical communion with the universal Christ spirit and also carries the amethystine vibrations of transformation. One of my 'matched pairs' of heart chakra bowls carries the violet vibrations. Another bowl is attuned to a certain fixed star (Regulus – in the constellation of Leo, a fire sign ruling the heart) that to the ancients was related to the archangel Raphael. I have one other bowl of this type of correspondence attuned to the fixed star Aldebaran, which was also named Michael, and that bowl is for the root chakra. With this Aldebaran bowl I found that the spiritual energy of the fixed star Aldebaran comes into our solar system via Jupiter, meaning that I need to form a triangle linking Aldebaran to Jupiter and then to earth.

I only recently discovered that in Tantra the *bija mantra*s of *strim* and *trim* relate to Aldebaran, and that is further associated with the planet Jupiter and with the goddess Durga–Tara. I recalled a past lifetime as a guru in India (spanning the eighth and ninth centuries) and I had some bowls in my cave then and one of these was attuned to a fixed star. This experience came during a visit to the late Ruby Tonks at her home in Heathfield, East Sussex. Ruby gave 'far memory' sessions using the 'Christos' technique and I went for a session lasting several hours wherein she conversed with me and I communicated with her from that past life.

Having sorted through over 9,500 bowls in over forty-two years I have found but two bowls with this aspect. If I had a mind to, I could imagine many more but the simple truth is that I only have found two such bowls. Similarly, I have four bowls attuned to great spiritual masters from the Hierarchy of Light but if I were simply using my intellect and not my spiritual gifts, I could claim many others to be so connected. I talk about these things because I experience them; they have been revealed to me during my spiritual quest through sacred sound, and I share them in case they can be of any assistance to others in their search into the dimension of sacred sound.

Time can be another factor, and patience is necessary because I may not be able to resonate with the energies of a particular bowl at a certain time – but then, after a period undergoing certain spiritual experiences, my understanding grows and I am able more fully to recognize what is living in or attached to the energy of the bowl in question. I am then ready to greet its subtler resonating frequencies and so actually able to work with its deeper levels.

Some Examples of Singing Bowl Encounters

White Tara Bowl. During the 1980s, my friend Melodicium worked for an antique shop off London's Portobello Road, called 'Frontiers', and he would contact me whenever they had just taken delivery of a shipment of singing bowls. On one such occasion I was sorting through around four hundred bowls on the shop floor with two other individuals when I overheard one of them play a bowl the sound of which grabbed my attention. I looked up and immediately saw the form of White Tara above the bowl and player, who was Melodicium. I already had a Green Tara bowl and this would make the perfect partner. Nevertheless, it might well have been the right bowl for Melodicium, and so I consciously withdrew my attention from it.

Soon, though, I heard the sound of the rejected bowl being placed back on the wooden floor. I therefore knew that some-where among these hundreds of bowls was this special one. Some time later in our task I picked up a bowl and as I played it I im-mediately saw the form of White Tara and so instantly placed it in my pile. The cosmos had seemingly decreed that I was allowed this partner for Green Tara. As chance would have it these bowls are very close, both in pitch and in size, and are *yin* (feminine) bowls – most probably from Tibet.

Several years later Melodicium was working at another store and approached me one day with a Shakti Bowl, asking if I would buy it and thus reduce my bill with them (they sold CDs of my music). I declined but analysed the bowl only to find that it was another White Tara bowl. Melodicium kept it for himself – so that a White Tara bowl joined him after all. Sometimes, having briefly heard the White Tara bowl of mine at workshops, a person might approach me afterwards and, being a devotee of Tara, ask if I could play this bowl some more. Invariably, male or female, their eyes fill with tears on hearing it.

Amogasiddhi Bowl. My ex-wife Christine would buy and sell bowls and I would assist in selecting these for her – and most often help purchasers to choose. I had already met Gaynor O'Flynn and she would often go out to work in the Himalayan region, and she got into buying, selling, and collecting singing bowls. Christine and I had gone to sort through her bowls, and during this session Gaynor decided she just wanted to sell everything. We bought a large selection of her bowls and among them were some large ones, from which I chose a few. There was another that I was attracted to, but felt that I must let it go, as dear Christine was trying to turn a profit on them. So I decided to pay no attention to it in case I found it irresistible. We sold it to a lady who rang me a few years later to ask if the bowl had bad energy (or black magic) as things had gone very wrong in her life since she had owned it. I said that I notice such bowls very quickly and would have nothing to do with such a bowl and, therefore, it was highly unlikely that this was the case. She'd asked several of her spiritual friends to alter its energy but every attempt failed.

So it was that I arranged to meet her at a *Caduceus* Sound Day in London (where I was giving workshops and a solo concert) to check it out for her during my lunch break. Whilst observing its energy, I saw the form of a Dhyani Buddha with the bowl and described the effects of the sound of this bowl – that of being totally focused and one-pointed – unwavering in one's path. A few weeks afterwards, watching a videotape of Joseph Campbell (Mythos II) speaking about the chakras and how the Dhyani Buddhas are met with at the level of the throat chakra in the Bardo state, I identified Amogasiddhi from his posture and *mudra* (hand gesture) as being the Dhyani Buddha concerned. Joseph Campbell went on to describe this Buddha's energy ('He who will not be turned from the achievement of his aim') and this exactly fitted my description of how to work with the sound of this bowl. The said lady further contacted me again some years afterwards saying she hardly used it and would I take it back – so I swapped it for a nice heart chakra bowl for her. I now am able to have this special sacred singing bowl, giving me bowls for all of the Dhyani Buddhas. For more on the Dhyani Buddhas see p. 282 and Appendix C.

Mercury Bowl. I found that one bowl in my collection had previously been used for black magic. I performed various rituals involving cleansing with water and incense alongside certain visualizations of re-empowerment to remove this accretion. Once it was cleared of such energies I meditated upon the sound and what it created and then re-consecrated it to its original purpose. I found that this bowl is very helpful in revealing our thought-patterns. I believe this is why it had been abused: the previous owner had used the bowl to reveal the thought-patterns of his victims. This is akin to looking into a mirror and so I named this bowl Mercury Bowl – for the planet Mercury. It is a one-off hand-hammered bowl. It has a fine patina and is very old.

For consecrating or re-consecrating a bowl see Chapter 6, 'Old and New Bowls' (pp. 118-9).

Whistling Bowl. On one occasion Alain had invited me to his home where he wanted to swap a strange-looking bowl for something of mine. I struck the bowl but it sounded rather awful. Nonetheless I was attracted to it, and I had Alain willing me to receive it. So I pondered this bowl and in doing so I clairvoyantly saw an amount of water inside it. I asked Alain if he'd tried it with water and he replied that he had, but that it didn't work. It has a very low wall with writing inscribed upon the outer rim and Alain told me that it translated from Tibetan as 'On the surface of sound'. This encouraged me to believe that water was associated with this bowl. So I accepted the swap. When I got it home I placed the amount of water inside that I had seen and played it only to find that it produced the most exquisite whistling sounds – stemming from the upper partials of this bowl. For optimum performance, the Whistling Bowl requires an extremely precise amount of water. It has an eerie sound and suggests to me the effect of rays of light reflecting upon ocean waves.

Jesus in the Garden Bowl. This is a beautiful little Tibetan singing bowl that I bought from Alain in 1983. It carries a joyful energy that I link to Jupiter. I characterized its sound as being that of 'Jesus in the garden' – the infinite and eternal garden in meditation. While I was playing it at a workshop close by in Romsey, Hampshire, the lady whose house we were using told me later that when I began to play it, around twenty-eight birds landed on the bush outside the window and when I finished playing it they all left.

Chintamani and Padmasambhava Bowls. Returning again to the story from 1981, featuring the middle-aged Tibetan, Joseph, I had few bowls at this time and was therefore anticipating these new and welcome additions – but simply had to let the event go and accept that I'd been conned. I pondered this meeting and considered whether or not it was a test of my greed – not that I had many bowls at the time.

A few years later the bowls I mentioned arrived, independently of one another, and both of them were attuned to specific visualizations that featured strongly in the White Eagle meditations. I therefore felt that these would serve me well in my work of creating music for meditation. They both cost me a similar amount – £250 for the one and £300 for the other (1983 prices!) and, as chance would have it, I earned the money for both by working on a converted barn in mid-Wales owned by an artist-philosopher-plumber friend, Roy Bowden. I would work on his conversion up in the Welsh mountains (miles from anywhere and anyone) for around two weeks at a time. It felt right that I should perform some kind of manual labour and service in return for these wonderful sacred instruments. I shall never forget removing endless barrowloads of old sheep faeces from the upstairs of the farmhouse over a few days and then mixing up endless barrows of concrete to seal the floor according to government standards.

The Chintamani bowl was damaged when I received it. It would appear to have been struck forcibly near its base from the inside and the metal broken and forced outwards and then rather clumsily pushed back and filled with some awful-looking paste. Once it reached a certain level of amplitude while being stroked, it would always make a rattling, buzzing noise. I eventually took it to my already aged bowl-friend, Hector Benson, up near Newmarket in Suffolk. Having been an engineer he had the necessary expertise and very kindly was happy to work on it – removing the paste and gently heating it and finally silver-soldering the break-age. Whilst he was engaged on mending the bowl I played a very old and special bowl of his to 'heal' my bowl. This old bowl of his had very special psycho-spiritual properties and it felt so right to play it throughout the entire process. Hector, himself, in a letter that he wrote to me, attested to these intensely psychic proper-ties of that singular bowl (he had been involved with Spiritualism and spiritual healing in his time) on account of certain experiences he'd had with it on occasions in his own home. I thought of it as alchemical, and it really did feel as though its balanced ener-gies assisted in the healing process upon the inner, subtler planes, whilst Hector worked upon the physical level. Thanks to Hector, my Third Eye Chakra bowl is now fine and no longer rattles when reaching a high volume.

Whitefeather had this to say about this bowl in 1985: 'Opens 'Inner Eye'; opens Third eye to see 'Inner World' of Spirit = INVISI-BLE world/s. Many Kingdoms in God's Universe. Brings Peace. Feel Safe in God's Universe. Bowl brings the Great White Brotherhood close. Circle – All Equal – Unity. God's Love. One Big family!'

The other (Padmasambhava) bowl was found at my friend Ray Man's musical instrument shop on 28th August 1984. He is originally from China and ran a jazz club called 'The Crucible' in London's Soho area (New Compton Street, now built over). I was 'house drummer' for the club (after my first appearance on the evening of the day in early January 1970 upon which I had moved back down to London from Mildenhall, Suffolk). When he finally closed the club he set up a shop selling ethnic musical instruments (particularly from China and India). I had suggested that he stock the Chinese *qing* bowls and, while he wasn't convinced they'd sell, he ordered two sets and I was allowed to choose those I liked the sound of, to create one set for myself. During one visit to his (sec-ond) shop I found that he had recently procured a large quantity of Tibetan bowls from a large store, where they weren't selling as fast as they had expected.

I told Ray that I'd like the bowl and explained that it was attuned to a meditation from my spiritual Master, and enquired how much was it. He said that he wanted it for himself, as it went well as he played his *xiao* (a Chinese end-blown flute), but that he'd think about it. Around 10:55 that evening Ray turned up where I was staying at a friend's in Hampstead, London, and said I could have it for £300. In my view, if a bowl is really for you then you simply have to pay whatever is asked of you. When I got it home and could meditate and study it properly I discovered the very strong spring green that it generates on the astral plane, that it was attuned to Saturn, and also resonated with the two thoughts of Serenity and Tranquillity upon the higher mental plane. The Chintamani Bowl also resonates with these same two contempla-tive thoughts, only with the colours of blue and white light, and to the planet Venus. That bowl is also in tune with the meditation upon the circle of white brethren and also the Master K.H.

Shy Bowls

Some bowls can be temperamental. Hector Benson one day lent me his largest bowl. When I visited him he eventually showed me this bowl and explained that he couldn't get it to sing. I tried with my big ebony wand and it worked. Hector asked, 'is that the sound of the vacuum cleaner?' I said, 'No, it's your bowl!' He couldn't believe it, and excitedly called for his wife to come in and hear it. Afterwards he took precise measurements of the wand in order to reproduce one for himself.

I had decided to record a piece using only Tibetan instruments. I also chose to work with three chakras – solar plexus for the first seven minutes, heart for the central seven minutes and throat for the final seven. Hector's large bowl was for the solar plex-us and so started off the entire piece. This was at the studio of Jon Hiseman (founder and drummer in the group Colosseum). We tested it to get a level and then we'd record it but every time it under-performed. So I eventually decided to trick it by telling Jon that I'd play it again for a test but kept it going for seven minutes. It worked out fine. So it was evidently rather shy! This was for the LP, 'New Atlantis', side 2: 'Rays of Sunlight Touch the Healing Waters' (1983).[5] After the sound of this first bowl was recorded everything went well for the rest of the piece.

Wisdom from My Guides

Aldebaran Bowl. 'Bowl speak of Sound/Thought. Must have Direction once enter Spirit world; must know where go Look! Golden Hawk See with "eye"; see Golden Sun; know where look to find That which bring Life - Light to the world. Speak of Great Power of Spirit to cut through mind of Earth. Open mind and heart to Space - Manitou - Great White Spirit - Home of Soul. Sound focus of Spirit. Like LIGHT - like STAR, Make 'home' in Space. Sound of Bowl like planet; like Star of GOD-SELF within. This bowl link bright Star Aldebaran. Bowl speak of Great Space, Many Beings in that Space; Great Brotherhood of LIGHT! Travel with this bowl through space – then must have aim; must look for STAR; STAR of God-Self Within!'

Vairocana Bowl. Whitefeather, 1986. 'Great SOUND of Universe! Great WORD of GOD! Great White Spirit! Bowl speak of Power of Great WHITE LIGHT. Soul go straight to Higher Worlds. Bring Stillness; Peace; Light and True Vision.'

And an example of one of my own contemplations:

Blue Sunset Bowl (1983). 'I see men riding away. Bowl is for praying. Monk would pray and burn incense before taking up bowl. It inspires confidence in the Supreme Spirit – it's intended to remove anxiety – to relax. It brings sense of oneness – also sense of being in IT Here and Now! First, I saw White Light then Indigo Blue with some pale blue and a little pink. Then it turned pale gold and then affected brow chakra (once emotions stilled – desirelessness/Buddha) warm sensation, also present at throat. Like Buddha one sits as a "little Child" with mind and soul open (bowl) to the Father/Mother God for strength. Peace and Strength and raising of consciousness. Equilibrates and pacifies etheric currents making circle. Assists in reading the Akashic Records. Hot. Water – Flowing. Solar Plexus. Peace, quietening, stilling & centring.'

These unedited records are offered as an encouragement to record your own feelings around your bowls.

Unexpected Verification

While I was part of the teaching faculty at Emerson College
Summer School (an Anthroposophical college, and at the invitation of Michael Deason-Barrow) during the 1980s, the eu-
rhythmists were seeking to find a way of working with gongs,
made by Manfred Bleffert, that had just been brought over from
Germany. Steiner had given body positions for the various musical notes and what he said was typically related to the piano,
so that gongs, with their longer tones, required another method of working. The gong player couldn't be awakened on the
Wednesday afternoon and so I stepped into the breach, offering
to stroke my bowls for up to ten minutes or more for the senior
eurhythmist John Logan to move with. After I played the Padmasambhava Bowl he came over and exclaimed that he couldn't
understand why, but he found that he kept wanting to go into
the position for Saturn and also for the colours green and red –
thus confirming my observations with his refined body. So John
was experiencing which eurhythmy position went most harmoniously with the sound field of each bowl played.

I played two or three bowls in all and each time he would unwittingly confirm my observations in this way, even though this
was not the purpose behind our experimentation at all. While
stroking the bowls in question I simply played them and did not
concentrate upon adding any of my own subtle observations. I
just concentrated upon playing the bowl and keeping the sound
constant, whereas usually whilst playing such a bowl I would be
attuning myself to its effects in order to add to (or anchor within the human kingdom) the psycho-spiritual potential inherent in
the bowl. Nonetheless, the experience proved invaluable to me
inasmuch as it inadvertently provided confirmation of my inner
observations.

It was interesting for me to ponder that in Steiner's system Saturn is not green, but rather dark blue or black, whilst in the school
of wisdom that I am linked with (as well as in my own inner experience) Saturn is related to the colour green. So John would not be
expecting to associate green or red with Saturn.

'Voice of the Great Master' Bowl

The bowls don't speak to everyone. There are certain instances where after many years of not using a particular bowl I have set aside time to study it and a deeper level has revealed itself. A certain lesson from life has been learnt and a quality developed within my nature, one that then facilitates the ability to resonate with that same quality contained within the sound energy of that one bowl.

'Voice of the Great Master' Bowl is my name for the Talking Bowl that came via Alain Presencer from H. H. Dilgo Khyntse Rinpoche in 1982 (see the film 'Spirit of Tibet'[6]). This Talking Bowl resembled a grail cup in shape. I received it a year after performing a concert for the Almeida Festival in 1981 with David Hykes (one of the world's leading experts in 'throat singing' and founder–director of the Harmonic Choir of New York). We both performed solo and then as an improvised duet. After our first evening a woman came up and, without any introduction, simply informed me, 'It's all rubbish about these bowls. They're just fruit bowls. You can buy them by the pound in India.' She then turned to David Hykes and asserted, 'I can do overtone singing and I'm better than you!' So saying, off they went for a duel! The funny thing is that among the over four hundred instruments I had just performed with, there was only one Tibetan Singing Bowl ('Golden Voice of the Sun' Bowl) and it was attuned to the heart chakra and also to the Master Jesus (head of the healing ray) – a kind of fruit, I suppose! If the 'fruit' arising from sounding this bowl is to align me with the Great Healer then, for me, it is a most precious fruit bowl indeed! For some reason she just didn't get it. So, with the 'Voice of the Great Master' (Talking Bowl) resembling a cup I did begin to wonder whether I'd gone too far or not. Was it in reality simply a cup? Was my heart chakra bowl simply a fruit bowl? Were my intuitions regarding these bowls misguided?

The first time I meditated with the Talking Bowl the only words that I could use to describe the state of consciousness engendered were, 'I and the Father are One!' and I found it was tuned to the nirvanic plane. Some time shortly afterwards any self-doubt was vanquished when I was invited to meet a *geshe* (the Tibetan teacher of Jane Werner's Tibetan husband), whom I was told specialized in sound, amongst other things. I took along the Talking Bowl ('Voice of the Master' Bowl) and the 'Silver Ray of the Great Master' *ting-sha*. After playing the Talking Bowl, Geshela said that he heard it chanting a mantra. Jane translated the words he heard as, 'To cross the sea of *samsara* and enter *nirvana*'.

Any idea of these sacred sound tools being 'fruit bowls from India' left me forever. Geshela and I were on the same page! This bowl provides a good example of the effect of sound upon consciousness: that is, one has to transcend the earthly ears and simply experience within oneself (resonate with it). If we were informed that here is a bowl that is attuned to *nirvana* we might well imagine it to sound most beautiful, and yet this bowl actually sounds cracked! However, being together with its sound can raise one up to this nirvanic plane.

The ability to resonate with the subtle energies of any one bowl is a delicate matter. For this to happen there needs to be something of a reciprocal spiritual vibration already existing within the listener that can be awakened during the sounding. What follows is an account of another sound worker experiencing this same twelfth-century heart chakra bowl.

In 1981 I met Mikhail Harwitz, who visited me as a member of the Chishti order of Sufis. He told me that he had found a copy of my fourth solo album 'Deep Peace' (1980)[7] upon a Sufi altar of his Order and had tracked me down in order to buy copies to sell to the Sufi members of his group and customers of his musical compilations used in illustrated talks by his spiritual Master the late Pir Vilayat Inayat Khan (son of musician and Sufi Hazrat Inayat Khan, 1882–1927), the Head of the Chishti group of Sufis. I invited him to my home for the LPs, and when he then informed me that he specialized in sound I suggested that we compare notes regarding the effects of certain of my instruments – including those invented and handmade by myself. We were agreed in each case – the ancient Tibetan *ting-sha* I have ('Silver Ray of the Great Master') he could only say was attuned to a very high state of meditation and had something to do with Padmasambhava (as indeed the yogi who passed it on to me also informed me). The last instrument on which we compared observations was this beautiful 'Golden Voice of the Sun' Bowl. Afterwards, he simply looked at me with very great love in his eyes as if to say, 'What can you say?' 'How on earth can I put this experience into words?' We were in absolutely no doubt at all that this spoke of the Master in the heart as we communed in the heart with our respective spiritual Masters on the love ray.

'Silver Flame' Bowl

This is the Panic Bowl. On one occasion in February 1982 Alain Presencer wanted a *gshang/shanta* cymbal (Bonpo cymbal) plus a gong of mine and offered to give me a Panic Bowl in return. I agreed, and Alain took the instruments but phoned me a while later to explain, 'I'm sorry, Frank, but the chap has turned up on my doorstep with some cheap German imitation rubbish and so I don't have the Panic Bowl!'

I wasn't too worried – at least, my audiences wouldn't have to panic! Around six months later, on the eve of the day of receiving a wonderful Talking Bowl via Alain from one of the greatest Masters of the twentieth century – H. H. Dilgo Khynste, Alain rang to say, 'You'll never believe this, but the chap who was supposed to bring the Panic Bowl is standing on my doorstep quivering like a lump of jelly saying, "Don't ask me what happened – Please just take it". So, I now have the Panic Bowl to bring you tomorrow!'

The following day Alain brought the Panic Bowl down to me. What an exceptional weekend that was! I realized that the Panic Bowl was for exorcisms and by this time I was ready to accept it into my collection, as in spiritual healing I had been told that I had a special gift for treating exorcisms. This Panic Bowl creates a very strong Silver Flame on the inner levels of being and so is extremely useful for exorcisms. Alain later told me that this type of bowl is used for exorcisms in Tibet.

Members of the Nataraja Yoga Centre in North London used to arrange to come to my home for a private concert. I would erect a horoscope for the time and place to serve as a 'score' for the energies present. On an occasion around six months after receiving the Panic Bowl I had done this and arrived at a title: 'Gift from a Humble Heart'. With everyone present I was about to begin improvising when blues music came through the wall behind me. This was the only time that I ever heard music from the neighbour. I understood that malevolent forces were at work and so determined to begin the concert with the Panic Bowl. At the end everyone commented on how wonderful it was that the blues music stopped after the bowl. One lady said, 'What was that first instrument? I thought I'd never get my brain back!' It was recorded and we heard his music going all through. Fortunately, the neighbour listened to his blues music and my audience heard only the sounds of mine.

On another occasion I was in Norfolk giving a weekend workshop in a converted barn. It was a hot sunny day and we had the windows open. From outside came this horrendous noise. I commented how it was fortunate to be able to compare sacred sound with noise. Those present suggested we send the man love. The owner said, 'Love? He's a horrible man!' We sent love for some minutes as the noise continued. It was the farmer cutting his hedge with a tractor right outside the window. I continued with the workshop, finally telling the story of the Panic Bowl. I then played the Panic Bowl and everyone there will affirm that as the sound of this bowl faded into silence, so, too, did the noise of the tractor. Whilst the farmer fully intended to make noise all day long, we found after lunch that he'd gone away. This is the real McCoy. Needless to say, I use it for exorcisms of places or people or for removing dark energies.

'Silver Ray of the Great Master'

In my twenties, I had already recalled several past lifetimes in Tibet and in 1971 I had telepathically asked the leader of the family circle (the spirit known as Whitefeather) for an instrument to represent these. I had instruments representative of other past lives in India, China and Japan. Around two years later, and two days before my twenty-fifth birthday, a yogi from Tibet contacted me on the telephone saying he'd been asked to pass on an ancient Tibetan Meditation cymbal. We met the next day. This has an extremely powerful sound and although I'd been meditating, healing, and on the spiritual path since 1964 it completely changed both my music and my life! I have never heard, or experienced, another *ting-sha* like it before or since. Even to this day! As he struck it for the very first time I instantly saw an intense brilliant flash of bright white-blue silvery light. I listened with my eyes closed, to focus upon the sound, and immediately wondered how they got the light into this cymbal.

My new friend told me that it was from his master of the Nyingma sect. This cymbal is estimated to be around eight hundred years old by the crystallization in the metal (see Chapter 4) and other factors. My last Tibetan incarnation was at this very period. It is high in silver content and includes meteorite. I asked the yogi how much he wanted for it but he simply replied that it was from a sacred tradition and money should not change hands. However, if I wished to contribute to his fare back to Tibet he would oblige. I named this cymbal 'Silver Ray of the Great Master'. In the late 1970s Simon Bentley (a colleague from the White Eagle Lodge) visited our home and with his 'perfect pitch' he told me that it goes through the same note in five octaves – close to an Ab (which some schools give as the note for the astrological sign of Cancer – which was the ruling sign at the time of receiving this gift). He commented on what a tremendous feat of engineering it was to produce the same note over five octaves!

Oddly enough this experience was somewhat verified while I was taking part in the 'Earth Sings' Festival at Findhorn in 1980. After my solo performance, Findhorn told me that I was going to be filmed for them. The cameraman approached me saying that he wanted to film me from inside of my equipment (I was encircled by around five hundred instruments to create my sacred space). I desisted but he insisted and so I relented. In order to aid his filming, I told him that I'd begin with this *ting-sha* followed by a Sun Ray and then a Densho but didn't know what I'd play next. No sooner had I played the *ting-sha* than he dropped the camera to his side and said, 'I've just seen this blinding flash of white light!'

I simply said, 'Yes'. He informed me immediately that he would be filming from the other end of the hall using a zoom lens!

Crystal Tuning Bowl

On another occasion, a lady rang to enquire if we had a bowl that she could use for cleansing her crystals. I sorted through our selection of bowls for sale and found one suitable and rang her back. When she arrived, days or weeks later, she brought a few friends along and one used a pendulum. So, disregarding my findings, they sorted through the entire selection of bowls (maybe between thirty and forty), and when the pendulum rested over the bowl I'd selected, lo and behold it confirmed my findings. So we were all agreed on that being the bowl for the purpose. Then they had to find a wand and the entire divining procedure again agreed with my previous findings. The lady worked with her eyes closed and so I even replaced the wand that had come out best back into the sequence and it chose that one again! I seem to recall that several bowls were purchased and one was very old. I was asked how old. I used psychometry and it said 493 years and out came the pendulum again only this time it was not in agreement but said that the bowl was 485 years old (my memory may not be exact here, as this is not really something I'm particularly concerned about). Anyway, there was that amount of disagreement only regarding its precise age!

There is a link between bowls and crystals – apart from both being of the mineral kingdom. As mentioned above, there are some bowls the energy of which can be applied to cleansing or re-tuning crystals. And I have used crystals to re-tune my older bowls. Many years ago now (last century!) I underwent certain inner initiations into the Great White Light and I had a large quartz crystal that had been given to me by a friend and I charged this with the Light. The mineral kingdom is obedient, and so it became a good storehouse for retaining energies. If I ever stray and so need to reconnect with the Light for whatever purpose I can simply hold this crystal. If I have certain old bowls possessing powerful spiritual energy that may have encountered contrary energies or psychic accretions during their travels – when their need for cleansing isn't so drastic (as with my Mercury Bowl) – then I will leave this quartz crystal inside them for several days and nights before my altar. It is very useful to dedicate an area (or room if possible or desirable) to spiritual work. Repeating spiritual practices in this space builds up the spiritual power, and this can be helpful for those times when our energies are a bit low or our connection is a bit weak. As the power builds over many years it becomes a sacred space and it is here that the rededication or purification of singing bowls is best accomplished. It is also in this space that spiritual work with sound using our bowls is best undertaken.

Correct Uses of Spiritual Bowls

A friend of a friend contacted me to explain that he had a bowl that he loved to listen to but that over time he had become paralysed down his lefthand side. I happened to be giving a workshop close to where he lived, so we arranged for him and his bowl to come along. I found that it had been used for a specific meditation. This was one that I would not usually advise but at the turn of the last century spirit mediums sometimes did recommend it. It is to visualize blackness with the idea that it would be helpful for trance work as it would somewhat blank the mind. Because it had not been worked with consciously it had produced this paralysis. But don't worry. As I've already stated, such bowls featuring a certain power are very rare and it is unlikely that your bowl would produce such a result.

13. Teachings from the Bowls

THE BOWLS carry teaching in themselves, and this stretches from the immediate physical reality up into rarefied heights of consciousness. For instance, if we return home perhaps from a busy and fractious day we can sit ourselves down before our bowl and let its sound help us find our peaceful centre again. The bowl in this instance is teaching us to turn to the sound of silence within and find our inner peace, and so become in tune with our spiritual centre.

Similarly, if we take the symbol of the circle what does this teach us? There is no beginning or end to a circle. It is a symbol of the indivisible. Every point on the circumference is equidistant from an invisible centre, teaching us unity – or the principle of oneness. The circle is as smooth as possible, containing no angles whatsoever and it divides the space up into within and without. This symbol of the circle will mean different things to different people but it will serve to convey a significance that most can agree upon. The circle surrounds a point and to some this indicates a

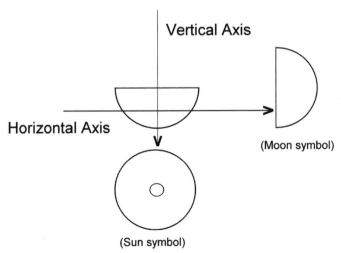

Vertical Axis

Horizontal Axis

(Moon symbol)

(Sun symbol)

Diagram #3

reminder of the state of non-duality (the infinite being without beginning or end) prior to embodiment symbolizing mindfulness or a good reflection in form of the formless. The diagram on the previous page begins by showing the circle and its 'dot-within' symbolism; this symbol serves as an archetype for every bowl.

There are two symbols used since time immemorial to represent the sun and the moon, and the diagram is intended to show how the archetypal shape of a singing bowl demonstrates the union of male and female principles in its design and shape. We have in the Tantric Buddhist *yab-yum* symbol (depicting the deity in union with their consort) just such a depiction of union between these two principles. With the bowls, it is interesting to note that we find the symbol whilst taking a view aligned with one such polarity. Thus the vertical view (will and masculine), the view from above, provides us with the astrological symbol for the Sun (masculine) – namely, the dot within the circle. The central dot is often present in the form of an inner circle upon the inside base of the bowl. Taking the horizontal view, that is, looking from the side, it is possible to find the symbol for the Moon (wisdom and feminine). Admittedly, we need to rotate the bowl 90° to find the exact symbol for the Moon (as in the diagram – horizontal line) but I find no problem with this. There are designs of bowls that cannot be said to conform to a semi-circular shape – 'Thadobati' bowls have straight sides for instance – but the other type, 'Jambhati', having curved walls, obviously more closely resemble the symbol for the Moon. The 'Thadobati' bowls look more like half a square, which symbol is linked to earth. These symbols for the Moon and the Earth are both feminine in nature. It is quite within the nature of the feminine to be flexible and so I find that the archetypal symbolism holds good.

The handle of the *ghanta* (the Indian handbell) is often cast with a depiction of the deity to which the bell is linked. The sacred form of the bell is derived from the abstract symbols of Brahmanism. In these, the universe is represented by a circle, and the form aspect of the universe by a semicircle. The semicircle is similar to a womb from which everything that is created emerges. The Hindu bell, as a sacred symbol, actual or depicted, was composed of these three symbols: the circle, which is the loop by which it is held; the hemisphere, which is its crown or top; and the lotus, which is stylized in its sides, flaring to a circular rim. This is normally stated with regard to the usual suspended bell, although the resting bell has three areas also.

Let us further contemplate this beautiful symbolism (intended or otherwise) of the union of masculine and feminine principles as shown in the shape of the bowl. Of the two lights in the sky, the Moon is queen of the night sky, full of billions of stars and galaxies, while the single Sun rules the day. The union of the Father and Mother principles brings forth the Child or the Son/Sun – the divine light in the heart of all of us. Each singing bowl, being a union of these two principles, therefore can come to symbolize the child. As the moon reflects the light of the sun, so, too, within the robe of the Great Mother the divine light is brought forth and reflected within each of us. We can visualize this central Sun as being a great bowl of light – a tri-unity of Father, Mother and Child (the threefold AUM of a bowl, if you will). As we each play our individual singing bowl we can be linked with this central Bowl/Sun as to a universal family of light and sound. Represented by the countless stars in the night sky, the sounding of bowls by many individuals around the globe can reflect or resound in each case the consciousness of this central bowl of light embracing all. Sounding the celestial note of that one central bowl we unite in a childhood (brothers and sisters) of tones where all is oneness. Each time we play our humble singing bowl we can consciously unite with this global family of the bowl and so enter the universal family through the door of sounding light.

Certain ancient (and indeed modern) religions have conceived of the creator as being both father and mother and viewed every single part of life as being the child, the product, of this union between spirit and matter. We can meditate on this deep symbolism simply by holding our bowl and contemplating its beautiful shape. In a way this archetypal form could be indicating to us that the aim of a bowl is to suggest to us, through the language of symbolism, the union between opposites. In this union there is a transcendence of dualistic thinking, so that the bowl shape points towards that level of awareness that is beyond those aspects of life that are impermanent when separate – and yet, surrendering to unity with the spirit of the permanent reality – partake of oneness from the greater view of a more enlightened being. As the ancient Buddhist philosopher Nagarjuna said, '*Nirvana* and *samsara* are one'.

The bowl itself is of one piece, yet can also be seen as composed of these two symbolic forms. It thus provides us with unity (or biunity) and multi-unity (a form of unity not reduced to a singularity but rather embracing all via coordinated differentiation). In Tantra we find the male and female principles in union (in statues depicting this, it is often interpreted by others to be a sexual embrace), to symbolize no division between the two great principles in life. Form and emptiness are one. Emptiness and form are one. In the form of spirituality taught by White Eagle (which can be considered esoteric Christianity) we are taught that God is both Father and Mother with the final member of the Trinity being the universal Christ Spirit. We can see the union of the Father and Mother Principles thus reflected in the union of the Sun and Moon symbols found in the archetypal design of the bowl.

The archetypal symbolism of each bowl, thus set out, can be a useful opening, if we so wish, to Tantric philosophy. We might regard the core belief of Tantra to be, 'Be in the world and *of the world*' – because the Tantric philosophy embraces spirit and matter as being just two sides of the same coin. In such a philosophy the suggestion is that through our bodies ('of the world') we can experience the spiritual. Also Tantra teaches us that if we accept our limitations (and our unconscious) we can progressively work through them, transforming them, whereas on the Sutric path (with which we are perhaps more familiar, it being that of the monk, the renunciate) we deny bodily attachments; we turn away from the world. Tantra, on the other hand, teaches us to work with what we are – or what we have – although such a path often recommends beginning from the Sutric position! In the main, Buddhist monks follow this Sutric path of renouncing the world – which can be seen as being a denial of life, exemplified by celibacy, the shaved head, abandonment of possessions, and so on. The sense of hearing may thus thereby be denied too, but through the Tantric Buddhist stream it is included – and leads to the use of sound as part of the path to enlightenment.

Attachment to sound can be transformed into a transpersonal approach to sound. It becomes the vehicle for the gods (such as with *bija* mantras). As an example of how Tantra works with what we have, let us consider anger. We can deny our anger (where it can then become hidden, unconscious, as sometimes along the Sutric path), or we can accept it and work to transform this energy so that it becomes a spiritual ally. In one school of Tibetan Tantric Buddhism anger is of the Vajra family (being the distorted manifestation) whereas its highest level brings clarity. This is perhaps easier to understand when we realize just how focussed we are when angry and how, were we to put that focus onto a loftier subject (such as meditation), we would accomplish far more – being far less likely to be distracted. We are seldom distracted from the focus of our anger when absorbed in anger.

Let us return to contemplation of the bowls. Viewing our bowl along the horizontal axis and finding the semicircle we can perhaps meditate or contemplate the fact that half of the bowl is *in* the physical and half of it is *out* of the physical. That is to say, the bowl's very curved walls suggest to us that it is half of a sphere or globe. We can conclude that perhaps this signifies that birth into the physical world should automatically call forth a corresponding need for connection with the other, non-physical half of life? This would thereby unite the world of form to that of the formless – our non-dual view. We can see in this a reflection of the hemispherical 'planetary pattern', which is found, for instance, in the astrologer Dane Rudhyar's holistic approach. The nighttime half (Moon) balances the daytime half (Sun). Day and night begin their respective cycles at dawn and dusk – the times when meditation is considered most efficacious – and thus at the symbolical Ascendant/Descendant, which is the horizontal axis. This is in turn reflected in the shape of the bowl when it is at rest or being played. This line is the axis of relationship between self and other, self and not-self, which is fundamentally the law, 'Love thy neighbour as thyself' – and therefore the connection between love, fire and light.

In astrology, the hemisphere of the Ascendant is to do with self

– that is, what we know – whereas the hemisphere of the Descend-
ant is of the unknown, or 'other(s)'. This is also the horizon of
awareness – the part of us which experiences change. In relationship, do we open ourselves completely to the 'other' and so become
absorbed into them, or do we retain our own separateness and
isolation? At what point along this scale do we place ourselves?

It is as if we start off with half of the picture and then set out
to find or discover the other half either in ourselves or in others.
Perhaps in the final analysis it is all One? The image is of the God
Within and the God Without – or of the Individual and the Universal, the drop and the ocean.

To explain this further, there's the physical and human being
that I think of as myself, here upon the planet, walking about, and
then there's the essential aspect of myself – the part that caused my
involvement with this material form. When I can more fully open
up to that essential Self, then I can truly sound my own unique note
within the universal orchestra – within the music of the spheres.

I then find fulfilment as a complete being. This also includes
the male finding his inner female and the female finding her innermost male energy. But above and beyond this it is entering into the
great silence and the stillness to hear that inner life coming from
our own heart. The flame of our true spiritual identity is then
given a chance to shine forth – it is given the space to grow. Then
that which was formerly invisible becomes visible as it begins the
process of incarnating into our physical lives – individuation! True
individualization, which process begins archetypally at the age
of twenty-eight, is the time of our Saturn return and of our progressed Moon. This planetary 'pair' is connected with father and
mother (bowl with male and female, Tantra with Father–Mother
God) and also with our fundamental identification of self, which is
so important in its influence upon how we enter into relationships
(the horizon).

We have physical ears, emotional ears, and mental ears. Our
emotions and thoughts are vibrational sound waves. Emotional
moods and mental attitudes are thus conditioned by sound.

Our life is nothing but a succession of exchanges made with
the universe. Cosmic life enters us, we permeate it with our

own emanations and then we return it. Again we absorb this life, and again we return it. These continuous exchanges are what we call nutrition, respiration and also love. And the moment when these exchanges cease is what we call death.

So we must make exchanges with the earth in order to live on the physical level, exchanges with water to live on the astral level of the heart, and exchanges with air to live on the mental level of the intellect. And lastly, we must make exchanges with heat and light in order to live the life of the soul and the spirit.

Everyone knows that the physical body needs food to survive, but the heart, mind, soul and spirit also need to be nourished. It is ignorance of this truth that causes humans to lose all sense of life's meaning.

Omraam Mikhael Aïvanhov[1]

The Shape of the Bowl

In order to see whether the three areas of the bowl can find a link with an appropriate trinity familiar to Buddhists and Bon let us consider the practice of *dzogchen*. Both Bon and the Nyingma school of Tibetan Buddhism have *dzogchen* as the highest level of attainment. Although *dzogchen* is the 'single great sphere', for convenience it is described as having the three aspects of base, path and fruit: 'base' because the ground of *dzogchen* is the primordial state of the individual; 'path' because *dzogchen* is the supreme direct and immediate path to realization; 'fruit' because *dzogchen* is the consummation of enlightenment, namely liberation from the cycle of illusory samsaric transmigration in one single lifetime.

Although the bowl is undoubtedly a single instrument, yet it has three aspects too, namely the Rim, the Base and, uniting these two, the Wall. Were we to seek to align these with the three aspects of *dzogchen* we could perhaps find that the 'base' relates to the base of the bowl; the 'path' to the wall of the bowl, and the rim to the 'fruit'. The base of the bowl would then represent the stillness out of which the potentiality of sound is to be realized and the wall of the bowl would indicate the variegated path into manifestation. Finally, the rim forms the point at which stimulation is applied and actualization is achieved and where the consummation of the purpose of the sounding device is materialized.

When we come to consider this threefold structure of a singing bowl we can further relate these fields of sonic activity to the three main vehicles that we all possess while living on earth – that is to say with our thinking, feeling, and willing, which are associated with our mental, astral, and physical bodies respectively. Actually, the sounds produced by emphasis upon any one of these areas within an individual singing bowl reflect a relationship with the trinity of principles that comprise our individuality. In Tibetan Buddhism we find another trinity: the mind of Buddha, the voice of Buddha, and the body of Buddha. Again, we can link it to the *triratna* (the 'Three Jewels' of Buddhism) with the *dharma* at the base, the *sangha* in the wall and Buddha (the 'Awakened One') at the rim. Then we have *yang* or *yin* rims that we could link to the Sutric and Tantric paths respectively.

To continue our analogy, the rim of the bowl thus relates to the head, the wall relates to the heart, and the base to the will and action. A lot of bowls will be comparatively dormant in their base, reflecting the intention of the bowlmaker to produce a bowl that will assist us in our meditation practices, where physical inactivity furnishes us with the opportunity to focus our energies upon higher, non-physical things. Still within the basic variety of designs possible from our primary trinity, there are other bowls intended to place a particular focus upon another area of the bowl design and so awaken through its resonant field yet another area of consciousness.

Among these are bowls with a considerably thicker rim than normal. When we have a bowl with a very thick rim it will produce a higher tone than a bowl of similar size lacking the thicker rim would. We are often surprised to find such a large bowl sounding a higher pitch than smaller bowls, and it is precisely because of this thicker rim. The higher tone affects the upper regions of our body – the throat or head region – so that these higher pitches call forth qualities residing in our higher mind, and in particular the quality of wisdom. Without the thick rim we have the mellower sound of the wall of the bowl and these lower pitches reach the

area of our torso and so resonate more with our heart energy –
with our love energy.

When we have bowls possessing an active base (such as Water Bowls and Jumping Bowls) we enter more into the sphere of
action, where it is easier to receive images of water flowing over
rocks, of prayer flags blowing in the wind, of the pennant fluttering over a mountain peak, of tall grasses blowing in the wind, or
of patterns of light flickering across the ripples of the sea or upon
the surface of a lake in the dark of the evening, and sometimes of
fishes or animals darting in and out of vision. Or again, we easily imagine dolphins swimming and singing in the sea. Somewhat
rarely we may also hear the voice of a teacher in the murmurings
of an appropriately sounding jumping bowl.

Certain special Water Bowls (such as the one on the left in
the photograph above) have a low wall and a thin rim, and this
design places more emphasis upon the base of the bowl, which is
then far larger, relatively speaking, than is usually the case with
singing bowls. With these bowls perhaps we can deduce that we
are 'activating' that area of our being which is normally silent?
Those non-physical realities are becoming awakened within ourselves with attendant mystery – as reflected in the sounds. There
are several varieties within this category. Some respond very well
to being tapped underneath – where the sound of the bowl's pitch
is bent, producing a somewhat eerie sound. Others produce more
of a whistling sound through their high partials whilst the bowl is
being stroked. All of these can serve to enhance our listening ability to the point where we hear sounds within the sound and so expand our hearing to other dimensional realms of vibratory reality.

Head and heart must work together, and for the Tibetan Buddhists this combination takes the form of wisdom and compassion.

Let me now summarize what I've already said about these three primary areas, namely the rim, the wall, and the base.

The **Rim** can be either thick or thin (*yang* or *yin*) and then the thickness at the rim can be built up upon the outside of the wall, or upon the inside, or going both ways, or the rim can be bent inwards or outwards acutely without any thickening of the metal. I've one rare form of bowl where the wall continues upwards at a similar thickness to the wall but there is an outward *yang* lip finishing beneath the *yin* wall. In my collection I have types of the latter bowls, where the wall has been bent inwards at the rim but the overall shape of the wall is bent outwards (see the Shakti Bowl pictured below, p. 266 – this is best stroked). The opposite situation is where the rim is bent outwards whilst the rest of the bowl's wall was bent inwards towards the rim in a shape resembling a cone (Tantric Bowl, pictured below, p. 267 – this sounds best struck). With Bengali bowls nowadays the deposit of extra metal at the rim tends to be as a kind of block, whereas with other bowls there can be a more gradual thickening (inwards, outwards or both ways) resembling more of a triangle (in cross section). For thickening outwards, see the Padmasambhava Bowl below, p. 263. This can be a wide thickening at the rim, or not quite so noticeable. The effect of this feature is to give qualities akin to a tuned gong (these carry the various names bossed, domed, or nipple gongs), whereby the range of harmonics is lessened, and the desire is to focus upon one tone rather than a wide variety of tones. However, it is unlikely that these were intended to be tuned bowls: rather, the effect upon the sound is to produce a high-pitched note that is very clear, with few distractions, whereas with *yin* bowls there are more harmonics (as with a symphonic gong). Some bowls are uneven at the rim, meaning that the height or length of the wall varies around the bowl; this produces a larger range of partials.

The **Wall** can be comprised of a rather sharp bend upwards, rising as though at 90° to the base (as with bowls from Orissa – which are plentiful in the market as I write) or any kind of curve (sharp or smooth) either coming all the way from the base up to the rim or curving only part way up and then straightening onwards up to the rim. This straight (or flat) wall can be turned inwards or outwards. Sometimes the bowl features a continuous curve, but then straightens for about half an inch below the rim. The bowls I have termed Vase bowls uniquely curve inwards below the rim and then back outwards up to the rim. Further variations also occur with regard to the wall, which may be curved (somewhat resembling the contour of a circle so that the rim is not the widest diameter of the bowl); again, it may curve upwards to a certain level and then turn inwards in a kind of conical form. These latter types have been called Elephant Bowls, as they resemble an elephant's foot. They can be either *yin* or *yang*, and originate from Bharampur (see photo on p. 266). The *yin* variety I've lately seen called 'Remuna bowls'. The wall itself can be thick or thin – the ancient Chinese discovering that this had a considerable effect upon the sound of the bell or bowl. *Yin* bowls provide the wall with maximum flexibility, thereby producing a greater range of partials.

The ***Base*** can be either wide or narrow. In the centre of the base there can sometimes be a kind of dimple (where the base has been hammered into a dome rising upwards in the inside of the bowl) or there can be a hollow form here that is more conical in shape (so-called Lingam Bowls, or otherwise Meru Bowls). The latter usually have a very thick rim too and a thicker base. The Lingam is the Cosmic symbol of the One Supreme. Manipuri Lingam bowls have this dome on the inside centre but the outer base of the bowl is flat – leading one to conclude that this central form is solid. More recently a three-dimensional Buddha-like figure may be found on the inside centre of a bowl. With the Water Spirit bowls the base is convex (in the side-on view) with an upward-raised dimple in the centre, while the walls splay outwards (see photo on p. 267). In other variants the meeting place between the flat base and the curved wall can be very acute – as if pressed out using a machine – while on other occasions the distinction between base and wall may be scarcely discernible. The base can also be very thin or the same thickness as the walls or thicker. It may have become thin through years of being wiped clean after being used for eating or drinking.

Various combinations of these several factors can be called upon when a singing bowl is created, which leads to a wide range of forms.

There will of course be different ratios pertaining between the diameter of the base and the diameter of the rim of the bowl. Some bowls are much wider at the rim than at the base (Shakti Bowls, for instance), whilst others are wider in their base and narrower at their rim (such as Elephant Bowls – which are also known as Chama bowls). Yet others are a similar size (bells from Orissa, Bhutan, Burma, etc) giving a straighter wall. In the former category, of bowls wider at their rim, are ones from Assam, Manipur, and other places.

So the **Wall** (from base to rim) can be:

Growing Wider (Water Spirit Bowl)
Growing narrower (conical, as in Elephant Bowl & Tantric Bowl)
Very gradually curving
A sharp curve finishing one third up the wall or lower
Spherical
Straight (See Thadobati, below)
In or Out near the rim
In near the rim (Elephant Bowls, Mani Bowls, Bengali Bowls)
Wider at rim (Padmasambhava Bowl)

Padmasambhava Bowl – wider rim (yang), built up on the outside of wall.

Often the presence of a line or two around the outside wall will be where the changes in the contour of the curves in the wall take place. This may be similar to the markings upon modern Paiste gongs that show where changes occur in the formation of the gong as it transforms from a flat plate into the gong shape. Such signs serve to indicate to the instrument maker where alterations take place regarding the shape.

Some bowls have a markedly uneven rim producing variations in the height of the wall. This effectively provides us with different lengths in the bowl's wall so that longer or shorter lengths produce deeper or higher tones respectively. This thereby produces a larger number of partials in the sound that can result in the phenomenon of doublets because these variations are only slightly different in pitch providing an oscillation between partials so close together audibly heard as 'beats'. A low wall will produce a higher tone (masculine/thinking) while a tall wall brings a lower sound (feminine/feeling).

The **Base** can be:

Flat (smooth or coarsely hammered)
Curved (Concave)
Curved (Convex)
With a base added (welded on or cast as part of the design)

Moreover, it can:

be wide
be narrow
have a small raised dome upon the inside centre
have a raised conical indentation upon the inside centre (Lingam bowls)
have a solid raised dome upon the inside centre but with a flat base (Manipuri Lingam)
be very thin
be thick

Nowadays we can find a three-dimensional casting of the Buddha or else a mandala-like pattern of deities (or Dhyani Buddhas) and the like, present upon the inside base of the bowl.

These are all recent innovations and are not be present in genuine antiques.

There are potential differences in the area where the base meets the wall:

From the flat base a gradual curve up to the wall (*above left*)
From the flat base a sharper curve up to the wall (*above right*)
From a wide flat base a very sharp curve up to the straight wall (*below left*)
From a medium-sized base with a sharp demarcation line onto the wall (*below right*)

And needless to say bowls are created from all variants of these factors.

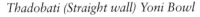

Thadobati (Straight wall) Yoni Bowl

Sharp angle from base to wall

The Shakti Bowl, getting wider as the wall rises, resembles the downward-pointing triangle. Downward, descending: meaning

response from the higher regions above, perhaps.

The Elephant bowl (pictured below), getting narrower as the wall rises, has some resemblance to the upward-pointing triangle. Aspiring upwards, it reminds us of deities – Kali, Shiva, Sanat

Kumara, Durga – that assist us in rising above our worldly cares, concerns and interests in a process of self-refocalization. Several of mine are consecrated to such deities.

> The hemisphere stands for the dark and motherly forces of the earth, the transforming power of death (and rebirth), the concentration of yoga and asceticism (ascetics and yogins always preferred cemeteries).

The cone as well as the similar pyramidal forms, characterized by one-pointedness and vertical direction, stand for the forces of the sun: light and life, represented by the fire altar (*harmika*) and the tree (spire).[2]

The Water Spirit Bowl

This Tantric bowl has a rather dissonant sound and seems to be best struck

Aum, and the Trinity of Love–Wisdom–Power

The holy Word OM is also spelt AUM. If we contemplate how the human voice produces this three-part sacred Word, then we find that A (ah) is sounded deep down in the rear of the throat. The U (ooh) then resonates within the central cavity of the mouth and M (mmm) is produced by the lips, with the mouth closed.

We find correspondence between this three-part Word and the bowls. 'A' functions as the base of the bowl, 'U' as the wall and 'M' as the lip or rim.

'A' relates to that Power which is behind all things. 'U' carries the sustaining energies that assist us along our journey between 'A' and 'M'. M is the end and yet not the end. Our mouth is closed yet our voice is still sounding. If you practice this sound with a loose, relaxed jaw, then the lips will vibrate and you can feel this stimulating the head area. It thereby links us with our wisdom.

We can find a number of other related trinities if we further link these three sounds to the three *marga* (the three main paths of spiritual unfoldment) in the *Bhagavad Gita*: *karma* [action]. *bhakti* [love], and *jnana* [wisdom].

AUM	Marga	Bowl	Trinity	Threefold body	Gods
A	*karma*	base	power	willing	Brahma
U	*bhakti*	wall	love	feeling	Vishnu
M	*jnana*	rim	wisdom	thinking	Shiva

Ponder an Egyptian pharaoh sitting upon his throne and you may catch a sense of the power behind that supports him. With the 'A' sound (as in father), there comes a similar connection to the invisible power that brought us into being. The 'A' sounds at the back of our throat. As the form of the 'A' rises to its peak so, too, it points towards that which is beyond (or behind) form. The Pharaonic throne was often a cube, representing stability, for with its six identical square surfaces a cube provides a more stable physical foundation than any other solid form. There is that stability which comes from being rooted in the divine consciousness or to one's spiritual teacher (as in the *guru yoga* tradition). There is also a sense of the Hindu creator god Brahma, and a sense of omnipotence.

The bowl has a flat base (no matter what the size of this) that rests upon earth, preventing the bowl from wobbling once struck.

This stability is an important quality to develop within ourselves. We may see a resemblance to the tree, whose trunk is immovable, indicating to us that when it comes to fundamental principles we should be unwavering. But the branches move and sway with the passing winds. So we may give way on matters of little concern and thus avoid inflexibility, but we must strive to become absolutely stable when it comes to our deepest convictions and inner loyalties – the deeper principles within ourselves. We must remain constant in our efforts to 'walk our talk', or to put into practice those deeper truths revealed to us during moments of insight and inspiration. In this there is a recognition of where we have come from – or, as it is said, 'Show me your face before your mother was born'. As an exercise we can link our listening to the inaudible 'nada' sound-current (experienced by most as a high-pitched tone), the 'absolute sound', and link the 'A' to our first two chakras. As we listen to this inaudible sound as an 'A' we do so as if the sound was originating from these two lower chakras. There is much more on this inaudible sound in Chapter 17.

'U' (as in true) brings the quality of being sustained along the journey. There is therefore a link here to guides, or to the Christ Star (or North Star, the Pole Star) that we follow to the birth of the Great White Light within our spiritual heart. This time, as an exercise, listening to the nada 'absolute sound' with the 'U' can bring this sense of flowing. We feel the relentless movement towards the sea that a river has, even as it cuts something of a U shape in the landscape. This feeling may link with the solar plexus, the hrit padma chakra (between the solar plexus and heart chakras), the heart and throat chakras: those that relate to the flow of energy. So, again, we listen to the inner sound current as if it were stemming from either one of these chakras. The guiding six-pointed Star represents a balanced power, even as our heart chakra rests in the centre of our seven main chakras – a balance point. A balance between life and death (A to M) places U at the centre. If we were to slice the bowl in two we would find a U revealed. The basic definition of a bowl is stillness at its centre. We can experience ourselves within the bowl, resting upon the base of the U-shaped form, and feel enfolded by walls of support guiding us along the journey. There in the silent centre of the bowl we would be linked to the centre of all, with our central Sun bringing the light for us to see our way. The elements of fire and water link to this energy. A sounding bowl calls attention, showing how we can attract spiritual support and assistance along our way. We unfold the quality of trust. This 'U' sound fills the space of our mouth, bringing to mind the quality of omnipresence. Filling our mouths, it enlivens the sense of presence: presence with regard to what lives within something. The sound is on a journey outwards into manifestation. There is a link here to the Hindu god, Vishnu the Sustainer.

'M' produces a gathering of power or a focal point at the boundary between the within and without of ourselves. Saturn was known as the 'ring-pass-me-not' and thus represented a boundary. Saturn rules the bones, foundations and condensation into solid form. As we seek to materialize anything it must be condensed down into coarser material substance. A lot of mantras (*bija*) end in 'M'. 'M' sounds like a drone and this humming sound fits neatly with the absolute sound of the *nadi* yogis. Listening to the inner sound as if it were coming from either of these two chakras, third eye and guru, it is easy to sense a merging of the two. The sound and the chakra are somewhat inseparable, leading to conditions of consciousness that transcend dualistic thinking. Saturn is linked to concentration, even as there is this concentration of energy at the lips. 'M' is the final point of this process of sounding. At this point it is almost as if one hears the words, 'I have arrived. I am totally here – or, I've arrived to beginning!'

The process began in heaven (the invisible) and it came down to earth; it now returns to heaven (the formless realm). 'M', being the final sound of the AUM, is the last sound coming out of the throat; therefore it represents completion and the final stage, which, in the process of manifestation, would be Form. As the sound began with the A, was followed by the U and ends with this M, we have completed a cycle of sounding. A cycle is also a circle – a magic circle. Sound continues, vibrates, inside the closed form. What lives in the form is a presence! The Presence of what lives in all? – the presence of the essential spirit that is at the root of each one of us. The high overtones produced by sounding the M stimulates the head area and (as a final exercise using the AUM), silently sounding the M with the *nada* 'absolute sound' stimulates the crown and guru chakras. We can find this divine presence as our awareness of self awakens.

A rock is the end of a process (form). What lives in a rock? How much self-consciousness lives in a rock? The Tantric path concerns itself with what lives within the body and in transforming what we find there. The third member of the Hindu trinity, Shiva, links to this sound. If Shiva destroys anything, then what is destroyed are the illusions that keep us from pure consciousness – our true essence. When internally we sound the M alongside the nada absolute sound we focus upon the upper chakras of throat and head, with the element Air linking to mind and thus wisdom and so to omniscience.

At times we may find bowls that have an affinity to one of these vibrations – the 'A,' or the 'U,' or the 'M'. This is due to their sound quality and not necessarily to their shape. For if a bowl has its rim emphasized it does not necessarily mean that it is in tune with the 'M'.

The three areas of the bowl then further give rise to three other possible categories of singing bowls, categories that arise from the traditional trinity of wisdom, love and will or power. Thus there are Will Ray Bowls, Love Ray Bowls and Wisdom Ray Bowls. As I mentioned in Chapter 12, the two rays linked to will are the first ray and the seventh ray. The love ray is found in the second and sixth rays. The two rays for the wisdom quality are the third ray and the fifth ray. Finally, there is the fourth ray, the one that all of humanity is said to be on.

Some bowls carry energies linked to all three major rays (love, wisdom and power) and others can resonate to two rays and, yet others, to a single ray. All of this has more to do with the energetics of the bowl rather than to its design or shape. In other words, a *yang* bowl might not necessarily relate to a will ray.

Bowls that work on the **Will** ray (given in the *Bhagavad Gita* as the path of *karma yoga*) may also be concerned with magic, but

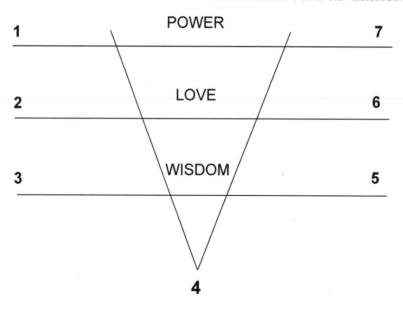

Diagram #4

they are certainly to do with centring ourselves, and with other matters of self-discipline and alignment – especially along the vertical axis. This could be a matter either of connecting to regions above and beyond this earth or else of bringing transcendental experiences and spiritual states down into earthly expression or actualization. To an extent the process of individuation resonates to this will ray. Bowls more closely associated with ritual would also come under this category, along with bowls that have a use in space cleansing or exorcisms. In the West we are more directed along the path of will or power. One example of this is our desire to control nature, which the various sciences explore. Will is linked to action, so that gaining some control over our actions in order that they serve a higher purpose is part of this will ray. Rather than responding instinctively to life's challenges, we strive to act from the highest that is within us – from the Christ Self or Atmic plane.

Aligning our will to the universal Will can often involve subjugation of our self-will to the whole. This relinquishment of self-will likewise connects with dedication and issues of commitment and the source of strength to continue along a chosen path even when the obstacles are great. Self-discipline can also mean a withdrawal from outer activity and thus a restraining of the senses.

When called upon to give up our self-will we should act from a centre of love, be at peace through acceptance, be motivated by the impulse to work for the good of the whole, and be prepared to lay aside our earthly nature that the divine may dwell within and direct our lives along ways of service.

As the sun gives its life-bestowing rays freely upon us all, so the *karma* yogi (in the realm of action) performs an action without attachment to the fruits of that action, but simply because it must be done. Key words here are change and willpower (for example, the willpower needed to give up alcohol, smoking, sugar or any habit). Mantra is used to bring about change in our lives and some bowls carry such energy.

> Remember, if the steep slope would be too smooth, the ascent would be still more difficult for thee. The stones not only do not hinder thee, but support thee. Do not forget it and bless these stones, for they may be used as steps.[3]

Listening to the Panic Bowl, we are aware of actual changes in the brain. Such bowls carry the energy of initiating new energy or new levels of being – new beginnings – along with the energy of striving, aspiring, emerging, change, direction, innovation, potentiality, adventure and sacrifice. They often possess an intense sound or energy, thereby arousing an effort of will.

Bowls working on the **Love** ray (which in the *Bhagavad Gita* is given as the path of *bhakti yoga*) would certainly include the heart chakra and healing bowls and those connected with water: not just 'water bowls' but bowls that otherwise have a link with this element. Perhaps through a visualization they seem to carry with them a peaceful lake or stream, or a strong sense of 'going with the flow', or fire. For the follower of *bhakti* the love of God is all. A musician along this ray has no need to know how his or her music works, for all that matters is the sense of being absorbed into a sense of oneness with all life. Such bowls can awaken qualities of devotion within our heart and rededication to our spiritual path. Deity Yoga Bowls would likewise enter this category as also Yab-Yum Bowls (see p. 253), and bowls awakening our compassion for others, simply uniting us with a broader loving awareness, ones that raise us up into feelings of ecstasy. This category includes bowls that carry the warmth of communion (or union – a sense of merging into) with a greater being, bowls that bring the feeling of a deep peace and a stilling of all restlessness – a broadening of our love until we can embrace all life and all the experiences of our life (both pleasant or painful), moving us ever towards unconditional loving. Forgiveness is born of love, as is self-sacrifice, along with generosity and a desire to give freely. A Master once said, 'We ask you to love everyone, but we don't ask you to like everyone!' A beautiful form in art (created from love) serves to align us with the harmony that inspired it. Bowls that carry a sense of beauty are likewise part of this love ray.

The phrase, 'Love thy neighbour as thyself', hints at a balance between selflessness and self-interest: not to love others more than we love ourselves, neither to love ourselves more than we love others – a gospel of perfection. What we love in our hearts will dictate our actions. Beautiful-sounding bowls serve to bring us into contact with feelings of gratitude for the source of all goodness. For the *bhakti*, all that matters is to feel love for and the love of their beloved – the Lord.

> Those who have met the Teachers in life know how simple and harmonious and beautiful They are. The same atmosphere of beauty must pervade all that approaches Their region. The sparks of Their flame must penetrate into the lives of those who await the Soon-Coming. How to meet Them? Only with the worthiest. How to await? Merging into Beauty. How to embrace and to retain? By being filled with that Fearlessness bestowed by the consciousness of beauty. How to worship? As in the presence of beauty that enchants even its enemies.[4]

Bowls connected to this ray carry a sense of establishing, stability, focus, beauty, cohesion, consolidation, defining, changelessness, cyclicity and rhythmicity.

Bowls linked to the **Wisdom** ray (in the *Bhagavad Gita* given as the path of *jnana yoga*) broaden our consciousness beyond the confines of our limited personality and into a sense of spaciousness – but a living space filled with being. They are bowls that we might say bring about some form of enlightenment or 'teaching'. As this could also relate to our awakening, we can include bowls that assist us in our understanding or appreciation of sound itself. Otherwise, this ray would include bowls that focus upon our minds, bringing clarity (during periods of indecision), or stillness, or transcending the rational lower mind (and even time) through linking us with a mythical sense of time or unfolding philosophical qualities. Such bowls could also affect our attitudes and thus help us adjust to 'impermanence'. Perhaps we can include here bowls that possess a voice that seemingly speaks to us – such as Jumping Bowls or Air Spirit bowls – or bowls that free our consciousness from over-involvement with the material world of form. The category includes bowls that encourage us to become silent within to catch their message, awakening wisdom within us. Wisdom is not necessarily intellectual knowledge but often 'inner knowing', contacted within during periods of stillness and silence. Bowls that help to still our minds or emotions carry this wisdom ray.

The mind has two aspects, namely the higher and the lower mind. These two levels to the mental realm are distinguished by the presence of form or formlessness. Bowls that awaken this intuition and assist us in rising up above the rational level of thinking bring something of this wisdom ray. Discriminating wisdom is a keyword here. For the *jnana yogi* the avoidance of entanglement with anything other than the ultimate truth of essential consciousness – the I AM – is the ultimate transcendent wisdom of simply Being. All that remains is the witness.

> Women, it is you who are to weave and unfurl the banner of peace. You shall stand guard over the amelioration of life, you shall light at every hearth a beautiful fire, creative and inspiring. You shall tell your children the first word about beauty. You shall teach them the blessed Hierarchy of knowledge. You shall explain to the little ones the creative power of Thought. You can preserve them from disintegration and at the very beginning of their lives inculcate in them the meaning of heroism and self-sacrifice. You shall be the first to speak to the children of the advantages of spiritual values. You shall say the sacred word Culture.[5]

These bowls bring discriminating awareness, adaptability, flexibility, seeking, quest, discernment, self-knowledge, transition, enhanced communication, duality and non-duality, the above and the below, and choices. Here is a summary of the rays and the qualities the Gita puts with them:

WILL Ray : *karma* (action)

LOVE Ray : *bhakti*

WISDOM Ray : *jnana*

Some bowls resonate to one of these ray qualities, others to two, and some to all three. This trinity of wisdom, love and power represent the three spheres of being; mind, energy and body symbolized by the syllables *om, a'a,* and *hung* such as are found on the underside of modern *ting-sha* (we encountered them in Chapter 4). The forehead is the sphere of emptiness, the throat is the sphere of energy, and the heart is the sphere of form.

Some More Trinities of Awareness

These can be seen to be represented in the three areas of resonance within each bowl. The rim corresponds to the forehead; the main energy body (wall) to the throat, while the torso would correspond to the lower part, the base, of the bowl.

It is also true that there can be a focus within any one bowl upon one of these areas. For instance, some bowls may have an 'active' base (*hung*) – as in Jumping Bowls and Water Bowls. This is usually the silent area of a bowl – so, perhaps this is the voice of the silence? Other bowls, particularly *yang* bowls, focus upon their rim (*om*) by virtue of having a thick lip, while there are also bowls which have a focus upon their sides (*a'a*) – which are correspondingly either thick or thin or else tall (as a dominant feature in the bowl shape). I've noticed that with these latter, there is often a healing quality about their sound – very stilling and soothing.

Similarly, it might be possible to find a link between these three areas and the three Tantric spheres of being – known as *dharmakaya, sambhogakaya* and *nirmanakaya*. Ngakpa Chogyam writes:

The three spheres of being are called: *cho-ku, long-ku* and *trul-ku*. These terms are so exorbitantly rich in meaning that it is not at all possible to give them concise one-word equivalents in Western languages – our vocabularies are simply not adequate to the task. However, as a starting point, we can relate to them as *emptiness, energy and form.*

Cho-ku – emptiness – is the sphere of unconditioned potentiality.

Long-ku – energy – is the sphere of intangible appearance.

Trul-ku – form – is the sphere of realized manifestation.

In Sanskrit these are known as *dharmakhaya* (cho-ku), *sambhogakaya* (long-ku) and *nirmanakaya* (trul-ku).

Cho-ku, long-ku and trul-ku, exist as a singular field – the fourth, or indivisible sphere of being. This is also known as *dorje-ku* (indestructible sphere) or *ngo-wo-ku* (essence sphere). Cho-ku, long-ku and trul-ku manifest as three inherent modes of access to the unitary experience of reality.[6]

The 'Banner of Peace' symbol of Nicholas Roerich (illustrated) offers a handy depiction of this interrelationship.

Higher-pitched bowls stimulate our consciousness–awareness–thinking selves, insisting on more of a concentration upon their sound and their overtones – and so, too, what 'ideas' (compositionally) are behind the sounds. *Medium-range bowls* work more upon the feelings. We open up to their warmth of tone and aren't so aware of overtones or musical direction. We are being led by our feelings, whereas with the higher-pitched bowls we're being led by our thoughts. In each case our focus should be upon the Light. *Deep-sounding bowls* bring us the sense of power and thereby link to will. This has to do with manifestation, and in order to build power we need to use rhythm. We can do this by way of the regular rhythmic timing of our strikes or when stroking a bowl with strong regular audible pulses (or beats – for more on this see Chapter 16). The sense of stability that arises from this regular sound leads to a greater sense of security and safety. The depth and power can then be related to mountains and even to the mythical Mount Meru, the centre of the universe, where our individual self-will merges into the universal will.

Elephant Bowls have a clean, crystalline sound that is purifying. This captures the sense of a return to the source, such as befits the aspiration upwards. There is a reduction in the number of partials present with this design that perhaps suggests a diminution of our outer activity and accompanies a return to the essential stillness of our centre, with a focus upon simplicity. In the White Eagle tradition, to which I belong, the metaphor is that of becoming still under the six-pointed Star. It is not simply a withdrawal from outer activity (relaxation or holiday) but also an aspiration to return to, or focus more upon, the spiritual plane – to link with the higher self, shifting our activity from the everyday outer level up to the inner – a level of vibration. It is akin to rising up into the mountains, where the air is fresher. We enter more into this air element with the angels of the air assisting us in rising above the lower mind; at this higher elevation of consciousness we can be open to the inspiration of a more ideal life and the discovery of the creative power of thought. With the rim strongly emphasized, there is a focus upon the mind, or wisdom, or *jnana yoga*. With this emphasis, we become more centred upon being than upon doing, and residing in our being we may more easily hear the voice of the silence, or the inner sound, the *nada*. Our attention becomes fixed upon this vertical axis, aligning that which is above to that which is below.

We could ponder this trinity within three types of bowls:

Begging Bowl – accept whatever is offered or given for food (i.e., experience).

Sacrificial Bowls – offerings of water or food to the gods.

Sacred Bowls ('voice' and 'mind' versus 'physical' bowls) – bowls psycho-spiritually charged and dedicated to a deity for use in Tantric deity yoga.

Let us look to other trinities in relation to the singing bowls.

To summarize, I place bowls into three main categories that can be linked with the three aspects of Buddha:

Buddhism and three bodies – Body, Voice and Mind of Buddha:

| Bowls | = | Physical | = | Body | mere sound. |
| Bowls | = | Voice | = | Soul | psychic content |

Bowls   =   Mind   =   Spirit   spiritual energies

And so there is the physical body of the bowl, then there is the sound (voice) of the bowl (*prana*) and then there is the spiritual dimension (mind) behind or contained through and within the action of sounding the bowl.

Aware of the three main areas of every singing bowl (rim, wall and base) you may consider the numerous trinities that you might wish to contemplate in that connection. So that whilst playing you could concentrate upon the rim with its link to thinking, or upon the wall of the bowl and its link to feeling or upon the base of the bowl and willing. Otherwise, you could consider which of these three may be prominent in your bowl. If a *yang* bowl then it would be the rim, if a tall bowl then the wall and if a jumping bowl or water bowl then the base. Then you could consider some of the links suggested to that area in the list below:

Matter exists in THREE states:	Gaseous	Liquid/fluid	Solid
= Link to the three bodies	Thinking	Feeling	Willing
= Link to the three types	Wind	Phlegm	Bile
= Link to Ayurveda	Vatta	Kaffa	Pitta
= Link to Hindu gods	Vishnu	Mahavesvara	Brahma
= Link to Chinese	Qi	Yin	Yang
= Link to three Hindu paths	Jnana	Bhakti	Karma
= Link to three Buddhist poisons	Greed	Anger	Passion
= Link to the Holy Trinity	Wisdom	Love	Will (Power)
= Link to three Bon divinities	Sky	Water	Earth

When sounding a bowl we are creating a point of change. Something is emerging from the invisible worlds. It is a birth of light. Durga (consort of Lord Shiva), in her form as Parvati, held a bell of divine power in her left hand and it was prayed to in this manner: 'OM to the bell striking terror to our enemies by thy worldwide sound! Drive out from us all our iniquities. Defend and bless us, O Lord'. The bell is here associated with the goddess and so with the divine world and its 'worldwide sound' appertains to its limitless spiritual force sounding not only to the listening ear of the petitioner, but, alongside the cosmic vibration of *om*, permeates the entire world or universes when it is struck! Therefore, consider what it is you wish to let loose for it affects the universe!

Herein we find another trinity or threefold cyclical pattern. These are easier to apply when striking the bowl and, while not necessary, you may wish to perform a simple meditative exercise using one or other of the progressions listed below:

Silence	Sound	Silence
Night	Noon	Night
Darkness	Light	Darkness
Bardo	Life	Bardo
Inaudible	Audible	Inaudible
Inaction	Action	Inaction
Alone	Together	Alone
Invisible	Visible	Invisible
Emptiness	Fullness	Emptiness
Within	Without	Within
Unmanifest	Manifest	Unmanifest
Darkness	Radiation	Darkness
Unconsciousness	Consciousness	Superconsciousness
Sunrise (gong)	Noon	Sunset (Bell)
Dawn	Day	Sunset
Incarnating	Purpose	Excarnating

14. Elemental Bowls

THE SHAMANIC and animist indigenous faith of Tibet has been grouped here, primarily in Chapter 3, under the heading of Bon, and in Bon we find an awareness of the beings of the invisible world that has carried over into Tibetan astrology. In animist belief, each of the elements contains a world of spirits (in our tradition these have names like undines, sylphs, fairies, gnomes, dryads, angels, and salamanders). For the Tibetans, a mountain god would abide in a certain mountain, and so on through creation. The Tibetans thus shared their world with beings living in the other realms of nature. A great many so-called 'primitive' cultures do this, but they may be reflecting a wisdom now lost rather than merely a superstition that today we dismiss.

In fact, modern traditions – including the way we look at bowls – may owe much to these ancient beliefs. The Theosophist, Geoffrey Hodson, in his book THE KINGDOM OF THE GODS, illustrates many angelic beings – gods of mountains, angels of healing, etc.[1] When I have seen angelic beings myself, they have resembled those depicted in Hodson's book. There are people who are capable of seeing into the subtle realms of nature and who can teach us about the brotherhood of all life. It is even possible to recognize a sound spirit living within certain singing bowls. The shaman Joska Zoos, for instance, painted the sound and light spirits that he saw.[2] As I've said, there are bowls that possess a strong spiritual power of quite precise qualities and characteristics. Just as there are great spiritual beings that abide within a human form (e.g., H. H. the Dalai Lama is considered to be a manifestation of Chenrezig, the patron deity of Tibet) so, too, the physical body of certain singing bowls may be considered the dwelling place for certain spirits.

One way of categorizing singing bowls evolves from such an understanding of the elements, and some singing bowls have an affinity to one or another of them, or even to several different

282 HIMALAYAN SOUND REVELATIONS

elements. It is also possible to find a link to one of these elements
simply from the sound that the bowl produces. Since 1986 I've
become convinced that certain of my bowls have been consecrated
to specific Dhyani or 'Meditation' Buddhas, while since 1983 I
have been discovering links to the elements with other bowls. This
is an aspect of the singing bowls that opened up for me since then.
The characteristics, symbols and qualities of the Dhyani Buddhas
is set out in Appendix C.

The five Dhyani Buddhas (or, more correctly, 'Jinas') and the
five Dakinis (their female consorts) are linked to these elements
within Tibetan Buddhist teachings. One of them, Amogasiddhi, is
depicted opposite, identified by his hand gesture or *mudra*. This
is not to say that any such (elemental) bowls are automatically
for use with the deities concerned (although there are some so
consecrated), rather that they have an affinity with the element
concerned. It may prove helpful to study the influence that the
sound of any one bowl sends forth from within this context of the
elemental world. Using the structure of the Dhyani Buddhas we
can see whether any of the several elemental qualities can be applied to the sound virtues of any of our singing bowls. This could
open a door into the effects from the sound of a bowl upon the
subtler dimensions – a gateway or portal to the inner dimensions
of sacred sound.

Dhyana means meditation, and we can see these buddhas as
referring to a fivefold process of meditation. They are all part of
the meditation process yet each comes into its own as we follow
the progression. There are a number of planets within our solar
system. We cannot live on all of these at the same time. For us,
here now, we are living on earth and our focus is upon earthly things. In a similar way we each have certain of the elements
in our psychological constitution more strongly than others. To
work with one of the deities will assist us in achieving a more
awakened manner of manifesting that element (or two). As 'Jinas'
they are conquerors – they have conquered isolationism. 'The one
is in the many. The many are in the one.' In Buddhism one is striving to overcome any sense of separateness but this does not mean
the annihilation of differences with a reduction into a singular

unity but rather awareness of the differences that doesn't disturb the overriding awareness of unity (a multi-unity). It is rather similar to a *nada yogi* performing music without ever losing the connection to the inaudible sound. It is difficult to express non-dualistic thinking within a dualistic language, and in some ways I'm trying to express the inexpressible in what I say here.

Each of the elements – wood, fire, earth, metal and water in the Tibetan system – represents a particular mode of action of cosmic energy in this terrestrial realm – respectively mobility, destruction, solidification (coagulation), cutting, and permeation (humidification). Another categorization is pacifying, increasing, empowering and wrathful (this fourfold version omits Vairocana as he is considered to be the ground of all). Wood is our familiar Air element while Metal is our Space element or Ether. It is possible to find that the sound of a bowl has qualities that can be referred to one or other of these elements. What follows is offered as a means of identifying if this is the case with your bowl(s). We begin with the Space element (the Buddha family – which has the eight-spoked wheel for its symbol).

While we listen to the sound of the bowl we might feel expansiveness, or a vastness, or a sense of spaciousness, or expanded awareness, and we could find ourselves experiencing more clarity as we become one with the sound and feel a sense of ease with life. If so we are being enfolded in the Buddha family headed by the Dhyani Buddha Vairocana ('One Who Completely Manifests' and also 'Supreme and Eternal Buddha', 'The Radiant One') and the bowl has a link to the Space element, bringing the wisdom of emptiness. The sense of radiance is as the light of the spiritual sun – the birth and source of light. A bowl linked to this energy can transport us straight into the spiritual worlds when we hear its sound. We immediately lose all association to this earth.

Some bowls might lead us into a pleroma (fullness) of space, where there is a delicate balance between our little human personality and our spiritual individuality – a connection with the void.

The colour for the Buddha family is the blue of its element, Space, which can either be just dull and blank or alive with the ubiquity of intelligence. The eight-spoked wheel is the symbol of the Buddha family, indicating all-pervading rule. The Buddha embodies sovereignty. For the female consorts of the Dhyani Buddhas differences exist in the Tantric texts so for consistency I shall use those found in *The Tibetan Book of the Dead*. The Dakini of Vairocana is Akashadhateshvari ('Sovereign Lady of the sphere of infinite space'). Each of the Dhyani Buddhas carries certain wisdom, and for the Buddha family this is the wisdom of emptiness. Tenzin Wangyal Rinpoche in his book, HEALING WITH FORM, ENERGY AND LIGHT[3] gives us the image of a vast open sky over the desert or the plains. In the same book he informs us about the spiritual development of each element, and for Space he writes, 'overcoming anger, increasing love'. Against each description of the Dhyani Buddhas below I have set a three-line summary from Tenzin Wangyal Rinpoche's book.

While we are listening to the bowl, do we find a strong sense of peace, or a sense of flowing with things, or again calmness and a sense of being relaxed and comfortable, maybe even with a more sensuous quality? Feelings of humility, or compassion, or intuitive and empathic qualities, or generosity of spirit are maybe awakened within us. We may feel as if we are gazing over a vast calm lake up in the mountains. There may also be a stillness linked with increased clarity or a sense of calm clear reflection – such as we'd find upon the surface of an absolutely still lake. If so, then these are qualities linked with the water element or the Vajra family ruled over by the Dhyani Buddha Akshobhya (the 'Unshakeable' or 'Immovable' One). The five Buddha principles constitute the basic mandala. Vajra's direction is the east, which is connected with the dispassionate clarity of dawn. The *vajra* (*dorje*), the thunderbolt sceptre that betokens indestructibility and precision, is the symbol for the Vajra family. He embodies steadfastness. The consort for Akshobhya is Locana ('She with the eye'). The colour of this element is white.

The wisdom of the Vajra family is mirror-like wisdom.
Image: vast, calm lake.

Spiritual development: overcoming jealousy, increasing openness.[4]

The sound of the bowl might inspire in us the sense of a great mountain and we may therefore find the qualities of strength, steadiness, security, focus and stability or groundedness. It may seem to provide us with a sense of direction, or else (through the sense of equanimity), it might bring the quality of humility, or tolerance. Otherwise we might feel connected to a sense of richness, profundity, or of the majestic, in which case there is a link to the Earth element and to the Ratna family, headed by the Dhyani Buddha Ratnasambhava (the 'Source of Preciousness', also 'Source of Precious Things' or 'Jewel-Born One') who brings the quality of the wisdom of equanimity. We are unlikely to find such qualities in small bowls as these will tend to produce a high tone (too high to suggest being grounded) although steadiness could be implied if the tone has that still quality (no warbling, fluttering or vibrato). Warmth and full sunshine and the lushness of the South is associated with the Ratna family. Its colour yellow can express either the putrescence of pride or the richness and wellbeing of gold. The Ratna family symbol is the jewel, which fulfils all wishes. He embodies compassion. Mamaki ('mine maker' [mother of all]) is the Dakini.

The wisdom of the Ratna family is wisdom of equanimity.
The image given is: powerful, solid mountains.
Spiritual development: overcoming ignorance, increasing wisdom.[5]

If we find that there is a sense of warmth with the sound or inspiration, creativity, or bliss, great energy, or a sense of strong will, then there is a link to the element Fire. Fire is also linked with light, so that if we have any sense of spiritual light being present, or a vibrating or pulsating light with the sound, then it has affinity with this element of fire. With spiritual light this is the quality of self-development, linked to the spiritual path with its attendant obstacles, the things that the fiery will overcomes. The Dhyani Buddha Amitabha ('Infinite Light') is associated with fire and the Padma family, and also the quality of discriminating wisdom.

Padma is connected with the West and with the brilliant display of the colourful qualities of existence expressed in the sunset. It carries the strong colour of red, evincing the seduction and heat of passion or the all-pervading warmth of compassion. The symbol of the Padma family is the lotus of compassion, the purified form of passion. He embodies Light. Pandaravasini (the 'white-robed one') is consort for Amitabha.

> The wisdom of the Padma family is discriminating wisdom.
> Our image is: fiery volcano.
> Spiritual development: inner fire, overcoming desire and
>   greed, increasing generosity.[6]

Again we might find that there is a certain quality of liveliness, a freshness, or quickness about the sound; the sound helps us to feel more flexible or adaptable or responsive and more easily open to change. The sound brings about an enquiring mind, or a love of knowledge, or desire for freedom, or a greater respect for community (perhaps even embracing non-human realms such as the angelic or elemental worlds) – the *sangha*. When some exceptional bowls are sounded, a sense that all will be accomplished can come. In fact, it already is accomplished – we are linked in with the field of energy embodying the potential to manifest anything. As with its element, the air, it is everywhere present – in which case these are air qualities linked to the Karma family. The Dhyani Buddha Amogasiddhi ('One Who Accomplishes What Is Meaningful' and also 'Almighty Conqueror' or 'Lord of Karma') rules the Karma family and signifies all-accomplishing wisdom. His consort is Green Tara ('all-accomplishing wisdom'). The Karma family connects to the cold, stormy energetic quality of the north. Its colour is green, expressing either envy or the energy of all-pervading action. The Karma family symbol is either a sword or a double *vajra*, both of which denote the fulfilment of all actions. He embodies dauntlessness.

> The wisdom of this Karma family is all-accomplishing
>   wisdom.
> The image is: fresh wind through the valley and across the
>   mountains.

Spiritual development: overcoming pride, increasing peacefulness.[7]

With the main elements of nature we have something that we all experience in some degree or another. We can commune with the earth through trees and flowers or walking barefoot upon the earth. To link with the air element we can listen to the wind through the trees, tall grasses, or even through the mountains. In Mongolia it is said that the origin of overtone singing comes from hearing the wind whistling through the mountains. Many of us have had the pleasure of being seated before a roaring fire, enjoying its warmth during cold times and listening to the cracking of the flames or watching fiery sparks rise up to rejoin the stars in the night sky. At other times we have enjoyed the warm rays of the sun upon our being, telling us that life is good. We are all friends with water, washing ourselves each day, and we love to swim in its 'body' and listen to the gurgling sounds of streams, the soothing sound of a fountain, or the rhythmic breathing and other sounds of the drawing and breaking of the ocean waves.

We can go even further and explore the angels of these elements. The great Angel of Earth provides all the variety of forms for life. The Angel of Water may be like the spherical form of a mass of water with countless tiny points of light that come from waves reflecting the sunlight. The Angel of Fire can be a mighty being of Golden Light directing the life-giving ray to all. The Angel of Air, blowing into each being the very breath of Life, raises us up into the higher regions.

Sitting in contemplation beneath a tree we may feel the closeness to the great mother of the world. It is the mother who provides creation with a range of physical forms with which to evolve and experience life upon planet earth.

Water and Air Spirit Bowls

I first came up with the idea of classifying certain of my bowls according to the elements around 1993. With Ululating Bowls and Water Bowls I had already made links to the elements of air and water respectively, but now I decided to see whether I could find bowls for the remaining elements. I had been buying bowls from the shop 'Frontiers', which was close to Portobello Road market, London, for some years, when I decided to ask David (who was in charge of selling the bowls) if he could keep an eye out for any unusually shaped bowls and to let me know if and when he had some. The shop dealt in tribal antiquities but also sold singing bowls, and subsequent to my request I received a call to say that a new assignment of bowls had arrived including some unusual ones. Among the hundreds of bowls I found three bowls of a design I'd not encountered before. These were shallow bowls with a sharp angle to their short walls that widened outwards; there was also a slightly convex shape to the outer underside of the bowl and a raised concave dome in the centre. I intuited that these were designed to work with water. I asked David for a container of water and placed an intuited amount inside and while I was stroking heard the most wonderful and astonishing sounds! Not wishing to be greedy, I decided to select two out of the three but as I listened to them it became apparent that they were a set, inasmuch as they were tuned together. So, somewhat reluctantly, and foregoing my desire to leave one for somebody else, I bought all three.

© Rose Perry

Water Spirit Bowl

The technique I used was outlined in Chapter 10. Listening to their sounds, sounds that so stimulate the imagination, the realization arose that what came from any one of these bowls would

2

6

7

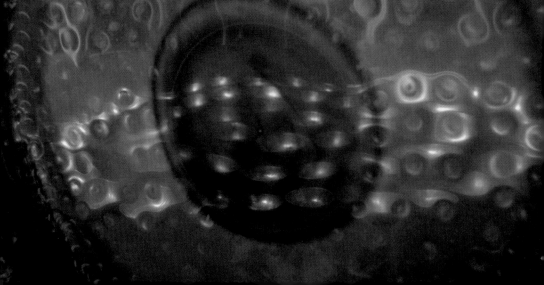

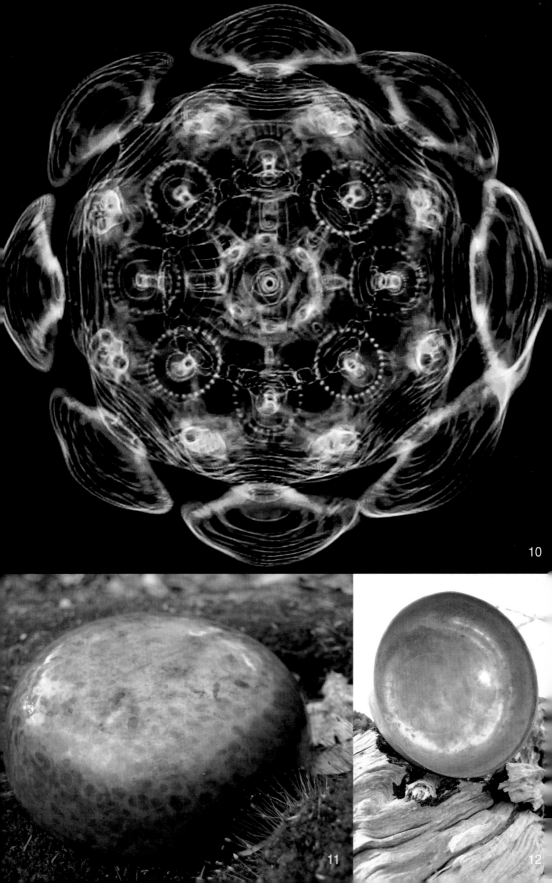

10

11

12

13

14

Pictures in this Supplement

Key to the Photographs

First page) 1. 'Padmasambhava' Bowl gleams in the middle of a line-up of others.

Pages two and three) 2. Going with the flow' (*Rose Perry*). 3. 'Silver Ray of the Great Master' *ting-sha*. 4. The author with 'Ocean of Great Bliss' Bowl (*Vlasta Marek*). 5. Spiral of *yin* bowls before gongs (*Oliver Nares*).

6. 'Blue Sunset Bowl', cymatic photograph (*John Stuart Reid*). 7. Fountain Bowl in action.

Pages four and five) 8. 'Divine Mother' Bowl, cymatic photograph (*John Stuart Reid*). 9. Yin spiral of bowls reflected in rear of Paiste Sun Gong (*Oliver Nares*). 10. 'Song of the Mountain Waterfall' Bowl, cymatic photograph (*John Stuart Reid*). 11. 'Under the heart' (*Rose Perry*).

12. 'Decay' (*Rose Perry*).

These pages) 13. 'Great Star Mother' Bowl, cymatic photograph (*John Stuart Reid*).

14. 'Silver Ritual' Bowl, showing strong evidence of silver mineral content (*Raphael Perry*).

15. 'Padmasambhava' Bowl, cymatic photograph (*John Stuart Reid*).

Final page) 16. 'Song of Crystal' Bowl, cymatic photograph (*John Stuart Reid*). 17. 'Oirot, Messenger of the White Burkhan', painted by Nicholas Roerich in 1925 (mentioned on p. 220).

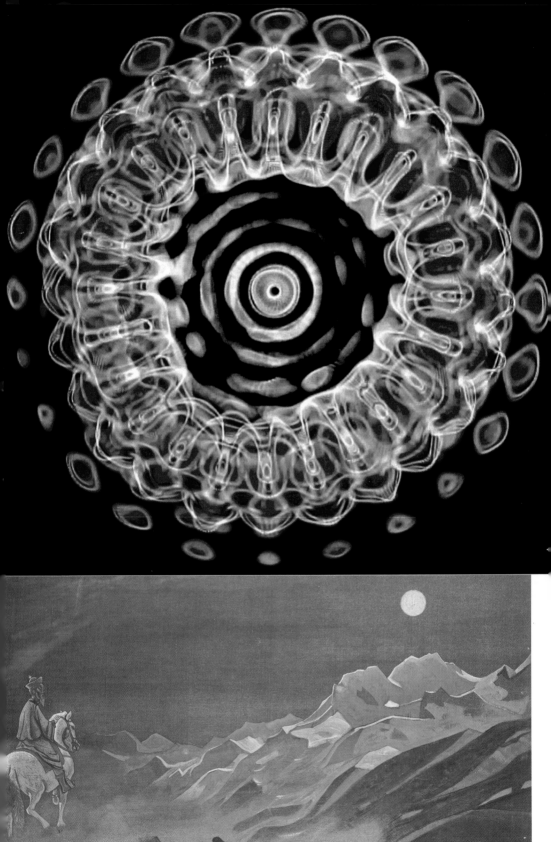

be very helpful to a student of astrology who was especially seeking to understand or empathize with the spiritual quality of the element water. I saw that they would help the student understand the soul lesson of persons either born under a water sign or with whom the element of water featured strongly in their horoscopes. They would also help whenever water was emphasized in Tibetan astrology. Listening to such a bowl would allow one more easily to enter into the water element and discover more about what lives in this element. Listening to these specific bowls I could so easily hear the sounds of the water elementals as they joyously rode the froth of the wavelets in mountain streams or swam with the water over rocks or diving down waterfalls. And so it was that I conceived the appellation Water Spirit Bowls for these bowls. I realized that, to an extent, all water bowls could be related to this water spirit or to those creatures that live in the water element, such as dolphins. Certainly there also comes a soul-like quality from the mysterious sounds of good water bowls. This particular set of three bowls was truly exceptional, though, and seemed to be so directly linked to water spirits that they transcended other water bowls.

Another aspect of engaging with the beautiful water bowls lies in their unpredictability. When you move the bowl around to produce the effect, you have no absolute control over what precise sound will come out of the bowl. It really is playing in the water. This helps us to get back in touch with our innocent childlike nature, if we have lost that. It opens up (within the language of sound) the strange realm of quantum physics and may serve to remind us that all came forth out of so-called chaos.

When we consider the numerous forms that water assumes – such as the springs and streams at the source, moving on to the flowing rivers, the still lakes, and then the ocean itself – we can catch a glimpse of the variety of worlds that Water Spirit Bowls can suggest. Let us consider for a moment the relentless rhythmic flow of the river towards the ocean, the entering into the ocean (and all the creatures that live and sing in the ocean) and how the water subsequently turns into clouds to float over land – and again descend as rain, to enter the same streams in that cyclic dance of life. Water features strongly in the Taoist philosophy of ancient

China. There, symbolic of taking the path of least resistance and 'going-with-the-flow', it contains something of the feminine or *yin* approach to life. This lends itself well to a procedure more akin to following the sound of the bowl home to where it lives, rather than a *yang* approach, effectively dominating a bowl. If a large rock from an avalanche finds its way into a river the water works around it – it does not reject it. This quality of acceptance is helpful for us along the path of initiation.

Some water bowls have a simple sound that moves alternating between two tones, but others can be far more complex and can contain a range of voices. To the ancients the water element was related to psyche, the soul. Some water bowls produce deep and mysterious sounds and reflect those great mysteries and the powers available from the greater initiations of life – even at times from the 'dark night of the soul'.

For the air spirits, as I explored the elemental connections further, there was a set of bowls already in my collection that were excellent for performing the ululation technique, and I immediately went towards these. Again, the technique is explained in Chapter 10. Here, I refer to a set I have built up that works particularly well using this technique, but primarily through stroking of the bowl. You may well need to experiment with how high the rim of the bowl is in relation to your open mouth and lips before you get the effect. Soon one tone will become louder than the others and you have it. I mostly use a back and forth action with the wand opposite to the mouth. These are also shallow bowls, most probably from Assam. I have found that they always have similar decorative patterns around the rim of the bowl, leaving me to conclude that they are made especially for this purpose.

Because they strongly connect with the spiritual aspect of the air element I originated the term Air Spirit Bowls for this type of bowl. I have another shape of bowl that works very well for ululating, but chiefly while it is being struck, and I have come across a few others of like design that work in the same way, again contributing to the view that these are their purpose. This ululation technique can sometimes be applied to other shapes of bowls, but the two types I've mentioned are so exceptional in applying this technique that I can only conclude that it must be an intentional part of their design.

Another purpose behind the struck version of such remarkable bowls would be for opening the hearing of the student of sound to the several notes contained within a bowl. Because the overtone structure of each bowl is unique, it would only apply to the actual bowl being listened to. Nevertheless that would serve to demonstrate how each bowl creates a number of audible subtones that together form its complex world of sound. I was visited several times by someone seeking sound healing who asked me afterwards how they would be able to tell if a bowl was good or not. I struck a bowl and asked him how many sounds he could hear. Although he had a degree in sound and worked as a sound engineer he replied 'One'.

'Well, you have a problem, then', I said, smiling, 'for I can hear seven! Hearing all of the sounds in a bowl and how well these co-exist together constitutes how we grade it'. I suggested he buy a certain CD of mine that had a track featuring specific bowls and designed to enhance our listening capacity.[8]

With the struck version of these bowls there is sometimes an optimum position along the rim of the bowl where all of the partials are almost equal in volume (there are typically from five to seven partials obtainable). This will not be marked upon the bowl, so it is again a question of experimentation. Some struck ululation bowls have a straighter wall so that no tilting of the head is necessary.

With all my Air Spirit Bowls the angle of the walls is quite acute. I need to tilt my head backwards, which is a useful but somewhat submissive position, inclining to the worship of higher Being. To the ancient initiates the element Air concerned itself with the ability to discriminate between the higher mind and the lower mind. The ability to hear the song of birds in the sound of such bowls assists us in contemplating how the song of the male bird attracts the female. It can be seen as a reflection of the song of our higher mind attracting the attention of our little earthly mind to rise, or fly upwards, into the higher dimensions of reality.

Laying aside the critical, reasoning, logical mind can be difficult for many of us. This aspect of the mind is very useful for everyday practical affairs, but we also need to exercise the more formless area of the mind, which deals with abstract idealism and philosophy and mystical insights into deeper levels of truth. Like the bees we can learn to extract the life-giving substance from out of the flowers of our earthly experiences.

Earth, Fire and Space Element Bowls

Turning towards yet other types of bowls from my instrumentarium, I remember having associated certain of these bowls with particular mountains (for instance, 'Mount Kailas' Bowl and 'Mount Kanchenjunga' Bowl), and it became obvious to me that they could be categorized as being of the Earth element. There is a certain sense of being grounded that comes with the sound of these bowls, or else they may produce a very deep, centred sound (giving the impression of largeness of size), upon which we are seemingly resting. They can thus give us a sense of feeling supported by life. We can take this sense of being supported further by contemplating that the laws of the universe do, in fact, truly support us, whereas all else is impermanent.

When being stroked with the leather wand a bowl will sound slowly, the four pulses providing us with the symbolism of the square, or of the cube (both earth symbols), either of which increases this sense of stability, solidity, substantiality, security and dependability. From it we also get the symbol of the cross within the circle, and so we have the four elements as four equal-sided arms. They may provide us with a sense of stillness at the centre of the cross or the 'hub of the wheel'. It is only when we are stable and secure upon the physical plane of being that we have the time to devote to higher things. Focus upon the deep-sounding fundamental of large bowls is particularly helpful in linking with this earth element. There will also be a sense of stillness with such bowls – in contrast with many whose sound is exciting or very active, or that have a fast pulsation in the first partial. There is also the sense of being centred and stable and of not moving very far from the physical body. We may be reminded of rocks or stones and the sense of resting still, and the absence of physical movement. Or we may have the sense of rhythmic movement, away outwards into external life and then returning home with our experiences as soul food.

My 'Golden Voice of the Sun' Bowl produces a very warm feeling and, through the enlarged gold content – attuned as that is to the sun – has a definite warmth to its sound, accompanied by a childlike joyousness. I could see that this, along with what I term 'Chod Rite' Bowl (actually a Jumping Bowl that produces an inspiring effect of watching flames leaping around oneself and destroying all the negativity within – but has no emphasized gold content), went well with the element Fire. To the ancients the element Fire was related to the initiation of Divine Love and therefore it is also possible to relate any bowls awakening warmth within, or the love quality, to this fire element. Heart chakra bowls resonate with the love energy within the heart chakra – be that divine love or human love (compassion for others). There can be a dispassionate quality here wherein little self-interest is present, and these bowls possess a certain coolness alongside of the quality of warmth. The quality of love, having risen above desire, expands into more selfless regions and is related more to agape, or spiritual love, than to the other Greek words for love such as eros. It is blissfulness. Another example of fire finds expression in 'Golden Song of the Sun' Bowl (a throat chakra Jumping Bowl) that produces a lovely golden light on the astral plane. This is very helpful in relieving symptoms of depression, for fire inspires and ignites our spirit.

Lastly came the Space element, and that lent itself very well to certain bowls that are connected with certain Tibetan practices that embody this Space element such as *shi-ne* and Sky Gazing, whilst the Chintamani Bowl and Padmasambhava Bowl also had qualities in their sound that brought the energies of the Space element. Both of these bowls resonate with the thought of tranquillity and stillness, which is in tune with this space element.

I also like to include in this categorization other bowls, the energies of which resonate with the spiritual consciousness of the Buddha known as the *dharmakaya* body, or *nirmanakaya* body. These latter carry a real sense of vastness, great spaciousness, or of super-consciousness, and convey the sense of an expansion of one's awareness into that One Great Universal Being. They can mirror that connection with vastness of space found in performing the '*soham* breathing' that connects us to the divine I AM – uniting our individual dot with the universal circle, our wave with the whole ocean. Traditionally, this is a silent breathing meditation. The ancients taught that breathing in produced the sound of *so* and that of the outbreath was *ham*. While breathing we inwardly listen to these two sounds. Furthermore, we contemplate the *so* as being the wave of our individual existence (the dot) and the *ham* the ocean of life (the circle). This helps to balance the archetypal relationship between the lower and higher self.

I trust that I am making it clear that (perhaps with the exception of the Water Spirit Bowls) such appellations are strictly according to the capacity of certain bowls to resonate with one or more of these several elements. I am not linking the elemental qualities to any specific design features and so I cannot advise you simply to seek a specific pattern or shape in order to procure a bowl for any one element. You must decide for yourself, as few sellers can be trusted, most especially when the price tag goes up with the names and what they claim (now that I have written this I fully expect to see bowls on sale with all these names)! It has far more to do with the properties inherent in the sound and energy of the bowl. Ultimately, it is probably the case that the only way to determine whether any one single bowl possesses a link with one of the elements comes from acquainting ourselves more fully through meditation with these elements and doing so chiefly from within the Tibetan culture and the Bon tradition in particular. I have never been told when purchasing a singing bowl myself that it is for one of these elements. I cannot state with any certainty that this application was intended or even known about – apart from centuries ago by certain sound masters. Nevertheless, it is an obvious inroad towards the subtler levels of sound and the singing bowls.

For more on the Five Buddha Families see RAINBOW OF LIBERATED ENERGY by Ngakpa Chogyam[9] and the aforementioned HEALING WITH FORM, ENERGY AND LIGHT by Tenzin Wangyal Rinpoche.[10]

15. Sound Made Visible

IT IS POSSIBLE to 'see' music in the context of the forms sound can create, either by watching the effect of its physical vibrations in a medium like fine sand, or by using electronic imaging technology. This chapter not only extends our knowledge of the acoustics of bowls, but also serves as background for the cymatic photographs of bowls in the colour supplement.

In the West, the study of the shape-forming potential of music began around 1785 when Ernst F. F. Chladni (1756–1827), a German acoustical physicist and amateur musician, experimented with sand on vibrating metal plates. In 1802 Chladni, in his book DIE AKUSTIK, published remarkable demonstrations of the power of sound to affect physical matter – using his now-famous 'Chladni plate' to create regular patterns known as Chladni's figures. In one sense, bowls or bells are nothing more than a flanged circular Chladni plate.

For a moment looking much further East, in Mongolia, in Tuva (part of southern Siberia), in Tibet, and from the Sayan to the Ural mountains (i.e., across a further stretch of southern Siberia), certain advanced vocal techniques are practised that allow one to sing several tones simultaneously. This is known to us as 'overtone' or bi-phonic singing, and traditionally as throat singing (*khoomei* in Mongolian and Tuvan, or sometimes *xhoomei*). Within the tone produced by the human voice are a hierarchy of overtones obedient to certain laws. Through this vocal technique, it is possible to focus upon one or another of these several overtones up to the sixteenth overtone. Just as all of these sixteen tones are ever-present as potential, so too, a complete series of overtones (or harmonics) are potentially present in the Chladni plate. Through variations in the basic technique of bowing the plate different sounds can be elicited, with their accompanying patterns specific to each sound.

In 1787 Chladni published his book, DISCOVERIES IN THE THEORY

OF SOUND. Here, he shared with the world his now famous patterns or figures. Chladni accidentally discovered (while he was investigating another phenomenon known as Lichtenburg figures) that by centre-clamping either a square or round metal plate, sprinkling fine sand or spores onto the surface of the plate, and then drawing a violin bow vertically along the horizontal plate's rim, he produced geometric figures which were altered according to which point on the edge of the plate was bowed and the degree of intensity of the pressure applied. In this manner, different harmonics of the plate were stimulated, producing varying forms.

Simply speaking, this is because when a plate is vibrated, it has both vibrating areas (antinodes) and non-vibrating areas (nodes). The particles of sand jump from the vibrating areas to the almost stationary nodal areas of the plate. We are, therefore, also witnessing a playful 'dance' between the so-called 'audible' and 'inaudible' areas of the vibrating plate, and revealing a certain orderly pattern. It is the inaudible (silent) areas of the plate which display the mandala-like patterns.

For a determined sound on the plate a very precise network of nodes and antinodes were created. Chladni was thus able to lay down the experimental principles of acoustics. This technique

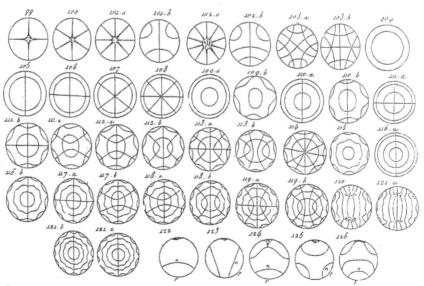

Diagram #5

allowed musicians actually to 'see' in a dynamic manner the powerful effects of sound upon substance – even witness it as a kind
of 'sacred geometry' or 'sound mandala'. The patterns are similar
to a photographic negative whereby we see a reverse image of
what is actually happening. In other words, the patterns we see
are where the plate is inactive, not where it is active. The mandala's form would be determined by the particular overtone elicited
from the plate.

The effect could be repeated. For instance, the 'fundamental'
(the lowest note possible) of any plate was a cross, drawn from
the four corners (if the plate was square) or otherwise displayed
across the surface of the plate. This could also be comprehended
as two primary directions diagonal to each other and manifesting
as two lines 'crossing' each other at the centre. The higher overtones produced highly complex patterns in the sand as the vibrating areas of the plate became far more sophisticated in their division. In the diagram on the previous page, taken with permission
from LES SCULPTURES SONORES by François Baschet (1999, p. 14) are
shown several original Chladni figures, beginning with the simple
four-, six- and eight-based patterns, of which we shall hear more.

According to tradition, it is said that the first to make music
with a bow and iron was an Italian musician, who was hanging
up his bow on a nail on the wall in his house. One evening in the
dark, his bow slipped as he was hanging it up and in the haze of
his fatigue, he rubbed it against the nail. The nail whistled and the
musician forgot how tired he was as he played a tune on the row
of nails.

Here are Chladni's own words regarding how he came to experiment in this way:

> As an admirer of music, the elements of which I had begun to
> learn rather late, that is, in my nineteenth year, I noticed that
> the science of acoustics was more neglected than most other
> portions of physics. This excited in me the desire to make good
> the defect, and by new discovery to render some service to this
> part of science. In 1785 I had observed that a plate of glass
> or metal gave different sounds when it was struck at different
> places, but I could nowhere find any information regarding the

corresponding modes of vibration. At this time there appeared
in the journals some notices of an instrument made in Italy by
the Abbé Mazzocchi, consisting of bells, to which one or two
violin bows were applied. This suggested to me the idea of
employing a violin-bow to examine the vibrations of different
sonorous bodies. When I applied the bow to a round plate of
glass fixed at its middle it gave different sounds, which, compared with each other, were (as regards the number of their
vibrations) equal in squares of 2, 3, 4, 5, &c.; but the nature
of the motions to which these sounds corresponded, and the
means of producing each of them at will, were yet unknown
to me. The experiments on the electric figures on a plate of
resin, discovered and published by Lichtenberg, in the mem-
oirs of the Royal Society of Gottingen, made me presume that
the different vibratory motions of a sonorous plate might also
present different appearances, if a little sand or some similar substance were spread on the surface. On employing this
means, the first figure that presented itself to my eyes upon
the circular plate already mentioned resembled a star with ten
or twelve rays, and the very acute sound, in the series alluded
to, was that which agreed with the square of the number of
diametrical lines.

Entdeckung. In d. Theorie d. Klanges, 1787.
(Metal plates and Chladni figures)

Although it is Chladni whom history has chosen to acknowledge for this class of phenomena, the knowledge is older. Today,
an exercise is taught in schools which consists of covering a drum
skin with grains of rice and beating it to produce a lively display,
yet primitive societies were not altogether ignorant of the vibrational effects of sound either. Accounts exist of African shamans
placing small grains upon their drum skins in order to produce
sound pictures from which to divine future events. Nonetheless,
no great contribution to the science of physics was obtained this
way. We know that the acoustical knowledge of the ancient Chinese was well developed from the evidence of their 'Spouting Bowl'
that demonstrated visible sound. It has been found since the Han
Dynasty, i.e. fifth-century BCE China, and is discussed above, p. 83.

The Spouting Bowl is a round metal bowl with two handles on opposite sides of the flat rim. The bowl is filled with a quite specific amount of water and the hands are wetted. Then the wet palms begin rubbing the handles. The vibration applied to the handles from the wet palms makes the bowl audibly vibrate and the water in the bowl begins to spout upwards symmetrically in four equidistant places around the bowl. Often, there are four fishes depicted upon the inside base of the bowl, and where their mouths open is exactly where the water spouts upwards in its formation of four fountains. It is stated that an expert in this technique can raise the water around a metre high. The fact that the fountains appear where the fish have their mouths open not only demonstrates the predictability of this acoustical phenomenon but also makes it clear that the ancient Chinese knew that the acoustics of the bowl produce a fourfold fundamental.

Recent research into ancient mounds in Great Britain and Ireland suggests a very marked awareness of sound in prehistoric times. At Newgrange in Ireland there are many rock art carvings within the chamber, and one in particular features a zigzag pattern with twelve peaks. It was found that the entrance passage produces standing sound waves, twelve in number. This could be a coincidence. It is suggested that with a ceremony taking place within at the winter solstice fire and incense, creating smoke, filled the passageway and when the chanting reverberated the passage the standing wave would form and the light of the sun would then make visible its twelvefold zigzag pattern. Other carvings feature concentric circles. These resemble the action of sound viewed from above and possibly experienced by the participants when moving through the chambers at the same time as sound was being produced whereby, and as they moved between the nodal and antinodal areas, the sound would appear and disappear. Many clairvoyants testify to sound creating such concentric patterns upon the inner planes. It has also been found that many such ancient monuments resonate at 110 Hz or thereabouts.[1] This is within the range of a male baritone voice.

There is an account of sound being used to levitate rocks by lamas in Tibet from a Dr Jarl, a Swedish doctor, who himself saw this phenomenon back in the early 1940s. This would be a most impressive form of visible sound! The Doctor was of the opinion that the phenomenon had more more to do with the geometric layout of the sounds than with the sounds themselves.[2] Myths and legends from many ancient cultures tell of the movement of huge stones by sound. The enigmatic scientist Nikola Tesla (1856–1943) is said to have done some experiments with anti-gravitational sound. Here is the verdict of a modern spiritual teacher.

> The buildings of the past had peculiar acoustic properties. The Masons of old possessed knowledge which enabled them to create chambers which proved receptive to sounds from the invisible worlds. Today some occultists attempt to invent instruments to receive the finer sound waves, so that messages can be received from the astral plane and possibly from the planets. Then, this was common knowledge; voices from afar were heard and actual communication from other planets were received, this fact establishing a great harmony, a linking-up of the human with many other aspects of life contained within the solar system and the spheres above, beyond and beneath or within the earth.
>
> White Eagle[3]

We find this partly borne out with one example found in the 'Oracle Room' within the Hypogeum (underground) of Paola, Malta, dated to 3,000 – 2,500 BCE. This chamber has the peculiarity of producing a powerful acoustic resonance and we find advanced acoustic sound technology in its design, for within it a word spoken out loud is magnified a hundredfold and is heard throughout the entire chamber – and indeed throughout all three levels of the Hypogeum. Again, interestingly, the resonant peak is found to be 110 Hz. In case we feel this is accidental, there is a niche in one of the walls that is clearly intended to be sung into, for it produces these acoustical phenomena in the most pronounced way. In our modern scale and current pitch standard of A at 440Hz, 110 Hz would be an A two octaves lower.

There are indications from certain writings that others down the centuries have made experiments with sound that produced visible effects. These include the Renaissance Italian, Leonardo da Vinci, followed by Galileo Galilei, and the Englishmen Robert Hooke, Michael Faraday and John William Strutt, Third Baron Rayleigh. This process culminated in the publication of Chladni's figures.

Since Chladni the field has opened wider, and we find the works of Margaret Watts-Hughes and (more recently) Hans Jenny supplying us with further images in their publications, for a further step along the way of visibly demonstrating the power of sound arose with the invention, in 1885, of something called the Eidophone. The Welsh singer Margaret Watts-Hughes (1847–1907) published THE EIDOPHONE VOICE FIGURES (1904), following on VISIBLE SOUND (1891). In them, geometrical and natural forms produced by vibrations of the human voice are shown (as an example, see right, 'Tree Form'). Her method was to stretch India rubber discs over numerous 'receivers' ranging in size from 1 to 37 inches in circumference. These produced a range of geometric shapes when the apparatus was sung into via a tube. Having found a disk circumference responsive to the singer's voice, she would ask that singer to move up through the musical scale and notice the shapes produced. It is said that she

TREE FORM.

actually developed this system in order to improve her own singing voice. Nonetheless, it is another example of visual representations regarding how sound influences form. It also seems likely that she had been inspired by the work of Faraday, as she uses his term 'crispations' when discussing the patterns she observed.

An account of one of her presentations is found in the book MUSIC AS YOGA (1956) by Swami Sivananda (1887–1963):

> The first manifestation of God is Ether or Sound. Sound is the Guna or Quality of Ether. Sounds are vibrations. They give rise to definite forms. Each sound produces a form in the invisible world and combinations of sound create complicated shapes.
>
> The textbooks of science describe certain experiments which show that notes produced by certain instruments trace

out on a bed of sand definite geometrical figures. It is thus demonstrated that rhythmical vibrations give rise to regular geometrical figures.

The Hindu books on music tell us that various musical tunes Ragas and Raginis have each a particular shape which the books graphically describe. For instance the Megha Ragha is said to be a majestic figure seated on an elephant. The Basanta Raga is described as a beautiful youth decked with flowers. All this means that the particular Raga or Ragini, when accurately sung, produces aerial etheric vibrations which create certain characteristic shapes.

This view has recently received corroborations from the experiments carried on by Mrs. Watts Hughes, the gifted author of 'Voice Figures'. She recently delivered an illustrated lecture before a select audience in Lord Leighton's studio to demonstrate the beautiful scientific discoveries on which she has alighted as the result of many years of patient labour.

Mrs. Hughes sings into a simple instrument called an 'Eidophone' which consists of a tube, a receiver and a flexible membrane, and she finds that each note assumes definite and constant shape, as revealed through a sensitive and mobile medium. At the outset of her lecture, she placed tiny seeds upon the flexible membrane and the air vibrations set up by the notes, she sounded, danced them into definite geometric patterns. Afterwards she used dusts of various kinds, lycopodium dust being found particularly suitable. A reporter describing the shapes of the notes, speaks of them as remarkable revelations of geometry, perspective and shading. 'Stars, spirals, snakes, wonders in wheels and imagination rioting in a wealth of captivating methodical designs' such were what were shown first....

While in France, Madame Finlang's singing of a hymn to Virgin Mary 'O Ave Maria' brought out the form of Mary with child Jesus in her lap and again the singing of a hymn to 'Bhairava' by a Bengali student of Banaras (India) studying in France, gave rise to the formation of the figure of Bhairava with his vehicle dog.

Thus the repeated singing of the Name of the Lord gradually builds up the forms of the Devatas or the special manifestations of the deity, whom you seek to worship and this serves as a focus to concentrate the benign influence of the Being, which radiating from the centre, penetrates the worshipper of the singer or Sangeeta-Premi.

When one enters the state of meditation, the inner Vritti-flow is greatly intensified. The deeper one goes into meditation the more marked is the effect. The concentration of the mind upwards sends a rush of this force through the top of the head and the response comes in a fine rain of soft magnetism. This feeling arising from the downward power sends a wonderful glow through the body, and one feels as though bathed in a soft kind of electricity.

The above experiments demonstrate the following facts:

1. Sounds produce shape.

2. Particular notes give rise to particular forms.

3. If you want to reproduce a particular form, you must recite a particular note in a particular pitch.

4. That, for that purpose no other note and no other pitch, chanting even the identical note will avail. For instance in '*Agnimile purohitam*' – '*Ile Agnim purohitam*' will not do. In doing so, the efficacy of the Mantra is gone. You cannot therefore transpose or translate a Mantra. If you do it, it will cease to be a Mantra. When a Mantra is defective either in Svara or Varna, it is incorrectly directed and may produce a result just contrary to what was intended.[4]

Being very much taken by the beauty of the forms, Margaret Watts-Hughes wrote:

I have gone on singing into the shape these peculiar forms, and stepping out of doors, have seen their parallels in flowers, ferns, and trees around me; and again, as I have watched the little heaps in the formation of the floral figures gather themselves up and then shoot out their petals, just as flowers spring from the swollen bud – the hope has come to me that these humble experiments may afford some suggestions in regard to nature's production of her own beautiful forms, And may thereby aid, in some slight degree, the revelation of yet another link in the great chain of the organized universe that, we are told in Holy Writ, took its shape as the voice of God.

Margaret Watts-Hughes, VISIBLE SOUND (1908)

During the 1960s in Switzerland, the scientist, artist, doctor, and anthroposophist Dr Hans Jenny (1904–72) made further experiments. He adapted the Chladni plate by using a circular disc that was stimulated via a piezoelectric crystal in the centre of its base and experimented with a variety of substances (lycopodium powder being a staple) and different pitch frequencies and amplitudes. Certain remarkable phenomena resulted. Later he developed discs of other shapes, such as triangles. Jenny was primarily interested in the cyclic phenomena of nature, and so he filmed the processes arising from the interaction between sound, the plates, and the substances placed upon them. Very many beautiful patterns resulted, resembling forms in nature and the cosmos alongside *mandala*-like patterns, whereby a specific frequency and amplitude would always produce the same symmetrical pattern on the plate using the same substance. Sometimes this would be of water or of oil or an admixture and then these *mandala* shapes would acquire an almost three-dimensional aspect.

Jenny also photographed the results of his experiments with sound, experiments that reveal to us all the power of sound and its role in the manifestation of certain forms and patterns. One cannot fail but be impressed and deeply moved by seeing material moved by sound into distinct patterns and shapes and cycles of activity. In order to show this cyclical aspect, Jenny would place a drop of dye into what appeared to be a static form, only for us to witness that spot of dye moving through the pattern and showing that it was, in fact, in constant motion. Jenny's famous Cymatics work forms a beautiful large book, a new edition of which, combining the previous two volumes with video/DVD films of these experiments, is available from Jeff Volk at www.cymaticsource.com.

Jenny derived the word 'cymatics' from the ancient Greek word, *kyma*, meaning wave. He was most interested in studying cycles. A musical note is a cycle (measured as cps, cycles per second) though it is depicted graphically as a wave. During one of his experiments, Jenny used a mixture of salt and water. Placed upon the plate and exposed to sound it moved in a cycle between form and formless-

ness; a pattern would emerge and later would disintegrate back
into a shapeless mass but then reform into the same shape as before. It produced a cycle of activity that fascinated Jenny.

In the UK, Dr Peter Guy Manners adapted Jenny's cymatic
work by creating the Cymatic Applicator for use in healing, but
a further expansion of the cymatic process has arisen far more
recently through the work of John Stuart Reid (b. 1948), who
has created his own machine, the CymaScope. Reid worked with
American design engineer, Eric Larson, to engineer the instrument
according to Pythagorean proportions. The intent was to reproduce certain of the phenomena discovered by Jenny in the 1960s.
However, of particular significance to us here is what John Stuart
Reid has further discovered, in what we might term the cultural
dimension of the cymatic phenomena. After a presentation of his
CymaScope, an individual known as Bear (having played a didger-
idoo) commented that what could be identified as aboriginal patterns had emerged upon the surface of the membrane. Bear grew
very excited, so he then played a Celtic horn and Celtic patterns
emerged. Next he played a Tibetan horn and Tibetan *mandala*
forms emerged. During experiments made by Reid himself, inside the Great Pyramid (1997), Egyptian symbols appeared – and
were also witnessed by the guide present in the chamber. John
performed a cymatic experiment using the sarcophagus:

> The sarcophagus is badly damaged and in order to stretch the
> PVC membrane over its open top and maintain a level surface,
> it was first necessary to 'repair' the broken south-west corner
> and to level the top edges which are largely broken away. This
> was achieved by means of expanded polystyrene sheets/adhe-
> sive tape and a pre-prepared aluminium right angle for repair
> of the corner. The membrane was then stretched over the sar-
> cophagus and weighted around its perimeter with 43 bags of
> sand, of approximately 1Kg each, to produce an even torsion
> across its surface…. The speaker had been positioned centrally
> inside the sarcophagus and connected to the sine wave oscilla-
> tor. Finally, a fine sprinkling of quartz sand was applied to the
> entire surface area of the membrane and the oscillator turned
> on, commencing at 20KHz and slowly sweeping down the

band whilst closely observing the sand grains for movement.[5]

It is intriguing that some of the images resemble ancient Egyptian symbols and motifs but I see these as natural manifestations, locked within the quartz-rich granite in the far distant past and released today by acoustic excitation. It is possible that the ancient Egyptians also experimented with sand patterns, in the Great Pyramid or elsewhere, and that they incorporated some of the imagery into their glyphs. If they did experiment in this way they would surely have seen the images as powerful magic, as is the case with present day shaman.[6]

John Stuart Reid has supplied cymatic images for several of my bowls featured in this book, and these are reproduced in the colour supplement.

Professor Thomas D. Rossing has taken yet another turn in this process through the use of 'holographic interferograms'. In this photographic technique it is possible actually to see the areas of instruments that are active or inactive in a graphic way, revealing great beauty. In the holographic interferograms of an 18cm-diameter *qing* bowl on p. 309, reproduced in his paper, you will see the areas of a resting bowl that are active during the production of the several partials of the bowl (from 343 Hz up to 6478 Hz). Professor Rossing shares with me a great love of bells, the sound distribution of which, or the nodal and anti-nodal areas of bells, he has rendered visible to us anew. Of special interest to us here is his work examining the acoustical properties of Chinese *qing* bells. These closely resemble the Tibetan or Himalayan singing bowls. He has made his scientific studies of many instruments (especially percussive instruments) available and you can read of these in his papers or books (notably 'Science of Percussion Instrument').

I should like to reproduce here, in its entirety, his short paper on *qing*:

Acoustics of The Chinese Qing

Thomas D. Rossing and Jianming Tsai
Department of Physics
Northern Illinois University
DeKalb, IL 60115

The qing (also known as shun or ching) is a bowl-shaped musical instrument, commonly used in Buddhist religious ceremonies, where it is often paired with a muyu or wooden fish of about the same size (as shown in Figure 1). Qing generally range from 10 to 40cm in diameter and 8 to 35cm in height, although one large qing from the Han dynasty (206 BC–210 AD) measures 75cm in diameter. When used in religious ceremonies, the qing generally rests on a silk pillow and is struck at the rim with a wooden stick. Figure 2 shows four bronze qing from 10 to 18cm in diameter. In ancient times, the qing was often engraved with the text of the Buddhist Sutra, whose wonders would be conveyed by the sound of the qing.

The principal modes of vibration result from the propagation of bending waves around the circumference. Viewed in the axial direction, these modes resemble those of a bell, the $(m,0)$ mode having $2m$ modes around the mouth. The $(m,1)$ and higher families of bell modes are not observed, however, Figure 3 shows holographic interferograms of some of the prominent vibrational modes of a 16 cm diameter qing (the largest one in Figure 2). Modes (2.0) through (9.0) are identifiable in the top two rows, but it is still difficult to assign more numbers at the high frequencies.

Mode frequencies are shown in Figure 4 as a function of m, the number of nodal diameters, for the four qing in Figure 2. Sound spectra from the 18cm qing, freely suspended from rubber bands and resting on the silk cushion, are shown in Figure 5. The upper spectrum in each case is recorded when struck, and the lower spectrum 0.5 seconds later. Note that the decay rates are comparable in the two cases, indicating relatively little damping from the cushion. In both cases, the partial radiated by the (4,0) mode has the largest amplitude. Frequencies of the main partials in a 18cm and a 15cm qing

Above: illustration from first page of Thomas D. Rossing's article, showing the Qing bell at right. Below, p. 2 of the article, showing the interferograms derived from the Qing bowl.

Table 1. Mode frequencies and ratios in two qing

Mode	18cm qing f_{mn} (Hz)	f_{mn}/f_{20}	15cm qing f_{mn} (Hz)	f_{mn}/f_{20}
2,0	346	1.00	434	1.00
3,0	953	2.75	1180	2.72
4,0	1751	5.06	2130	4.91
5,0	2691	7.78	3267	7.53
6,0	3748	10.83	4496	10.36
7,0	4644	13.42	6182	14.24
8,0	6255	18.08		
9,0	7363	21.28		

The authors thank Prof. Kuo-Huang Han in the Northern Illinois University School of Music for his enlightening discussions and especially for loaning us the qing used in these studies.

REFERENCES

1. Alan R. Trasher, "Qing" in New Grove Dictionary of Musical Instruments, Vol. 3, ed. S. Sadie (Macmillan, London, 1984).
2. Thomas D. Rossing, "The Acoustics of Bells," Am. Scientist 72, 440 (1984).

Figure 2. (above) Four qing with diamteters of 18, 15, 12, and 10 cm.

Figure 3. (left) Holographic interferograms of a 18 cm diameter bronze qing, showing modal shapes of the (m,0) modes (top two rows). Modes in the bottom row are not identified, except for the second one, which is the (7,0) mode at a higher amplitude than in the photograph immediately above it.

qing #1

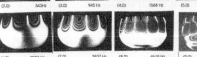

Figure 4. (below) Mode frequencies as a function of m, the number of nodal diameters for qing with diameters of 18, 15, 12, and 10 cm.

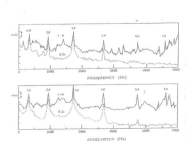

Figure 5. (above) Sound spectra of 18 cm qing freely suspended on rubber bands (upper) and resting on a silk cushion (lower). The upper spectrum, in each case, is recorded at the time of striking, and the lower spectrum 0.5s later.

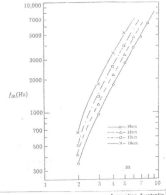

are given in Table 1, along with their ratios to the fundamental in each case. Note that no harmonic relationship exists among the partials. The pitch of the qing is determined almost entirely by the fundamental (2,0) partial, although the strong (4,0) partial is clearly heard as an overtone.

Taken from Acoustics Australia *Vol. 19 No. 3 – 73 and reprinted by kind permission of* World Scientific.

Again, more recently, we find published the work of Alexander Lauterwasser, WATER SOUND IMAGES (available from www.cymaticsource.com). Lauterwasser's takes Jenny's work as a starting point but primarily, if not exclusively, he works with the effect of sound upon water. He uses not just sound but, as with certain of Jenny's experiments, actual pieces of music too. His book is very well written and with a profusion of beautiful images each created from sound. Posters of his photographs can also be bought.

'Gary Robert Buchanan' has a number of videos on YouTube mostly featuring the healing application of cymatics. Particular health complaints are intended to receive healing energies from specific frequencies contained in certain cymatic films on YouTube under his name.

In the Hindu metaphysics of sound it is understood that the highest level of sound is not a vibration of any sort (such as supersonics), but rather it is thought. Bearing this in mind, we might see the work of the Japanese scientist Dr Masaru Emoto (b. 1943) as demonstrating the relation between thought and material manifestation. His books on water crystals reveal his experiments with thoughts and even more wonderfully the effect of words upon water, substances, and people.

Another of his experiments has consisted of projecting thoughts onto water. Via his website, a group of volunteers were rounded up consisting of four groups of parents and their children. Two glasses of water were taken from the Tokyo mains. To one glass the group express gratitude for one minute, both out loud and then silently with eyes closed. The other was left alone. Then the glass exposed to positive thoughts was removed to observe any changes. Three hours later, after freezing, and observation under a microscope, a small hexagonal crystal grew in this glass – clear and simple, in contrast to the 'untreated' Tokyo tap water that had a lack of beautiful crystals when frozen. Dr Emoto concluded that water could act as a mirror to reflect human thoughts.

Before turning to words, Dr Emoto had exposed distilled water from a drugstore to the music of certain classical composers. In MESSAGES FROM WATER, Book I (1999), he tells us that at first his team had no idea what music they would use and under what conditions they would conduct the experiment. But after considerable trial and error, they reached the conclusion that the best method was probably the simplest – put a bottle of water on a table between two speakers and expose it to a volume at which a person might normally listen to music for the duration of the piece. They would also need to keep the source of the water the same.

Beethoven's Pastoral Symphony, with its bright and clear tones, resulted in beautiful and well-formed crystals. Mozart's Fortieth Symphony, a graceful prayer to beauty, created crystals that were delicate and elegant. And the crystals formed by exposure to Chopin's Etude in E, Op. 10, No. 3, surprised them with their lovely detail. All the classical music that they exposed the water to resulted in well-formed crystals with distinct characteristics. In contrast, the water exposed to violent heavy-metal music resulted in fragmented and malformed crystals at best. Our body is composed of between 75 and 90% water and therefore it behoves us to consider the effect that words, sounds, and music have upon us (the water within our body).

Water was also taken from Fujiwara Dam before and after a prayer from a Zen Buddhist monk. Again, the water that had been prayed over showed a beautiful crystal. In the film, 'Water – the Great Mystery', we hear from a Tibetan, Dr Ogun Bolson, that even the simple act of reading a prayer or mantra will raise the quality of the water of which most of our body is composed.

It is also reported from history in the film that the Chinese hermit Shang Shung was alive when the country was ravaged by an unknown epidemic. The ruler of Beijing asked the hermit to protect the peoples. Shang Shung prayed and the sickness retreated. In reply to numerous expressions of gratitude, the hermit said,

'Prayer is not a thing. All it requires is Faith'. Thought and intention can be imprinted upon water but thought and will alone are
not as powerful as faith. Similarly, it has often been shown that
holy water sprinkled over sick animals or dying plants will revive
them. No chemist can understand this.

The researches mentioned, along with the anecdotes, abun-
dantly illustrate the power of thought, sound, or intention upon
various substances. In the book, THOUGHT FORMS (1901), Theosophists Annie Besant and C.W. Leadbeater show us the effects
of certain feelings or thoughts upon and within the human aura.
Colours and form are seen to be the language of the aura, with
such energies derived from certain thoughts and feelings, creating
the resultant shapes and figures. For example, angry thoughts or
emotions create red, arrow-like figures through the aura whereas vague pure affection is found to create a rather indistinct soft
pink cloud-like form. This book recounts the work of Chladni and
Margaret Watts-Hughes, also that of F. Bligh Bond.

Fundamental and Partials

As I have said, and despite some very real differences (most of
all that the bowl is not a flat plate and there is no sand in it
to demonstrate the pattern) it can be helpful to conceive of the
singing bowl as a flanged (or deformed) Chladni plate. Chladni
found the fundamental sound of the metal plate to produce a
fourfold pattern – diagonally across from corner to corner on
square plates or forming a cross within the circle on circular
discs. This pattern is the same as the one exploited in Chinese
'Spouting Bowls', described on pp. 83 and 298-9.

In keeping with this, the fundamental of every single singing
bowl is found to produce a fourfold pulsing – that is, four beats to
every circuit as we stroke it. With a special wand (rather thick in diameter and covered with leather) it is possible to get a medium-sized
bowl to sound its fundamental. The four pulses created are audible
as the wand completes one circuit of the rim of the bowl. It is as if
the bowl were breathing out and in as the sound grows in volume
and then approaches silence again, alternating between manifest

and unmanifest sound in this fundamental fourfold rhythmic dance.

I own three singing bowls that I named Fountain Bowls because they seem to have been created to demonstrate this acoustic phenomenon, namely the four fountains, witnessed with the Chinese Spouting Bowls. However, there are no handles! One of these is of the *yang* variety, whilst the other two are of the *yin* variety. These appear to be a singing bowl equivalent of the spouting bowl, for whereas some bowls possess markings upon the inside wall as decoration, these that I term Fountain Bowls all have a line inscribed upon the inside of the bowl in an unusual position. When water is filled up to this line and the bowl is then sounded, fountains appear in four corners of the bowl. For this reason during the 1980s I originated the term Fountain Bowl for this category of rather rare bowl, as it would seem reasonable to deduce that this was their intended purpose. Having sorted through over 9,500 bowls I have found only four myself. But since 2005 I've known of a fifth, for by then my friend Ian Dale had bought a consignment of bowls from the East and one of those was a Fountain Bowl – in my definition of that term.

The purpose of these Fountain Bowls could be to demonstrate acoustics, or perhaps to charge the water before using it during a period of fasting, or to demonstrate the power of vibration; I obviously don't know which for certain. I have seen merchants selling a so-called 'fountain bowl' and tilting the bowl at around 60° so that the water touches the rim. Hitting the rim, naturally the water splashes upwards – to gasps of wonder from gullible buyers! But the same effect could be obtained with a saucepan. With what I term Fountain Bowls there is no need for such antics. Filling the bowl up to the prescribed line, resting it horizontally on a table or the palm of the hand and striking or stroking it produces the desired and predicted outcome. It is true that many bowls when filled with a certain amount of water (roughly one third full) can produce these fountains, or at least movement upon the face of the water, while being played in a horizontal position, but I do not believe that this is their precise and intended function, for the water level marker is missing.

Theodore Levine, recounting a meeting with the shaman Lazo

Mongush at the Dunggar Society in Kyzyl, Tuva, in 2003, writes:

> Lazo rose from the bearskin cushion on which he had been
> seated, picked up the larger of two silver bowls from the cor-
> ner of his desk, and filled it with milk from the refrigerator in
> the corner. He sprinkled powdered juniper on the milk, stirred
> it with a twig, and added water. 'This is the best arzhaan (min-
> eral or spring water) for a shaman.' Lazo picked up a wooden
> beater and struck the bowl on its four sides. As it began to
> resonate, he traced the circumference of the top of the bowl
> with the beater, producing a chain reaction of shimmering
> overtones that piled up on top of one another until the bowl
> was ringing loudly. The excitation of the bowl made the milk
> 'boil' and sizzle.
>
> 'When you drink this, it purifies the human organism from
> the inside,' Lazo said, motioning for me to take a sip.
>
> 'It's like a Tibetan singing bowl! I exclaimed.
>
> 'The Tibetans don't use it correctly,' Lazo replied sharply.
> 'Shamans used these bowls before Buddhist monks, although
> I was the one who thought up the idea of filling it with milk.
> I haven't seen others do this. Silver is one of the nine valuable
> things that a shaman should have, and this bowl is one of my
> attributes – an *eeres*.' *Eeres* are physical objects that represent
> spirit-helpers called upon to assist a shaman with particular
> tasks or rituals.[7]

During an interview in 1976, I stated an intention to investi-
gate acoustics more. It led to the discovery of the partials of the
singing bowls and their numerical sequence – 4/6/8/10/12. Since
the mid-1980s, I have found ways to isolate these partials within
certain good singing bowls in order to demonstrate them during
workshops. Bowls have no rules for the frequencies of their partials but the numbers of their partials are constant.

After the four of the fundamental the next partial of a singing
bowl produces six pulses, and continuing the sequence we find
eight comes next followed by ten, and then twelve. I have not been
able to isolate anything beyond this fifth partial out of a single
bowl whilst stroking it. In one instance this is while playing an old
thin *yin* bowl ('Song of the Mountain Waterfall' Bowl), around

ten inches in diameter, and playing it with a hard ebony wand that is very thin (around half an inch in diameter). I invented this specifically for the purpose of eliciting the higher harmonics from bowls. I find it easiest to count the ten in the rhythm of three, two, three, two and the twelve as four threes. This sequence of numbers produced by a bowl is unalterable and, although the bowls do not conform to the law of overtones as this is usually understood and applied in music, yet they can be said to comply with this law of number. In the following chapter are provided some possible ways of working with these numbers that you may wish to use in exercises with your bowl(s). They are drawn from a range of disciplines and traditions.

It is surprisingly obvious how this fundamental of four comes about. When the bowl is struck, although we cannot see it doing so, the rim of the bowl moves inwards at that point and the rim in between expands outwards. This is the first and basic movement that takes place within the shape of the bowl. We have two modes of movement producing four points – rather similar to the day and night movement of the earth's orbit, which produces four periods of our day, marked by sunrise, noon, sunset, and midnight.

In Figure 1, opposite, we see this movement within the body of the singing bowl from the strike point (here at the bottom of the circle – or the position directly in front of oneself before the bowl – from this overhead perspective) and the moment after contraction, whilst in Figure 2 we see the two shapes combined – as, in fact, they are, when the sound is produced.

To put it more fully, where it is struck, the circular rim of the bowl moves inwards while the perpendicular region (in this instance – with the first partial or fundamental of the bowl – at right angles) of the bowl's circumference moves outwards. Then, as the struck area of the bowl moves back to its starting position, it overreaches that position, while the area perpendicular to it now contracts and moves inwards. The four points where these two movements cross are relatively static and provide us with our nodes and what is termed the fundamental of the bowl. Every single bowl creates its fundamental in the same manner. It produces the ancient symbol of the cross within the circle – a symbol the

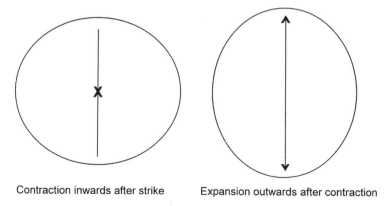

Contraction inwards after strike   Expansion outwards after contraction

Figure 1:
Contraction inwards after strike,and expansion outwards after contraction

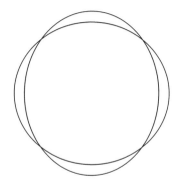

Figure 2:
The intersections are the four nodal points of the fundamental of the bowl

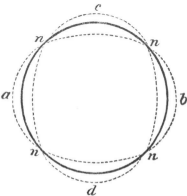

Figure 3:
The four nodal points around the circle of the bowl

teacher White Eagle tells us represents the ancient Great White Brotherhood – mentioned in earlier chapters.

When brought into activity, each bowl will produce a sequence of nodal points, dividing up equally the circumference of the rim. We find the progression to be four, six, eight, ten, twelve and so on. When the bowl is struck these all sound simultaneously, providing us with the several partials of the bowl. Therefore, when the bowl is stroked, and as outlined above, the first partial will produce four beats, the second partial six beats, the third partial eight beats, the fourth partial ten beats and so on.

The best way to experience this will be by stroking the bowl either with an aspen (or other very soft wood) wand or a leather-covered one. This will focus upon the fundamental (also known as the first partial) of the bowl. With each circuit of the rim of the bowl you will hear four beats and the times when the sound grows louder to produce the sensation of beats will be seen to occur at four equidistant points around the bowl.

Here we can see the origin of the four fishes and four fountains in the phenomenon of the Chinese 'Spouting Bowls'. They produce a visual representation of this rhythmical movement of the bowl between contraction and expansion from the strike point.

As we circle the bowl with a wand we can also hear a certain number of pulses. Whether we will hear these four pulses (or six, or eight, etc.), will depend on the wand.

The unfoldment of partials moves along the even numbers. If we want to focus symbolically upon the odd numbers while sounding the bowl then we must always (in our mind) include the centre of the bowl, thus providing us with the numbers 5, 7, 9, 11 and 13 (that is to say four plus the silent central spot (5); six plus the silent central spot (7); and so on). In Figure 3 (previous page), the bold circle represents the bowl and the four points marked n are the nodes, whilst a to b show the bowl after striking and c to d the moving back inwards and this time stretching at ninety degrees to our starting point (a/b).

16. Partials Exercises

IN THIS CHAPTER are exercises to accompany the isolating of one of the partials from your bowl. They offer a spiritual practice to go with the sounding of the partials, but also give us a way of becoming really familiar with the sounds and sensitizing the ear.

Exercises using the Fundamental of the Bowl

We can use this phenomenon of the partials as a foundation to guide our meditations while stroking the bowl. For instance, the fundamental of the bowl, producing the fourfold rhythm, lends itself to a variety of correspondences: the four seasons of the yearly cycle, the four archangels of these seasons – Raphael, Uriel, Michael, and Gabriel (spring, summer, autumn and winter respectively), the four times of the day (sunrise, noon, sunset, midnight); the four *yugas* (that is, epochs: see Sri Yukteswar's comments below, p. 322), the four states of matter for the alchemists (solid, liquid, gaseous, and igneous); the four elements (earth, air, fire and water), which can also correspond to our four vehicles (physical body, emotional body, mental body and spiritual body); the four major phases of the Moon (new, first quarter, full and last quarter).

To illustrate how this might work, we might choose to focus upon the four petals of the root chakra and, because this chakra is the very foundation of the sequence of chakras (and therefore of our spiritual path), we could contemplate this foundation of our spiritual activity and with the number four representing the earth element. This foundation would be the selfless one, namely that of service; or, in other words, the attitude of service to life lays our foundation upon a safe and secure footing. The root chakra with its four petals is in the shape of the cross, and in the symbol we may see the union between male and female principles via this cross. The masculine is symbolized by the vertical line and the feminine by the horizontal, even as in the act of playing the bowl, the wand is held in the vertical axis and the rim of the bowl is horizontal. Despite this, I have three bowls – 'Panic Bowl', 'Talking Bowl', and also a small Space-cleansing Chalice Bowl – that are played in the opposite manner with the bowl held in the vertical position and the wand in that of the horizontal.

When working with the four elements – earth, water, air, and fire – we must be ever mindful that these are governed by angels and that these angels are God's servants. This means that we can ask the Lord to send his angels to help us in our spiritual work as we stroke the bowl. Here is a prayer from the Master Omraam Mikhael Aïvanhov of the Great White Brotherhood that we can say:

> Lord God almighty, Creator of heaven and earth, I beg you to send me your servants, the four angels. The Angel of Earth, that he may absorb all the wastes of my physical body so that it may be capable of expressing your splendour, and that your will may be manifested through it. The Angel of Water, that he may wash all impurities from my heart and fill it with selfless love. The Angel of Air, that he may purify my intellect with an influx of wisdom and light. Send me, Lord, the Angel of Fire, that he may sanctify my soul and spirit, so that your truth may dwell in them, and so that I may work for your kingdom and your righteousness. Amen. Amen. Amen. So may it be![1]

As an alternative, we could use the acoustical properties of the bowl to work with the four directions of North, South, East and West. Another deeply significant manner of working with the fourfold fundamental is to contemplate what were termed by the ancients 'the four great initiations'. We find a manifestation of these four in the life of Jesus the Christed One – with the Baptism relating to the water initiation, the Sermon on the Mount to the air initiation, the Transfiguration to the fire initiation and finally the Crucifixion forming the earth initiation. Although this story shows the initiations in what might be termed an archetypal process, in reality we can be going through any one or any combination of these initiations during a single lifetime. Each of them requires certain spiritual qualities to come to the fore, or to be unfolded within us. We can contemplate these qualities whilst rotating our wand around the bowl, focussing upon each element in turn with water for our first round, air for the second and so on. For more on this subject of the four great initiations I particularly recommend the book, INITIATIONS ON THE PATH OF THE SOUL, by White Eagle.[2]

We may also wish to focus upon the fourfold process of sound, as found within the metaphysics of sound expressed in *nada yoga*. In India the OM is said to be comprised of four parts – A, U, M, and Silence. We can also use this fourfold approach with the primary mantra of Tibet, which is 'om mani peme hung' in Tibetan, or *om mani padme hun* in Sanskrit. The OM is the beginning of everything (the primordial sound-space or the closest we can get to the hum of the universe) located at the crown chakra. *Mani* means 'jewel', and so we focus upon the third eye chakra and the vision of that which we wish to create. Next is *padme*, where we bring the energy down into the lotus of the heart chakra, where the fire of divine love gives life to the vision. Finally, with *hum* we focus upon the throat chakra, where the effort of our will finally actualizes our vision in this physical world. Naturally, I advocate that this vision be selfless in nature and for the benefit of humankind, and certainly not simply for material gain or our own interest or for self-aggrandisement. As an example, our vision might be that of all humanity working together for the good of the whole.

The pre-Buddhist path of Bon in Tibet is found to grant a fourfold pattern to sound:

> Thought is the body of Sound.
> Sound is the body of Light.
> Light is the body of Consciousness.
> Consciousness is the body of humanity.
> The soul, once made, is the body of these.[3]

The Bonpo Master, Tenzin Wangyal Rinpoche, speaks of the Four Immeasurables and states what these qualities refer to, namely love, compassion, joy and equanimity. We can contemplate these while we play the fundamental of the bowl (if it is a large bowl, so that the pulsations are slow enough) or choose one of the qualities at a time (cycle by cycle) in order to unfold their enlightenment within ourselves during the meditative practice, rather than looking outside ourselves for answers to our needs.

If we add the centre to these four, then we have the fifth element, Space (see p. 283). The number four features in a great many spiritual/religious traditions. The most common form of Tibetan mandala has this four-plus-one, i.e. fivefold, rhythm as its foundation, either within a square or a circle. The Tibetans also apply this fivefold partition to the chakra system, to the elements, and it exists also in their stupas.

The fourfold rhythm is also to be found in the *Tetractys* of Pythagoras, the Sage of Samos. Here the one (the fundamental) would represent the Father; the two (the octave interval) the mother, the three (the interval of the fifth), the son, and the fourth (the interval of the fourth, also known as the second octave) the daughter.

During the act of playing the bowl and producing the fundamental, we create the symbol of the cross within the circle. The spiritual teacher White Eagle offers this as a symbol of the ancient brotherhood. Certain crosses within Celtic Christianity have the circle of the fiery sun (Son) upon the cross of earthly matter, symbolizing the human spirit rising above, or transforming, or transmuting, the limitations of matter – for instance, the St John's Cross on the Isle of Iona. The Celtic cross within the circle, unlike the Christian cross, has equal-sided arms indicating a balanced condition between the four elements.

According to the Theosophists, we are in the Fourth Cosmic Day within the sevenfold cycle. This means that the number four is the fundamental of our current cycle (or Cosmic Day of Brahma [*Manvantara*] and the [*Pralaya*] Cosmic Night), lasting many millions of years. The number four is the central number within any sevenfold sequence and it is also stated that the Christ impulse (the Christ event – the lifetime of Jesus the Christed One) took place at the very midpoint of this fourth Cosmic Day and thus of the entire cycle. However, this Fourth Cosmic Day is broken down further into another sevenfold sequence, or set of subdivisions, known in our period as the post-Atlantean epochs, and we are currently moving from the fifth of these into the sixth. Therefore, the numbers of five and six are also prominent at this time, modifying that of the primary number, which is four.

Taking the cycle of the moon's four major phases into consideration, I prefer to begin playing the bowl from the position right in front of me, and I see this corresponding to the new moon position, the commencement of the solunar cycle. When we reach the halfway point, farthest away from us, we have reached the position representing the full moon. From the holistic perspective of the solunar cycle we here have represented the involutionary hemicycle and the evolutionary hemicycle. That is to say, the first hemicycle represents the coming into being and the second hemicycle the process of moving away from the manifest realm back towards the source.

Playing, we may wish to be aware of the direction that we are facing when playing, so that we are facing one of the four cardinal directions. For instance, when chanting a mantra it is recommended either to face north or east. Anybody familiar with working with the cycles of the moon knows that it is best to begin an activity during the period from new moon to full moon as after this the energies are waning.

In each of the major periods of our earth's history one of the four elements (earth, water, air, and fire) has marked one such period by its predominance. Our present era will be dominated by fire, so that humanity will become accustomed to every form that fire can take. Because of this, we should strengthen our relationship with the element fire and befriend it. If we link ourselves to the sun, which is fire in its essence, through contemplating the sun (never look at the physical sun for any period of time as blindness will result), we can gradually change the vibration of our being until we feel that we have become one with it. Those who love the sun will avoid being affected by the negative aspects of fire. In truth we all live within the extended body of the sun, for its rays reach every corner of this solar system. We are each of us children of the sun. So while playing the bowl we can commune with the spirit of the sun and thus the spiritual flame upon the altar of our heart chakra will awaken. As the sun radiates its light to all members of its family, so too we can radiate the light of the spiritual sun out to all creation as we stroke the bowl – so that the light of the sun-star floats outwards upon the continuously sounding *om* vibration of the bowl.

We may also wish to ponder upon the four yugas. Many writers suggest that we are at present in the Kali Yuga age, but according to Sri Yukteswar (best known as the guru of Paramahansa Yogananda) the dates for these periods that have been handed down are incorrect. Dwapara Yuga started in 1700 CE, he says, so that we are not in the *kali yuga* – the darkest of the four – at all. He states that rather we are in *dwapara yuga*. Basing what he said upon ancient Indian writings Sri Yukteswar wrote in THE HOLY SCIENCE that as well as the daily rotation of our earth on its axis and yearly orbit of the sun, the sun itself orbits another star, with a period of about 24,000 years. One cycle of the four yugas lasts 12,000 years. However, there is a descending and ascending arc moving from *satya* to *tretya*, to *dwapara* to *kali* and then in reverse order, completing in the 24,000-year cycle, with One Day of Brahma being equal to twenty four million years and our earth being many Brahmanic 'Days' old.

We may know these ages already as the four Ages of Hesiod and the Greeks – Gold, Silver, Bronze and Iron respectively (descending). The idea of the Ages was shared by many ancient cultures such as the Celts and Norse, the Aztecs, Hopi, Egyptians, Persians and Sumerians. Yukteswar's teaching about the great yugas is related in Yogananda's THE AUTOBIOGRAPHY OF A YOGI.[4]

With regards to the fundamental of the bowls being Four, we find that the circle enclosing the cross denoted Paradise and its four rivers rising from the centre, the Tree of Life, and flowing in the four cardinal directions. It is also the Cosmic Solar Wheel, 'the vivifying principle that animates the universe' (Proclus); the four divisions of the cosmic cycle; the four seasons of the year and the ages of man, etc. The solar wheel-cross is always a symbol of good fortune and of change. In the North American Indian lodge the cross inscribed in a circle symbolizes sacred space and is a Cosmic Centre. The four directions of space in the celestial circle are the totality comprising the Great Spirit.

Stroking the bowl is a form of circumambulation that fixes the axis of the world in a particular sacred place such as a temple or a church; it also represents the relation and harmony of motion and stillness, the relation of the axle to the turning wheel; the manifest and the Supreme Reality. It defines a boundary between the sacred and the profane; it is also an imitation of the path of the sun. Making a ritual circuit was also associated with the revolving of the Great Bear, which indicated and controlled the seasons. The Hindu and Buddhist circumambulation of a sacred object (*pradakshina*), keeping the object always on the right hand, is symbolic of circling the world, the All, contained in the Self; it is a pilgrimage to find the Self. Circling the bowl clockwise likewise keeps the object on the right hand side.

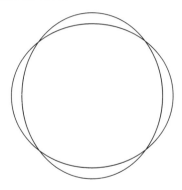

Figure #2

Bowl Exercises

Listen to your bowl, and either concentrate on the pulse your bowl most naturally produces (4, 6, 8, 10, or 12), or else find a wand that brings out one of the pulses, ideally the one you wish to work with. You may find through a choice of wands that your bowl will produce a number of the different pulses. The exercise will work best when we find the wand that brings a focus to one of these pulses in particular rather than generating several simultaneously. A medium to large bowl (say nine inches in diameter), because of its longer circumference, will produce a slower pulsing. There will be a longer period between each pulse, which can make the meditation practice easier. Otherwise, one can ponder the ten qualities (or whichever other pulse it is – 6/8/12) in your own time, without having to link each of these with the successive pulses. For instance, you may like to think of each one of the ten qualities (in our example) for each circuit of the bowl.

For the fundamental four pulses a wand covered with rather coarse leather should work; otherwise use a soft wood such as aspen. A thick wand will work best as thinner wands are generally intended to bring out the higher notes. For the next overtone (or six pulses) a regular wand, maybe from beech, should suffice. Most commonly this would be of two inches in diameter for bowls between six and nine inches diameter. For bowls around ten inches or larger, a thicker wand might work better – say three inches in diameter – whilst a softer wood, such as aspen, might help too. Once we get on to the other overtones of eight, ten, and twelve we will require wands that are ever thinner and made from harder woods until with the twelve we have a thin wand (around half an inch) made from a hard wood such as ebony, violet rosewood, kingwood, cocobolo or Mexican rosewood, depending upon the bowl.

There will be bowls that only produce one set of pulsations – this could be 4, 6, or 8, usually – and no matter what wands we try the same number of pulses will occur. In this case we are limited to that number of pulsations. If this happens to be number four and if it is the right kind of tone (middle octave or lower – but not too low) you could use it for a form of 'soul retrieval' practice. The four carries the energy of the Root Chakra, which relates to the element of Earth, and so can help in bringing the lost energies back to oneself. If it is the case that your bowl tends to form only one cycle of pulses then you can meditate on the various exercises that follow for that number of pulses.

You may choose to burn incense during the exercise and you may also like to light a candle. Because the exercise will involve concentration it is better to make sure that you won't be interrupted. Turn off your mobile/cellphone if you have one, and take any other steps ensuring this protection from outer disturbances.

Before beginning any of these exercises, remember that you can consider which direction you face as you do the exercise, namely

North, South, East, or West.

All the exercises in this section deal with the four-beat fundamental. They are numbered 1-10, and all begin in the same way, with the first five numbered instructions from Exercise 1, which now follows.

Exercise #1

YEARLY ASTROLOGICAL CYCLE

1) Having settled upon the fundamental (pulse of four) for this first exercise,

2) Sit on the floor, or choose a chair that will not impede your arm movements while you play the bowl.

3) Find the right wand to produce this fourfold rhythm with your bowl.

4) Find the right rhythmic speed for playing the bowl, so that you can free yourself from the concentration needed to sustain the sound in order to focus on these other thoughts. Too fast, or the wrong grip (too loose or too tight), or the wrong amount of pressure, and you'll get that horrible clanging noise I mentioned on p. 142 (unless you are using a leather-covered wand, as I mentioned previously).

5) Begin by playing the bowl in the position right in front of you (what I call the new moon position) and once you can produce a steady sound begin to listen to the pulses and focus upon your chosen overtone number (4, 6, 8, 10, or 12).

6) Now working with the fundamental of the bowl (four beats) begin to meditate upon the four turning points in the yearly cycle, beginning with Capricorn (for Earth and Service) right in front of you.

7) Then moving clockwise, think of Aries (Fire and Divine Love) on the next pulse,

8) Followed by Cancer (Water and Peace) at the point opposite our beginning and

9) Finally, on the last pulse, focus on Libra (Air and Brotherhood).

Exercise #2

SOLUNAR CYCLE

Once we have settled into the rhythmic cycle of our bowl, then we are free to notice the pulses and we begin to originate our meditation exercise from in front of ourselves. Again working with the Fundamental, repeat stages 2 to 5 of the first exercise, and then:

6) We begin with the new moon. The ancients would always begin a project at or around the new moon as this is the beginning of the waxing phase and the energy is directed towards manifestation. After full moon we have the waning period – that is, fading away from this world. At the second pulse, moving clockwise, we find the first quarter. This signifies a crisis in action whereby we are made aware of what obstacles lie in our way and so can take steps to remove them.

7) Next we reach full moon at the point opposite to our starting point. This phase represents understanding. We have reached as far as we can in manifesting our vision and now we can test to see how successful we have been.

8) Then finally we have the last quarter, where we must confront our consciousness – let go of the vision in order to be fully open to the new vision arriving at the next new moon.

If we wish to go a bit deeper with this exercise we can use the Sabian Symbol for the particular new moon that is occurring at the time we are doing the exercise. For these symbols, see AN ASTROLOGICAL MANDALA by Dane Rudhyar,[5] and ponder this fourfold rhythm of manifestation of that symbol. Should studying the science of astrology not have appealed to you before, but taking this approach does, then perhaps you will be able to find a friend (or professional astrologer) familiar with astrology to calculate which sign and degree the current new moon (or your current progressed Moon – see next paragraph) occurred on and then either they or yourself can refer to that Sabian symbol.

We might also wish to use this exercise to work with what is called our progressed new moon. Around every thirty years in our astrological (secondary) progressions we will come to a progressed new moon (that is our progressed sun and progressed moon are conjunct) and this will influence our next thirty years. For around three and a half years either side of this occurrence, we will feel that the impetus of the previous cycle has gone whilst the energy of the new cycle has not yet touched our earthly lives – that we can scarcely resonate to this new tone. This mirrors the physical new moon, which is invisible for three days either side of the precise event. Taking the Sabian symbol for our progressed new moon as our meditation (as I've said, you may need to consult an astrologer to do this), we focus upon the energy coming into our lives more and more until at the third pulse or beat we see it manifested fully in our lives, and enjoy that for a period of time before gradually moving away around the fourth pulse, when we enter a phase of purification and approaching emptiness for the next cycle.

As a rough guideline, if you were born at or around the full moon, then a progressed new moon will occur around the age of fourteen. If you were closer to the first quarter then it will come at around age twenty one, and if you were close to the last quarter phase then it will occur around the age of seven with multiples thereof occurring at around every twenty eight years. This means if you are born at full moon then progressed new moons will occur at around ages 14, 42, 70 and 98 and if at around first quarter then repetitions will come at age 21, 49 and 77 and so on with the other phases.

We can glean further insight into what it means for ourselves if we con-sult the Sabian symbol for the last new moon cycle in our lives in order to see how it harmonizes with the upcoming new moon symbol, in order to get some idea of the degree of change likely to occur in our life.

For excellent commentaries into the significance of the 360 Sabian symbols I've already recommended the book, AN ASTROLOGICAL MANDALA, by Dane Rudhyar. If you would like to gain more insight into the solunar cycle then THE LUNATION PROCESS IN ASTROLOGICAL GUIDANCE by Leyla Rael is also a good book. For details, see the bibliography.

Exercise #3

FOUR ELEMENTS CYCLE

In this exercise we are aiming to create a balance between the four elements within us. We may use the form of the pyramid where each of the four sides of its base is equal in size, or we may use the form of the equal-sided cross. Again, working with the fundamental, repeat stages 2 to 5, then:

6) We begin with the element Water. The element Water concerns itself with our feelings, with our soul, and the quality we are seeking here is that of peace.

7) At the next pulse we find Air. The element Air relates to our thinking – bringing the quality of sharing or the lesson of brotherhood.

8) This is followed by Fire. The element Fire represents our spiritual nature and also divine love (the divine flame or spark of spirit within our heart chakra).

9) Last is the element Earth, concerned with our physical life, body and actions, and the ultimate transformation of this body through the divine light. The quality we are seeking to experience here is that of service.

If the pulses of your bowl are too fast then you may wish to ponder one of the four elements per cycle (single revolution of the wand).

This sequence of elements comes from the cycle of initiation known from ancient Greece as the four great initiations. It also borrows from an initiation ritual in ancient Egypt found in the Crata Repoa. Finally, this archetypical representation of the four great initiations is found in the four axial moments of the life of Jesus Christ set out above, p. 318. It is helpful if we can identify which initiation we might be undertaking in the experiences of our life and also guidance concerning the way through such tests and an excellent book for this is that already mentioned by White Eagle.[6]

Should you wish to follow the five elements then simply add the fifth at the central point of the bowl. Perhaps I can suggest we follow the constructive cycle of the five elements in Chinese philosophy (see the next exercise)?

Exercise #4

FIVE ELEMENTS CYCLE

In this exercise we are aiming to create a balance between the five elements within us. These five elements are not simply the materials that the names refer to, but rather metaphors and symbols for describing how things interact and relate to each other. The original Taoist reference was about the seasons (or the heavens), and they would then be more accurately described as the five phases, even as we are following the phases in the sound of the bowl with the four pulses.

Again, working with the fundamental, repeat stages 2 to 5 and then:

6) We begin with the element Wood the equivalent of our Air element. The element Wood produces fire.

7) At the next pulse we find Fire. The element Fire produces Earth.

8) This is followed by Earth. The element Earth produces Metal.

9) The element Metal produces Water.

10) Now we come to the element of Water. We connect this here to the still point in the centre of the bowl. Water produces Wood.

However, this production cycle also has its companion cycle known as the control cycle, which is used to control excesses in the elements. That cycle is: wood controls earth; earth controls water; water controls fire; fire controls metal; metal controls wood. There may be times when you prefer to follow this cycle of the elements.

Exercise #5

FIVE BUDDHA FAMILY CYCLE

Again, working with the fundamental, repeat stages 2 to 5 and then:

In this exercise we are aiming to work with the five Dhyani Buddhas (see Appendix C), which we find in a typical Tibetan *mandala*. These are also known as the five Buddha families.

6) We begin with the Vajra Buddha family, which is linked to the element of Water.

7) At the next pulse we find the family of Ratna, linked to the Earth element.

8) Next comes the family of Padma, associated with the element Fire.

9) These are followed by the family of Karma and is the element Air.

10) Now we come to the Buddha family linked to the element of Space. Space occupies the centre of the mandala and hence the central point of our bowl.

Dhyani Buddha means meditation (or contemplation) Buddha and the five Dhyani Buddhas are: Akshobya, Ratnasambhava, Amitabha, Amogasiddhi and Vairocana respectively (beginning in the East and moving clockwise). For more on the Dhyani Buddhas see Appendix C. If you wish to you could visualize these Buddhas. You could choose to visualize and work with only one of them whilst playing the four pulses of the bowl. In a subtle way you could still be including all five of them as indeed they are interconnected.

Exercise #6

THE FOUR NOBLE TRUTHS

Again, working with the fundamental, repeat stages 2 to 5 and then:

6) In this exercise we are aiming to contemplate these Four Noble Truths first given by the Lord Buddha. At the so-called new moon stage we contemplate the first Noble Truth of Suffering;

7) At the First Quarter stage we think upon the Second Noble Truth of the Cause of Suffering;

8) Reaching the position opposite our starting point we reach the Third Noble Truth of the End of Suffering; finally,

9) When we hear the fourth pulse in our bowl as we reach the right hand side of the bowl we come to the fourth, the Noble Truth of the Path that leads to the End of Suffering.

Exercise #7

VAC: THE FOURFOLD PROCESS OF SOUND

Vac is the Hindu term referring to the four stages involved in the process of speech, although it should be said that to the spiritual vision of the Hindu seers *vac* is considered to refer more to sacred than ordinary speech. Notwithstanding that we shall focus upon the fourfold progress that has been found to exist between thought and the audible word. A fuller explanation of this is given in Chapter 17, on *nada yoga*. In this exercise we are aiming to follow the path of sound either from the highest to the lowest or retracing sound back to its abstract soundless source. At this point we should decide which direction we wish to follow. In our example I suggest the manifestation process; you would reverse the order if choosing to retrace sound, i.e. *vaikhari, madhyama, pashyanti* and finally *para*.

Again, working with the fundamental, repeat stages 2 to 5 and then:

6) Beginning at the new moon position right in front of us we attune to *para* sound – sound that is beyond any physical sound – the *nada* Brahma.

7) With the next pulse (halfway towards the other side of the bowl on our lefthand side in the clockwise direction) we ponder *pashyanti* or visible sound.

8) At our full moon phase (as far as we can go away out from ourselves) we then ponder *madhyama* sound, the in-between phase mediating between our vision and the final sounding.

9) We reach the final phase of *vaikhari* sound – the audible sound or the word.

We may wish to take a specific word or even a *bija mantra*. A suitable example here would be the *bija mantra* for Saraswati (goddess of music and literature), which is '*alm*' (pronounced like I'm). We begin with the thought of Saraswati, with the inspiration to attune ourselves to her wisdom, then we visualize her at the second pulse, then we bring into play our feelings of devotion for her and our thoughts regarding the mystery of this process of creating through sound during the third pulse (opposite our starting point) until we finally inwardly pronounce her *bija mantra 'alm'* on the fourth phase of the sounding of our bowl to our right-hand side.

We can ponder the synthesis of all these four parts as areas of the one body of the singing bowl, so that each person communicating on earth via words or sound is part of the one body of the goddess Saraswati. We begin to draw closer to her being (body of sound) as we move around the bowl, with each repetition following this cycle of manifestation. Or we might even choose to work with Matangi, the goddess particularly involved with *nada yoga*. Her *bija mantra* is *hrim* (hreem). If we choose an English word instead, we may find it most helpful if this is a spiritual quality such as humility, or patience, or peace, or joy, or generosity of spirit, and so on. In this case the inspiration is towards humility (for example) and then we visualize this quality manifesting within us. This is followed by a heartfelt desire to attain the quality, and finally sounding the quality of humility in our lives. In such a way we are following the same fourfold process but with regard to a spiritual or soul quality.

Exercise #8

OM MANI PADME HUM

Again, working with the fundamental, repeat stages 2 to 5, then:

6) At our new moon position we meditate upon the primordial sound of *om*.

7) At the next pulse we turn to *mani*, referring to the jewel of vision in our third eye chakra,

8) followed by our third pulse corresponding to *padme* when we bring the vision down into our heart chakra, for whatever we love we will manifest,

9) and at the final pulse we find *hum* resonating with our throat chakra (manifest sound of *vaikhari*).

In this manner we hear the mantra, which is in six parts, but work with it in a fourfold way in tune with the fourfold process of sound in the ancient Hindu metaphysics. We start at the crown chakra with *om* and move to the third eye with *mani*. Then down in the heart chakra we focus on the fire of divine love (from the Padma or Fire family) until we complete the procedure with *hum* at the throat chakra. We take the great universal sound of *om* and then visualize this manifesting in all people, lighting the fire of love for all life and our fellow beings and finally living this vision in our actions. In this way we purify mind, speech and body or thinking, feeling and acting by the energy of the universal *om*. Or we can use the threefold A-U-M – fourfold when including the silence between repetitions – as in the next exercise.

Exercise #9
A-U-M

Again, working with the fundamental repeat stages 2 to 5, and then:

6) At our starting point, directly before us, we ponder the sound 'A'. This sound arises from the back of our throats. We can spend time experiencing the power that is behind our life. As if seated upon a great throne as with the ancient Egyptian Pharaohs. We open to that power which is behind our lives – pure spirit.

7) With the next pulse we come to the sound 'U' and we feel this moving through our mouth, opening up into the space or cavity and moving forward towards the end of our mouth. Accordingly, here we feel the sense of being sustained and supported along our journey.

8) At the next pulse, reached at the position opposite the one we began with, we inwardly sound 'M'. This would reverberate on our lips if actually sounded and so excite certain areas of our mind. In order to assist in this exercise (but not while playing), try sounding the 'M', keeping your lips loose so that they vibrate. You will feel the energy in the area of your head (not necessarily during the exercise). Our mouth is closed, so we have reached the end of our journey, and yet it is still sounding!

9) At our final pulse we have reached the fourth phase of this sacred word, which is silence.

Exercise #10

CHAKRAS

In this exercise we once again follow the four stages of *para, pashyanti, madhyama* and *vaikhari* that we used in exercise no. 7, but use them in connection with the chakras.

It is important for our spiritual well-being to choose a high ideal. As Jesus said, 'Seek ye first the kingdom of God … and all these things shall be added unto you' (Mark 6 : 33). For this reason we may wish to select one of the higher chakras. The three lower chakras deal largely with our experience with the outer world. I recommend using any of these exercises for spiritual purposes and not in the pursuit of materialistic or utilitarian consumerism. Take the longer view of many lifetimes and work for those qualities that will sustain you throughout this agelong journey of spiritual unfoldment. Nevertheless, follow whatever seems best for you or leaps out at you. What follows is a list of the first six main chakras alongside their desires.

The safest method would be to work with the heart chakra. Many great teachers emphasize love as the key principle to the spiritual path and to life. The spiritual teacher White Eagle, for instance, recommends that we go to the heart chakra first and heal the others by way of the heart chakra.

For instance, if we are feeling ungrounded, outside of our bodies or unearthed – or what is sometimes called 'spaced-out' – we might select the root chakra or *muladhara*. I'll use this as the example, but the same instructions will apply with each of the chakras, except that you will have to take their qualities from the table that follows.

So, working with the fundamental again, repeat stages 2 to 5 and then:

6)   We begin at our crown chakra with the sound *om* and attuned to the field of infinite potential – the uncreated realm working with *para* sound.

7)   Next we visualize the selected chakra (*muladhara* in our example), which action takes us into the *pashyanti* stage. This is the earth chakra, providing us with solidity, etc. We see ourselves embracing the desires of this chakra – being grounded (security), finding stability, experiencing

the process of condensing our vision, feeling comfortable and relaxed with our physical body and our basic biological needs – such as breathing, warmth, feeling our heart beating, appreciating the shelter provided for us.

So it might help to sit upon a chair. Feel your feet firmly on the ground. Breathe a bit more deeply, really feeling that you are breathing yourself down into your body. See how this is the pole opposite to that of the Atmic principle of pure spirit. Here, in terms of holistic philosophy, we experience spirit and matter as two parts of one whole, often seen as father and mother in different spiritual traditions. In astrology, once again, the symbol for earth is the cross within the circle, and this is what we are creating as we play the bowl. We have our four pulses sounding as we encircle the rim of the bowl. We aim to have our head in heaven while our feet are placed firmly upon the ground.

8)   We seek a union of these two principles within our life and this corresponds to the third or *madhyama* phase of our process.

9)   Finally, in the fourth, *vaikhari*, phase we are right in our physical body, feeling gratitude for this opportunity to grow in wisdom, love and power during our earthly sojourn.

This exercise can continue, working with the chakras in sequence, or just focusing on one chakra, but always in the fourfold way described, which as we have seen derives from the Hindu metaphysics of sound, or *vac*. As a guide to working with the other chakras the following list is provided. 'Desire' is not intended in the Western, often pejorative, sense, but to identify how the chakras relate to our needs and the experience of being on the earth.

CHAKRA	ACCOMPANYING DESIRE
MULADHARA Pelvic plexus Perineum	To be grounded (security), physical comforts, stability, shelter.
SVADHISTHANA Hypogastric plexus Genitals	Family, to go with the flow of energy, to feel connectedness, to enjoy the fruits of life.

MANIPURA	To feel the peace of one's own power and inner
Solar plexus	strength or courage to resist outside influences.
Navel	
ANAHATA	Sharing, love, devotion, selfless service,
Cardiac plexus	compassion.
Heart	
VISUDDHA	Creativity, successful communication.
Carotid plexus	
Throat	
AJNA	Vision of the way forward. Insight into life or self-
Pineal plexus	realization, situations, wisdom and intuition,
Third eye	enlightenment.

Exercise #11

MANIFEST SOUND

Again, working with the fundamental, repeat stages 2 to 5 and then:

6) In this exercise we are aiming to follow the path of sound, beginning at the *para* level of soundless sound, attuned to the field of infinite potential.

7) Next, in our *pashyanti* stage, we visualize the quality of the sound. Feel which image goes best with the sound of your bowl. If you visualize peace, does the bowl resonate with this quality of peacefulness? Should you choose to awaken qualities of compassion, does the sound of your bowl resonate with such qualities? If you choose to focus upon total absorption into sound, does the bowl you are using resonate with this quality? If you choose to visualize a harmonious balance between your personality (lower self) and your individuality (higher self), then does the bowl's sound work with this vision? In this instance are there two prominent sounds from the bowl, with one higher than the other but sounding together simultaneously in balanced harmony and providing

us with a sound reflection of this union? Not all bowls can produce this acoustical phenomenon, and I call such bowls Yoga Bowls.

8) In the next stage of *madhyama* we assimilate the qualities (peace, absorption, balance) into ourselves. We feel the sound leading us along this chosen path. Taking our first example, we would then feel this wonderful sense of peacefulness. At this stage it is still a thought.

9) Again, finally, using our example we enter the *vaikhari* stage and, staying with our example, we listen to the peaceful quality in the bowl's sound. We are now experiencing within the actual sound of the bowl the manifestation on earth of the desired quality of peacefulness and stillness. At this stage in the fourfold process we focus upon the actualization of the desired quality, manifested within the actual sound vibrations of our singing bowl. If we had chosen the virtue of compassion, then we appreciate the compassionate qualities within the sound of our bowl. We can contemplate any such quality following the same process, whichever virtue we may select or whichever seems to go best with the sound energy of our bowl.

Exercises using the Second Partial of the Bowl

After striking, the vibratory movement around the rim reflects the phenomenon of contraction and expansion and where these two directions cross (see Figure #4) there is no movement. We see these spots for the second partial depicted by the six short radial lines. The same occurs when stroking, only we can hear these six points as brief moments of quieter sound between the 'beats'. When working with the second partial of six, we can visualize and inwardly sound the sixfold mantra of *om mani padme hum*, breaking it into individual syllables, thus: OM MA NI PAD ME HUM. The mantra translates as 'OM the Jewel is in the Lotus', Mani being the jewel and Padme the lotus. The sacral chakra is six-petalled, and so we may choose to bring our focus to that chakra as we listen to this partial. The *om mani padme hum* mantra is also the mantra for Chenrezig, the patron deity of Tibet.

There is a link with the heart chakra, too. The heart chakra possesses twice six petals, twelve in all, and – according to Rudolf

Figure 4: the Six Nodal Points of the Second Partial.

Steiner – all of humankind has evolved six of these qualities in our past evolution, leaving six to work on.[7] We can therefore make a link between the sixfold pulse and the remaining petals of the heart chakra. Chenrezig is the Tibetan name for Avalokitesvara, the Lord of Compassion: most appropriately for the love energy of the heart chakra. Using the balanced form of a six-pointed star, we provide a beautiful channel for our compassionate energies to radiate forth in blessing to all humankind.

The number six is the number for Venus. Venus has a link with beauty, as well as balance and equilibrium. The Hindu goddess Lakshmi and her *bija mantra 'shrim'* harmonize with this six-pointed star, because of her link to the planet Venus.

The six-pointed star is often known as the Christ Star, and we radiate its light out into life. We each become as a lighthouse, guiding all those tossed about on the waves of life to a safe shore. As the Star guided the Wise Men to the birth of the Christ so, too, is it guiding humankind through these troublesome times. By 2102 we'll have reached the maximum position of the Pole Star (*Stella Polaris*) in the 25,770-year cycle of the precession of the equinoxes (and the circumpolar cycle) or the 'Great Year' of Plato. During this 'circumpolar cycle', there are no less than seven different stars towards which the earthly North Pole will point in turn.

Although we have been using Eastern systems such as the chakras and their graphical symbols, they are profoundly inclusive and there is no conflict in using Christian vocabulary here.

Exercise #12

SIX-POINTED STAR

1) Having settled on working with the second partial and the pulse of six,

2) Sit upon the floor or choose a chair that will not impede your arm movements as you play the bowl.

3) Find the right wand to produce this sixfold rhythm with your bowl.

4) Find the right rhythmic speed for playing the bowl. The aim is that you can free yourself from the concentration needed to sustain the sound in order to focus on these other thoughts to which the exercise directs you. Too fast, or the wrong grip (too loose or too tight), or the wrong amount of pressure, and you'll get that horrible clanging noise (see p. 142).

5) Begin by playing the bowl in the position right in front of you, and once you can produce a steady sound begin to listen to the pulses or beats. Hear the six pulses as you circle the bowl.

6) Once you are in the rhythm of playing the bowl for the six pulses you can see the six points of the Star as you hear the six sounds. Gradually become completely identified with this Star. Feel that you and the star are one. Gradually become aware that the Star is as a sun radiating the light out into the world. Feel that you and the bowl are together a channel for this spiritual light of Christ love to shower forth its blessings upon all. The twelve-pointed Star rests within our heart chakra and the six-pointed Star has these twelve points once we include the outward-facing and inward-facing points.

Feel compassionate love flowing from the universe out to all humankind – like the sun bestowing its rays of light and warmth upon all. If you wish, you may link with a six-pointed Star way up above you, high in the heavens, shining down into the six-pointed Star of your higher self (about fifteen feet above you) and then resonating with the star in your heart. To tune in more deeply to this radiant spiritual light you may also wish to visualize the Master Jesus at the centre of this Star. It is the Star of guiding light and the gentle radiation of the universal Christ Spirit of divine love and light to all humanity.

The Christ Spirit is at the very heart of the Great White Brother-hood, itself uniting East and West, and Jesus was a channel for this universal Christ spirit. So, too, can we be, as 'I and my Father are One' resonates throughout our being and into the hearts of all those whose will is set on receiving this cosmic blessing. Alterna-tively, you can visualize any great teacher at the centre of this Star.

> The concept of Christ as a state of consciousness, as well as lin-guistic variants of the word itself, is very ancient, referring to the unchangeable Intelligence, the pure Reflected Conscious-ness of God, present in every atom of matter and every pore of finite creation – the Christ Consciousness, known from time immemorial by India's rishis as *Kutastha Chaitanya*.
>
> Paramahansa Yogananda[8]

The same Trans-Himalayan occult brotherhood informs Theo-sophical and many other teachings. In them, in their own language, we can find the six-pointed Star. The six-pointed Star is symbolic of the new era, or the sixth post-Atlantean epoch (sub-cycle). It represents the faculty of intuition, as distinct from the mental, or more rational or logical, quality of the number five. The majority of humankind is still working under the five of the fifth post-At-lantean epoch. If we view the six-pointed Star as composed of two triangles, then the upward-pointing triangle symbolizes the hu-man personality striving upwards towards God while the down-ward-pointing triangle is representative of the Individuality, or of the spirit of God, touching our individual centre. The famous Zen saying, 'The one is in the many and the many are in the one', ex-presses this idea beautifully. We could say this is the union of the experience of the God without and the God-Self within.

The points of the Star can be seen to radiate outwards and inwards, and from the outward points we can see radiating out-wards the six 'positive' signs of the zodiac. Equally we can find the six 'negative' signs (Taurus, Cancer, Virgo, Scorpio, Capricorn and Pisces) from those points seemingly moving inwards towards the centre. When this six-pointed Star is seen as one total whole (not as two interlaced triangles), then the union between self and Self, and also non-duality, is signified. It is also the symbol of Shiva–Shakti (the male god Shiva in union with his female consort Shakti), which is sometimes interpreted as Spirit and Matter united. This sense of flowing with the energy of the light of the Star links to the second chakra (*svadhisthana*) associated with the element of water in Hinduism or to the quality of service if working with the Tibetan chakra system – wherein the first two chakras are linked together as one (earth).

If we include the central point of the star we find the form of the seven circles within the one larger circle, with this central seventh point found in the central base of our bowl. By way of the three sets of three (e.g., circles 1, 7 and 4), we can find the three major paths of *karma marga, bhakti marga* and *jnana marga* and place them within the world of united opposites. In the occult philosophy of India, there are six modes of operation of the one life power – that is to say: Parashakti, Gnanashakti, Ichchashakti, Kriyashakti, Kundalinishakti, Matrikashakti – with Shakti being the name for the goddess.

Parashakti is literally the great or supreme force or power whilst also meaning the powers of light and heat (fire).

Gnanashakti relates to *gnana yoga* or the path of intellect or the real wisdom of self-knowledge. When liberated from the phenomenal material world and concerns, it also signifies clairvoyance.

Ichchashakti literally translates as power of the will, particularly as this relates to material manifestation.

Kriyashakti indicates the ability of thought to manifest itself. The apparent miracles of yogis involve the use of Kriyashakti and Ichchashakti. The ancients held that concentration upon an objective eventually manifests that desired aim.

Kundalinishakti signifies the serpentine or curving movements

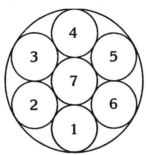

Figure #5

of opposite energies such as attraction and repulsion, whilst also indicating the universal life-principle apparent everywhere in the manifestations of nature. This brings to mind the symbol of the caduceus, associated with Mercury.

Matrikashakti is literally the force or power of letters or speech or music. The science of *mantra* is rooted in this shakti. St John's Gospel begins with the verse, 'In the beginning was the Word'. The power of sound and words to make creative changes in our world resides here. Masters of sound are said to be able to both destroy and create through such power.[9]

Exercise #13

SIX MODES

As in Exercise #12 follow the stages one to five:-

6) When you reach the pulse directly in from of you, at this new moon position, ponder the quality of Parashakti (Supreme Force) and as you hear the next pulse move on to consider the one following.

7) At the next pulse focus on Gnanashakti (power of self-knowledge)

8) At the next pulse focus on Ichchasakti (will power)

9) At the next pulse focus on Kriyashakti (power of thought)

10) At the next pulse focus on Kundalinishakti (chakra energies)

11) At this final pulse focus on Matrikashakti.
(Power of sound)

If the pulses from your bowl are too fast, then consider each quality during an entire repetition or two or three repetitions, but stick to the same amount for each of the six modes.

Exercise #14

THE SIX PERFECTIONS

There are three different lists of these Paramitas and they come from the Ten Paramitas of Theravada Buddhism. They are taken from several sources including the Jataka Tales. Mahayana Buddhism took a list of Six Paramitas from a number of Mahayana Sutras, including the Large Sutra on the Perfection of Wisdom (Astasahasrika Prajnaparamita).

Again, working with the second partial, repeat stages 2 to 5 and then:

6) When you reach the new moon stage directly in front of you upon the bowl's rim concentrate upon the first quality of **generosity**

7) Next focus on **morality**

8) Next focus on **tolerance**

9) Next focus on **energy**

10) Next focus on **meditation**

11) Finally focus on **wisdom.**

If the pulses are too fast, consider each quality during an entire repetition. The Six Perfections are nicely set out in Dale S. Wright's book of the same name.[10]

Exercise #15

THE SEVEN RAYS

Again, working with the second partial, repeat stages 2 to 5 and then:

6) When you reach the new moon stage directly in front of you upon the bowl's rim, concentrate upon the quality of ... the First Ray of Will,

7) then the Second Ray of Love-Wisdom,

8) then the Third Ray of Truth,

9) then the Fourth Ray of Harmony through Conflict,

10) then the Fifth Ray of Concrete Science,

11) then the Sixth Ray of Devotion and Abstract Idealism,

12) and finally be aware of the Seventh Ray of Ritual and Ceremonial Magic (and also Beauty) in the Centre (this is the Ray of Synthesis and currently the dominant ray for humanity).

Exercise #16

THE RAINBOW COLOURS

While we work with the seven colours we can focus upon their virtues as we rotate the bowl beginning with red at the new moon phase, etc., and placing indigo in the centre.

Again, working with the second partial repeat stages 2 to 5 and then:

6) Red, and the virtue of Love

7) Orange, and the virtue of holiness

8) Yellow, and the virtue of wisdom

9) Green, and the virtue of hope

10) Blue, and the virtue of truth

11) Violet, and the virtue of sacrifice

13) Indigo, in the central position with the virtue of stability

Alternatively, you may do seven rounds as you move through the cycle of colours, giving one colour and its corresponding virtue to each round. You may even choose to begin with Red at the new moon phase and next time round focus upon the virtue of holiness for Orange at the second pulse point and then the wisdom of Yellow at the third pulse point, and so on. In this way you are also maintaining the position of the colour to its pulse position around the rim of the bowl.

Exercises using the Third Partial of the Bowl

With the third partial producing the eightfold rhythm we are offered the chance to work with any kind of eightfold structure. We could focus our contemplation upon the Noble Eightfold Path or the eight phases of the Moon. The eight-spoked wheel is associated with Chenrezig (also with the Buddha family, Vairocana). If we seek a slightly more universal significance, we can see the eight as another level of the vibration of the number two, that involves itself with the process of actualization. Firstly, the division of the circle into two, then into four and then into eight: eight sections offer the 45° angle. We can also see this as the four seasons and their midpoints (found at the fifteenth degree of the fixed signs). This would be the point of maximum intensity (arrived at during the rhythmic or organized phase) for each of the four processes of the cycle. The four Gospels in ancient times were correlated to these four fixed signs so that this midpoint of intensity carries the signature of these signs. The links are Luke with Taurus, Mark with Leo, John with Scorpio, and Matthew with Aquarius. With the circle enclosing the double cross it is the 'Rose of the Winds', the four cardinal and four intermediate directions. Or, to change to a quite different civilization,

> I am the One that becomes Two that becomes Four that be-
> comes Eight. Then I am One again.
>
> The Hermopolitan Mystery, from
Old Kingdom Egypt (before 2000 BCE)

The number eight also provides us with our law regarding the octave. In our diatonic scale, the eighth tone of the scale is the same note as our starting note, only vibrating twice as fast. If we begin our scale with the note C, after moving eight places (white notes on the piano) we again reach a C, only it is vibrationally twice the speed of our first C. If, for convenience's sake, we say the first C is moving at 250 cps the next C above would be 500 cps. For Pythagoras this interval symbolized the two great Principles of Father and Mother. The fundamental signified the Father and the octave the Mother. It is interesting to notice that they share the same name (C in our example). In one sense they are the same; they are equal; and in another sense the female energy is different, moving outwards into manifestation away from the Source, the fundamental. When we are sounding the octave interval we can ponder upon this union between Father and Mother. Rudolf Steiner stated that the interval of the octave carries the energy of the God experience (or superconsciousness, if you prefer that term).

By the time we reach the third octave, we would have multiplied our original frequency eight times. Sticking with our example of C as 250, then the next octave would be 500; the next is 1,000 and then we have 2,000 (eight times 250). To the ancients, eight was the number for Saturn, whilst three (the third octave) was the number for Jupiter. These two planets come together every twenty years and in the same sign every sixty years, and for this reason the Chinese and Tibetan astrological cycles are based upon this sixty-year cycle. These two planets are likewise contrasting pairs, with Jupiter basically representing the principle of increase and Saturn that of decrease. Within our breathing cycle, these principles occur as expansion and contraction. Limitation is a prerequisite for expansion.

When they are in union, the comparatively limited personality (lower self – the upward-pointing triangle) and the real individuality (or so-called Higher Self – the downward-pointing triangle) also carry the energy of this musical interval. Therefore, it is helpful to meditate upon the relationship between these two poles of our nature while listening to this eightfold rhythm or pulsation in the bowl. We can then find a correspondence with the universal I AM. This is not the limited self of the ego (Saturn) but rather the universal I AM (Jupiter – named Guru in Hindu astrology).

Another way of entering into this experience is through *so-ham* breathing, which we met on p. 294. In *soham* breathing, on the inbreath we silently and inwardly sound the syllable *so*, and while exhaling we inwardly sound the *ham* (pronounced 'hum'). The *so* is as the individual wave on the surface of the sea and the *ham* relates to the ocean itself. In 'I AM: The Secret Teachings of the Aramaic Jesus' (a six-CD set by Neil Douglas-Klotz), we find Jesus making statements such as: 'Ii the Door'. Here he is linking the greater I (or Self) with the small i (separate self). Experiencing this union between our lesser being and our greater being can accompany the listening to this eightfold rhythm of this overtone of the singing bowl.

Again according to Rudolf Steiner, eight petals of the sixteen petals of the throat chakra have already been worked upon, leaving us eight to work with. We can consider that working with this third partial will assist in unfolding this chakra. The exercises he prescribes for working with these eight petals are linked to the Buddhist Eightfold Path (included in Exercise #18 below).[11]

Alternatively, we could inwardly chant the mantra for Padmasambhava, called 'the second Buddha' and also known as Guru Rinpoche (because it was he that carried Buddhism into Tibet and Bhutan) and by eight other names (or titles) – e.g. Shakya Senge (Padmasambhava as Buddha):

OM A HUNG BENDZA GURU PADMA SIDDHI HUM.

Exercise #17

PADMASAMBHAVA MANTRA

1) Having settled upon working with the third partial and pulse of eight,

2) Sit upon the floor or choose a chair that will not impede your arm movements as you play the bowl.

3) Find the right wand to produce this eightfold rhythm with your bowl.

4) Find the right rhythmic speed for playing the bowl so that you can free yourself from the concentration needed to sustain the sound in order to focus on these other thoughts. Too fast, or the wrong grip (too loose or too tight), or the wrong amount of pressure, and you'll get the clanging noise (unless using a leather-covered wand as mentioned previously).

5) Begin by playing the bowl in the position right in front of you and, once you can produce a steady sound begin to listen to the pulses or beats and hear the eight pulses as you circle the bowl.

6) When you reach the pulse directly in front of you upon the bowl's rim, concentrate upon the first syllable of the mantra OM, and so on:

7) A (as in ah)	11) PADMA
8) HUNG	12) SIDDHI
9) BENDZA	13) HUM
10) GURU	

Unless you are using a very large singing bowl, the chances are that the pulses are too fast, so it may work better to consider each quality during an entire repetition or constant number of repetitions.

Exercise #18

THE NOBLE EIGHTFOLD PATH

This is one of the Buddha's most famous teachings, after the Four Noble Truths.

5) Again, working with the third partial, repeat stages 2 to 5 and then:

6) Consider the first virtue at this pulse – right belief

7) Consider the second virtue at this pulse – right aspiration

8) Consider the third virtue at this pulse – right speech

9) Consider the fourth virtue at this pulse – right conduct

10) Consider the fifth virtue at this pulse – right mode of livelihood

11) Consider the sixth virtue at this pulse – right effort

12) Consider the seventh virtue at this pulse – right mindfulness

13) Consider the eighth virtue at this pulse – right meditation

If the pulses are too fast, then consider each quality during an entire repetition.

Exercise #19

THE WHEEL OF THE BUDDHA FAMILY

This is a kind of three-dimensional mandala where the wheel of the Five Meditation Buddhas is expanded into the third dimension of Space.

5) Again, working with the third partial repeat stages 2 to 5, and then:

6) Ponder the space before you.

7) Ponder the space behind you.

8) Ponder the space to the left of you.

9) Ponder the space to the right of you.

10) Ponder the space above you.

11) Ponder the space beneath you.

12) Ponder the space within you.

13) Ponder the space that is in each of these and omnipresent.

Exercises using the Fourth Partial of the Bowl

The fourth partial provides us with ten pulses. To the ancients, ten was the number symbolic of completion or perfection. The *manipura chakra* (or solar plexus centre) has ten petals. Manipura, meaning City of Jewels, is associated with our personal power – if we visualize the sun shining through this centre we can then associate ourselves with this inner spiritual sun sustaining our lives and our path. Our personal power is then not that of a forceful nature but rather one that is at peace with its inevitable invincibility. One way of working with this number is to approach it as two five-pointed stars. Then, one points upward, and is symbolic of the mind aspiring upwards towards the higher worlds, while the other points downwards. Where the creative energy of the mind is directed downwards into self-centred material aims alone this star is then associated with the practice of black magic, but using them together we can see the combination of the two five-pointed stars as two aspects of the One. We see two opposing forces working together to produce evolution.

The principle can be very difficult to understand, but we are here conceiving of God (or the Supreme Being or Oneness) holding both good and evil. It may help us to understand this conception if rather than thinking of wickedness, we see evil as the unevolved aspect of an energy or force. We might commonly experience this as selfishness or self-centredness, but in reality this is evolution in progress. From a purely visual perspective, the best way to understand the relationship is by comparing the opening of a jam jar, wherein our hands have to oppose one another in the process, else nothing happens. From a higher perspective, the two forces are always complementary and not opposing.

In listening for this ten-pulse, solar-plexus-related fourth partial, we could meditate on how we are moving along an evolutionary path. This might allow and help us to accept where we are now and not feel shame or guilt at not manifesting the highest potential (especially as we live in such a competitive society). With limitation a prerequisite for expansion, it is somewhat inevitable that we should make mistakes from which to grow and learn. Such an insight is more akin to the Tantric than the Sutric path, for on this we accept our limitations and work to transform them, rather than renouncing and seeking to subdue them. Sometimes, by denying the direction of the energy within us we become cut off from that energy and fall into dis-ease. When we are moving from an unconscious level of consciousness towards self-consciousness it is somewhat natural that a degree of self-centredness dominates our behaviour. Yet, as I've said, it is usually advised to begin by following the Sutric path before attempting the Tantric path.

The two planets associated with the dark side are Mars and Saturn. An unevolved reaction to the Mars energy creates a very strong desire nature. This in turn leads to selfishness, and the un-restrained fiery quality of the planet often results in arguments or warlike behaviour, its self-assertiveness manifesting as dominance. A similarly unevolved interaction with the Saturnian energies pro-duces a very strong ego, and this accentuated sense of a separate self creates the isolation and coldness that go with self-centredness – and the application of the will in the coercion of others. In both instances the will is directed towards achieving selfish aims, and this is typical of the lower levels for either of the two Will rays (first or seventh).

Within Tibetan Buddhism we are also reminded of the Ten Perfections (as opposed to the six we explored in Exercise #14). The Ten Paramitas are part of the Bodhisattva Code – and we can ponder these as we focus upon this harmonic of ten pulses. The Ten Virtues of the Bodhisattva Code and their derivation are:

Generosity, Ethics, Patience, Effort, Meditation, Transcenden-tal Wisdom, Skilful Means, Spiritual Aspirations, Higher Accom-plishments, and Awakened Awareness.

Here is a poem ascribed to Tibet's master yogi-saint Milarepa (shown below in a painting by Nicholas Roerich). It is called 'The Ten Transcendent Virtues of the Bodhisattva'.

> *Perfectly give up belief in any true existence,*
> *There is no other generosity than this.*
> *Perfectly give up guile and deceit,*
> *There is no other discipline.*
> *Perfectly transcend all fear of the true meaning of emptiness,*
> *There is no other patience.*
> *Perfectly remain inseparable from the practice,*
> *There is no other diligence.*
> *Perfectly stay in the natural flow,*
> *There is no other concentration.*
> *Perfectly realize the natural state,*
> *There is no other wisdom.*
> *Perfectly praise Dharma in everything you do,*
> *There is no other skilful means.*
> *Perfectly conquer the four demons (death and illness, defiling*
> *   obscurations, prideful ignorance and sensuality),*
> *There is no other strength.*
> *Perfectly accomplish the twofold goal (liberation of both self*
> *   and others),*
> *There is no further aspiration.*
> *Recognize the very source of negative emotions,*
> *There is no other primal wisdom.*

This tenth overtone is likely to be rapid and so it may be easier to think of each one of these virtues during a single repetition so that during our first cycle around the rim of the bowl we ponder the quality of Generosity, and with the second cycle Ethical Self-discipline, and so on through the ten qualities.

Exercise #20

THE TEN PARAMITAS

For the Ten Paramitas, see the book, BUDDHA IS AS BUDDHA DOES.[12]

1) Having chosen the fourth partial and the pulse of ten,

2) sit upon the floor or choose a chair that will not impede your arm movements as you play the bowl.

3) Find the right wand to produce this tenfold rhythm with your bowl.

4) Find the right rhythmic speed for playing the bowl so that you can free yourself from the concentration needed to sustain the sound in order to focus on these other thoughts. Too fast, or the wrong grip (too loose or too tight), or the wrong amount of pressure, and you'll get the clanging noise.

5) Begin by playing the bowl in the position right in front of you and once you can produce a steady sound begin to listen to the pulses or beats and hear the ten pulses as you circle the bowl. I find it easiest to count this as two fives – or, more helpfully, as three, two, three, two.

When you reach the pulse directly in from of you upon the bowl's rim concentrate upon the first quality, generosity, and continue thus:

6) GENEROSITY. This arises from unselfishness and non-attachment and it is kindness and compassion in action.

7) ETHICAL SELF-DISCIPLINE. Involves virtue and integrity, balance and moderation.

8) PATIENCE. Requires inner fortitude, inner strength, acceptance, and resilience.

9) EFFORT. Means courage in joyous and enthusiastic perseverance, never giving up.

10) MEDITATION. Implies mindfulness and awareness, concentration, reflection and introspection.

11) TRANSCENDENTAL WISDOM. Includes discernment, sagacity,

self-knowledge and knowledge about ultimate reality: thus, realization.

12) SKILFUL MEANS. Includes resourcefulness, skill in methods and imagination too – creativity.

13) SPIRITUAL ASPIRATIONS. These involve the noble intuition and strong resolve and determination to be of service to all, to contribute, to edify and awaken.

14) HIGHER ACCOMPLISHMENTS. These may be powers, empowerment, positive influence.

15) AWAKENED AWARENESS. This is summarized as total realization, as primordial, pristine awareness.

Exercise #21

THE TEN SEPHIROTH

With this exercise we move into the tenfold Cabalistic system of the Jewish tradition, perhaps more familiar to some Western readers. Again, working with the fourth partial repeat stages 2 to 5 and then:

6) When you reach the new moon stage directly in front of you upon the bowl's rim, concentrate upon the first quality of Kether – the Crown (*Primum Mobile*)

7) At the next pulse focus on Chochmah – Wisdom (The Zodiac)

8) At the next pulse focus on Binah – Understanding (Saturn)

9) At the next pulse focus on Chesed – Mercy (Jupiter)

10) At the next pulse focus on Geburah – Severity (Mars)

11) At the next pulse focus on Tiphereth – Beauty (Sun)

12) At this pulse focus on Netsah – Victory (Venus)

13) At this next pulse focus on Hod – Glory (Mercury)

14) At this pulse focus on Jesod – the Foundation (Moon)

15) At this final pulse focus on Malkuth – the Kingdom (Elements)

Exercise #22

THE LORD'S PRAYER

You may find it most congenial of all to use the Lord's Prayer. Again, working with the fourth partial, repeat stages 2 to 5, and then:

6) You reach the new moon stage directly in front of you upon the bowl's rim. Concentrate upon the first quality of Primum Mobile – Our Father

7) At the next pulse focus on the Zodiac – Which art in heaven

8) At the next pulse focus on Saturn – Hallowed be Thy name

9) At the next pulse focus on Jupiter – Thy Kingdom come

10) At the next pulse focus on Mars – Thy will be done

11) At the next pulse focus on the Sun – On earth as it is in heaven

12) At this pulse focus on Venus – Give us this day our daily bread

13) At this next pulse focus on Mercury – Forgive us our debts

14) At this pulse focus on the Moon – Lead us not into temptation

15) At this final pulse focus on the Elements – For thine is the Kingdom, the power, and the glory.

Exercise #23

THE TEN FUNCTIONS

Dane Rudhyar developed this idea of seeing the ten planets (including the Sun and Moon) as ten functions within the total whole of the solar system.

Again, working with the fourth partial repeat stages 2 to 5 and then:

16) You reach the new moon stage directly in front of you upon the bowl's rim. Concentrate upon the first function of the Sun: vitalization, energy and fuel.

17) At the next pulse focus on the Moon: distributing agency, circulation of life energy. Etheric.

18) At the next pulse focus on Mercury – communication between parts of the whole and the outer environment. Nerves. Intelligence.

19) At the next pulse focus on Venus – Judgment of what comes in – is it good or bad; does it help or injure?

20) At the next pulse focus on Mars – Mobilised to act. Our judgments are followed by muscular response.

21) At the next pulse focus on Jupiter – Growth, expansion. Social expansion and the things that bind – family, blood ties, ideologies.

22) At this pulse focus on Saturn – Stabilizes what Jupiter has expanded. Group laws.

23) At this next pulse focus on Uranus – Crisis and growth. Transformation through revelation or upheaval of ego-consciousness. Takes all previous functions and relates them to a larger unity.

24) At this pulse focus on Neptune – Dissolution of static and rigid Saturnian structures. Jupiter connects with others but only the family! Here is the vast feeling of Neptune. Utopia and idealism.

25) At this final pulse focus on Pluto – Reduction. Polarisation. Reduces all down to basic elements – essence! A re-focalization onto new lines related to cosmic greater whole.

Exercises using the Fifth Partial of the Bowl

When we reach the fifth partial we find the number twelve. Twelve unites the numbers one and two (placing them alongside one another) and yet it has them existing separately, as contrasted with the number three, where they are added together. To Pythagoreans, the number three was the first real number, as the numbers one and two signified the first two major principles from which all else derived. Accordingly, the third point reached in the overtone series, the major fifth, carries this creative energy and supplies the basis for our Western musical scale (as well as the Chinese), along the lines of what is musically termed a geometric progression. Of course, if we take our number four signifying materialization along with our four basic bodies and multiply this by the threefold

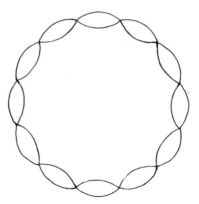

Figure #5

paths (or *margas*) we get the number twelve. Placed in a balanced form, the four and the three give us the pyramid. The number three of the triangle represented the element of fire to the ancients, whereas the cube, being derived from the number four, represented the element of earth. In other words, the fire of the spirit working within the physical earthly element produces the pyramid. In that form we have our four elements combined with the three modes of manifestation, balanced with one another.

Each element, as we have already seen (pp. 196-7) manifests along three major lines, known as cardinal, fixed and mutable. Symbolically, these represent will, love, and wisdom respectively. If we take the fire element as an example, then in Aries, the first sign of the zodiac, which is a cardinal fire sign, the fire is beginning, the flames are flickering from one piece of wood to the next and we are waiting for the fire to stabilize. In Leo, the fixed fire sign, we have our roaring fire and a rhythm that has been firmly established. Then we approach the dying embers of the fire in Sagittarius, the mutable fire sign, and we must choose between allowing the fire to die or rekindling it into new life.

Within the scope of a year, cardinal signs initiate one of the four seasons and then that season becomes organized into a regular rhythm (fixed sign). Then a period of adaptiveness occurs, bridging the two energies of the old and the new seasons (the mutable sign). Across the wheel of twelve signs this pattern creates three crosses, namely the cardinal, fixed and mutable crosses.

Listening to our bowl, I find that 12 is easiest to hear when we think of it as consisting of four groups of three, as in 1, 2 3

— 2, 2 3 — 3, 2 3 — 4, 2 3. Another way to count it, which may come more easily, is one-and-ah, two-and-ah, three-and-ah, four-and-ah. This partial is likely to be so rapid that placing a single thought alongside each of the twelve sounds as they rotate by is too distracting. In practice it is far less stressful if we focus upon counting the four trinities. However, you could draw yourself a chart with the twelve astrological glyphs and simply look at them. Otherwise, it is easier to focus upon the first of twelve during one (or two or three) rotations followed by a focus on the second for a similar number of rotations, etc.

The most obvious usage of four trinities lies with the twelve signs of the zodiac, as I have demonstrated, so that we can take this as our focus of meditation. We can choose to think of this, or visualize it, as a pyramid if we wish. Herein, a square base of four supports a triangle on each edge – the four elements supporting the three qualities. This provides us with four triangles, thus matching our method for counting this fourth overtone, or fifth note, of the bowl. We could here focus once again upon the lessons of the four elements or the four greater initiations, namely water (associated with peace), air (with brotherhood), fire (with love), and earth (with service).

If we choose to follow the order of the signs, then it would be fire (Aries), earth (Taurus), air (Gemini) and finally water (Cancer). Using our counting system from above this would be fire-and-ah, earth-and-ah, air-and-ah, water-and-ah. Round and round. That is to say, Aries-and-ah, Taurus-and-ah, Gemini-and-ah, Cancer-and-ah, Leo-and-ah, Virgo-and-ah, Libra-and-ah, Scorpio-and-ah, Sagittarius-and-ah, Capricorn-and-ah, Aquarius-and-ah, Pisces-and-ah, making three circuits of the rim in all.

Element	Fire	Earth	Air	Water
Sign	Aries	Taurus	Gemini	Cancer
	Leo	Virgo	Libra	Scorpio
	Sagittarius	Capricorn	Aquarius	Pisces
Count	Fire and ah	Earth and ah	Air and ah	Water and ah

Table #11: Order of the Signs through the Four Elements

In the attempt to isolate a single harmonic from within the bowl, this is the highest I have been able to reach – from any single bowl. If you can't achieve the twelve from your bowl, don't worry. It is just that this twelvefold exercise isn't for you, or for your bowl – at the moment. It is something of an advanced technique to produce this fifth partial, and even the fourth too.

There is nothing to stop you using the fundamental four pulses and completing three circuits to produce the twelve signs. Another way we can count this overtone, of course, is as three cycles of four: one-e-and-ah, two-e-and-ah, three-e-and-ah. Then, the threefold counting relates to our three principles of will, love, and wisdom (linked in the way we saw to cardinal, fixed and mutable):

Cardinal (Will) Phase = Spring/Summer/Autumn/Winter, or by the signs of Aries/Cancer/Libra/Capricorn, giving the elemental sequence of Fire/Water/Air/Earth, or

Fixed (Love) Phase = Taurus/Leo/Scorpio/Aquarius, giving the elemental sequence of Earth/Fire/Water/Air or

Mutable (Wisdom) Phase = Gemini/Virgo/Sagittarius/Pisces, giving the elemental sequence of Air/Earth/Fire/Water.

In the cardinal cycle, Fire initiates the sequence while Earth concludes. This could be seen as a mirror of the Hindu metaphysics of sound. Fire would be the spark of an idea. Water then reflects that idea as light – or vision. Then Air, via the characteristics of Libra, involves itself with attracting that which is needed from outside of ourselves (Libra rules relationships), so that finally the completed form is manifested in Earth. The cardinal cross relates to the quality of will and thus of action: 'Knock and the door shall be opened unto you'.

In the fixed cycle, the beginning and end, *alpha* and *omega*, are the most fixed elements of the four – Earth and Air. This fixed cross is related to the quality of love. Taking the soul lessons, we find a sequence that is based upon the beginning focus of service, which is followed first by love and then by peace; the sequence concludes with brotherhood. The entire sequence is centred upon the heart quality of spiritual love. Because it is said that one cannot hear the *anahata* sound of the *nada yogis* until one has reached the level of the heart chakra, perhaps this is the main sequence of elements that we should focus upon while we are working with sound. 'Ask and it shall be given unto you.'

In the mutable cycle, all the signs are dual except for Virgo, the Virgin; Pisces at the close relates to the drop of water entering into the ocean of universal life. Mercury and Jupiter are the two main planets found here. They are planets of the mind – the lower and higher mind respectively. The mutable cross correlates with the principle of wisdom. 'Seek and ye shall find.'

These three major qualities can also be related to the first three major rays – first ray of will, second ray of love, and third ray of wisdom (*karma marga, bhakti marga,* and *jnana marga* respectively) so that we could also meditate on one of these while working with this partial.

Two fours are eight and three fours are twelve, and if we wish to marry our two principles of male and female (symbolized within the odd and even numbers) then we could multiply twelve by nine (the eight plus the centre of the bowl) and reach 108 – a sacred number used in mantric repetitions. We also find our mathematical relationship between three and four present here as nine is three quarters of twelve.

Exercise #24

THE TWELVE ZODIAC SIGNS

1) Having chosen the pulse of twelve for this fifth-partial exercise,

2) Sit upon the floor or choose a chair that will not impede your arm movements as you play the bowl.

3) Find the right wand to produce the twelvefold rhythm with your bowl.

4) Find the right rhythmic speed for playing the bowl so that you can free yourself from the concentration needed to sustain the sound in order to focus on these other thoughts. Too fast, or the wrong grip (too loose or too tight), or the wrong amount of pressure, and you'll get that clanging noise.

---

5) Begin by playing the bowl in the position right in front of you, and once you can produce a steady sound begin to listen to the pulses or beats. Hear the twelve pulses as you circle the bowl. As I have said, I find it easiest to count this as four threes, although we have also looked at three fours.

When you reach the pulse directly in front of you on the bowl's rim, concentrate upon the first quality of the Cardinal Fire Sign of Aries. Our entire cycle begins with this creative Fire. The ancient Greeks linked Fire with the Tetrahedron, which has four Triangles (one underneath) and so it is that this first sign brings the energy of the triangle (each of the four elements has three signs or qualities) to our cycle of Signs.

6) ARIES, the Cardinal Fire Sign.

7) TAURUS, the Fixed Earth Sign.

8) GEMINI, the Mutable Air Sign.

9) CANCER, the Cardinal Water Sign.

10) LEO, the Fixed Fire Sign.

11) VIRGO, the Mutable Earth Sign

12) LIBRA, the Cardinal Air Sign.

13) SCORPIO, the Fixed Water Sign.

14) SAGITTARIUS, the Mutable Fire Sign.

15) CAPRICORN, the Cardinal Earth Sign.

16) AQUARIUS, the Fixed Air Sign.

17) PISCES, the Mutable Water Sign.

Exercise #25

THE TWELVE LABOURS OF HERCULES

This time our meditation is on the symbolic heroic tasks of incarnation.

Repeat the process from 2 to 5, then:

When you reach the pulse directly in from of you upon the bowl's rim concentrate upon the first Labour of Hercules – The Capture of the Man-Eating Mares. And so on, as below.

6) The Capture of the Man-Eating Mares.

7) The Capture of the Cretan Bull.

8) The Golden Apples of the Hesperides.

9) The Capture of the Ceryneian Doe or Hind.

10) The Slaying of the Nemean Lion.

11) Seizing the Girdle of Hippolyta.

12) The Capture of the Erymanthian Boar.

13) Destroying the Lernaean Hydra.

14) Killing the Stymphalian Birds.

15) The Slaying of Cerberus Guardian of Hades.

16) Cleansing the Augean Stables.

17) The Capture of the Red Cattle of Geryon.

See THE LABOURS OF HERCULES, by Alice A. Bailey, and the next exercise.[13]

Exercise #26

THE TWELVE SOUL STANZAS

Alice A. Bailey was the vehicle through which the Tibetan Master (D.K.) gave his teachings. Here we will focus upon the stanzas that The Tibetan gave for the twelve astrological signs. For instance, if you are a Virgo, then part 11 'I am the Mother and the Child. I, God, I, matter am' would especially be for you.

Repeat the process from 2 to 5, then, when you reach the pulse directly in from of you upon the bowl's rim concentrate upon the first 'stanza':

6) 'I come forth and from the plane of mind, I rule.'

7) 'I see and when the eye is opened all is light.'

8)	'I recognize my other self and in the waning of that self I grow and glow.'
9)	'I build a lighted house and therein dwell.'
10)	'I am That and That am I.'
11)	'I am the Mother and the Child. I, God, I, matter am.'
12)	'I choose the way which leads between the two great lines of force.'
13)	'Warrior am I and from the battle I emerge triumphant.'
14)	'I see the goal. I reach that goal and then see another.'
15)	'Lost am I in light supernal, yet on that light I turn my back.'
16)	'Water of Life am I, poured forth for thirsty men.'
17)	'I leave my father's home and turning back, I save.'

See Alice. A. Bailey, ESOTERIC ASTROLOGY (Volume III of 'A Treatise of the Seven Rays.')

Beyond the Fifth Partial

The fifth partial is usually as far as one needs to go with singing bowls. I have not been able to isolate the partials beyond this point while stroking a bowl. In any case it is not really necessary to go beyond this fifth partial, as there is another factor that enters in. It shows up in research into the acoustics of round plates that was carried out by Mary D. Waller, of the London School of Medicine for Women, in 1937, when she introduced nodal circles into the equation. So far we have dealt with the radii of the round plate or bowl (this divides our plate up into segments that are somewhat pie-shaped) but following her work we now must also include circles concentric with the perimeter of the plate.

As you can see in the inset diagram opposite, this provides us with a very rich interplay of frequencies. These are coloured black and white in order to signify that each adjacent section is always moving in the opposite direction at any given time. We remember once again that the singing bowl can be viewed as a kind of flanged Chladni plate: this adds more complexity to what is already an intricate acoustical study. In the diagram, we are dealing with a flat plate although the nodal circles are also found in studies by Rossing of western church bells, using holographic interferograms. Below is a diagram to illustrate the point using the nodal radii and the circles where (m) represents the nodal radii (here 2, 4, & 6) and (n) the nodal circles (here 1 & 2).

A bell is a very complex acoustical body. Bells do not follow whole-number ratios, as the voice, stringed instruments, brass instruments, and so on do. Therefore, what is referred to as the overtone series does not apply to bells. The overtone series arises from a simple arithmetic ratio – namely the same number added to itself (see Table #12, overleaf). However, with bells we find an adaptation of the acoustical phenomenon of vibrating plates (directly related to the Chladni plate). It has been found with both bells and plates that increasing the thickness of the vibrating material increases vibration, while increasing diameter decreases the vibration frequency. However, while this may be a rule-of-thumb, yet other variants come into the equation. We may place two bowls of similar diameter beside each other and yet be shocked to find that they sound dissimilar. One may be made from thicker metal (reducing elasticity) and this produces a higher pitch, while the other is constructed from a much thinner piece of metal and so produces a lower tone because it possesses a higher rate of elasticity. Our pair of bowls might also comprise a *yin* and a *yang* bowl. Here again, with the

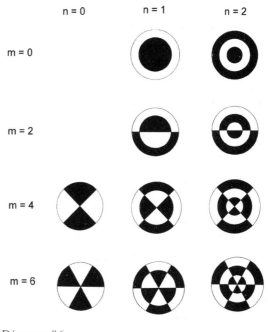

Diagram #6

thicker rim, reducing elasticity, gives us a much higher tone than with the thinner-rimmed *yin* bowl.

In the table opposite (#12) I list over four columns the overtones found in the arithmetic progression in music. Taking C as 256 cps, then in order to cover seven octaves we begin with 32 cps – three octaves below 256. To put it in the simplest terms, beginning with 32cps the musical interval found in the next number in the sequence (64cps) is an octave. 32cps we call a C and 64cps we also call a C, only it is one octave higher than the C at 32cps, eight white notes up from C on the piano. In the table the octaves are in bold, i.e. 32, 64, 128, 256, 512, 1,024, 2,048 and 4,096.

As we progress the number of divisions per octave increases, and this translates into ever-smaller musical 'intervals'. You can see this in the table for the whole of the two righthand columns are the sixty-four intervals existing between the C at 2,048cps and the next one at 4,096cps. Then following down the numbers in the table we find that the next octave (64cps to 128cps) contains two intervals – the 'fifth,' (this is the 'third' note to appear [96cps] but is found on the piano by playing the 'fifth' white note up from C – 64cps) then a fourth (four white notes on the piano down from C found at 128cps to the 96cps), then the next octave (from 128cps to 256cps) has four intervals, presenting a series of four ever-decreasing thirds ('three white notes' on the piano), etc. Each octave doubles the number of overtones present (1, 2, 4, 8, 16, 32, 64) – that is to say, it doubles the number of divisions within the octave – never equally but always decreasing in size during the ascending progression.

In the lower table (#13), we compare this arithmetic whole number series of overtone frequencies to the partials of one singing bowl. For the example I have chosen one of the bowls from the Solar Plexus 'matched pair', shown first in table #2 from Chapter 6, where we discovered how much it differed from its companion singing bowl. We now compare its sound with the normal overtone sequence.

For the sake of comparison I have chosen the same starting point, 91 cps. You will first observe that there are far fewer overtones in the singing bowl and you will also notice that the first

C	32	1,056	2,080	3,104
C	64	1,088	2,112	9,136
	96	1,120	2,144	3,168
C	128	1,152	2,176	3,200
	160	1,184	2,208	3,232
	192	1,216	2,240	3,264
	224	1,248	2,272	3,296
C	256	1,280	2,304	3,328
	288	1,312	2,336	3,360
	320	1,344	2,368	3,392
	352	1,376	2,400	3,424
	384	1,408	2,432	3,456
	416	1,440	2,464	3,488
	448	1,472	2,496	3,520
	480	1,504	2,528	3,552
C	512	1,536	2,560	3,584
	544	1,568	2,592	3,616
	576	1,600	2,624	3,648
	608	1,632	2,656	3,680
	640	1,664	2,688	3,712
	672	1,696	2,720	3,744
	704	1,728	2,752	3,776
	736	1,760	2,784	3,808
	768	1,792	2,816	3,840
	800	1,824	2,848	3,872
	832	1,856	2,880	3,904
	864	1,888	2,912	3,936
	896	1,920	2,944	3,968
	928	1,952	2,976	4,000
	960	1,984	3,008	4,032
	992	2,016	3,040	4,064
C	1,024	C 2,048	3,072	C 4,096

Table #12

SINGING BOWL	NORMAL OVERTONES
91	91
	182
261	273
	364
	455
503	546
	637
	728
806	819
	910
	1,001
	1,092
1,170	1,183

Table #13

interval (the octave) is entirely missing from our singing bowl (91 – 182 would be the octave; instead we have 91 – 261). There are no meeting points between the normal series of overtones and the partials of this singing bowl. The overtones present in the human voice and all instruments of our western orchestral music (woodwinds, brass, strings) all adhere to the arithmetic overtone series. Every single one of them can only produce the first overtone of an octave – nothing greater or less. In overtone singing it is impossible to produce a first overtone of a major third or fifth or any other interval starting from the same fundamental with our voice because the first overtone we can produce will always be an octave. The sequence of overtones is therefore unchangeable and very predictable.

Bells do not obey this law. Nonetheless, church bells are tuned, and it typically takes up to two weeks to do so. In this case the bell is placed upon a lathe and small amounts of metal are removed from specific parts of the bell in order to tune their partials to make them more musical-sounding. Of course, church bells are also cast, and not hand-hammered as with singing bowls (apart from modern machine-made bowls). However, with singing bowls this is not the case – they do not obey this law of overtones but instead each individual bowl has its own unique structure of partials originating from the fundamental. So, rather like the unpredictability of quantum mechanics, no standard sequence of overtones can be applied to singing bowls. I must also mention here that the overtone series is not the same as the twelve notes of our scale.

In order to demonstrate again the uniqueness of the subsequent partials in each singing bowl we now compare (opposite, #14) two large singing bowls. On the lefthand side is a thirteen-and-a-half-inch *yin* bowl that I name Olmo Lung Ring. And on the right, an eighteen-inch *yang* bowl that I call Zhang-Zhung – almost half as large again – with fundamental tones that are very close to each other (58.5 – 59.5 cps) and follow their progress through their individual partials to discover that they do not follow any regular order (their dominant pitches are in bold). Here they are played with soft lambswool gong mallets, so that not all of their partials were stimulated:

OLMO LUNG RING			ZHANG-ZHUNG	
• **58.5**	**Bb (-2) +6**		• **59.5**	**Bb (-2) + 36**
• 169	E (0) +43		• 182	F# (0) – 28
• 227.5	Bb (0) -41		• 185.5	F# (0) + 4
• 315.5	Eb (1) +24		• 361	F (1) - 42
• 318.5	Eb (1) +40			
• 334.5	E (1) +25			
• **338**	**E (1) +43**			
• 502.5	B (1) +29			

Table #14

This means that making 'music' with bowls is extremely difficult – it is more like organizing chaos. Nothing resembling western
harmony is possible unless we restrict our listening to the fundamental of each bowl, and even then we'd need to search far and
wide to find bowls with fundamentals exactly in tune with notes
of our western scale – before we even began to look into pitch
standards or tuning systems (Equal Temperament, Just Intonation,
Pythagorean, etc.). The nearest way to make music may rest with
microtonality, in which category we find the music of Harry Partch
(1901–74) with his collection of beer bottles, light bulbs and hub-
caps, and his Cloud Chamber bowls. Not wishing to misrepresent
Partch's music with these few examples I should also mention that
he built and constructed stringed and percussion instruments (and
adapted reed organs) for playing his music – in what he sometimes
called his forty-three-notes-to-the-octave scale (ours typically has
twelve) from 1930 onwards. Others likewise have questioned the
twelve-note scale in use and gone on to work with larger divisions – such as Ezra Sims, Alois Haba, Julian Carillo, Ivan Vysh-
negradsky, and then Iannis Xenakis, Ben Johnston, etc. As early
as 1924 (with sketches begun between 1910 and 1914), Charles
Ives composed a piece for two quartertone pianos. Following this,
other composers then pursued more subdivisions of the semitone,
moving into eighth tones, and then sixteenth tones was one way
to go with the (fretless) stringed instruments available. So it is
that we find 24, or 48, or 72, or 96 notes per octave. On You-
Tube I found people using a harp tuned to 400 notes per octave!

Music in India has twenty-two tones per octave, close to the quartertone, as opposed to our usual twelve semitones to the octave. But these other western composers mostly found working with stringed instruments easiest for such excursions into finer divisions of the musical scale (mostly in the form of string quartets). By contrast, Partch invented and hand-built instruments to play his scales.

Lastly, the development of electronic or computer music frees the composer considerably from the limitations of acoustic instruments and tuning issues. Ironically, perhaps, some of these composers have tried working with intervals mathematically outside of the overtone scale only to find that the human ear puts them back in! It seems we are bounded finally by the structure of the human ear itself.

Listening to some singing bowls we can hear a vibrato effect, a kind of fluttering in the sound. This occurs when the partials of the singing bowl lie very close together. In the table below you will see listed twenty-three separate partials that make up the sound

BLUE SUNSET	
• **159**	**Eb (0) +37**
• 460.5	Bb (1) -21
• 473	Bb (1) +25
• **879**	**A (2) -1**
• 885	A (2) +9
• 921	Bb (2) -21
• **946**	**Bb (2) +25**
• 1345.5	E (3) +35
• 1352	E (3) +43
• 1381	F (3) -19
• 1384	F (3) -16
• 1844.5	Bb (3) -18
• 1946.5	B (3) -25
• 2269	Db (4) +39
• 2592.5	E (4) -29
• 2614	E (4) –15
• **2831.5**	**F (4) +23**
• 3310.5	Ab (4) -6
• 3330.5	Ab (4) +4
• 3893	B (4) -25
• 4076.5	C (5) -45
• 4560.5	Db (5) +48
• 4694.5	D (5) -1

Table #15

of one ancient bowl. Strictly speaking, this bowl would then contain some sixteen different 'notes'. Many experts have dated it to around eight hundred years old – that is, to the twelfth century. It is an unusual shape and has a graceful dome in the centre. It is a thin-rimmed *yin* bowl and I have found that it is useful in remembering past lives or in seeing the past lives of others. The name I give this bowl is Blue Sunset Bowl.

I have drawn attention to where the partials are very close together via the arrow-shaped lines. This is quite a remarkable bowl, as within its sound are exact octaves, which as I have said is rare amongst bowls. You will notice that the second and third partials are Bb (1) – 21 and Bb (1) + 25, and the sixth and seventh partials are similarly Bb (2) – 21 and Bb (2) + 25 – exactly one octave higher. Elsewhere we find partials that are very close to the same frequency and these produce what I call 'beats' or 'vibrato' (rather like when two separate bowls are used together, such as my solar plexus 'matched pair' – shown in Table #2). With regular church bells, the effects are referred to as 'warbles' or 'doublets'.

To give another example, between the eighth and ninth partial there is only 8 cps difference (E (3) + 35 and E (3) + 43), and then again the following pair of partials are found to be F (3) – 19 and F (3) – 16, giving a difference of only 3 cps. When this bowl is heard, there are seven of these pronounced pulses (doublets) existing within its sound. Again, with different bowls that possess this vibrato effect it can occur in several instances – we might hear one, or two, or three vibratos (existing together after one strike), or more. This effect can be found in other bowls but not in all bowls. It might even be that not everyone enjoys the presence of these beats in the sound of a bowl. Sometimes their presence is very pronounced, yet with other bowls it can be less noticeable, making it easier for us to focus upon an overall continuous sound.

17. Nada Yoga

Seek the Sound that never ceases, seek the sun that never sets.
RUMI

The universe was manifested out of the Divine Sound;
From It came into being the Light.
SHAMAS-I-TABRIZ

The Sound is inside us. It is invisible. Wherever I look I find it.
GURU NANAK

NADA YOGA is the ancient yoga of sound – both the inaudible and the audible – and we have considered it from time to time already, noting the concept of inaudible sound quite carefully. It has been said by Alain Presencer that those Tibetans who worked with the bowls followed the sound into the silence. We have also noted that the ancient Chinese bellmakers were asked to create a bell that was most sonorous and that rang on for a long time. The dividing line between the sound of the bowl and silence can be very blurred when a bowl rings on for anything from one to over four minutes. Hearing sound turn slowly into the voice of the silence brings us quite naturally to the study of *nada yoga*. This non-linguistic element of music bridges our world with that of the formless. The singing bowls would be a natural compliment to *nada yoga*, offering one of the simplest forms of music. They provide us with the opportunity to enter into what lives within that one sound. With the bowls the sound does not move very far away from the silence. As the inner sound of the *nada* yogi is as a call to the spirit, so, too, the various bowls, each with their unique sound, call us to join with one aspect of the spiritual community of beings. One of the best singing bowls that I've found for this are the Manipuri Lingams.

From within the enormous number of thoughts that may arise from this one word, sound, let us begin with the lexical definition of *nada* that reads: 'A loud sound, roaring, bellow-ing, crying, any sound or tone, the nasal sound represented by a semicircle (in yoga philosophy) and used as an abbreviation in mystical words'. Etymologically, *nada* means 'flow of conscious-ness' and so it is that some speak of it as the 'Sound Current'. For the initiate, *nada* is the primal vibration, the divine ever-present creative sound and the very core of spiritual practice. The sylla-ble *na* means breath, the syllable *da* the fire (of intellect). Born of the union of breath and fire, intelligible sound is called *nada* (*Sangita-Mekaranda* 4.18.).

The expression, *nada yoga*, adds another word. The word *yoga* means union; that is, union with the divine source of all life, whilst *nada* is often translated as sound or river. The Hindu goddess of music is named Saraswati after an ancient river in India. As the divine is living within all things, so it is that there are many rivers or pathways to the divine. The major ones are probably *raja yoga, karma yoga, jnana yoga, hatha yoga, laya yoga, bhakti yoga, and mantra yoga*, but we find over forty others including *agni yoga, kriya yoga, shiva yoga*, and *nada yoga*.

In a sense, *nada yoga* could be seen as a branch of *mantra yoga*, as both are concerned with sound. From the views of both, *vac,* the Hindu metaphysics of sound (which teaches that sound has a fourfold process) and the inclusive Tantric perspective, *nada yoga* could be said to incorporate and include all forms of sound or music. However, in practice the *nada* yogi places his or her fo-cus upon what is termed the *anahata nada* or the inaudible (or to use the more literal translation, 'unstruck') sound. That is to say it represents a sound that is not made as a result of two or more objects striking one another. It is, in fact, a sound not coming to the human ear from outside of the body but rather from within. However, it isn't an imagined sound – such as might happen were we to recall a sound or a piece of music to ourselves and sing it in silence, mentally. Neither is it an 'earworm' – the phenomenon we know so well when we have some song or tune irritatingly repeat-ing itself over and over inside our heads. Nor is it like the sound inside our ears during take-off in a plane, as it rises up higher and higher, or like the sound inside a deep lift shaft – or any other such

physical situations where we experience the sensation of a sounding inside of our ears. Neither is it tinnitus.

The way of the inner sound is found in certain spiritual organ-
izations established in their tradition where one can safely unfold
this gift. Being rooted in an eternal truth, it is also ever-present for
those who can provide the right conditions for its manifestation
independently. I know of a few such that have been blessed with
this gift. *Nada* is a form of yoga suited to those who are attracted
to work with sound. There have been periods in history when this
form of yoga has had little appeal and only a very few yogis have
followed the demands of such a path. It is only relatively recently
that it has become known in the West. The aim of the *nada* yogi
is to find the inaudible sound within and, meditating with this experience, to enter into communion with the Supreme Being and so
attain liberation. Listening to the inner sound is a way of purifying
the nadis – or subtle channels within the body.

It is not uncommon nowadays for *nada yoga* teachers to be
involved with music-making, too. The exploration of music has
been developing since the Middle Ages but it is only in the past
few centuries that a connection between music and *nada yoga* has
been established, although it remains one of the least documented
streams of sacred sound. With musicians who choose *nada yoga*,
the structure of the musical tradition forms part of their *nada yoga*
practice. For instance, the singing of musical scales, or the playing
of the notes of a raga and, with Yogi Hari, the particular method
of playing the Indian harmonium, comprise the practice. But in
essence it is the practice of listening to the inner inaudible sound
that has been the way.

Some practitioners of *nada yoga*, working with sound, may
prefer the human voice and in the form of chanting, to using a
physical instrument. There are three traditional forms of chanting in *nada yoga*: *mantras, kirtans,* and *bhajans*. These divisions
are not to be confused – as they often are in workshops. Because
yogis or saints have generally composed these, they are considered
to carry a pure energy and to have a harmonizing effect upon the
physical body, astral body and mind. The word *mantra* refers to
assisting our mind in stopping its endless chattering while trying to

meditate. Via *mantra* (the repetition of certain sacred sounds) the mind that is attempting to meditate is prevented from its aimless wanderings and is given a focus (or perhaps a careful diversion) to aid its concentration. There are different speeds for chanting mantras – from very fast, to medium, to slow – suitable to the demands of varying degrees of mental distraction. Once we can find the quiet mind, it becomes easier to listen to silence and possible to hear the inner sound that lies beneath, behind, and within all sounds. *Mantra* is, therefore, concerned with the power of sound to transform our consciousness, or being. Likewise, *nada yoga* concerns itself with Self-realization through the transforming power of sound; only here that of inaudible sound; the sounding of the Inner Being – divine sound. *Mantra* or the making of sacred music can be considered its outer expression although *nada yoga* doesn't concern itself with rituals governing mantras or their pronunciation, mystical meanings, or embodiment of energy. If scientists can demonstrate that machines can utilize mechanically-produced sound vibrations for healing, then imagine what using our own voice can do!

To summarize, *nada yoga* is the path of union with the Divine through sound or music. Many great religions also state that the origin of life is sound or vibration. Once we are able to reach that place of great stillness and silence deep within our hearts, we are able to hear this 'Music of the Spheres'; we are able to approach the source of our being through this gateway of vibration – or via this path of sound and deep inner silence. Indian yogi mystics speak of outer sound, then of hearing ten inner sounds and finally of hearing the One Sound – divine sound. This is a path of spiritual practice – attuning to this inaudible sound and thereby hearing the voice of the inner teacher – the Word of the Supreme Transcendent Oneness. *Samadhi*, or union with the *paramatman*, or totality, can be entered into through *nada yoga*. At one and the same time the process incorporates the Transcendent and the Divine Imminent.

After attuning to this quiet inner 'voice' deep within, it eventually becomes possible for us to find the inner stillness and silence associated with it at any time in our lives – and of course most especially during times of crisis, stress, or misfortune. We thus enable ourselves to face difficulties, and to transform and evolve the inner elements of our being with the supreme strength of the transcendent sound of absolute Oneness. We thus receive the great love of the divine Comforter. Becoming at one with this divine sound-current opens us up to resonance with that stream of Universal Love consciousness experienced as flowing throughout the entire body of nature, including all the galaxies and the whole universe. I reach this conclusion also because the term *anahata* is given to the heart chakra and it is likewise stated that we cannot hear this inner sound until we have progressed along the spiritual pathway to the level of the heart chakra and have, therefore, been born again within the heart of the Divine Being. Interestingly, the heart chakra is the central chakra in the major sevenfold chakra system.

The great yogi Paramahansa Yogananda communed with the Master Jesus to receive insights into the original meaning of His teaching. Here is one passage in which we see links with *nada yoga*.

> Then said Jesus to those which believed on him, 'If ye continue in my word, then are ye my disciples indeed; and ye shall know the truth, and the truth shall make you free'. (John 8: 31-32)
>
> If ye will persist in attunement with the Cosmic Vibration (as heard in meditation) and with the Christ Consciousness in that sacred sound, then indeed you may consider yourselves my disciples, disciplined and guided by my word or Christ Intelligence within you.... By 'continue in my word', Jesus advised his followers to heed conscientiously his words of wisdom about faithfully practising the meditation technique of contacting the Holy Cosmic Vibratory Sound and the Christ Consciousness in it, thus becoming his true disciples.[1]

Sound is in relationship to silence as the light of the stars is to the darkness of space. Some music has silence built into it – the Zen Buddhist *shakuhachi* (end-blown bamboo notched flute), for instance. However, the silence that we might experience whilst listening to certain music is not the silence of the *nada* yogi. The human ear can hear vibrations up to 20,000 cps. Beyond this lie supersonics, and more. But none of these are the silent sound of the *nada* yogi, for that is beyond a measurable vibration and more akin to thought.

In the silence, in the stillness, in the deep stillness of the heart we can find God. This is the foundation of *nada yoga*. *Nada yoga* has this philosophical aspect to its teachings and practice. It asks us to listen to that voice sounding deep within the silence and to follow our conscience, or the voice of our higher Self, that is one with all. Part of this process of spiritual unfoldment through sound is learning to listen and hear the inaudible sounds so that our mind gradually reaches this stillness. The manner in which snakes are entranced by sound can be seen to reflect the way our busy earthly mind learns to cast aside its worries and concerns with this earthly existence when engrossed with the stillness of the *anahata* sound.

Music of the Spheres

Sometimes this *anahata nada* experience can take the form of music that we seem to hear although nothing of this music actually exists upon the earthly plane. Such rather mystical experiences are often referred to as the 'music of the spheres' by those who encounter them. This is not the same as imagining sounds. At any time we could run through our mind a certain song that we like and imagine that we were listening to it, but this is not the same experience. Rather it is more like listening to some unknown music that our neighbour is playing – only to find that our neighbour is not playing any music at all!

The book TALK DOES NOT COOK THE RICE, Series 2, by Guru R.H.H. (a follower of the Russian artist Nicholas Roerich) written down by his disciple, contains the following words.

> While on the subject of the music of the spheres, there's an interesting story of an incident that happened to my Guru, his wife and son George, and some of my spiritual brothers and sisters. They were all at a meeting in a large room, and through the doorway they could look into an adjoining room where the keyboard of a piano was visible.
>
> They were speaking of Scriabin, who was a great mystic and had written special music to color. My Guru knew him. Suddenly there was a chord struck on the piano and it was unmistakably Scriabin. They saw the keys go down, but there

was no person sitting there. It was a whole number that evidently Scriabin had never written before. Apparently it was
triggered by the simpatico of these people and their love and
speaking his name.

There was another incident that happened one night in
Sixty-third Street in New York. There were about thirty-two
people in the room and suddenly music came from the middle
of the room. It was like no music that was ever written. Only
about seven or eight people heard it. We rushed to see if the
radio was on. It wasn't, and then there was nothing coming
from the outside. It was coming from the center of the room. It
was about eight bars of the most glorious music I've ever heard
in my life, and then it vanished.

We were doing a special healing at the time, and all thirty-
two people were working on the case. The patient was a man
who had no experience with this esoteric work whatsoever,
but he had a complete healing at the moment he heard the
music. He kept asking where the music was coming from. He
said it was the most beautiful music he had ever heard.[2]

In October 1968 my parents and I moved from London to
Mildenhall, Suffolk. I worked in the same factory as my father
(the firm had moved from London to Mildenhall onto a new industrial estate) and I was kindly allowed to practise music regularly in the works canteen each weekend, which I did for between
eight and thirteen hours at a time. I lived in Mildenhall until January 1970, and it was while I was living there that I had one of the
most wonderful experiences of my life. Upon the Sunday morning
of one such weekend practice session, on a warm summer's day, I
walked along the road through the woods from our home to the
factory, when I was drawn to stop by a gate on a bend in the road.
Here I paused to look out across a piece of wild land lying before
another part of the forested area.

While I was looking at all the several wild flowers, shrubs,
and grasses, I found that I could hear them rather like the music
of a symphonic orchestra – although not sounding similar to any
earthly instruments except, perhaps, a large gong. The effect was
as if the whole of nature before me was sounding a wonderful

om composed of many intermingling tones. My thoughts were led to ponder how every wild flower was growing exactly where it needed to be; where conditions were exactly right to support its growth. The result of nature growing in obedience to the higher laws of the Creator was this beautiful inner music that I was listening to. All the sounds were in perfect harmony. Everything was just as it should be – nothing was dominant but all existed together in harmony. The entire floor could have been covered with a single type of plant but, instead of that, there were little clusters here and there, of a wide variety of wild flowers. Everything was organized by an invisible gardener who knew exactly where each individual flower belonged in this symphony of nature.

Rightly or wrongly, I think of this as an aspect of the harmony of the spheres – a phrase attributed to the ancient sage of Samos, Pythagoras. However, this term is interpreted nowadays from our own mechanistic world-view and not from the philosophical context that prevailed at the time of Pythagoras around 600 BCE. For at that time we had the 'sphere' of the Fixed Stars! Esoterically, Pythagoras is now thought of as the Master Koot Hoomi who, alongside two other Masters, was responsible in guiding the beginnings of the Theosophical Society and whom I referred to on p. 224.

In 1974, during each of the daily meditations on a week-long retreat at New Lands (the headquarters of the White Eagle Lodge in Hampshire) I heard this Master playing divine music upon his 'organ' in the inner worlds. This was also confirmed by Minesta (Mrs Grace Cooke – White Eagle's medium and the founder of the White Eagle Lodge) who spoke of this Master being present and also of hearing his music during her sharing at the close of the daily meditation sessions over which she presided.

Another occasion that again will stay within me for my entire lifetime arose when my wife and I first got together in the spring of 1974. She had just made the decision to end a difficult (or even non-existent) relationship and we were simply lying down together relaxing after her trauma. I found myself listening to the wonderful singing of a choir of heavenly voices (I shall always think of them as coming from Venus for some reason). Suddenly, my wife-to-be asked if I could hear the music she was hearing. The choir seemed to sound a rejoicing song celebrating our finding of one another. This shared experience supported me during years of marital trial. I was astounded to find this inaudible sonic experience being shared, and momentarily wondered whether or not I was being bewitched! It is the only time that I have shared these experiences of inaudible music conjointly with another. During our honeymoon on the Isle of Iona, just after the summer solstice in 1975, I recall passing the 'fairy mound' there, and I could hear the fairies singing, seemingly from inside this earth mound.

On the subject of fairies, I worked as head gardener at Hornsey High School for Girls for Haringey Borough Council between 1973 to 1977, and in periods when there was little work to do I went out to work with 'gangs'. On one such occasion we were removing the spring flowers to replace them with summer ones and I felt so sorry for their lives being cut short. Then I found that I heard the flowers singing for joy – and they explained to me that this was out of gratitude because their life had touched a human heart with compassion. It was a truly joyful and humbling experience for me!

There were some lovely standard roses in the grounds behind the gymnasium at that school. One day I beheld a beautiful rose fairy at work with a velvety purple rose. Such a wondrous creature, and nothing like any artist's paintings have depicted. There were no 'wings': the rose fairy was simply an energy being made of white light, imparting its vibrations to the flower, and not earthbound at all.

Yet another instance worth mentioning, which might be said to come under the caption of *nada yoga,* was a rare occurrence that took place at the birth of our first child Raphael (pictured opposite) in the autumn of 1977. We had planned a Leboyer home birth, and one of the first things that the midwife explained to me was that the baby was in the wrong position and we were heading for a breached birth. Alongside giving my wife spiritual healing for her pain, I spent several hours working with the healing angels and we managed to rotate him 180° so that he was now the right way round. I was then told that the posterior lip (part of the cervix with the anterior lip) was proving a problem. I could visualize where this was, and so I worked on that and once again we were on track.

After nineteen hours my wife's cervix still had not dilated, meaning that continuing with a home birth was now legally inadmissible. It was at this point that, to my surprise, I was given from spirit a precise inaudible sound which  I was to make upon the inner planes, and it was explained to me that this was the sound that would wake up the elemental of the muscle concerned. I sounded this very high note inaudibly once upon the inner planes and within less than thirty minutes she was fully dilated.

The first stage of delivery was now completed. However, we had gone over the legal limit of hours and so, unknown to me, arrangements had already been made for us to transfer to the Whittington hospital. The doctor and other hospital staff retired to a corner of the delivery room until the very last minute, leaving me beside my wife the entire time, massaging her legs and wiping her brow between contractions and doing the breathing alongside her until the crowning. It was a twenty-eight-hour labour but I shall always think of this experience as my special 'birthday present' from my son – an initiation into the further miraculous depths of sound. In fact, I understand that his spirit guide is named Chibiabos (the singer for the legendary Hiawatha) and so a worker with sound, alongside the spirit guides for my father and myself (both Comanche) who told me decades ago that they are both masters of sound.

Another illustration of a *nada yoga* experience occurred for me over a period of three days around ten years ago now when I was constantly hearing the inaudible sound of tiny bells (similar to Indian crotals on a string). It was very beautiful and I felt immersed in the sound. I could carry on as normal, listening to everything else, and did not find it uncomfortable at all – possibly as I love the sound of bells. Later I read in Swami Rama's teaching that this is the highest level of *nada yoga*.

In a certain kind of way, from within the philosophical context of *nada yoga*, it can be said that in order to contact our master we have to 'sound our own note'. This note then resonates within the auric field of our master and he or she responds, as part of the law of resonance. This note arises when we are in resonance with that One Sound; that One Great Note! We can go on farther to envisage this inner 'abstract sound' as the upper partials of a cosmic gong. Our sense of being an individual separate self, with this particularized sound within us (our *nada yoga* experience), 'resonates' with the outer harmonics of a cosmic gong – each attuned to the central solar gong-tone or central spiritual fire.

It is only when we can lose ourselves into the One Self that we can resonate with the central tone of this cosmic gong. Extending the image, just as we find polarity with the individual waves upon the surface of the one ocean, so the planets may be seen as the gongs of this solar system and therefore resonating with that one great central gong – the galactic centre. As there is the one light at the back of all the different colours, so too there is the One Sound (*nada*) behind all manifestations of sound. Something of that sound exists within each one of us – the individual 'parts of the whole'. Such a field of resonance, or wave, is the master's ashram, or aura, within which all of the separate 'particles' (disciples) live and together constitute the One Great Being (gong) reflected in that particular wave within the one cosmic ocean of being. So, too, during the practice of *nada yoga* we can experience ourselves, and these individual disciples of sound (*nada* yogis), as 'particles' within the one wave of the sound of God.

Hazrat Inayat Khan expresses this same oneness in the following passage.

> Abstract sound is called Saut-e Sarmad by the Sufis; all space is filled with it. The vibrations of this sound are too fine to be either audible or visible to the material ears or eyes, since it is even difficult for the eyes to see the form and colour of the ethereal vibrations on the external plane. It was the Saut-e Sarmad, the sound of the abstract plane, which Mohammad heard in the cave of Ghar-e Hira when he became lost in his divine ideal. The Qur'an refers to this sound in the words, 'Be!

And all became.' Moses heard this very sound on Mount Si-
nai, when in communion with God; and the same word was
audible to Christ when absorbed in his Heavenly Father in
the wilderness. Shiva heard the same Anahad Nada during his
Samadhi in the cave of the Himalayas.

The flute of Krishna is symbolic of the same sound. This
sound is the source of all revelation to the Masters, to whom
it is revealed from within; it is because of this that they know
and teach one and the same truth.[3]

The subject termed *nada anusandhana*, or an enquiry into the
mystic sounds, describes the *anahata* sounds or the mystic sounds
heard by the yogi at the commencement of his meditation. This is
a sign of purification of nadis or astral currents due to *pranayama*.
One is advised to listen through the right ear.

The mind exists so long as there is sound, but with the sound's
cessation, there is the state called *unmani* of *manas* (the state of
being above the mind). We are enabled to make contact with
the omnipresence of the transcendent being and are no longer
identified with the ceaseless chain of thoughts. Entering the non-
dual realm, the sound is absorbed within the indestructible and
the soundless state is the supreme seat. There is the beginningless
and endless circle of the eternal.

After experiencing the ten inner sounds echoing our sonic environment, we are advised to go beyond these to a constant sound
that resembles nothing; a soundless sound. This is the final aim,
and once we have located this sound we are further advised to listen intently and begin to discern ultra sounds or overtones of this
one soundless sound. We may at times hear two distinct sounds
or more, whereupon we must determine which is the highest and
gently shift our focus to this higher tone. Always we are moving
towards the highest.

In the Upanishads we have an account of these musical notes. It
is stated that these resemble to a certain extent the gentle murmurs
of the vast sea, the low rumbling thunders of the distant clouds,
the continuous splash of a waterfall, and ultimately merge into
the sound of a conch, and develop into the blast of a trumpet,
a thundering drum, sharp violin and a flute. We find these ten

variously described below. First, Mahatma Charan Das, in his book, BHAKTI SAGAR, has described ten types of melodies – the sweet warblings of birds, the chirping of green hoppers, tinkling of bells, sound of the gong, conch, playing of cymbals, thunder of clouds, the roar of a lion, violin and flute.

Then, in the classic *Hatha Yoga Pradipika* we have an account of ten kinds of *nad*, like the buzz of flower flies, tinkling of anklets, sound of conch, bell and cymbals, flute, drumbeat and other musical instruments, and the roar of a lion, etc.

In SAR BACHAN, Swami Shiv Dayal Singh Ji gives a wonderful account of the divine orchestra, comprising ten musical notes resembling what has been said above, as one enters into *sahansdal kanwal* or the region of thousand-petalled lights.

Madame Blavatsky, whose works, ISIS UNVEILED and THE SECRET DOCTRINE, remain controversial, writes in her book THE VOICE OF THE SILENCE:

41. Before thou set'st thy foot upon the ladder's upper rung, the ladder of the mystic sounds, thou hast to hear the voice of thy inner God (Higher Self) in seven manners.

42. The first is like the nightingale's sweet voice chanting a song of parting to its mate.

43. The second comes as the sound of a silver cymbal of the Dhyanis, awakening the twinkling stars,

44. The next is as the plaint melodious of the ocean-sprite imprisoned in its shell.

45. And this is followed by the chant of vina.

46. The fifth like sound of bamboo-flute shrills in thine ear.

47. It changes next into a trumpet-blast.

48. The last vibrates like the dull rumbling of a thunder-cloud.

49. The seventh swallows all the other sounds. They die, and then are heard no more.

50. When the six are slain and at the Master's feet are laid, then is the pupil merged into the One, becomes that One and lives therein.

51. Before that path is entered, thou must destroy thy lunar body, cleanse thy mind body and make clean thy heart.

The glossary in this volume explains: 'The "Soundless Voice",
or the "Voice of the Silence". Literally perhaps this would read
"Voice in the Spiritual Sound", as Nada is the equivalent word
in Sanskrit, for the Senzar term.' THE VOICE OF THE SILENCE (1889)[4]

Amir Khusro, a great scholar and mystic poet (the disciple of
Kh. Nizam-ud-Din Chishti), has described these sounds thus:

> First is the hum of the bees and the second is the sound of
>   anklets,
> The third is that of the conch and the fourth that of a gong,
> The fifth is a trumpet-blast and the sixth that of a flute,
> The seventh is of a Bhir, the eighth of a mardang (drum beat)
> and the ninth of a Shahnai (Naferi).
> And the tenth doth resemble the roar of a lion,
> Such indeed is the Heavenly Orchestra, O Khusro.
> In these ten melodies a yogin gets absorbed,
> The senses get stilled and so doth the mind, saith Khusro.
> With the flourish of limitless Music within,
> All the lusts of the flesh and the deadly sins fly off,
> The Master too has a wonderful world of his own,
> Khusro is now fully engrossed within himself.

All these sounds arise within as the pilgrim soul starts on
the Path; but of all these, one must catch the sound of a gong
or a conch for these in particular are connected with the higher
spiritual realms, the various mansions in the house of our Father.

> *None knows where the abode of the Beloved is,*
> *But sure enough the sound of the gong comes*
>   *floating therefrom.*
>   HAFIZ

The ten sounds are generally described like this.

The first is the sound *chini* (like the pronunciation of the
word); the second is *chini-chini*; the third is the sound of a bell;
the fourth is that of a conch; the fifth is like that of a lute; the
sixth is the sound of cymbals; the seventh is like that of a flute;
the eighth is the voice of a drum (*bheri*); the ninth is the sound of
a double-drum (*mridanga*); and the tenth is the sound of thunder.

Traditionally we are instructed to hear the internal sound through the right ear. Change your concentration from the gross sound to the subtle. The mind will soon be absorbed in the sound and transcendence of this earthly plane will be attained.

Shri Brahmananda Sarasvati (Ramamurti S. Mishra M.D), a great *nada* yogi who taught in the U.S., writes the following in his book NADA YOGA: THE SCIENCE, PSYCHOLOGY AND PHILOSOPHY OF ANAHATA NADA YOGA. In his account, the sequence of the sounds is somewhat altered.

For the sake of our understanding, various tones and tunes of nada have been noted by sadhakas or adepts. The Gheranda Samhita describes the following classes:

1. *Jhinjhin-nada:* This is a sound like the chirping of crickets or other grasshopper-like insects, like the sounds heard in the evening in the garden when insects sing.

2. *Vanshi-nada:* This is the sound of the flute, but it is different in frequency and charm from the flute of an orchestra.

3. *Megha-nada*: This is a rumbling sound, similar to rumbling thunderclouds. Thus it is called the thundering nada. It is frequently accompanied by clicking sounds so powerful that it can seem to the meditator that his or her bones are being re-aligned or even broken. Yet with this sound we experience a new, electrical atmosphere.

4. *Jharjhara-nada:* This is the sound like the rattle of the drum.

5. *Bhramari-nada:* This is the sound like the humming of bees, quite musical and sonorous, like certain beetles and bees.

6. *Ghanta-nada:* This may be compared to the sound of church bells.

7. *Turi-nada:* This is like the sound of gongs or large, clanging cymbals.

8. *Bheri-nada:* This includes sounds similar to the kettledrum, the trumpet, high-pitched flutes and various other wind instruments.

9. *Mridanga-nada:* This sound is like a military drum or a snare drum.

10. *Tantri-nada*: Various string instruments are heard in this state, like the violin, cello, sitar, vina and harp.[5]

The *Nada Bindu Upanishad* (31–6) describes a process of yogic meditation wherein the aspirant listens to eleven different internal sounds in successive degrees of subtlety:

> The Yogi being in the Siddhasana (posture) and practising the Vaishnavi Mudra, should always hear the internal sound through the right ear. The sound which he thus practises makes him deaf to all external sounds.... In the beginning of his practice, he hears many loud sounds. They gradually increase in pitch and are heard more and more subtly. At first, the sounds are like those proceeding from the ocean (jaladhi), clouds (jimuta), kettle-drum (bheri) and the waterfall (nirjhara) ... after further practise it will be like the sound produced by a tabor (mardala, or small drum), bell (ghanta – handbell) and horn. At the last stage, those proceeding from tinkling bells (kinkini), flute (vamsa), vina (South Indian stringed instrument – lute-like) and bees (bhramara). Thus he hears many such sounds more and more subtle. When he comes to that stage when the sound of the great kettle-drum (kahala) is being heard, he should try to distinguish only more and more subtle sounds.

The *Darsana Upanishad* (6.36-8) describes the perception of sounds in the highest position, or chakra, in the body known as the Brahma-randhra, located in the region of the head:

> When air (prana) enters the Brahma-randhra, nada (sound) is heard also produced there, resembling first the sound of a conch blast and like the thunder-clap in the middle; and when the air has reached the middle of the head, like the roaring of a mountain cataract. Thereafter, O great wise one! The Atman, mightily pleased, will actually appear in front of thee. Then there will be the ripeness of the knowledge of Atman from yoga and the disowning by the Yogi of worldly existence.

Swami Sivananda tells us:

> Anahata sounds are the mystic sounds heard by the Yogin during his meditation. It is a sign of the purification of Nadis. Some students can clearly hear it through any one of the ears and some by both the ears. There are loud as well as subtle sounds. From the loud, one will have to contemplate on the

subtle and from the subtle to the subtler. Beginners can hear
the sound only when the ears are closed. Advanced students
can concentrate on the Anahata sound even without closing
the ears. Anahata sound is also termed Omkara Dhvani. They
proceed from the Anahata centre of the Sushumna Nadi.[6]

You cannot expect the sound immediately after you close your
ears. You should concentrate and keep your mind one-pointed.
The particular sound that you hear today, you may not hear
every day. But you will hear any one of the ten Anahata sounds.
     The description given above is Laya through Nada, Anaha-
ta sound. In the same manner, Laya can be effected by concentration at the tip of the nose (Nasikagra Drishti), at the space
between the two eyebrows (Bhrumadhya Drishti), meditation
on the five Tattvas, on Soham Mantra, Aham Brahma Asmi,
Tat Tvam Asi Mahavakyas and other methods also.[7]

Although it is stated above that one hears one sound during
a session, for my own part one day many years ago now I chose
to listen to the inner sound as if it were 'music'. Music played by
God. I have only practised the traditional technique once. It was at
the retreat centre in Sussex, England, called Hourne Farm, when
I was first introduced to *nada yoga*, and I will be talking more
about the work we did there shortly. I have since listened for the
nada sound without touching my ears or doing anything else. My
approach here was: 'Listen. Stop everything and just listen to this
Sound'. The result was that during this one session every so often
a 'sound' would enter into my head. After the first, I'm not sure
of the order of the following, except for the final sound, but here
is a list.

- The very first sound was that of two pieces of wood being
  'clapped' together – like they might use in Zen to 'wake
  you up'. It also resembled the sound of bones breaking!
- Then I heard the sound of tinkling bells (like an Indian
  dancer might wear around her ankles);
- then that of conch-shell trumpets;
- then that of *sarangi* (an Indian 'violin');
- then the sound of shawms (Indian/Chinese/Tibetan 'trumpet');

- then the *bansuri* flute (transverse bamboo flute of India);
- then a *sarod* (Indian 'lute');
- then a 'cymbal' which sounded very similar to my Tibetan 'Milarepa' meditation cymbal – light (single *ting-sha*);
- then a sound like very low drums but also similar to thunder;
- then finally a 'dum dum' drum (with pellets on either side) this was quite high-pitched – whereas I'd 'imagined' that drums would be lower, like in African drumming.

The fact that many of these instrumental sounds were Indian came as no surprise to me, but I realized how it would be a bit absurd for an ancient Indian yogi to describe a sound as being that of a brass trumpet when he would never have heard one! When I previously may have imagined these sounds my thoughts returned to ones familiar here in the west – for example, western cymbals (crashing), western flute, western lute, etc. It might be the other way round, of course: that the instruments invented by the ancient Indians were to resemble the sounds heard during *nada yoga*. And before instruments were invented what were these inner sounds likened to?

The following quotation is intended as a guide for those who may take up *nada yoga* with their bowls. Having described the ten sounds from the chapter on sound in the *Hansopanisad*, Swami Yogeshwaranand Saraswati ji Maharaji goes on to write:

> Now, we shall describe the fruits of such sounds when heard in samadhi. The description is intended for the yogis.
>
> The first one causes the sound of 'chinchini' in the physical ears, the second one the pain in the body. The third one produces a feeling of sorrow, fourth vibrations in the neck or head. The fifth one produces a flow of sweet fluid in the palate. The sixth one gives the feeling as if nectar or ambrosia is falling in drops on the tongue; this sound has been much praised in the scriptures. Sweet juice flows from the brahmarandhra and the tongue tastes it. This experience has been called the drinking of ambrosia. The result of the seventh sound is the attainment of the esoteric knowledge, the knowledge of self and God which bestows on the yogis the feelings of joy, peace and bliss. The

fruit of the eighth sound is the rise of the four types of sounds – para, pashyanti, madhyama and vaikhari – which enables the yogis to gain all types of knowledge and the ability to describe it. The ninth confers on the yogi the power to become invisible; even if the yogi is sitting in front of you he remains invisible. He is able to attain profound inward meditation and his vision becomes divine. He is able to see others but himself remains screened. The fruits of the tenth sound is the realisation of Brahman, becoming almost like Brahman. The manas is absorbed in it and all the thoughts and impressions are pacified. Such a yogi rises above sins and merits and becomes like Shiva or all-pervasive like the omnipotent soul. Becoming like the divine light, he shines or becomes enlightened and assumes the form of pure, eternal, tranquil knowledge.

Here we have described the sounds of the Hansopanisad and their fruits. This path is a short one and capable of granting liberation....

For those who decide to follow this path and who seek further guidance along the way, the book by Shri Brahmananda Sarasvati would be helpful especially the section entitled 'The Ganthis: whirlpools of Energy'.[8]

At the heart of Tantra is *kundalini yoga*, and central to this is *laya yoga*. Tantra is a spiritual tradition that became more formal in the first few centuries CE, reaching its zenith around 1000 CE. Tantra, when we work with our physical body, is known as *laya yoga*. Here we evolve upwards through the chakras, experiencing the elements therein so that with the throat chakra we are dealing with sound. To these ancient tantrics, sound has four stages, regarding which we read:

Sound is about to sprout in para (Supreme) form; it becomes two-leafed (that is just manifested) in pashyanti (radiant) form; it buds in the Madhyama (subliminal) form; and it blooms in the Vaikhari (acoustic) form. Sound which has been developed in the above-mentioned manner, will become unmanifested, when the order is reversed.

Yogakundalya Upanishad, 3. 18-19

Personal Experiences with Sound

It was during the late 1960s and early 1970s that I began having my
own mystical experiences of the world of sound. I later discovered
that they were a form of *nada yoga*. Twenty years after, in the late
1980s and early 1990s, I was regularly invited to attend weekends
at Hourne Farm (which I mentioned earlier in this chapter) where
the Sound Research Group, organised by the owner (the late Peter
Rendel) met annually alongside other special sound events in their
calendar. It was at one such weekend in the late 1980s that we were
all invited by Peter to an extra session, and those so inclined all
settled down to try traditional *nada yoga* practices. I immediately
heard the *anahata nada* at its highest level. I can't recall whether
or not anybody else said that they had experienced it. Being a
musician involved in spiritual sound I naturally incorporated the
sound experience (not the traditional exercises) into my daily
routines – as I can tune in at will.

During another such weekend we were introduced by Peter to
siva yoga, and each of us was lent a *siva linga* to meditate with.
Afterwards, we were each asked what we experienced. After I related my own experiences Peter responded by saying I could keep
the *siva linga* (he was given it by *siva yoga* master Kumaraswami).
At another such weekend Muz Murray was giving one or two
sessions to lead us in mantra. He also asked us about our experiences. I had experienced specific shapes and colours in a certain
chakra whilst chanting and this was confirmed by Muz to be what
the master yogis predicted for that mantra.

There are two chakras in the head that govern clairvoyance
and clairaudience – or sight and sound. According to occult astrologers, the third eye chakra or pituitary gland is ruled over by
the planet Uranus, while the pineal gland (at the base of the brain)
has the rulership of Neptune. It is rather noteworthy that with the
third eye chakra we can choose what we wish to visualize – be it
a candle flame, a star, a tree, a lotus pool, a garden, a temple, or
a master, whereas over the third ear (or pineal gland) we have no
control whatsoever while it is involved with listening to the *nada*
sound. In the early stages we might be able to shift our focus of
listening and thereby enhance another harmonic from within the

sound, but we are unable to say, I'd like that 'sound current' pitch to be an octave higher, or a major third lower, or whatever we'd wish it to be. We do not choose the sound; rather, we discover it. Being self-arising it is what it is and although we control what we visualize at the third eye centre, here, with the pineal gland, we have no control. This lends itself very well to the idea of submitting to an other, or a Supreme Being, or God, or greater whole beyond our ego, mind, thoughts, will, or self-control. The sound is quite simply beyond these, and it requires a degree of surrender. Call it selflessness, or self-transcendence, we must simply accept it as is.

In acceptance it becomes easier to experience ourselves as individual waves upon the great ocean of life. So we enter into the brotherhood of life and the oceanic consciousness of Neptune (dissolving our sense of being separate ego beings). Neptune is considered to be the most spiritual of all of the planets in our solar system and when prominent in a horoscope it often indicates the mystic. This phenomenon of the inner *nada* sound points to the transpersonal God Self (Atman); to an extension of our self-awareness into higher transcendental levels for this sound is both within us and beyond us, and we can experience this sound as doing us rather than us doing it (or creating it). We have no control and so we can think of the sound as arising from outside ourselves despite it undeniably sounding inside ourselves. It is self-arising and lies beyond boundaries. It is non-dual. *Nada* forms a kind of bridge between the God within and the God without, uniting the two as one. Through its sounding the boundary of our selves, which is our skin, becomes as if transparent. This phenomenon reduces for us the distinction between where 'we' end and where the rest of life begins.

Composer, musician, and 'Renaissance Man' Dane Rudhyar (1895–1985) relates something of this *nada* experience in his book THE PLANETARISATION OF CONSCIOUSNESS (1970):

> I am the adventurer. I close my eyes. I try to quiet down and still the surface-waves of sense-impressions, the emotional eddies and the currents of thought which affect my consciousness. Then I try to let go entirely, to forget that 'I' exist, that anything exists. All is void. And yet … a heart beats, lungs expand and contract, motions are dimly felt. Through whatev-

er is now sensed, there is a great peace – the silence of a calm ocean unmoved by winds. Within this silence, as it deepens, an awareness of quiet, rhythmic activity seems to arise. It may best be spoken of as a soundless 'tone', a vibration of definite pitch, though it seems also to contain a myriad of overtones. What is this 'tone? It is so pure, so simple. It is; it so definitely, irrevocably 'is'! It seems to spread through that great peace of which I am aware; but is there an 'I' that is aware? Whatever is aware is implied in this 'is-ness,' in that undeniable fact – that tone, that peace, that no-whereness and nothingness that spreads everywhere. Yet it is centred. It is rhythmic and imperturbable movement; but so still, so pure! It is perhaps what men call 'existence.' Whose existence?[9]

The pineal gland is shaped very similarly to the male sex organ. It is mostly blue in colour and it is in two parts (actually some see it being in seven parts – to connect it via vibration to the glands). The pituitary gland is 'female' (receptive and like a grail cup) and linked to psychic activity.

The pineal gland is related to sound whereas the pituitary is naturally related to light or vision. The energy of the pineal gland is along the vertical axis – it has the effect of making us strive to rise up 'straight and true', whilst the pituitary has an energy that is far more horizontal, rather like a wide screen television. It carries an energy of expansion and width, wherein we experience an 'opening up'. It is concerned with inner visualizations which, like our physical vision, are definitely horizontal – it would be strange for our 'visions' to run the other way!

The traditional *nada sadhana* includes certain 'locks' found in *hatha yoga*. This should only be attempted by those advanced in *hatha yoga* or under the supervision of a competent teacher – such as Jenny Beeken, Principal of the Inner Yoga School. Overleaf is an exercise less potentially dangerous or demanding.

The Fourfold Process of Sound

Let us return for the moment to the process of sound, *vac* in Sanskrit, which we first encountered in Chapter 10 and met again in Exercise #7, in the chapter previous to this.

Exercise #27

NADA YOGA EXERCISE

Here is a traditional practice called Bhramari (the Bumble Bee). 'With regular practices of this pranayama (Bhramari) bliss arises in the yogi's heart', says the *Hatha Yoga Pradipika*. Unlike other exercises, this does not involve advanced *hatha yoga* abilities.

The name Bhramari is derived from the word for the black Indian bumblebee, and is said to describe the characteristic humming sound produced during exhalation in this breathing exercise.

In India the exercise is practised sitting in a meditation pose with a straight back. You place hands on your knees and close your eyes. Inhale deeply through the nose and hold the breath. Lean forward a little so you are supported by straight arms and place the weight upon your knees. Now bend the head down so that the chin touches the chest. This is followed by pulling up the pelvic floor, the perineum and anal muscles together. Hold the breath awhile. Release the contractions, raise the head, relax the shoulders and sit up straight. Close the ears, as before, by closing the small flap of the ears with the index or middle finger. At this point the elbows are held out to the sides, leaving the chest open. Then exhaling through the nose and keeping the mouth closed, but holding the jaw loose (teeth apart), a smooth, deep and relatively strong humming sound, like that of a bumblebee, is produced.

Allow yourself to become one with the sound vibrations and feel them filling your head or even your entire body. After the exhalation let your hands rest on your knees and breathe normally.

Repeat this nine times.

The *anahata* sound is also called *omkara dhvani*. It is due to the vibration of *prana* in the heart. Many people wonder where *anahata* sound comes from and believe that they have found the answer in the story of the American composer John Cage (1912–92), who once entered an anechoic chamber. He had been informed that in this there would be absolute silence. However, he discovered that he could hear two sounds. He enquired of the sound engineer where these sounds were coming from. The engineer replied that the higher sound was that of his nervous system and the lower sound arose from his blood circulation.

A further slant on this story comes from the composer and improvising accordion player Pauline Oliveros. In her book DEEP LISTENING it is related:

> When John Cage went into this room (an anechoic chamber) he heard a high sound and a low sound. And the story went that the high sound was the sound of his nervous system and the low sound was the sound of his blood going through the veins. Well – that's the story. However, there is more to that story that is not generally known. John Cage died of a massive stroke just before his eightieth birthday. A physician has said that you wouldn't hear blood pressure the way John described it. There was plaque in the arteries building up and that if someone had taken heed of what he had said, they would have known it was building towards a stroke. That was one thing. The other – the nervous system does not make a twang that you can hear like that either – it was also part of the condition that led to John Cage's stroke. So that is another part of the story that hasn't been told.[10]

Of course, the higher and the lower sound conform well to the patterns of sound we have been describing, and they represent a third explanation of Cage's experience. In 'Mantra: the potency of sound' in TANTRA: THE PATH OF ECSTASY by Georg Feuerstein we read:

> What the various models describing the evolution of sound or vibration have in common is the idea that there are at least three levels at which sound exists. The Tantric scriptures distinguish between the following:
>
> 1. *Pashyanti-vâc* (visible speech) - the most subtle form of sound visible only to intuition
> 2. *Madhyamâ-vâc* (intermediate speech) – sound at the subtle level of existence, which is the voice of thought
> 3. *Vaikharî-vâc* (manifest speech) – audible sound trans-

mitted through vibration of the air

Beyond these three is the transcendental level called parâ-vâc or "supreme speech," which is Shakti in perfect union with Shiva. It is soundless sound, hinted at in the Rig-Veda (10.129) in the phrase "the One breathed breathlessly."

The three levels of sound correspond to the three forms or levels of the serpent power:

1. Urdhva-kundalinî (upper serpent), the kundalinî primarily active in the âjnâ-cakra and tending to ascend toward the thousand-petalled lotus at the crown of the head;

2. Madhya-kundalinî (middle serpent), the Goddess power active in the region of the heart and capable of ascending or descending;

3. Adhah-kundalinî (lower serpent), the psycho-spiritual energy primarily associated with the three lower cakras.[11]

Four forms of Nada Brahma are also enumerated in the *Yogasikha Upanishad* (3.2–5):

There is the *para* power (shakti) ... inherent in the Muladhara (Root Chakra) of the indistinct form, known as *bindu* and having *nada* as its support. From that alone rises *nada*, even as the sprout out of the subtle seed. That, by means of which the Yogis see the universe, they know it as *pasyanti* (also known as *anahata* [or unstruck]) ... In the heart (wherein is the *anahata*) is placed this sound (*ghosa*), which resembles that of a thundercloud (*garja* the roaring of the elephant, or the rumbling of clouds). It is known as *madhyama*.... That alone is again known as *vaikhari*, when, in conjunction with the *prana* vital air, it goes by the name of *svara* (when it takes the form of articulate expression).

David Frawley (Pandit Vamadeva Shastri) in his book, MANTRA YOGA AND PRIMORDIAL SOUND, introduces an explanation with a Vedic text:

Four are the levels of speech. Those of spiritual wisdom know them all. Three placed in secrecy cannot be manipulated. Mortals speak only with the fourth.

Rig Veda 1.164.45

The essence of Tantra is *mantra yoga*, which is not only the repetition of sacred sounds but encompasses all means of energizing the mind. According to Tantra the mind consists primarily of sound. Working with sound, whether as *mantra*, music or vibration is central to energization of the mind.

According to Vedic and Tantric thought, the goddess is the divine Word, which has a feminine nature. According to the Vedas, in the beginning was the Word and the Word was the goddess. Speech has several levels of manifestation, which are keys to the nature and function of the goddess, and Tantra, like the *Vedas*, recognizes four levels of speech.

Name	Speech	Location	State
VAIKHARI	Audible Speech	Throat	Waking State
MADHYAMA	Thought	Heart	Dream State
PASHYANTI	Illumined Speech	Navel	Deep Sleep
PARA	The Transcendent	Root Centre	Samadhi

David Frawley[12]

The fourfold process of the word, as described by these experts, has some relevance to my own experience. Early, I outlined my childhood discovery of mediumistic power. Our spirit guides, as I mentioned, preferred to use what was then called 'light trance', explaining that 'deep trance' took a lot out of the medium. In the latter the medium's own consciousness is taken away and he or she has no idea what has gone on during its absence, but with light trance the medium is still fully conscious. So it was that while the spirit guides were speaking through my physical body I would get the gist of the thought or idea that they wished to communicate. I would see this forming into a vision and then they would search the vocabulary in my brain for the word or words to relay this vision to the earthly listeners. I note in this the same fourfold process.

In the Tantric metaphysics of sound there are these four phases – *para, pashyanti, madhyamika* and *vaikhari*. *Vaikhari* usually translates as 'word' so that we have here a process of speech. In my light-trance experiences there is first the impulse, then it forms as a mental vision, then we search our vocabulary for the words that best express our idea, and then we speak. Naturally, it is no problem to transfer this fourfold process to the act of making sound. Perhaps we can convey this process in another manner, whereby first there is the thought that we are hungry, then comes the vision of the food we would like (let us say a cake – we visualize a chocolate cake, granny cake, Victoria sponge, whichever), then comes the process of finding all the ingredients and the pots and pans, alongside the process of baking and, finally, we have the finished cake.

Three of these sounds are non-physical, with Vaikhari being the only stage that is heard by the human ear. However, we can also reverse this process and follow the path back to the source. We take the word, or words, and follow these onto ever-subtler levels until we enter their source.

The former path of gradually assuming a more material form until the manifested word is sounded resembles the sound action of the gong, whereas the latter way of retracing the steps of a word or sound more closely fits the direction of the sound from a bell or singing bowl.

Returning to this fourfold process from its subtlest level to the manifested realm of words, as found in relation to the chakra system, we could find explanations in greater detail in the Vedic exposition of sound that has been adopted in the Tantras. In this tradition, Shiva says:

> The source of nada (sound) which is called para (causal) arises in muladhara; that sound being in swadhishthana, becomes manifested and is called pashyanti; that sound going up to anahata, becomes reflected in the conscious principle and is called madhyama; then going upwards in vishuddha in the region of the neck, by the instrumentation of the larynx, palate, the root and tip of the tongue, teeth, lips and nasal cavities ... it becomes Vaikhari.
>
> *Tantrarajatantra*, 26.5–9

Pointing towards realms within the para dimension of sound we find:

> Maheshvara said: 'What is called Shabdabrahman, the nature of which is nada (causal or unmanifest sound), is one aspect of Supreme Infinite Being. Shabdabrahman as Shakti (power), is

in the form of bindu (supremely concentrated conjoined power), and being in Muladhara that Shakti becomes Kundalini, from that arises nada (sound), like a sprout from a minute seed, called pashyanti by means of which the yogis see the universe. In the region of the heart (that is, in anahata), it becomes more pronounced, resembling thunder in the atmosphere. It is called madhyama. Again it (Madhyama) becomes swara (voice) by the expiratory help this is called vaikhari.

Yogashaktiopanishad, 3. 2-5

Para sound is beyond vibration. *Para* means 'transcendental,' 'beyond' or 'the other side.' It is indicative of the super-conscious transcending sense-perception. We must not confuse this stage with ultrasonics or supersonics, which are still rates of vibration. Rather it is more akin to thought and not of this physical world at all. The human ear cannot hear sound frequencies beyond 20,000 cps. There are sounds or vibrations produced in life that far transcend these but for us humans they remain outside consciousness, as such sounds (having a very high frequency) are transformed into silence.

Various texts mention that *para* has no sound vibration. It is a sound that has no movement and therefore no frequency. It is still a sound, although we cannot conceive of a sound without vibration or movement or motion. *Para* is a cosmic transcendental sound devoid of all movement. It is both still and infinite. It is the 'absolute sound' of the *nada* yogis. It refers to that 'soundless sound' from out of which the whole of life issues forth.

Pashyanti sound translates as light. From this it can be concluded that sounds produce light or colour but what is also intended here is to indicate that this process has reached the stage where sound is visualized or envisioned. Here the sound current has reached the level of the solar plexus chakra, which relates to the element of fire (light, vision) in the Indian system and in the Tibetan system to the water element – 'reflecting' our vision and generating the power of desire. This stage may be referred to as a mental sound, to a subconscious sound pertaining to a quality of mind. They are imagined sounds, however. Saying 'Krishna, Krishna, Krishna' out loud, we properly call *vaikhari*, but if we close our eyes and mouth and mentally repeat 'Krishna,' while visualizing its colour and form with our inner eye, it would be *pashyanti*.

Madhyamika also translates as 'middle' so that what is indicated here is having reached that point in the process that lies between the spoken word and the vision. It is the intermediate stage. As *para* lies beyond form, we concern ourselves with the three remaining stages with *madhyamika* resting in the centre. It is sometimes referred to as a whisper – not as fully embodied word. We are thinking about our vision and how we can best manifest it. This level corresponds to the sound having reached the heart chakra, indicating a degree of loving devotion to our vision. No matter the wonderful noble ideals we might harbour, our spontaneous actions will be dictated by the spiritual qualities living within our heart. This is the final creative stage of the process prior to manifestation. Our vision has attracted all of the necessary parts from which to assemble the corresponding form.

Vaikhari is the final stage, as the manifested word. Here what began with *para*, was envisioned in *pashyanti* and then organized and assimilated in *madhyamika*, finally appears – that is, is heard – in the physical realm. It is the end product of the fourfold process of sounding. *Vaikhari* is audible and producible, being the grossest phase of the movement in sound – a word. For a musician it is the actual sound produced upon his or her instrument (including the voice) and heard by all. Here the sound current has reached its culmination in our throat chakra. This is the only stage that is actually heard as audible sound.

Exercise #28

CONTEMPLATION OF THE FOURFOLD WORD

Find a singing bowl that offers at least four different partials when struck. I have found some of the so-called Manipuri Lingam Bowls to be excellent for this. However, such bowls are rare and, therefore, expensive. With four distinct sounds it can serve as a reflection of this fourfold process and, as a metaphor, aiding our contemplation. The lowest sound from the bowl would correlate to *vaikhari*, the next sound higher up would then be *madhyamika*, and the next highest sound would be *pashyanti* and the highest sound(s) would be *para*. Listen to these four sounds (some of them might be like a vibrato effect, an oscillation either rapid or otherwise) and see if there is one that is more prominent in the mix and also which tone rings on the longest. It might be that the tone relating to *madhyamika* phase is slightly more prominent, ringing on until the end and then we can focus upon this stage of the process. *Madhyamika* would lie between *pashyanti* and *vaikhari*. This is the creative phase and can be seen to relate to the process of intention and result whereby the artist strives to reduce the gap between these two.

In our spiritual life we have an intention or an aim and we strive to realize this in our daily lives in our thinking, feeling and acting. In general the highest tones are the first to return into the silence. So, generally, we are concerned with pondering either one of the three phases of the reversed fourfold process of sounding the Word. If all three are equal we can ponder that situation where the Word has been made manifest perfectly.

Unlike other systems of yoga such as *raja yoga* and *hatha yoga* (which are set down clearly and in considerable detail), *nada yoga*, being an oral tradition, was less fixed and there were also differences in the teachings. For this and many other reasons, our ability to tell whether or not a teacher is actually listening to an inaudible sound is tested to its limit.

Whenever I wish to focus upon the *anahata nada* I do so (that is, I 'turn it on') and in this respect it's the opposite experience from tinnitus, which the sufferer cannot turn off. Eric A. Gustafson, in THE RINGING SOUND, suggests that sufferers train themselves to listen to the inner sound as in *nada yoga* practice. Gustafson further relates that tinnitus sufferers have experienced a lessening of their condition through the use of such a meditative approach.

It is further possible to listen to the absolute sound as if it were stemming from various locations in our body. We can hear it coming from the heart chakra, from the third eye chakra or from the *bindu* (one of the head centres) chakra. In each case certain aspects of our being are unfolded: for instance, listening from the heart chakra naturally develops the *bhakti* qualities of love and devotion. I will close with some quotations which seem to be referring to the absolute sound, directly or by analogy.

> *High above in the Lord's mansion ringeth*
> *the transcendental music.*
> *But, alas, the unlucky hear Him not;*
> *They are in deep slumber.*
>   Guru Nanak, sixteenth-century Sikh guru

> *Sound, stars, and light are all inside.*
>   Maharaj Sardar Bahadur Jagat Singh

> *Seek the true Master with faith, love, and patience.*
> *He will give the Light to find the hidden entrance.*
> *If with constant effort you attune the Inner Ear,*
> *The way to God opens and the Path will be clear.*
>   Tulsi Sahib (nineteenth-century master of sound and light)

> *Listen friend, this body is his dulcimer.*
> *He draws the strings tight, and out of it comes*
> *the music of the inner universe.*
> *If the strings break and the bridge falls,*
> *then this dulcimer of dust goes back to dust.*
> *Kabir says: The Holy One is the only one who*
> *can draw music from it.*

> *What comes out of the harp? Music!*
> *And there is a dance no hands or feet dance.*
> *No fingers play it, no ears hear it,*
> *because the Holy One is the ear,*
> *and the one listening too.*
>
>   Kabir

> *The flute of interior time is played whether we hear*
> *   it or not,*
> *what we mean by 'love' is its sound coming in.*
> *When a love hits the farthest edge of excess, it reaches a*
> *   wisdom.*
> *And the fragrance of that knowledge!*
> *It penetrates our thick bodies,*
> *it goes through walls –*
> *Its network of notes has a structure as if a million suns*

were arranged inside.
   This tune has truth in it.
   Where else have you heard a sound like this?

Kabir

Disciples may be likened to the strings of the soul-echoing Vina; mankind unto its sounding board; the hand that sweeps it to the tuneful breath of the Great World-Soul. The string that fails to answer 'neath the Master's touch in dulcet harmony with all the others, breaks – and is cast away. So the collective minds of Lanoo-Shravakas. They have to be attuned to the UpaDhya's mind – one with the Over-Soul – or, break away.

H. P. Blavatsky[13]

The body may be compared to an instrument and the Ego to the player. You begin by producing effects on yourself; then little by little you learn to play on the tattvas and principles; learn first the notes, then the chords, and then the melodies. Once the student is master of every chord, he may begin to be a co-worker with Nature and for others. He may then by the experience he has gained of his own nature, and by the knowledge of the chords, strike such as will be beneficial in another, and so will serve as a keynote for beneficial results.

H. P. Blavatsky[14]

Esoteric science teaches that every sound in the visible world awakens its corresponding sound in the invisible realms, and arouses to action some force or other on the occult side of Nature. Moreover, every sound corresponds to a colour and a number (potency, spiritual, psychic or physical) and to a sensation on some plane. All these find an echo in every one of the so-far developed elements, and even on the terrestrial plane, in the lives that swarm in the terrene atmosphere, thus prompting them to action.

H. P. Blavatsky[15]

18. Mantra

THE WORD *mantra* derives from two words, *mana* (meaning thinking) and *trai* (meaning to protect or freedom). Therefore, in general, mantras are a means of protecting our thinking. The repetition of a mantra serves to focus the mind on spiritual matters. The vibrations of sound are essential for our wellbeing. By producing certain vowel sounds, our glands are made to vibrate and so cleanse our system of impurities. The yogis have developed a special yoga named *mantra yoga* designed around the powerful effect of sound vibrations upon our physical system and our mental and spiritual being. Mantras are compositions of sound comprised of both meaningful and meaningless words plus vowels that are chanted in a specific manner. Over and above this, mantras serve to blend the beings of both the deity and the one reciting.

In the case of mantras composed of sounds having no linguistic meaning, one cannot ponder the sense of the words but must simply enter into the vibration of the sound. Singing bowls come close to such a wordless sound; what they produce is a vibration that serves to put us *en rapport* with the divine source, or else the spirit owning the sound body. So it is that the world of *mantra* may improve our insights into the sounds of the singing bowls.

> In the beginning was the Word. And the Word was with God and the Word was God. The same was in the beginning with God. All things were made by him; and without him was not anything made that was made. In him was Life; and the Life was the Light of man. And the Light shineth in the darkness, and the darkness comprehendeth it not.
>
> Gospel of St John, 1 : 1–5

> *Prajapati (God as Progenitor) indeed was one*
> *And alone. The speech was his own being.*
> *The speech was second to him.*

> *He said:*
> *'Let me send forth this speech –*
> *She will go and become all these various things.'*
> *So he created, sent forth*
> *The speech to become the various things.*
>   *Kathaka-Samhita* XII.5.27.1

These verses remind us of the tremendous power of sound. We are taught here that, through the power of sounding the sacred Word, that which was before unmanifested came into manifestation on every plane of being. By inference, the words also inform us that we need to be very careful with sound. We are dealing here with a kind of magic (that is, the bringing into manifestation of the unmanifested) and we must acknowledge the caution that is required in this act of creation.

Concerning the unmanifested state, it is said that a mantra in its original state is called *anahata mantra*, non-originated, yet self-existing, and this condition takes place at the *madhyama* level, being the level just above that of audible or spoken sound (*vaikhari*) – where it is said that the *shabdatanmatra* (sound of a finer nature than physical – etheric/astral) can be heard by the pure-hearted yogi.

The sound that most closely approaches the great hum of the universe (the sacred Word) has three sounds, and these are A-U-M. In the first millennium BCE, *nada* yogis focused extensively upon this mantra, being taught by Patanjali that *aum* was the 'sound that expresses the Divine Absolute'. However, it need not be simply a matter of sounding these three letters of the alphabet. We can find a link there to our three bodies of thinking, feeling, and willing (or wisdom, love, and power). Symbolically speaking, the experiences along the path of spiritual unfoldment teach us to sound each of these vibrations in our reaction to life's challenges. As we grow ever stronger in spirit, and can meet our challenges in life along these three rays from that central point of the divine within our innermost centre, so we grow stronger in sounding our own note, which will admit us into the temple of the mysteries – or initiation.

Precious little will be manifested from a simple repetition of these alphabetical letters. The inner meaning of the sounds (*mantra*) is intrinsic to pure results. One has to learn to merge one's innermost being with that Being who is at the source of each sound in order to work the magic. It is akin to listening to spiritual teaching from someone who is reading the words beautifully, but only beautifully, compared to someone else who reads it with soul-wisdom, as if from the original source – their words a living flame. In the latter case the words retain their original function to serve as a bridge into the realm of light and their vibratory sound resonates with this inner dimension within the hearts of both the speaker and the listeners.

The throat chakra is associated with sound (speech) whilst the name for this chakra is *visuddha*, meaning pure. Therefore we should focus upon using the power of sound (or *mantra*) for the purpose of purifying ourselves. A *mantra* such as *soham*, for instance, translates into 'I am that' but not in its narrow, or lower, expression as our separate ego or self-identity. Rather it refers to the universal or cosmic I AM. When the Hindu speaks the words; 'I AM God', he or she is allowing this universal spirit to resound throughout their being in an effort to rise above the separate, ego self and expand their awareness, merging with the universal Self or *atman*.

In the world today, many persons primarily seek a practical outcome to their activities. But in our approach it is especially necessary to be respectful and careful about the use of sound or mantras – not simply seeing it as a means to achieve material results for our physical life. Jesus says: 'Love thy neighbour as thyself': in his teaching, self-interest is balanced with selfless interest. We can see something of this law expressed in the *soham* mantra, where we also find the astrological symbol for the Sun – the dot within the circle. Here, the *so* is the central dot and the *ham* is the circumference of the circle. In other words, as we breathe in for ourselves we actualize the consciousness of the dot (our individual, and apparently separate, being) and whilst we breathe out we expand into the universal wider circle and so balance our self with the Self. This is also the symbol for Shiva–Shakti – the union of male and female. It is taught that the sound of inhaling produces so while exhaling sounds like ham.

The circle is also as the great Mother, creating a safe space

for the child or spark (the dot in our metaphor), the spark of the
divine, to enter into physical form. In the spiritual astrology of
the White Eagle Lodge it is considered that at some point in space
and time we experience a desire to incarnate upon earth. This initial desire sets up a kind of chord, or combination of various im-
pulses, and when outer circumstances (principally the planetary
formations) correspond to this initial chord we then come back
into incarnation. With a similar harmony between the inner and
the outer, our intention when using certain sounds (for example,
bija mantras) should match the vibratory energy-field of the deity
the mantra connects to. Taking the intention to purify ourselves,
thus giving a focus to the throat chakra and thence to sound, we
would work with the *bija* mantra *aim* (pronounced like 'I'm') of
Saraswati or *hrim* of Matangi – an alternative deity to Saraswati,
favoured by many *nada* yogis. Saraswati is linked to the planet
Mercury and in a minor way to the Moon. Appropriately, Mercury rules the astrological sign of Virgo (the pure Virgin) and the
sixth house, of health, in the horoscope. This could also be an
expression of the virgin birth (a symbol in the ancient mysteries
of divine wisdom), or also the 'second birth' (mentioned by Jesus)
whereby one is born again of the spirit.

In Tantra the *mantra* is the sound form of the deity that reveals
its inner truths. We could say the *mantra* is the sound body of the
deity and thus the *bija mantra, aim,* is experienced as being the
sound body of Saraswati. It is to be noted also that mantras have
inner power only to the extent that we are truthful in life. Truth
and sound go hand in hand, as the phrase 'to sound true' makes
clear. Therefore, if truth pervades our mind and thoughts, if we
'walk our talk', if our words can be seen in our actions, then it is
far more likely that that mantra will work for us. Working with
mantras reflects this power of our speech – reflecting back to us
just how much we have cultivated this gift of the living word.

> He must daily withdraw from the turmoil of his outer exist-
> ence, and seek the place of silence within his own being. Here
> he will be brought into contact with God, the Great White
> Spirit, because the little spark of spirit within his own being
> will be touched, be responsive to that infinite and eternal, that

sweet and holy power.

This experience cannot come to you by reading books, or studying the history of the nations, or studying the religions of all time. It can only come as you endeavour to seek that silent power, that gentle, pure love which you will find deep within your heart. Some people rush about the world trying to contact some sacred centre or to meet some holy man with whom to talk. All the while if you will only turn within, to that silent centre within, all the holy men of past and present will draw close to you in your own sanctuary, in your own home. Their light and power and companionship will be with you instantly.

White Eagle[1]

In order to ascend into the higher levels of consciousness the mind needs to become silent and empty of the clutter of worldly thoughts. Sri Aurobindo has said that once the mind is still, then truth will have a chance to be heard in the purity of silence. In such stillness and silence there is little room for worldly desires and ambitions. The ancients took the symbol of a mountain to represent the consciousness of the adept who has risen above the plane of duality and abides in those lofty peaks, away from the cares and troubles of this world. It is perhaps best if mantras can be repeated from such a lofty state of consciousness.

Nowadays there are some individuals who sell, or teach, mantras as the means to obtain one's worldly desires, wants, or demands. There are three main ways of working with mantra and that is one of them – the Rajasic! Regrettably, few of these teachers point out the negative *karma* that can accrue from such an application. However, there are a few other teachers who extol the original spiritual objectives of this ancient spiritual science. I do not recommend using them in the Rajasic way (as a kind of spiritual materialism), but rather as spiritual aids along the path, aids that help to purify our nature and help us move towards sounding our own true note within the grand symphony of the brotherhood of all life.

One literal interpretation of the word *mantra* is 'freedom from the mind' (the cognitive, creative mind). We can go on to interpret these words as representing the freedom we find when we transcend our everyday thinking (called the lower mind) and become absorbed in the supra-mental levels of being (the higher mind) via sacred mantric sound. Sri Aurobindo tells us that mantra 'is a word of power and light that comes from the overmind inspiration or from a very high plane of intuition'.[2]

Returning to the word *mantra* and the root *man* (from *manas* – the thinker) and the suffix *tra* (indicating instrumentality) we find that an 'instrument of thought' is another possible translation. In his Vimarshini commentary on the Shiva-Sutra (1.1.), Kshemaraja explains that a mantra is 'that by which one secretly considers or inwardly reflects on one's identity with the nature of the supreme Lord'. In this instance the connection between *mantra* and *manana* ('thinking, considering, reflecting') is exploited. In yet another etymological interpretation, *mantra* derives from providing protection (*trana*) for the mind (*manas*). In other words, in order to save us from the distractions of each passing thought, our mind is focused upon repetitions of the mantra; turning it towards contemplation of a deity helps protect our minds from worldly interests.

The bowl, as it is stroked, provides us with the repetition of one sound or vibration, the degree of complication of which depends upon the bowl and what is being used as a wand. But, compared to the mass of sonic stimulation we find in most music, it is a simple sound that we can even refer to as a single sound.

This simple act of repeatedly stroking the bowl brings to mind the repetition of the *bija* mantra of a god or goddess. Saraswati, goddess of music, is a suitable example: while we repeat her *bija* mantra (*aim*) we become attuned to her consciousness and being and expand our awareness up to the atmic level of the one Self. It is possible for us to experience the whole of life as music played by the goddess upon her *vina* (a South Indian stringed instrument). We can envision a monochord (or a single string of her *vina*) stretching between the highest realm and this earthly abode. Our ability to respond places us at varying heights along this string according to whether we are more focused upon the earthly region, the watery, the fiery, the airy, or the etheric, never forgetting that it is all One string! We may even experience our entire life as a piece of music wherein certain key events that have occurred during our lifetime are as key moments in the unfolding music of our life (here it is helpful to compare the four main movements of the classical symphony with the four great initiations). We realize that everything occurs at the perfect time and that we ourselves are the composer/improviser of all that happens to us.

As we've seen, Saraswati is said to connect with the energies of the planet Mercury – and those of the Moon, too. Mercury has connections with the throat chakra (and via one of the signs that it rules, Virgo, it also relates to purity), and the caduceus (one of the symbols related to Mercury) features in the healing arts. The archangel Raphael is also linked with Mercury. Mercury is connected with communications of all sorts (especially through its other sign, Gemini – speech and expression/language). This is how Saraswati comes to be the goddess of music, knowledge (books, etc.), and speech.

The name Gemini refers to the Twins. Being an air sign, Gemini is associated with the mind; here we have the twin aspects of the mind, first the lower mind (rational) and then the higher (intuitive). In yogic thought it is said that there are two factors working through all words and these are 'sound' and 'meaning'. Sound is said to be Shakti (or the feminine principle of energy), and meaning to be Shiva (the masculine principle of being). In this analogy, sound is a vehicle for meaning.

From the philosophical standpoint meaning is more important than sound. Speech is reflected in sound, whereas meaning reflects the mind – or awareness, or consciousness. There is the sound of the bowl and the meaning behind that sound – where applicable. Some bowls, being 'off-the-shelf' or 'machine-made', carry very little significant meaning relative to mind.

The *bija mantra* is the seed mantra of a deity. The Advaita philosophy being essentially non-dualistic, we can either view this deity as being outside of ourselves or as an aspect of our own inner nature – whichever answers the need of the moment – or transcend dualism altogether. Mostly, in mantric formulas, we find a sequence of sounds – such as *om sri sarasvatyai namah* or, most famously, *om mani padme hum*. But it is also the case that we can work with the *bija mantra* (as is the case with the chakra sounds), and we can do this in one of three ways. We can say the mantra out loud, we can speak it as in a whisper (movement of the lips with no actual sound), or we can sound it internally in our mind. The latter is considered to be the most powerful, for here the attention is fixed exclusively on the inner meaning of the mantra. Perhaps listening to the sound of a singing bowl has affinity with this mental repetition wherein we produce no audible sound.

Repetition of the mantra *soham* will likewise achieve the level of awareness where we connect to the universal being and our lower mind and our sense of being a separate ego is left behind for the *arupa* or formless level of the mind. A connection to a more universal awareness takes the place of separateness. It is like the unity between the ocean and the waves. We lose our sense of identification with the separate wave upon the surface attachment (or over-involvement with our earthly self) and reconnect to the vast ocean. Each separate breath as we inhale enters into our little individual earthly body and is similar to a passing wave, while breathing out we retain connection to the source – to the oceanic level of being.

The number of repetitions is important with mantra, and it is traditional for this to be measured by the use of a *mala* (a set of beads similar to a Christian rosary). Usually, one is advised to make 108 repetitions, or multiples thereof. *Mala* come in different numbers (divisions of 108, e.g. 36) but a *mala* with 108 beads is probably the easiest to use. Actually such *mala* contain 109 beads, with the extra one being called the *guru* bead (also called Mount Meru – a symbol for the central channel, or *susumna*), and this marks the end of the cycle of 108 repetitions. If we wish to do more than 108 we simply begin over again. The numeral 108 has been held sacred and auspicious in India since ancient times. It is taught that the heart chakra is where the spark of the divine rests and that from this chakra 108 *nadis* (or channels) radiate out to all parts of the subtle body. By chanting 108 times we will send to all channels.

Another possible reason for this lies in ancient Indian astronomy, where it was found that the average distance from the earth of both the sun and the moon is 108 times their respective diameters. This number is also symbolic of the mid-region of the space between earth and heaven. In this regard, the 108 beads can come to represent a kind of ladder stretching between the earthly region and the luminous region of divine reality. Each repetition moves us another step nearer to our goal. Most high-minded practitioners are reluctant to use mantras for anything other than the greatest human goal – namely liberation.

Perhaps because of the link between sound and the throat chakra (and thereby purity), one's lifestyle is another factor that is considered significant in getting the most from *mantra* recitation. A vegetarian diet is favoured, even if only for the period of days that you perform the *mantra* – usually forty days are recommended.

The Sanskrit teachings inform us that three prime vowels are the basis of all other sounds. These are A, I and U. I understand these as conforming to the parts of the bowl, already set out, as follows.

BASE OF THE BOWL	The primal sound 'A' (a as in *father*) is the most basic sound that forms the root of all other sounds. It relates to the Absolute (Brahman), pure existence, the infinite, the void, the unmanifest, and the changeless. It is said to be the Supreme Shiva and pure light.
WALL OF THE BOWL	The primal sound 'I' (i as in *pin*) is the sound of contraction, focus and direction. While the 'A' sound indicates inarticulate sound, the sound – 'I' is the basis of articulate sound. The sound 'I' relates to Shakti or energy, the One, the atomic, the point or *bindu*, the seed power of will and desire through which all creation proceeds. As the sound reverberating in the centre of the mouth, the greatest number of letters is connected to it.
RIM OF THE BOWL	The primal sound 'U' (u as in *flute*), made with the lips, has an expansive power that is strong, harsh or even explosive, almost opposite the contracting or focused power of the sound, I. It relates to the Shiva principle in developed, expressed or articulated form, arising to pervade all things, in a successive and graduated manner. It is said to have the power of knowledge.

Bija mantra for health include:

AIM ('I'm')	Best for the mind. Improves concentration, thinking, rational powers and speech.
SHRIM ('shreem')	Promotes general health, beauty, creativity, and prosperity.
RAM ('a' as in 'car')	Promotes strength, calm, rest, and peace. Good for an excess of the Air element and for mental disorders.
HUM ('u' as in 'put')	Wards off negative influences. Promotes digestive fire.
KRIM ('cream')	Improves the capacity for work and gives power and efficacy to action.
KLIM ('kleem')	Gives strength, control of emotions, and sexual vitality.
SHAM ('shum')	Promotes peace, detachment, and contentment. Good for mental problems.
HRIM ('hreem')	After toning, promotes cleansing, purification, energy, joy, and ecstasy. An aid to detoxification.

In Indian scriptures, we find explained that the *bindu* is itself composed of three parts, namely *nada, bindu,* and *bija* ('seed'). The first part has a predominance of consciousness (i.e., Shiva), the second a preponderance of energy (i.e., Shakti), and the third part an equal presence of consciousness and energy. We also see here a reflection of the family concept of the Supreme as being Father, Mother and Child (the Child being an admixture of the two main Principles). We can also find an application to our singing bowls with the rim being *bindu* or energy, *nada* being the base and *bija* being the wall linking the two poles. Such terms might be unintelligible to some of us but after we make progress along this path of mantric science they become increasingly meaningful.

Many centuries have passed during which the Vedic and Tantric masters have conceived, or rather envisioned, a variety of other sounds for the release of primary power besides *om*. These seed-syllables, or bijas, as they are called, can be used singly, or as is more usual, as part of a sequence of other power sounds forming a mantric phrase. In the *Mantra-Yoga-Samhita*,[3] there are eight such primary *bija mantra*, and these are helpful in various circumstances yet they reveal their deepest mystical meaning only to the yogi:

AIM (pronounced 'I'm')	guru-bija	'seed syllable of the teacher'; also called *vahni-jaya* ('Agni's wife')
HRIM	shakti-bija	'seed-syllable of shakti', also called *maya-bija*
KLEEM	kama-bija	'seed-syllable of desire'
KRIM	yoga-bija	'seed syllable of union', also called *kali-bija*
SHRIM	rama-bija	'seed syllable of delight'; Rama is another name for Lakshmi, the goddess of fortune; hence this seed-syllable is also known as *lakshmi-bija*
TRIM	teja-bija	'seed syllable of fire'
STRIM	shanti-bija	'seed syllable of peace'
HLIM	raksha-bija	'seed syllable of protection'

There are other texts or schools that provide us with a different list of names for these eight primary *bija*, whilst yet another, and better known, list of *bija mantra* is found associated with the five lowest chakras and the five elements, namely *lam, vam, ram, yam,* and *ham*. True revelation is not mere words read from a book. Rather it is found in the mantra revealed in the state of awakened listening, revealing the essence of truth. This state of awakened listening serves to open the head or crown chakra, whose organ of reception is the ears. True *mantra* is not just about speaking: it has more to do with listening. Unless one is able to listen to the spirit of a mantra, the secrets of the mantra remain withheld.

We find that the application of *mantra* rests with the intention attached to it. These intentions are defined according to the three gunas or qualities of nature that are widely considered in yogic thought: *sattva* (harmony), *rajas* (aggression), *tamas* (inertia). The interaction of the three constitutes all of life in the philosophy of yoga. To attain real happiness and wellbeing, we are encouraged to promote the *sattvic* guna – that is, the clear quality necessary for the mind to rest in awareness and for our heart to be at peace – for which the right use of *mantra* is possibly the most important method.

Mantras and the Three Gunas

I promised earlier to mention the three types of *mantra*. There are:

Sattvic Mantras. These are for liberation, the wellbeing of all, the fulfilment of deeper soul wishes, and gaining our real needs in life, like our legitimate needs of security, home and family.

Rajasic Mantras. These are for the achievement of outer goals in life like wealth, career, power or relationship, as if these were the highest aims, to gain power and prestige for the ego.

Tamasic Mantras. These offer ways to control, harm or hypnotize others or employ mantras in an ignorant or destructive manner.

Naturally, it is advocated by the masters of *mantra* to draw from the collection of *sattvic mantra* only. As an example, with this in mind, the following exercise is given.

Shiva is the dot and the circle is the active, feminine, Shakti. As I began to say earlier, we can find a representation of this relationship between the two great Principles when looking down onto of a singing bowl. The rim (circle) is then the feminine and often there is a circle inscribed upon the inside centre of the singing bowl, representative of our dot. Otherwise, the narrow base will serve as the dot at the centre and will correspond with the sound A – the source emerging out of the silence. The U then corresponds to the wall of the singing bowl, even as the mouth fills with sound while producing the U. We feel the journey of the sound from the back of the throat forwards to the lips, and see the sound moving from the base of the bowl towards the sounding rim. Our journey within the Divine is as a circle (*ouroboros* in Greek – the circle of a snake biting its own tail) with no beginning and no end – even as the wall is shaped as a circle when looked upon from above.

Then the major part of the sound resides in the vibrating circular rim, which corresponds to the M sound. This is the sound of dissolution – with the vocal sounding of AUM the process ends here with the closed lips, although the sound continues within our mouth and throat, and is found to reverberate more in the head region. For this reason it is more related to self-awareness and with *gnana yoga*, the yoga of knowledge, too. The flow of sound has met with an obstruction here at the lips and yet triumphs over this by continuing to sound. In this case the wall of the bowl would

Exercise #29

AUM EXERCISE

Take a full breath. If possible, do a full yoga breath. Breathe in, down through the abdomen, releasing the diaphragm, and then fill the chest cavity (the middle lungs). Finally, raising the shoulders a little, expand the breath up into the upper lungs.

Hunch your shoulders while you hold your breath. On the outbreath relax the shoulders quickly – almost as if down into a slump. If you've ever watched a pet slump down (cat or dog) then you'll know what I mean.

Also drop, loosen and relax the jaw – allow it to drop right down. You may find that you yawn a lot but that is a good sign. Now keeping the teeth apart raise the jaw a little, maybe midway between shut and fully dropped open, but still relaxed.

Find a pitch that is comfortable for your voice to sing in, neither too low nor too high. Now produce a long 'A' (as in Amen or father) and sound the A from the back of your throat and right down in the throat.

Repeat the first three steps.

Produce the long U as in (food) and experience the sound resonating inside the spatial cavity inside your mouth.

Carry out the first three steps once again.

Produce the M sound with lips closed. Feel your lips vibrating with this M sound and also feel the resonance in your head.

Thus the AUM moves from the rear of the throat through to the closed lips. Feel it as a fourfold rhythm. Begin with silence (as you breathe in), and then produce the A-U-M.

It is as a journey representing WHAT we have come from; HOW we are travelling forwards and onwards; and WHERE we are going to end up. This also relates to that power behind us; that wonderful support that sustains us; and the transformation possible of turning an ending into a beginning or into an eternity.

relate more to *bhakti yoga* (the yoga of love and devotion) and so, too, the sounding of the U, leaving us with the A sound and the base or root of the bowl relating to *karma yoga* and the power of the will. So we again find our trinity of thinking, feeling and willing – otherwise known as wisdom, love and power. Alternatively we might think in terms of mental body, astral body and physical body and their higher counterparts – the causal body, buddhic body, and the atmic body respectively.

The will unites spirit and matter with the upper pole, *atman* or the Self, and the lower pole (base of the bowl), which represents physical activity. Therefore, during the act of playing the bowl, or making a sound, we can also experience this link between the Self and our activity as an apparently separate self.

Some bowls have wider bases – giving something of an emphasis upon the A and the will aspect. Bowls that are active here, where normally there is inaction, include Jumping Bowls and Water Bowls, and these would relate more to the long 'A'. Bowls from Orissa in east India tend to have these wider bases and these were largely available, passing for Tibetan singing bowls in the marketplace, until fairly recently. Others have their rims emphasized: *yang* bowls in general, and Elephant Bowls (also known as Chama Bowls or Mani Bowls – from Bharampur), along with Lingam Bowls (also known as Meru bowls). These tend to create a very strong sense of focus, clarity, and attention.

Finally, we find bowls with the walls emphasized either via a slow curve expanding outwards from the narrow base, or else in tall or high wall bowls. These often have a grounded feeling, or else a warmth to their sound.

Many of the bowls that I own that have a very shallow wall produce excellent results with water inside their wide bases. None of these feature a thick or *yang* rim. Otherwise they are connected with subtle realms. One induces 'out-of-the-body' experiences for me; another resonates with the guru chakra, and yet another creates moving concentric rings of golden light on the inner planes, etc.

For many decades now I have followed the path of sound first vouchsafed to me by Lom Phook Trenglam in 1971. Finding nothing like it elsewhere, I simply had to accept that this is how it is for me, whether I like it or not. I was simply 'out on a limb', with only my faith and personal experience to keep me company. My truth had revealed itself to me through an innate ability to divine what subtle qualities, if any, were found embodied in certain sacred (or otherwise) bowls. I was recently encouraged and heartened to learn that there is a tradition in India that follows a similar approach to sacred sound – in the excellent book, MANTRA YOGA AND PRIMAL SOUND: SECRETS OF SEED (BIJA) MANTRAS by David Frawley.

Maybe without difficulty we can see the direct link here between the base of the bowl and the sound A, and then with the root chakra qualities of stability and groundedness. This is the area of the bowl that rests upon the earth, providing stability for the bowl itself. As we contemplate the shape of the bowl we can consider our own stable foundations for the spiritual path. Jesus said: 'Whosoever heareth these sayings of mine, and doeth them, I will liken him unto a wise man, which built his house upon a rock: and the rain descended, and the floods came, and the winds blew, and beat upon that house; and it fell not: for it was founded upon a rock' (Matthew 8 : 24-6).

We can also experience ourselves as rooted in the absolute sound of the *nada* yogis from which comes forth light or the fiery love found in the wall of the bowl, finally manifesting in the resonant vibration of awareness at the rim. Upon this stable foundation we can rest assured of the spiritual law of evolution supporting us, and there is no need to be in any hurry. We have countless lifetimes ahead of us and it is better to take each step carefully and not make mistakes that can be very painful to undo later along the path. We can rest within the universal laws that support us. We can rest within the supreme ultimate.

Should you wish to study this subject further then David Frawley (Pandit Vamadeva Shastri) and Thomas Ashley-Farrand (Namadeva Acharya) are two dependable sources for *mantra yoga*. See 'Recommended Reading'.

19. Planet Bowls

'PLANET BOWL' is a term that I began using in 1981 upon receiving the 'Golden Voice of the Sun' Bowl and used again in 1985 in respect of a bowl from Alain Presencer of rare design and featuring an attached base. I called it my 'Chintamani' bowl and found it was attuned to a specific planetary influence, that of Venus. This is the context in which I originated and applied such terms. The same applies to chakra bowls – they were bowls that I found to resonate with specific chakras while I was making a selection. I have also written about a couple of bowls that happen to be attuned to spiritual masters. Up to that time nobody used the terms of Chakra Bowl, Master Bowl, or Planet Bowl. We had Tibetan Singing Bowls and a Talking Bowl, a Panic Bowl, and Star Bowls (a bowl with a star engraved upon its inside base) and that was it. I should like to share how these terms came about for me.

As I've already said, I found that the Padmasambhava bowl resonated with the planetary energy of Saturn just as the Chintamani Bowl did with the planet Venus, the 'Golden Voice of the Sun' Bowl with the Sun, and so on. I had begun my study of spiritual astrology in 1973, and in the White Eagle School of Astrology one is encouraged to meditate upon the different planetary rays and become familiar with their influences by that means. Because of this discipline, it became possible for me to identify when the sonic resonance of any one bowl vibrated in sympathy, or channelled the particular qualities, of one of the planets. And so it was that since 1981 I have mentioned in some of my workshops this relationship between certain of my singing bowls and the planetary rays. Not surprisingly, the term 'Planet Bowl' arose. Here I shall clarify what I meant when originating this term – which is different from what it might have come to mean since, when the classification is used by others.

My intended meaning has nothing whatsoever to do with a

straight system of correspondences, just as the relationship between the notes of the Western diatonic musical scale and their relationship to the chakras has no relevance to the way I link bowls
with the chakras. Some practitioners refer to the work previously
mentioned (p. 178) by Hans Cousto, wherein a certain frequency
is said to be the note of a particular planet. That system is derived
from the physical properties of the periodic planetary cycles, either speeded up or slowed down, via the musical octave, to be
brought within the realm of human hearing. In accord with such
a system, if a singing bowl produces the appropriate note (or close
to it, depending upon just how particular one is with regards to
the degree of exactitude to the precise frequency) then it is called
a Planet Bowl.

As an example, let us take the note 'A' (actually 221.23 Hz
[Cousto]). The concert pitch for many orchestras is A = 440, and
the octave below, being 220 Hz (not 221.23 Hz) is said in this
system to be the note for the planet Venus. So if your singing bowl
produces an 'A' (221.23 Hz) then, according to Cousto's system, it
is called a Venus bowl. Of course, Cousto gives precise numbers,
which would place this A into its specific octave. Regardless of
this, many bowl sellers would call any bowl that sounded close to
any 'A' a Venus planet bowl, whatever octave it was in.

Cousto's system is derived from the time periods of the planetary orbits. By using the 'law of octaves' one can either reduce
or speed up the figures to bring them into the range of human
hearing. We will see this is unavoidable when we consider that the
sidereal period of the Moon takes some 27.32 days to complete,
whilst that of Pluto takes around 90,465 days! Our hearing ranges
from 20 to 20,000 cps (16 to 23,000 according to some writers).
If we allow 1 cps to equal one day then we would end up with the
very deep note of 27.32 cps for the Moon and a very high note
of 90,465 cps for Pluto. You will notice that 90,465 cps lies way
beyond the 20,000 cps limit of our hearing! If we reduced the
cycle of Pluto by five octaves we would then reach 18,093 cps,
which would be audible to us in our upper register. The number of
octaves required to raise or reduce the time periods for the several
planets would therefore vary. Thus no consistent application can

be used excepting the 'law of octaves'. For instance, in this system we find that the planets Mercury (closest to our sun) and Pluto (farthest) and Mars, Saturn and Earth have close frequencies: 141.27 Hz, 144.72 Hz, 147.85, 136.1 Hz, and 140.25 Hz respectively – just over one semitone. This results in a mere 11.75 Hz to span half of the planets from a range of almost 20,000 Hz. That is to say 50% of the planets from a mere 0.059% (approximately) of our audible range.

Well, once again, I do not wish to limit myself to working with these instruments simply with my physical ear. When I am seeking to discover what may live within the sound of any single bowl I seldom have regard for the name of the musical note that it may come close to producing. By contrast, if the quality of the energy produced by its sound (including, furthermore, what may or may not be present upon the planes of subtle energy) happens to vibrate sympathetically with the qualities of a particular planet, then I refer to that bowl as being a Planet Bowl.

Needless to say, I am not stating that such a bowl comes from that other planet. Quite simply, the system of correspondences (between bowls and planets, or colours, or elements, etc.) that I use allows me to recollect quickly what lives in the sound of any one such bowl, the better to prepare me to serve more efficiently. By that I mean that whenever I am intending to work with a bowl that I feel possesses a certain power behind its sound, I should prepare beforehand by attuning myself to those individual energies so as to be in tune with the subtle levels. That way, I can assist in conveying those properties more faithfully into the current situation. Such a situation might be within a one-on-one sound-healing situation, a sound meditation during a workshop, or a live improvisation, or a recording session in a studio. This is also compatible with my aim to work with the singing bowls as extensions of the fullness of my being – even as my physical life may be seen as an extension of my higher non-physical being.

There are a number of varieties of bowls available, whether we class them by shape or by their acoustical properties. A number of merchants and workshop leaders have attended my workshops down the years, and they sometimes take terms originating from me and, either through misunderstanding or for a sales pitch, adopt my categories and simultaneously misrepresent them, to a certain extent.

That may not sound very serious, but I have had a number of people coming to me stating that they've bought a Master Bowl, or a Talking Bowl or a Panic Bowl, but when they produce the bowl or describe it, it becomes clear that they own nothing of the sort, in my terms. There are bowls that we have come to term Jumping Bowls[1] in the UK to distinguish them from Talking Bowls, because a Talking Bowl is a very precise shape and sound, seldom seen or found, but these Jumping Bowls (mostly from Orissa) are often mistakenly called Talking Bowls – and Water Bowls are even more often called Talking. Apart from being specific forms, both the Talking Bowl and the Panic Bowl are held in a manner completely different from other bowls. Both possess bases and must be held by these and they are played on a vertical rather than horizontal axis, as Chapter 8 described.

I do not find, either, that a Planet Bowl necessarily becomes a Chakra Bowl because of the relationship between planets and chakras. It is just not that simple. Rather, I find it to be the case that one planet can have a relationship with several chakras. For instance, I have a bowl attuned to Venus that works on the third eye. Actually, there is a relationship between these two, but it is not the one derived from a straightforward system (in which Venus would be placed at the throat centre). I also have another bowl attuned to Saturn that is a throat chakra bowl, whilst the aforementioned system, widely in use, places Saturn as ruling the lowest (root) chakra!

The whole subject of Planet Bowls, I should like to suggest, is an intuitive science and not a method that can be applied simply by anybody who can remember a system. Sometimes, when I play my ancient heart chakra bowl, mentioned at the beginning of the chapter – conveniently also my Sun Bowl, which I regard as attuned to the solar ray and the spiritual master, Jesus – I ask the group whether they can imagine the 'Iron Lady', Margaret Thatcher, playing the same bowl and giving the same effect! Everyone has their own relationship with a bowl – and so it isn't all down to the bowls, either! If all such psycho-spiritual influences originated from the bowl itself, then anybody playing that bowl could exert the exact same influence with no conscious awareness being required. We know that intention is a significant factor when working consciously with sound frequencies.

One has to feel these things intuitively, with the heart and soul, or view them clairvoyantly, or understand them clairaudiently. In order to come safely to such an understanding one has to aim at being very still and working from within the voice of the silence – with a quiescent openness and selflessness within a spiritual heart that contains no desire, passion, or egotism – one that simply seeks the truth in order to be of service. Try to get behind the sound of the bowl to the spiritual or subtle dimensions (remembering that not all bowls function upon these additional dimensional realms). This is not a psychic faculty, nor a mere vague feeling as might arise from the solar plexus centre, but a direct result of working with the third eye chakra and also the third ear chakra.

One of the benefits of working with bowls is there is no real alternative to really listening, and being absolutely clear about the impressions you pick up. You thus develop authenticity – but may also need to be humble about your intuitive powers. Other people's judgment is no substitute – least of all, the judgment of someone who has a profit to make from a sale. Let's take a specific example.

'Golden Voice of the Sun' Bowl

At the very first instant of playing this bowl I felt it working in my heart chakra and linking to divine love. Then I became aware of the presence of the Master Jesus and saw him – the lord of love. I next saw that this bowl created a golden colour on the astral plane, followed by a soft pink and finally a beautiful blue. The ancients placed the astrological sign of Leo with the heart so bringing a link to the Sun at the centre of our solar system, even as the heart chakra is the centre of the seven main chakras. In this way they placed divine love at the very centre and heart of life.

Communing with this spirit of divine love involves abandoning oneself. It's rather like becoming absorbed into the spirit of music during an inspired improvisation or abandoning oneself to the spirit of love when in a romantic liaison or the great silence during a mystic reverie with nature. It's also about becoming childlike: 'Except ... ye become as little children' (Matthew 18 : 3).

We all live in the sun's light, the life-giving rays of which reach throughout the solar system. We are built of sunlight. Such is the universal Christ spirit that found such a well-suited abode within the Master Jesus. Speaking through Jesus, Christ said, 'I and my Father are one' (John 10 : 30). This is the Son/Sun of God. Opening my heart to this spiritual sun – or son – is as natural as the flower-like shape of the bowl releasing its beautiful golden radiance out into the world and bringing light, love and life to all beings. This bowl serves as an anchor to focus this spirit of the universal Cosmic Christ within the heart chakra for the benefit of all. Such is the purpose for charging bowls – to act as a lighthouse or as a guiding star for all seeking direction.

Moments of insight or inspiration visit us all, yet often these sudden flashes pass us as soon as they arrive. We must strive to hold on to some of these to allow them to perform their transformational processes within our lives. The charging of sacred objects (including singing bowls) serves the purpose of providing an anchor or focus for the unfoldment of particular spiritual qualities within our lives.

The fiery spiritual sun fans the flame of divine fire, which is found as a seed or spark of divine life vouchsafed in the heart chakra of each one of us. This grail-shaped bowl of mine carries me upon its waves of sound, up into the flaming light upon the great altar of life. I become one with the body of sacred flame, leaving nothing of myself, only joining the angels of Christ in the body of divine love.

Planets and Elements

In the ancient science of astrology, the planetary rays are further modified by the element through which they are passing. In traditional healing methods of the *bonpo* the elements are also very prominent. The elements are also associated with the chakras, just as are the planets. In Chinese acupuncture the five planets (that is, minus the Sun and Moon – the two 'Lights' in the sky – and the more recently discovered 'extra-Saturnian planets') are associated with specific elements:

Wood, with Jupiter,
Fire, with Mars,
Earth, with Saturn,
Metal, with Venus,
Water, with Mercury.

In order to work with Planet Bowls it is obviously necessary to have spent time meditating upon the several Planetary Rays. How do we work with a bowl attuned to Neptune, Pluto, Venus, or Uranus, for instance? It is then necessary to understand how to work with these Planet Bowls within the context of sound healing. Just as in the form of spiritual healing in which I am trained certain colours are seldom used, if at all, so in my sound healing work the energy of some planets will rarely be used. I do not use a Newtonian mechanistic paradigm that is based upon the assumption that a planet rules a certain chakra and then if that chakra is out of tune, I simply need to play that one Planet Bowl to the chakra in question in order to restore harmony. In that system we either have a chakra running well or we don't. We have the view that it should be running at a precise frequency and, if it isn't, then it simply needs to be retuned to that specific frequency.

For myself, each planet is associated with a number of soul qualities and it is these that I need to bring to a chakra once I have analysed why it is not functioning as it could. I am seeking to attune the soul of the patient with the soul quality that they are inwardly lacking, from the archetypal soul qualities of that planet or chakra. This reunion with spiritual harmony will gradually filter through as change, or alter the physical condition – the particular manifested disease. Life would be easy for me if I simply had one bowl for healing all of the chakras or just one for helping the heart chakra. Instead, when considering the heart chakra I must make some initial considerations. Am I to use a bowl that very gently opens the heart (for someone whose heart is closed, or who has suffered emotional pain, or who is extremely wounded and shy)? Or am I to use a heart chakra bowl that is attuned to divine love, seeking resonance, or am I to turn to one that cultivates in the heart a more human quality of compassion? Alternatively, which combination of heart chakra bowls will I create for the client's needs from out of my eleven available heart chakra bowls? Putting it graphically, in their effect heart chakra bowls can vary from sunlight through clouds, right up to 120°F in the shade!

More of this can be put forth in a future book on my form of spiritual sound healing with Himalayan singing bowls.

Sound Magic, Old and New

What I am doing here is linked to a far more ancient form of sound magic. It arises from the nature of what can be found to reside within the tones themselves. Such ancient sound magic would also attribute meaning to a tone, and would not attribute the same significance to that tone in whatever octave it appears. Actually it would deal independently with that precise note or sound. A good bowl, producing a range of notes, cannot really be said to produce a single note. In fact, only a sine wave would do that. In fact, any musical instrument will produce a range of notes, or frequencies, and these constitute what is known as timbre. These are more obscure than are the companion notes or tones within the sound of a good singing bowl.

Nonetheless, octaves do exist and we can equate the seven octaves on the piano to the seven great ages, or rounds, that are then associated with certain planets. For instance, in our current round, we are in the middle (fourth, or central) Earth section. The first, or lowest octave, is seen to represent the very earliest phase of humankind's evolution, known by certain esotericists as the Saturn Age. In the next octave up we have the Moon Age, then the Sun Period, then Earth (now) and then Vulcan (Roman god of fire), next Venus, and finally Jupiter.

In Western music today, this ancient way of working with sound magic is almost entirely lost. The notes on the piano are now all equal. All that matters are the intervallic relationships between these notes as found in melody and harmony and printed in black and white on the score. As long as the sequence of intervals and chords remains the same it may not even matter to composers what key their compositions are played in. A singer may find the published key awkward and transpose the piece into one in which it is easier for them to perform; generally, this would be considered a minor change to make. This is because the composer is not dealing with what lives in the precise tones used in their works, but in the emotional quality of the intervals. As long as the structure and relationship between the notes remains the same, the precise frequencies are of little consequence.

Some composers of course do have a sense of meaning for each key while others (including Messiaen, Scriabin, Rimsky-Korsakov, Beethoven, Feldman, Scelsi and Takemitsu, for instance) also have a sense for each note and chord, be that by virtue of synaesthesia or otherwise. As a synaesthete Messiaen is a case in point; he sees sounds as colours and composes accordingly. I listened to an LP of his music back in the early 1970s. I intentionally didn't read any of the liner notes beforehand but listened and 'watched' the music. When I read the LP notes later I found that I had seen exactly what Messiaen had seen and intended, just as he described. However, this is not the usual way that I would look for any astral colours with singing bowls.

In Western music, different combinations within the sequence of whole tones and semitones created the ancient Greek modes. Only two of these are in common use today and composers and listeners alike can distinguish between the (sad) minor and the (outgoing, positive) major keys. In some ways the evolutionary developments of modulation and chromaticism have freed the composer from the rigidity of keys and provided the entire resounding keyboard as a tonal palette from which to select notes and chords. Poetically, we could come to see the sounding board of the entire piano keyboard to be reverberating almost like a huge giant gong, only with a capacity to focus upon every single tone within its entire oceanic sound-world. Admittedly, with the piano, it is very hard to perceive this in the current equal-tempered system. It is easier in alternative piano tunings that have been devized recently

– such as that used by Terry Riley (5-limit) or La Monte Young (11-limit).

But I am relating far more to that which lives uniquely within the one sound itself – apart from any other. A handful of composers have likewise stepped into this world and considered what of spiritual significance can be found within a single tone. In particular I can mention the Italian composer Giacinto Scelsi (1905–88) who continued to experiment with this new way of listening from the middle of the twentieth century. He was interested in spiritual philosophy (particularly that of the Far East), as were Dane Rudhyar and Cyril Scott – both of these being Theosophists. Theosophy influenced many hundreds of artists at the start of the last century – most notable of which were Wassily Kandinsky, Piet Mondrian and Nikolai Rerikh (Nicholas Roerich). Theosophy had teaching to offer around the sevenfold constitution of Man and so dealt with the manner in which the five senses operated upon these subtle layers of life. Dane Rudhyar was particularly concerned with what lived in the actual tone as we find in his writings and (at the close of his life) in his book THE MAGIC OF TONE AND THE ART OF MUSIC.[2]

Rudolf Steiner too was a Theosophist before beginning his own movement, Anthroposophy, which included many Theosophical teachings and ideas. Steiner gave several lectures upon the subjects of sound and colour which have been made available in books. An important seminal work published by the Theosophical Society was the book THOUGHT FORMS by Annie Besant and Charles W. Leadbeater (1901). This book contained a chapter on the experiments of sound by Ernst Chladni as well as Margaret Watts-Hughes and also offered clairvoyantly-observed depictions of certain thoughts and emotions via coloured diagrams. The final chapter ('Forms Built by Music') includes clairvoyant observations of three pieces of music, namely: the ninth 'Song without Words' of Mendelssohn, the 'Soldiers' Chorus' from *Faust* by Gounod, and finally the Overture from *The Mastersingers* by Wagner. Each was performed upon the same church organ, and Wagner's music form was observed to be towering some nine hundred feet above the church. The authors of THOUGHT FORMS state that such forms remain coherent for an hour or two afterwards at least. [3]

Two more books that feature clairvoyant observations of what is created out of subtle matter by the performing of music are two books by the Australian Theosophist, Geoffrey Hodson, one of which is MUSIC FORMS (1976 – in which he looks at Handel's 'Largo', Bach's Prelude in C# Minor, Mozart's Fantasie in F Minor, Haydn's 'Emperor's Hymn', Handel's 'Hallelujah Chorus' and 'Harmonious Blacksmith' (from *Messiah*, and Harpsichord Suite no. 5), and Wagner's 'Preislied' and Overture (*The Mastersingers*).[4] The other book is CLAIRVOYANT INVESTIGATIONS (1984). The second portion of the latter book provides us with descriptions of the following pieces of music: 'Ave Maria' by Schubert, 'Songs My Mother Taught Me' by Dvorak, 'Agnus Dei', some Plainsong chant, 'Greensleeves', 'Londonderry Air', Prelude in C sharp Minor by J. S. Bach, 'Our Worship Rises Like a Soaring Flame' (anonymous), 'The Prince of Denmark March' by Jeremiah Clarke, 'Horn Concerto no. 1' by Haydn, 'The Vain Suit' by Brahms, 'Pavane' by Fauré, the 'Coriolan" Overture by Beethoven, and 'Pie Jesu' from the *Requiem* of Fauré.[5]

The current explorations into the properties of water by Dr Emoto in Japan produce pictures akin to these early studies into the effect of thought upon substance. The effect upon abstract painters of Besant and Leadbeater's THOUGHT FORMS (which had been published earlier in 1896 in editions of *The Theosophical Review*) was obvious. Its treatment of sound likewise opened doors, especially through introducing these experiments that enabled one to see sound.

The rich harmonic world of the singing bowls can hardly be referred to as one single note, yet by approaching each bowl and focusing upon its single sound (relatively speaking) one enters into the inner world created by prolonged exposure to the individual sound-characteristics of each bowl. Only certain bowls carry subtle energies and, the more sacred or elevated the energies are, then the rarer is that bowl. It is obvious that anyone contacting the bowl manufacturer could request that they produce bowls that are 'tuned' to our western scale in order to supply demand. However, it would require someone to keep hammering until the bowl produced the correct number of cps – and this, I'd imagine, would be reflected in the price, owing to the number of man-hours required. Also the bowlmaking factory would require equipment providing an electronic means of testing the pitch frequency – such as that used by the Swiss gongmakers Paiste when manufacturing their tuned symphonic gongs.

When one is wishing to use bowls in sound healing according to a system specifying a certain note or sound for use, or for the chakras, then it is useful if these can be manufactured. One source is Peter Hess, who has factories in Nepal making bowls to sell for use in his sound healing method. I imagined, for instance, were I to come into contact with a selection of his heart chakra bowls in a shop, that being hand-hammered each would differ from the others in the individual sound they made. When I met a seller of sound healing tools and mentioned this, he commented that he sold these bowls through his own shop and had many of them – and indeed they each sounded different. This means that were we to refer to a system of correspondences between specific notes from our western musical scale and the chakras, or planets, and apply this through the singing bowls, such a course would not be easy.

Just as there are few predictions that can be made with regard to the sound of a bowl and its size (in a performing layout, where the bowls are placed according to pitch, there is no visibly discernible order of size: a couple of small bowls between two large bowls produce a pitch inbetween the larger two) so it is impossible to predict, by size alone, where any one single bowl might lie in a sequence of pitches. Similarly, a bowl attuned to Jupiter, the largest planet of our solar system, may be half the size of one attuned to Mercury, a tiny planet. Put quite simply, either it is or is not attuned to a similar vibration of one or more of the qualities of the planet concerned or to its archangelic influence.

Just as a planetary mantra will serve to put you *en rapport* with the planetary energy, so you may find a bowl that carries these selfsame energies and characteristic qualities and may serve to expand the influence of that planetary ray within the listener's being. Interestingly, I have found that some ancient antique bowls of four hundred years or older connect with the energy of the planet Uranus, although we in the West have only known about this planet since its discovery in 1781. Nevertheless, the spiritual qualities of that planetary ray may have been experienced by the follower of sound centuries ago within their inner spiritual life, irrespective of any external planetary attribution.

Planets

Next, I shall provide a guideline to the qualities of the several planets used in astrology for a possible insight into the potential uses of any one singing bowl, thinking of their healing and balancing effects particularly. You may well find that one or more of your bowls is linked to a planetary ray irrespective of what its frequency is.

All of the glyphs for the planets come from the following three main symbols: -

The Circle – symbol of Spirit
The Semicircle – symbolizing the Soul
The Cross – here representing Matter

The Sun is represented by the symbol of the dot within the circle. It is the centre and source of life for this solar system. This ball of fiery light that illumines our sky therefore corresponds to the energies of the metal gold. Some of my singing bowls do contain more gold than usual and it is possible to both hear and feel the difference when more of this metal is present. It is a spiritual vibration that is very positive in nature. Thus related to fire, these bowls possess a warmth that increases the love vibration within us. Fire, being related to divine love by the ancients, often awakens this beautiful love vibration within our heart chakra but it is not necessarily the case that every bowl with more gold than usual is for the heart chakra. The ancients aligned the zodiacal fire sign Leo with the heart. Leo is ruled by the Sun and so we have this link between the fire element and the heart so that most heart chakra bowls have something of this sun influence of divine love. In Tibet the heart chakra is related to fire.

The heart energy can go in one of two main directions, 'vertical' or 'horizontal'. That is to say, it can rise in pursuit of divine love, in which case we aspire to transcend our lower nature and connect with higher states or beings; alternatively, it can spread out in the horizontal direction by offering compassion and love for our fellow beings, those that we meet on our own level of life. Both the Sun and Moon possess counterparts within our being and, although strictly speaking they are not planets at all, they assert an influence over us all in the same way that planets do. The astrological glyph for the Sun indicates the spark of light and life lying at the centre of each human heart and at the centre of all life. When we can feel fully in tune with the central source of life, we can be said to be living in the sun and in a state of at-one-ment. It is associated with the principle of the father. Such bowls carry the sense that all is well; their message is that the sun has returned, bringing warmth, light, love, life and creativity!

The Sun is linked with the metal gold, the archangel Michael and the colours gold and orange.

The Moon is represented by the semicircle. The Moon is the feminine principle, and is always related to the mother. The astrological sign of Cancer is ruled by the Moon and to this sign the ancients gave rulership over the breasts, the 'protective' rib cage and the stomach. The metal silver is governed by the moon, and there are some bowls in my collection that visibly display more of a predominance of this metal than bowls in general. The semi-circular symbol of the moon represents the soul, and also our feeling body, symbolized by water.

For ages past the moon has been associated with ritual and magic. The Moon generates no light of itself but rather reflects the light of the Sun towards earth during the night time. It can represent our outer personality – which in turn reflects our inner nature. In an individual horoscope the Moon can be an indicator for past-life influences. The Moon, to appearances the swiftest of the celestial bodies, accordingly rules over everyday events. But as it is the planet of the Great Mother it is its nurturing quality that comes to the fore.

In respect of healing, both of these two principal planetary rays, the Sun and the Moon, carry a cleansing quality. With the Moon, this comes via the sign of Cancer, which relates to Water and the washing away of accumulated deposits and has a purifying and transforming energy. With the Sun, the link is the sign of Leo, which is related to Fire and has a more purging, or transformational, effect. In the context of the watery Moon, it is to be remembered that it is only when the surface of the water is absolutely still that we can receive a pure and clear reflection. Therefore, while striving to intuit the energies of any one bowl it is essential to keep our feelings or emotions absolutely still. Only this enables us to work with true intuition.

Bowls bringing the sense of Divine Mother, protectiveness, nurturing, tenderness, or unconditional love for all, or a reflection of light, or peacefulness, may be said to link to the moon. The Moon links to the metal silver, the archangel Gabriel and the colours of silver and violet.

Mercury has a glyph featuring a most harmonious blending of all three symbols with a horizontal semicircle resting upon the circle of spirit above the cross of matter. Mercury is usually related to reason, logic, the lower mind, argument, intellectual knowledge, communication, mental excitement and the flow of stimulating ideas and thoughts. Increased awareness of our own thoughts, or even the observation of those thoughts that are attracted to our individual minds, will come under its sway. The name for this planet in Hindu astrology is Buddhi: perhaps we can include those bowls that relate to various forms of meditation – particularly those concerning observation of our breathing or else related to *gnana yoga* practices (self-inquiry) or to *trekchod* (the Tibetan equivalent). In short, we link it to meditations that help to still the mind. Mercury is the metal used in the impartial mirror. So this planet has a higher side, and via its link to methods of communication it is also a connection with the world of symbols. Bowls that carry the quality of stillness to the mind or emotions, or bring mental clarity or reflectiveness (the mirror), or encourage dispassionate observation (even something like an objective 'witness' position within our awareness) can relate to Mercury.

The planet Mercury relates to the metal Mercury, the archangel Raphael and the colour yellow.

Venus sees the circle of spirit above the cross of matter. Of all the planets in our solar system, the orbit of Venus around the Sun is the one that most closely resembles a circle. She is given rulership over the metal copper, and all over the globe the majority of bells (and bowls) are made from a basic alloy of 80% copper and 20% tin, with tiny amounts of other metals and trace elements. Copper is a warm metal and Venus is traditionally associated with the quality of love and harmony. Other qualities associated with Venus are beauty, idealism, a sense of values, meaning, peace, gentleness, consideration, calm tranquillity, attraction and culture. The bowl I have for this planetary energy carries the energy of tranquillity and serenity.

Venus rules the air sign Libra, the sign often equated with balance. Once, during a workshop, I played this bowl for others to observe. Many actually experienced changes leading to a greater sense of balance as they listened. It also rules the Sign of Taurus, which the ancients linked to the throat centre, giving many of its subjects a lovely voice or an appreciation of sound and music. The word 'culture', which is strongly linked to Venus, could be broken down as 'cult of Ur' – that is, of light. Bowls that inspire the sense of universal brotherhood – the one great family of all life – could be linked to this Venusian Ray – otherwise, they bring peace, gentleness, harmony, balance, equilibrium, beauty, or idealism, and they carry ennobling qualities.

We associate Venus with the metal copper, the archangel Haniel and the blue ray.

Mars sees the cross of matter above the circle of spirit (in its more modern symbol, the cross takes the form of an arrowhead). The ancient god of war, ruler of the metal iron (and steel and weapons), gives us courage, energy, self-assertion, desire, action and self-will. Mars's nature is hot, and so it is sometimes impulsive and almost always impatient. An excess of dark red in the aura brings us into relationship with base desires and selfishness, but with the raising of the vibration through white light we enter into the shades of rose pink that reflect unselfishness and compassion. From the vantage point of earth it is the first planet leading out of our solar system to worlds beyond. Thus courage to explore or pioneer new worlds is also linked to this planetary ray. So a bowl that helps us to feel fearless in moving forwards, engenders self-reliance or self-confidence or self-assurance, courage, invincibility, or indomitability, or else is full of flowing, unconditioned energy, or offers a move towards activity, could resonate with this planetary ray.

Mars rules the metal Iron, the archangel Samael and most associate it with the red ray.

Jupiter sees the semicircle of the soul on the lefthand horizontal arm of the cross – reaching out to other worlds or dimensions. Jupiter rules over the metal tin (the other metal used in bowls) and expansion, the higher mind, philosophy, understanding, peace, creativity, wisdom, religion – and also joy. It brings with it a sense of grandeur or majesty and of greatness and vastness. Jupiter strongly relates to healing, so that any bowl found to resonate with the healing ray could be considered to have a connection to this planet. It has a soothing quality and an unshakable inner certainty and faith that everything will turn out right. Jupiter tells us that we are supported by immutable laws (even if one of them is impermanence!). It has for its final goal the attainment of peace.

Certain bowls do bring this sense of inner peacefulness or a state of being at rest. Many bowls have a relaxing sound (especially for those who are unfamiliar with spending any time alone) however; this state of deep inner spiritual peace transcends that of mere relaxation. Bowls associated with Jupiter bring a sense of profound deep peace, or freedom born of the higher mind, joyousness, aspiration, expansiveness, ascension, being above the world and free of all sense of limitation, or breadth of vision relate to this planetary ray.

Jupiter resonates with the metal tin, the archangel Zadkiel and to the colour of indigo blue.

Saturn has a glyph featuring the semicircle of the soul beneath the cross of matter. Its influence can often be depressing, as we might imagine from the symbol! Saturn rules lead, the heaviest of metals, giving us such qualities as contraction, seriousness, concentration, self-discipline, self-centredness, isolation, and ponderousness; in the bowls, the element it rules is lead. Saturn's is a cold energy, which can be useful for dispassion and cooling down, but it also possesses a cleansing quality. Saturn is a serious planet, whereas its complement, Jupiter, is more carefree and joyful in its nature. Saturn was for some time considered the farthest planet in our solar system; coupled with the symbol of its rings, this led it to be associated with boundaries – including the enforcement of those boundaries! Jupiter and Saturn make a pair – expansion and contraction, respectively – even as Mars and Venus make a pair (ability to execute and idealism). Bowls that carry contraction (maybe as concentration or focus), a sense of self-discipline, seriousness, coldness (dispassion), responsibility, stability, meekness, humility, impermanence, stillness, patience, clarity (piercing through illusions), groundedness, condensing of ideas into form, strong focus, or purifying could come under Saturn's Ray.

Saturn we link to the metal lead or antimony, the archangel Cassiel (or Jophiel) and the colour Green.

Uranus combines a cross above a circle with two semicircles on either side of the horizontal axis of the cross. It is the first planet beyond the 'ring-pass-me-not' of Saturn and so the first of the three trans-Saturnian planets (the inter-galactic messengers). One of its tasks is to break down the boundaries of Saturn. This planet has a link to revolution, as well as individuality and originality, and in spiritual astrology it is considered to be the octave of the Sun. This links it more with will qualities – even as the Sun gives us the power of life. Its energy is that of independence and it is also the planet that carries the energy of truth.

We can also relate to this planetary energy as 'being in the Now' – being aware of the instant of time – or being stripped of all else and left abiding in the spiritual essence of things. In contrast to all of the other known planets it rolls along rather than spinning on a 'vertical' axis. 'Awakening' is a feature of this planetary ray, although not necessarily an awakening in worldly terms so much as what is implied by the name of Buddha – which means 'the Awakened One'. The sudden flash of a revelatory spiritual breakthrough moment or the awakening that accompanies certain spiritual initiations; a revolutionary awakening that changes our lives: that is Uranus.

It rules the third eye chakra or pituitary gland. Bowls that awaken our Buddha nature, or heighten our sense of being in the Now, or align us with Divine Will, or otherwise encourage us to change towards a new more evolved future, awaken our sense of individuality, and the power to go beyond, will link to this planetary ray.

Uranus we link to the metal gold and the colour electric blue.

Neptune is represented by a cross with a semicircle crossing its upward arm. Neptune is seen as the octave of the Moon. It is the least material of all planets and carries with it the energy of dissolution. This dissolving away is also part of the oceanic experience of at-one-ment, or of unity, and Neptune often relates to mysticism or the mysteries of life. By its very nature it is difficult to define. It rules the centre at the base of the brain (the pineal gland – third ear), related to sound. We can best describe its energy as being that of the wine of cosmic communion within the oceanic Cosmic Christ consciousness: spiritual union with the rarefied quality of divine love. Divine Mother has been represented by the sea, the ocean, and Neptune is linked to the Mother by virtue of being an octave of the Moon (the mother principle).

Neptune rules over the zodiacal water sign of Pisces – the final sign of the zodiac – and so it is related to endings or the final stage of a process. This is a very high state and few bowls would reach this plane; perhaps it even shows us the nirvanic plane! Bowls that enfold us in mystery or inspire such mystical union with the Divine Mother (or the mysteries of Isis, etc.), reveal the hidden mysteries to us, provide teaching that unfolds as a flower, provide a deep sense of going with the flow of a great and larger life; bowls whose sound dissolves our sense of being an isolated or separate ego, or that encourage a divine mystical union with the transcendent One: all these could have a link to the planetary ray of Neptune.

Neptune is linked with the metal silver and the colour pale blue-green.

Pluto, just like Mercury, includes all three basic glyphs. It comprises a cross with a semicircle upon its upper arm and a circle suspended within the semicircle. Pluto is considered to be the octave of the planet Mercury, and most consider that it rules over the zodiacal water sign of Scorpio. Scorpio is related to the inner (secret) worlds and this knowledge has been handed down to us by its link with death. Pluto is therefore also characterized as concerning itself with re-beginnings. Whatever passion we may have, it will run out of energy at some future point, and then our passion is up for renewal. Do we wish to sacrifice our energy into our art, our marriage, our music, or whatever field we have been focused upon, in order to renew it and begin a new cycle of activity? A sacrifice of our spiritual energy is required in order to bring life back again – even if this is simply the desire to live! In order to recreate and to begin again we need reconnection to our deepest level of being. Similarly, the process of reorientation is linked to this planet. Bowls that seem to speak of deep mysteries hidden beneath the surface, seem to speak of the process of initiation, release deep hidden inner forces, or else serve to reorient us to the deepest spiritual realities of the fiery world of spirit, could connect with this ray.

Pluto I link with the colour purple.

*

Of course, I am not stating that every bowl will be linked to one or another of these planets. Still less do I wish to imply that every bowl for sale from every shop or dealer has been intentionally made to work with one of the planets! I am simply providing a set of qualities that one can look for in the sounds of bowls, while also accepting that maybe nothing will be found. In that case, perhaps we look for any qualities that can be found within the elements, or chakras, or mantric resonances. It may be that the bowl has no such links but is simply a sounding bowl, meaningful and valuable to us all the same.

If the issue of treating the human energy-field or chakra system were simply a matter of using a note from one of the white keys on a piano, then the fact of it being a Tibetan, Himalayan, or glass bowl, would be rather superfluous. For within the context of these correspondences any one of the seven notes of the C major scale, whether played upon a violin, a saxophone, a vibraphone, a flute, a piano, or some other instrument, must have the same effect. In fact, it would be better to play such a note upon one of those instruments, for they are less rich in harmonic overtones and therefore more focused upon the exact note declared to be ruling that part of the body or chakra in such a system – in contrast with the sounds that come from Tibetan or Himalayan singing bowls. The other side of the coin is that the extended harmonic language of the singing bowls allows the listener to enter into level upon level of sound and ultimately layers of meaning – and thus to glimpse something of the magical presence of the Great Spirit.

By making attributions from the most popular table of correspondences (the seven notes of our C major scale) we are, in effect, projecting twenty-first-century Western mental constructs upon Himalayan bowls, in the same way as many of us may struggle to live according to unnatural twenty-first-century Western scientific, agnostic, or religious ideologies, or economic dictates, or even self-improvement programmes, rather than trusting to nature and following the voice of our heart (including the nature within ourselves – the Anthroposophia). Admittedly, following this inner voice found in the silence of the heart is a mystical way and, in our modern culture, we are not so educated.

It is natural to want to make the bowls part of ourselves. New Himalayan bowls are often covered with Buddhist symbols – an attempt on their makers' part to consecrate the bowls to Buddhist ends. More cynically, it might be said that several sellers and manufacturers want purchasers in the West to believe the bowls to be Buddhist objects and they are decorated to promote this view. None of the older bowls that I have seen have any such markings. The most one would get would be some writing and this normally refers just to the maker or owner of the bowl, in the same way that Western church bells often have writing upon them – either details of the dedicatee or a message describing the effect of the bell.

At the time that the truly ancient bowls were being made, bowlmakers would never have even heard of our Western diatonic scale. Chinese music is pentatonic whilst Indian musical scales are derived from a different interval altogether (to be precise, the Eastern scale is derived from the natural interval of the fifth in the former and the sixth in the latter). So, none of the surrounding countries would be using our diatonic scale either – but in truth the bowls were not created to fit into any musical scale at all. A so-called tuned set of antique Tibetan singing bowls is rather improbable. Nowadays, however, with so many Westerners going out there to buy for resale, and the merchants knowing the need for selling bowls with certain pitches, it could be possible for modern bowlmakers to 'tune' a bowl – providing the bowl had a clearly discernible and prominent fundamental (or whatever partial was sufficiently pronounced as to be clearly audible above all the other sounds of the bowl) – to one of the concert pitch standards used in the West. The manufacturer would need electronic equipment to keep measuring the frequencies. Certain websites selling bowls in Nepal and elsewhere state that they would expect to have to sort through around three thousand singing bowls in order to find one with the correct frequency for a note from our scale.

We must remember that as far as we can tell, bowls are made for ritual, ceremonial or meditation purposes and not for playing tunes upon. It's also highly unlikely that any of the countries of their manufacture would have associated any planets or chakras with our western diatonic scale – if with any 'musical' note at all. Being created to ring on for a long time they are also unsuited to playing most written or melody-based music.

When it comes to applying a note of our scale to the chakras, it might be well to ponder that in yoga the chakras have a single *bija mantra* (*lam, vam, ram, yam, ham* and *om* – with silence for the crown chakra – see p. 412) associated with each one, while the number of petals for each chakra also have their own sound (derived from the Sanskrit alphabet) with four for the root chakra (*Va. sha. Sha. Sa* [Shyamji][6] or *vang, shang, kshang, sang* [Johari])[7] and six for the sacral chakra (*bam, bham, mam, yam, ram, lam* – Ashley-Farrand[8]) and sixteen for the throat chakra, etc. Not one sound – in that sense. Masters differ in their teaching as to which mantric sound is for which chakra – so it's best to work either within your own school or with whatever system works for you. These *bija mantra* are not sounded to notes of the musical scale, for in most renderings that I have heard emphasis is placed upon the individual sound of the *bija mantra*, often with scant regard for any musical note – as these several Bija mantras are often chanted upon the same note. However, there will be traditions of sounds associated with the chakras handed down from history that may well sound close to a certain musical pitch.

Ultimately, all healing comes from a heart full of universal love, and the healing angels can and do often make any necessary adjustments to our intended treatments. So, my final advice is that there is no need to get bogged down in details so that we 'can't see the wood for the trees'. Each person must work in the way best suited to their nature, and with the spiritual ray upon which they are working, if they work with spirit beings or groups. Nonetheless, it is also incumbent upon us to have our feet firmly placed upon the ground at the same time as lifting our heads up to the heavens.

Patience is also a virtue, and we shouldn't press ourselves upon the sick and needy as their healers before we are truly ready to provide a beneficial service. Patience is necessary for entering the deeper layers of sound. It is not advisable to be in a rush concerning such things for (as it is written) if we try to force the temple door we are likely to find a two-edged sword. Accept where you are along the path and that at the appropriate time what you need will be supplied – always.

20. More on the Chakras

I HAVE previously mentioned connections between singing bowls and chakras and the purpose of this chapter is to elucidate this further. The ancient wisdom teachings inform us that we have several bodies, formed out of different materials and all interpenetrating one another. Maybe we can understand this if we consider the three bodies as a physical one, an emotional (astral) one, and a mental one. That is to say, we can see ourselves as creatures of acting, feeling, and thinking, but the three are never entirely separate. We also possess a subtle body that has seven main focal points of entry, which are loosely related to certain points along the spinal column. These are traditionally called the centres, or the 'chakras', a word that means 'wheels'.

Chakras can be seen by clairvoyants either as a rotating wheel of different coloured lights for each chakra or as flower-shaped appendages. There are also traditional diagrams to accompany each chakra. According to those, each of the 'flowers' is constructed with a specific number of petals. The chakras are also known more poetically as the windows of the soul, because they are where we receive impressions from outside of ourselves. The location of each of the major chakras is given on pp. 335-6, and should you feel that spot awakening as you play a bowl then there could be a link between that chakra and the bowl.

It is generally considered that the fourth or heart chakra resides at the central point with three chakras beneath it and three above. However, it must not be misconstrued that the three higher chakras are preferred over and above the lower chakras. It is truer to say that the lower triad supports the upper triad and the entire system is interrelated and interdependent. In the Hindu system each chakra has certain letters of the Sanskrit alphabet associated with its petals, a presiding deity and a seed-syllable *bija mantra*.

The chakras are non-physical in nature and so it would be a

mistake to think of them as we would muscles, to be exercised or developed. Rather, we 'unfold' them, which to some extent is simply to develop our awareness of them. It is said that according to our temperament (spiritual path) we would start at any one of the chakras in order to unfold them. Therefore, our temperament would provide a centre of activity that may be in the physical, astral, lower or higher mental or in higher bodies still. You are free to work upwards or downwards from any starting point.

White Eagle suggests working from the heart chakra and allowing the other chakras to unfold safely from this central position since it is rooted in the Christ Love. As we continue to unfold along the spiritual path we change the emphasis of our focus on the chakras. In this way we evolve from a focus upon one chakra onto the next. As I've already said, some antique aged bowls have been used for working with specific chakras, while other bowls (old or new) can be used in this way. The following paragraphs are meant as guidelines for working with the chakras using singing bowls but by way of identifying whether a bowl of yours can be used in this manner.

There exist a number of models for the system of the chakras, with the traditional seven main chakras figuring in each one. One view taken divides the seven at the heart in the centre with three beneath and three above (these latter may be referred to as the golden triangle). H. P. Blavatsky speaks of three types to the main seven chakras giving us twenty-one in all. In one of the Tibetan manuals of higher magic, in a rite to produce transference of consciousness, we find twenty-one centres mentioned, and these not spaced after the usual manner. Another system from the Indian sages speaks of a further seven chakras beneath the root chakra (which chakra is the first in the usual order of seven). Yet another provides us with an additional seven above the crown – thereby also providing us with another order of twenty-one chakras. Another speaks of the seven main chakras plus centres in the hands and feet. Sri Shyamji Bhatnagar speaks of 147 chakras, all rooted in the seven main chakras. The Radha Soami school refers to twelve chakras, being two sets of six with the traditional seventh or crown chakra being the first of the next six higher chakras. Then we have the

main seven chakras with three additional chakras namely, Hrit
Padma, the higher heart and the *guru* chakra making a tally of
ten chakras. I have found bowls for these ten chakras plus the
soma chakra. Thomas Ashley-Farrand[1] provides us with a list of
twelve chakras: *muladhara, svadisthana, manipura, hrit padma* or
hridayam, anahata, visuddha, lalani or *kalachakra, ajna, manas,
soma, guru, sahasrara.* Shyam Sundar Goswami gives us thirteen
chakras: *muladhara, svadisthana, manipura, hrit, anahata, visuddha, talu, ajna, manas, indu, nirwana, guru,* and *sahasrara.*[2]

Nothing in the above is intended to show disagreement upon
the subject, nor is it to inspire ridicule, but rather to demonstrate
that the findings are determined by our tradition and approach
and also that the subject is more complex than we might at first
imagine. It is also a subject with a very long history. There is some
mention of chakras in yoga Upanishads of around 600 BCE and later in the yoga sutras of Patanjali, which date from around 200 BCE.
The chakra system features very little in early Buddhist teachings
but a key to this is assumed to be that Buddha traditionally lived
from 563 to 483 BCE, placing him almost before the idea came into
written record. Giving a slightly different date for the Upanishads,
Mircea Eliade writes:

> The idea of the subtle vital force (prana) and the channels
> along which it flows (nadis) appear in the earliest Upanishads
> (seventh or eighth century BCE). The heart was said to be the
> centre of the 72,000 nadis or subtle channels, and the place
> into which the senses are withdrawn during sleep. As with
> many ancient civilizations (e.g. Egypt, Homeric Greece), the
> heart was also considered the seat of waking consciousness.
>
> But it was only in the later Upanishads – the earlier of
> which were composed somewhere between the second century
> BCE and the second century CE – reference is first made to basic
> Tantric concepts such as chakras, mantras, and so on.
>
> The *Brahmopanisad* (11, 9) expounds a curious theory of
> the 'four places' inhabited by the *purusa*: the navel, heart, neck,
> and head. Each of these regions has a corresponding state of
> consciousness: the navel (or the eye), the state of diurnal wak-
> ing; the neck sleep; the heart, dreamless sleep (*susupta*); the

head, the transcendental state (*turiya*). In the same way the four states of consciousness respectively correspond to Brahma, Visnu, Rudra, and Akshara (the indestructible).[3]

There are two minor chakras mentioned in the ancient texts, the *soma* chakra, located just above the third eye, and the *anandakanda* lotus of the heart chakra.

The serpent power, or inner spiritual fire (*kundalini*), coiled at the root chakra, is really a force of withdrawal. A sound may begin in the unstruck region but once it strikes a material object the sound produced returns to its source via a series of ascending overtones. As with a sounding object, the journey of *kundalini* is from the base chakra up to the crown of the head. So *kundalini* reverses the process of creation so that we return to the source or to the One (crown). I believe this is a possible interpretation of the words of St John the Baptist, 'Repent. Make straight the way of the Lord'. Because of this process of reversal the spiritual fire of *kundalini* cannot function until we reduce external involvement and attachments.

I am not going to give musical notes for the chakras. Not only are singing bowls untuned to any particular note of the scale, but above all we must have real, pure, and true awareness of the chakras in order to work with sound upon them. A system codifying them with the notes of our C major musical scale that requires no understanding or true awareness of what or where they actually are is misleading, and the healing practitioner needs firsthand awareness of this subtle system, not embellishments to a list; they cannot merely adhere to an abstract musical system, however pragmatic and utilitarian it may be to have one.

While testing singing bowls, I may become conscious that one or other of my chakras is being awakened through the sound of the bowl. The second chakra, according to Leadbeater, is found at the spleen as well as the hypogastric plexus (see p. 335), yet I felt the two bowls that I have so far found actually resonate with and awaken into activity the sacral chakra where it traditionally resides. The hypogastric plexus is situated near the pelvic region, but the alternative location would be at the first lumbar vertebra, over the splenic centre. However, Leadbeater also advises that it is less dangerous to work with the second chakra from the spleen centre. As another instance, I have a large singing bowl that stimulates the third eye chakra, despite it offering a deep sound and not at all the right 'note' according to the system in vogue. In fact, even when I simply hold the bowl, without sounding it at all, my third eye is very strongly stimulated.

We can approach the chakras with two main models of access to levels of consciousness. One represents states of consciousness (therefore open to anybody at any time) and the other, representing stages of consciousness (mutually exclusive between one and another), is more vertical and somewhat hierarchical in nature and derives from our evolutionary unfoldment. For the purpose of this book (and for identifying whether a bowl will work on a given chakra) I shall provide an outline for the seven main chakras from the first (base) to the seventh (crown). Our experience of the chakras will change with our personal growth, so what I write is intended to have some sort of developmental axis within the context of our evolution along the spiritual path. The chakras' locations in the physical body are given again as a prompt to notice any sensation there.

1. *Muladhara* ('root base foundation') chakra is situated at the base of the spine. This chakra can be viewed as being reminiscent of the roots of a tree. Whereas the branches and twigs give way to the passing weather the roots and trunk remain stable. The symbolism is that with regard to our deepest principles we should remain immovable, but we should be flexible on small things. As the great oak grows from the tiny acorn, so the seed of our spiritual life awaits the right conditions to awaken.

> Behold, a sower went forth to sow; and when he sowed, some seeds fell by the way side, and the fowls came and devoured them up: some fell upon stony places, where they had not much earth: and forthwith they sprang up, because they had no deepness of earth: and when the sun was up, they were scorched; and because they had no root, they withered away. And some fell among thorns; and the thorns sprang up, and choked them: but other fell into good ground, and brought forth fruit, some an hundredfold, some sixtyfold, and some thirtyfold. Who

hath ears to hear, let him hear. (Matthew 13 : 3-9).

This chakra is linked with the earth element, suggesting the very stability and security that are demanded for us to apply a safe approach to unfolding the chakras and provide the best conditions for the 'seed' to take root and grow to fruition.

2. *Svadisthana* ('one's own place'). In my spiritual healing work by 'laying on of hands' I work from the spleen (splenic) centre, but for the purpose of analysing bowl sounds we will adhere to the customary position that is situated at the base of the genital organ. This chakra can reflect that everything in nature needs a habitat that will support its needs. We may learn to trust that we are exactly where we need to be for the best possible opportunity for growth, seen from the vantage point of eternal life: this would be our spiritual growth. In ancient societies and civilizations everyone had their place, be that as a cook, a farmer, a warrior, a teacher, a king, a potter, a child, a parent, or whatever. Knowing our place in life we can feel content to be contributing our link in the grand chain of life. We can fulfil our own *dharma* – for which we were created – rather than the *dharma* that others consider we should be doing. It is said that humankind is placed midway between the animal kingdom below and the angelic kingdoms above. To know our place here would mean receiving from those above us and giving to those who come up after us.

3. *Manipura* ('City of Jewels') chakra, situated around the solar plexus, leads us to ponder issues of power, for who is it that holds the precious jewels if not the king? How did the first king come to be? Was this one a natural born leader, or did he or she show expertise at warcraft? Perhaps they were simply a bully or maybe they had some power to persuade others and to galvanize the people around a common cause. The 'jewel in the sky' is the sun and all revolves around the sun in our solar system. In a like manner all the several aspects of our life must revolve around our central inner spirit. Perhaps the finest example would be an ashram where all are as satellites around the central, guiding Master. We can go further and see everything in our own lives as contributing towards our good. Then we can understand that in

order to grow we will have chosen certain difficult experiences
to go through during our incarnation, so that these unpalatable
experiences that we attribute to the outer world may be seen as
originating from our real Self and ultimately serving our real spirit
– the jewel within. Bowls connected with this chakra bring peace
and relaxation to help us through the 'warring' times of Mars.

4. *Anahata* ('unstruck') chakra, in the region of the heart (between the ninth and tenth thoracic vertebrae) translates as 'unstruck sound'. What is this sound if not the great hum of the entire
universe, or that which we hear from inside, or the voice of our
intuition that is found within the spiritual heart centre? At those
times when we are merging into divine love we surrender to a feeling of at-one-ment with all life and we enter the circle of eternal
now. The 'beginning' is constantly being created in each instant.
Life comes forth from out of chaos; it establishes itself and then
is destroyed – only to be reborn. This is our circle or cycle of
life formed out of desire, or love. It is a sound not made of two
things hitting (see p. 54), possibly hinting that here we rise beyond
dualistic thinking. That arises from the sense of being a separate
self – an ego. We transcend ego (not-self) and experience the One
Self. It is the central chakra, perhaps referring to that one central
tone or note experienced during absorption with divine love. *Anahata* is the chakra linked to *bhakti* or devotion. It is here that
we can encounter feelings of universal compassion and devotion
to love itself. Once having opened our heart to this great love we
no longer relate to others as being 'not-self' or 'it' but rather as a
'thou' alive with the tone of creation, for this great hum is at the
back of all living things uniting us all.

5. *Visuddha* ('pure') chakra is located at the juncture of the
spinal column and the *medulla oblongata*, behind the throat (la-
ryngeal or pharyngeal plexus). *Visuddha* is variously translated as
cleansed, clarified, perfectly pure. This centre gathers impressions
and experiences from the lower chakras and purifies them. At this
stage of our spiritual unfoldment through the chakras we remove
blockages and pollutants on all levels. As the *anahata nada* purifies the *nadis*, so, too, we may find that we are no longer attract-

ed to drugs, alcohol, meat, smoking, or any substances of lower vibration (such as artificial stimulants – even coffee or tea). The required method here is the turning around of the energy. The aggression of the solar plexus chakra directed towards conquering or correcting the outer world is now turned towards purifying oneself. It is as *visuddha* opens that we clarify our senses. Here we learn to sound our own note. Here we develop inner listening, unfolding our true wisdom. We listen to our deepest conscience and we follow our own truth from the central heart within. Clairaudience in its intuitive form arises here.

As we tune ourselves to our real note so we tune in with others better. Through purification, we enable the creative expression of our 'true' inner self. To be true to our original nature is to be pure and, as a mirror, to remain uncontaminated with anything not of our true virgin nature. We learn to speak from our heart. 'In order to receive and be nurtured as well as be creative and expressive, the yogi strives to clear his mind of secondary things to experience the unveiled voice and light of Brahman (God).' Divine sound or *mantra* resides here. Silence is also associated with this chakra, wherein our personal voice is lost in the divine Word. In the silent sound we merge into cosmic ether in which the essence of absolute sound abides as eternal wisdom. At the level of the heart chakra we entered the spiritual path and here at the throat we begin to clear away the accumulations of our lower nature (ego) and the misinformation or manipulation of the media and the street and so put into action our newfound direction, possibly through the practice of *mantra*.

6. *Ajna* (command) chakra, situated between the eyebrows, commands the various states of concentration realized through meditation. Its name is also translated as authority, order or unlimited power. It is stated that there are two petals here (two is the number of the Moon), however each petal has forty-eight smaller petals, giving us a total of ninety-six. The sixth and seventh chakras, *ajna* and *sahasrara*, are the two ways of experiencing what is known as 'God,' either as 'with form' (*saguna* Brahman – the 'qualified absolute') or as 'without form' (*nirguna* Brahman – the 'unqualified absolute'), alongside the two methods of

meditation – *savikalpa samadhi* ('discriminating absorption') and *nirvikalpa samadhi* ('undifferentiated absorption'). Accordingly, the third eye chakra refers to the radiant image of one's idea of 'God'. It is at this chakra that the currents of the two main *nadis* (*ida* and *pingala*) meet and join the *susumna* to form the single energy channel that continues up to the crown chakra. Although the word translates as 'command', this is a feminine chakra, and therefore our inner being 'commands' what vision shall be placed there. It is entirely our choice – whereas the *nada* sound we have no control over. It is said that here the state of enlightenment that is sought in Buddhism is experienced.

7. *Sahasrara* (thousand) is the 'Lotus of a Thousand Petals' located about four finger-breadths above the crown of the head; it is also called Brahmarandhra and is the meeting-place of the *kundalini shakti* with Pure Consciousness. It is bright with the brilliance of ten million suns, or so we are told. Here we find 960 outer petals and twelve inner ones, providing us with a total of 972 .

This centre connects us with divine consciousness. It is the Divine in its primal manifestation. 'In the beginning was the Word.' Sound is the primordial nature with the absolute sound of the *nada* yogi, bringing absorption into a nameless and formless realm of transcendence. As this chakra relates to a 'God' without form as well as a meditative state of 'undifferentiated absorption', there is nothing to say. Some teachers give no sound at all to this chakra, whereas those yogis who have entered into the higher states of *samadhi* can find no words to express their experience. I receive sensations in my crown chakra at the point of the fontanel while playing my crown chakra bowl.

In the Tibetan system the top two chakras and the bottom two are united as one, providing us with five chakras. The elements are thus distributed differently in this system – *muladhara* and *svadishthana* linking with Earth, *manipura* with Water, *anahata* with Fire, Visuddha with Air, and the top two, *ajna* and *sahasrara*, with Ether or Space.

If we take five teachers on the subject of sound vocalizations for the chakras, we can see that they each have their own attributions. Although they do not differ widely, it can be seen there is no set system that they all agree upon to be applied here. This is also the case with various gurus. Choose whichever works best for you!

Chakra by number	Jonathan Goldman	Randall McClellan	Kay Gardner	Peter Hamel	Anodea Judith
7	EEE	MMM	EEE	EEE	NG (ING)
6	AYE	EEE	IH	EEE	MMM/NN
5	EYE	AYW	EH	EH	EEE
4	AH	AH	AH	AH	AYE
3	OH	OH	AW	OH	AH
2	OOO	OOO	OH	UH	OOO
1	UH	OOO	OOO	UH	OH

Table #16: Chakras and Tones, Vowels and some other sounds

Practical Recognition of Chakra Links

Since 1972 I've found certain of my antique sacred instruments from the East to be linked to specific chakras and I've shared this knowledge in my workshops since 1978. There is little doubt that this has led to the term 'Chakra Bowl', unless someone else used the phrase prior to 1972. For myself this is once again an intuitive approach (not a mechanistic paradigm attributing specific frequencies to chakras) and I will now offer some hints to help you identify if you have a chakra bowl.

Apart from occasions when the sound of a bowl is felt directly in the location of a chakra we may yet be able to find a link through the sound characteristics of the bowl. To state these in summary, for chakras one to seven, the following word-associations may be helpful.

1. Stable, rooted, still, deep, grounding, safe, secure, relaxed, sense of trust, family, and home. Often larger and deeper bowls, but not exclusively so.

2. Flowing, energizing, accepting, letting go, pleasure, nurturing of self, and ability to change.

3. Powerful, regal, relaxing, centred, self-esteem, confidence, and at peace with oneself. Mostly larger bowls (ten inches plus).

4. Warm, loving, expansive, compassion, devotion, empathetic, altruistic, and relationship. These are normally medium-pitched bowls but with pronounced partials that awaken heart feelings. Quite gentle and warm in sound, so that we can easily feel enfolded.

5. Cleansing, heightening one's awareness of sound, resonance, creativity and symbolic thinking.

6. Inspiring, bringing visions, clarity, wisdom, imagination, illumination, and increased intuition. The pitch is usually in the upper regions (even if only a strong upper partial).

7. Transcendent experiences linking with a Divine Self. The enhanced sense of a connection to the very essence or source of All. A sense of transcendence of our normal consciousness. These are typically very high-pitched bowls sounding the third or fourth partial.

As I've mentioned before, a *basso profundo* singing the part of a baritone or bass brings a certain depth to the tone. In a similar way it is sometimes the case that the fundamental of the bowl is not the tone that affects a chakra but rather one of the partials, and playing with the appropriate wand will help us to focus upon this partial that stimulates the chakra in question. Because it is a partial there is warmth to the tone coming from the supporting fundamental below.

> Ajna has been compared to an eye, a crystal ball or a magic mirror. The virtues of this Chakra are passive, feminine: it is a mirror in which every event in the universe is reflected. Ajna can give you the power to see everything but this does not mean that you have the power to act: Ajna cannot give you that. It gives you vision, it allows you to see images, but it does not allow you to change the course of events or of forces. For this you have to reach the last Chakra, Sahasrara, which is emissive, dynamic and masculine and which can give you the power to act. When the Kundalini force reaches Ajna an Initiate receives a clear vision of reality but he is not yet all-powerful. He is still vulnerable, exposed to antagonistic forces, still tossed to and fro between good and evil. This is why he must attain the crowning point: Sahasrara.
>
> In almost every Hindu temple in India you will see a carved

symbol in the form of a flat horizontal stone surmounted by another, vertical stone: this is the Lingam. The horizontal stone represents the feminine principle and the vertical stone, the masculine principle. The Hindu Faithful, men and women, girls and youths, all pray and prostrate themselves in veneration before this symbol, which is often decorated with garlands of flowers, for it is the symbol of generation, of the fertility of men and of gods.

Omraam Mikhael Aïvanhov.[4]

Now, let me give you a very simple exercise to help you to develop the throat Chakra, Vishuddha: from time to time, devote your whole meditation simply to Listening. Don't think at all. Just try to listen, try to hear the voice of wisdom, the voices of the spirits of light. Of course, at your first attempts you will probably not hear anything, but if you persevere you will eventually hear the Inner Voice, the gentle Voice of God, that voice which is so faint and subtle that it is sometimes called the Voice of the Silence. When you hear this voice your whole being will vibrate and tremble – words are powerless to describe the experience.

Omraam Mikhael Aïvanhov.[5]

A method you can use to develop Ajna is to imagine that you are looking with your inner eye at the earth, the sky and the whole of space, with all its countless inhabitants, that you can see all worlds, both visible and invisible. You simply gaze at them with great love: that is all that is necessary to begin to awaken your spiritual vision.... Try to listen, as it were, to your own two ears; in this way it is another, a third ear, which is awakened. Similarly, if you focus your gaze on the wonders of the invisible world, it is your third eye which will be opened.

Omraam Mikhael Aïvanhov.[6]

21. Conclusion

FOLLOW YOUR passion, follow your heart; follow your bowl and follow the sound. Enjoy the adventure and create your own road map from your Self as it unfolds along this musical way. But be in no rush. Avoid the urgency and pressures of the competitive world and avoid comparing yourself with others and be content to unfold as the flowers do – from within.

Our journey has embraced sound, inaudible sound, form, esoteric Christianity, Buddhism, spirituality, acoustics ancient and modern, the four – or five – elements of nature, ancient initiation, chakras, the history of bowls and bells, metallurgy, symbolism, invisible beings, meditation, techniques of playing, and my personal experiences from over forty years working in these fields.

The many bowls that I have come across vary in a great many ways as to their shape, sound and spiritual properties. The bowls have taught me many things and I have wished to share these sound revelations with you. Through the centuries that the bowls have existed some have been consecrated for use in spiritual practices. I have found that the sound of such bowls matches the vibration of the spiritual energies to which the initiate has 'tuned' them. If we own such a bowl then it will be important at some time to work with its energetic content and purpose. If we own a metal bowl that makes a sound, and we wish to deepen our practice with this bowl, then it is possible through certain types of Tibetan yoga to work towards this alchemical transformation. Uniformity is a law of nature so that what happened once can happen again.

There is more that I have to say on the subject and a further volume is envisaged which will continue on from this one with more on the chakras, while the bulk of this second volume will concern itself with sound healing in the context of the Himalayan singing bowls.

Hopefully, some of the content of this book, alongside the several exercises, can enhance your own experiences in using your bowls as you continue to experiment. The categorization of bowls and techniques of playing, alongside the range of wands and mallets described, should furnish you with a vocabulary that tells you where you are on the road. You may have found energetic links between your bowl and one of the planets, or chakras, or elements, or even one of the Buddha families. Perhaps, in some small way, the contents of this book, written in order to help you, can contribute towards your playing and use of bowls as well as your understanding of the world of singing bowls.

You can visit my website, which is at www.frankperry.co.uk, for various articles, discography, biography, graphic scores, and details of my CDs, with some sound clips. You can find me on YouTube under Frank Perry, where there are currently ninety-eight videos of live concerts, interviews on my sound healing work, videos on the shape and sound of a variety of singing bowls, plus a complete workshop from the 1990s. There are a number of my recordings available to listen to on the OMN (Overtone Music Network) website; also on MySpace under Frank Perry III, and sound bites on SoundCloud under Frank Perry 4. CDs of my music are also available on the web from Wilde Ones – http://wildeones.com (under 'Meditation Music') – while my mini-wands are available in the USA from http://bestsingingbowls.com.

Appendix A: Metal Analysis

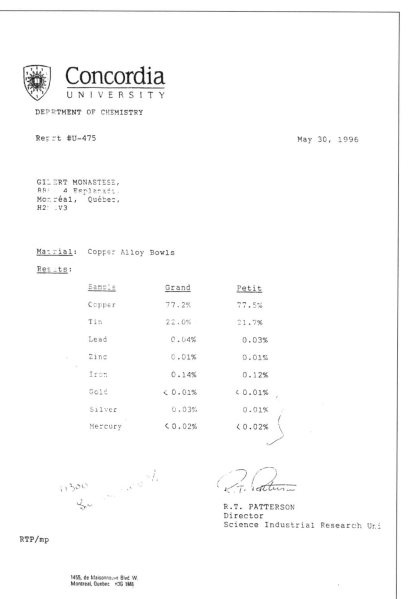

Concordia
UNIVERSITY

DEPARTMENT OF CHEMISTRY

Report #U-475

May 30, 1996

GILBERT MONASTESSE,
884 4 Esplanade,
Montréal, Québec,
H2W 1V3

<u>Material</u>: Copper Alloy Bowls

<u>Results</u>:

Sample	Grand	Petit
Copper	77.2%	77.5%
Tin	22.0%	21.7%
Lead	0.04%	0.03%
Zinc	0.01%	0.01%
Iron	0.14%	0.12%
Gold	< 0.01%	< 0.01%
Silver	0.03%	0.01%
Mercury	< 0.02%	< 0.02%

R.T. PATTERSON
Director
Science Industrial Research Unit

RTP/mp

Metal analysis of copper alloy bowls

Appendix B: Categories of Singing Bowl

IN MY EXPERIENCE there is a wide variety of singing bowls and I will now list those that I have categorized within my own collection of some three hundred and fifty bowls gathered over the forty-two years since 1971. I have sorted through over 9,500 bowls, and the main source for the longest period in this time-span (John Mead) sorts through around 8,000 bowls to end up with perhaps 200 that I then select from! In one sense every single bowl is a unique creation although there are some discernible designs and towards the end of the 1990s the majority of bowls upon the market (in the UK at least) were from Orissa and closely resemble one another and the demands of the market were met, but the manufacturing process of hand hammering guarantees a fair degree of dissimilarity. The majority of new bowls originate from Nepal and are of a unique design and covered with Buddhist symbols, plus either engravings or three-dimensional figures in their base. My aim here is to demonstrate the major differences in bowl design and then in their differing acoustical sound properties and then in the supersensible characteristics abiding upon the subtle planes of experience and existence.

There are a number of factors that can be and are variously joined together in the structuring of a singing bowl and there remain several other possible combinations that I have not encountered yet that may or may not exist. The following list is drawn from what I have found from my time of over forty years collecting and playing these wonderful instruments. The list is organized according to physical features first, followed by sound characteristics and finally qualities existing upon the more subtle planes of existence that can be found to correspond to other terminologies.

As I mentioned in the main text of this book, besides the present categories I would also divide any list into three basic partitions:

1. A purely physical bowl – it is what it is pure and simple with nothing extra-special about it and you either like it or you don't – but it is purely a piece of metal in a particular shape, off the shelf and sometimes machine-made, that makes a noise.

2. Next are bowls that can be used within a psycho-spiritual context in order to awaken and encourage the development of certain soul qualities such as courage, patience, joy, peace, humility, tranquillity, etc.

3. Finally, there are bowls that have been used by yogis or Tantric practitioners, when working alone, in varying degrees of commitment and involvement along the path of sound yoga, to accompany or assist in spiritual practices such as meditation or healing and often these still retain these supersensible energies or hidden powers embodied within their sound through decades or even centuries of spiritual work.

However, I should like to add that the potential for the suitability of working in a certain way with a bowl must also abide within the actual sound quality of the singing bowl and not be forcibly superimposed upon the instrumental object. In the spirit of Taoism one should 'go with the flow'.

Here is a full list, as of now. Italicized names are my own and Roman are not. 'A.k.a.' stands for 'also known as' and 'NFY' for 'not found yet'.

1. Identified by Physical Features (forms, shapes & designs)

Yang Bowl – Outer Lip
Yang Bowl – Inner Lip
Yang Bowl – Both / Central Lip
Yang Bowl – Chamfered Edge
Yang Bowl – Extra Thick Rim
Yang Bowl – Medium Rim
  Thickness
Yang Bowl – Small Rim Thickness
Yin-Yang Bowl – A Yin bowl with a flared Yang lip that ends lower than the Yin rim.
Shakti Bowl – Deep Thin (Yin) Lip-Inwards Yang Bowl

Tantric Bowl – Conical Thin (Yin) Lip-Outwards Yang Bowl
Tantric Lingam Bowl – as above, with the inclusion of a lingam
Flared Bowl – Bent out same-thickness Yin Lip
Flared Bowl – Flared rim slightly thicker (Yang) with chamfered edge
Flared Bowl – Yang (thicker rim not chamfered)
Yin Bowls
Talking Bowl

Panic Bowl

Whistling Bowl

Dome Bowl – a bowl with a form of 'lingam' that is more dome-shaped than conical

Dome Water Bowl – medium height (between shallow and normal) curved wall Yin

Dome Flat-base Bowl (Manipuri Lingam)

Crescent Bowl

Tall Bowl

Shallow Bowl

Yang Vase Bowl – a.k.a. Ultabhati

Yin Vase Bowl – a.k.a. Ultabhati

Waist Bowl

Narrow Base Bowls

Wide Base Bowls

Flat-bottomed Bowl – very flat with a sharp demarcation line at the base of the wall

Shallow Flat-bottomed Bowl

Spherical Yang Bowl

Spherical Yin Bowl

Resting Yin Bell-Bowl – with its own base (different from *Chalice Bowls*)

Chalice Bowl   Yin

Chalice Bowl   Yang

Elephant Bowl *Yang*

Elephant Bowl *Yin*

Elephant Jumping Bowl Yang

Conical Water – a.k.a. Remuna

Conical Jump – Elephant *Yin*, also called Remuna

Lingam Bowls – also called Mt Meru or Chama

Fountain Bowl Yin – unusual inner line position (a water mark)

Fountain Bowl Yang – unusual inner line position (a water mark)

Water Bowls   Yang

Water Bowls Yin

Shallow Water Bowls – *Yin* straight wall with wide base

Shallow Water Bowls – *Yin* curved wall with wide base

Very Shallow Water Bowl – *Yin* curved wall with wide base

Water Spirit Bowl – with lingam, flared wall, and convex base

Star Bowl – engraved star upon inner centre base

Lotus Bowl – strongly indented Lotus petals around outer wall

Air Spirit (Ululation) *Bowl* – stroked

Ululation (used for Overtone Meditation) Bowl – Struck

Iron Bowl

Silver Bowl

Gold Bowl

Dragon Bowls – by shape and colouration (black outside/inside)

Yoni Bowls – suns & downward-pointing triangles of suns in four quarters

Sun Bowls – sun decoration around outer rim

Pearl Bowl – decoration like strings of pearls on outside

Indian Bowls – highly decorated inside &/or outside

Bengali Bowls

Southern Bengali Bowls

Assam Bowls

Manipuri Bowls *Yin*

Manipuri Bowls *Yang*

Bhutanese Bowls

Burmese Bowls

Orissa Bowls *Yin*

Orissa Bowls *Yang*

Bharampur Bowls

Chinese Qing Bowls – a.k.a. Buddha bowl – Temple Bowl

Chinese singing bowl – machine

made
Japanese Rin Bowls – *Yin* (Zen)
Tang
Taiho
Nara
Kiho
Michiyuki
Uneri
Unryu
Shaka
Kyoto
Dharma
Shomyo
Shomyo lacquered
Uchinarishi
Japanese Kei (*Yang*) Temple Bowl

Nepalese 'Tibetan' Bowl – modern, machine-made
Nepalese (machine-made) Bowls
Thailand Bowls
Korean Bowls
Tibetan Bowls *Yin*
Tibetan Bowls *Yang*
Bowls decorated with Suns – on top of rim
Bowls decorated with Moons – outer rim
Bowls decorated with both Sun and Moon symbols – outer rim
Bowls with engraved writing
Machine-made Bowls

There will be others that are unusual in their characteristics and most likely these are all but categories of one: in a class of their own. Whoever knows how many of these there are?

2. Arranged by Sound Characteristics

The following (all named by myself) display their characteristics while being struck.

Fast-moving Fundamental Bowl
Medium movement Fundamental Bowl
Slow-moving Fundamental Pulse Bowl
Slow Breathing bowls – very slow oscillation between tones
Vibrato Bowls
Ululation Bowls
Overtone Bowl – clearly defined partials (Manipuri Lingam)
Singing Yang Bowls – loud partial
Singing Yin Bowls – loud partial
Ascending (Fire) Bowl – lower partials quickly fall away
Descending (Water) Bowl – upper partials quickly fall away

Central (Air & Earth) Bowl – both upper and lower partials fall away
Abiding Space Bowl – where all the tones last from beginning to end
'Sound Meditation' Bowl – enhances awareness of sound
Centring Bowl
Ritual Bowl – to prepare for commencement of ritual
Complex Sound – many partials some close together (doublets)
Simple Sound – very few partials, strong focus
Unconditional Bowl – for formless meditation practices – free of any specific energies
Jump Bowls – *Yin & Yang*

The following display their characteristics while being stroked.

Air Spirit Bowls
Yoga Bowl
Flying Bowl – Yin
Flying Bowl – Yang
Pulse/Mantra Bowl
'Space-Cleansing' Bowl
Exorcism Bowl

'Soul Retrieval' Bowl
Messenger Bowl
Consummation Bowl – Session
  Ending or Closing
'Passing Over' Bowl (Bowl to
  assist those with terminal illness)

The following can display their characteristics either way.

Earth Element Bowl
Water Element Bowl
Fire Element Bowl
Air Element Bowl

Space Element Bowl
Three-in-One Bowls (Ululation/
  Water/Jump)
Stillness (Astral and/or Mental)

3. Arranged by their Supersensible Qualities

These I find resonate with the qualities in question due to the structure of their sound and others, in addition, may also be charged with these self-same subtle qualities. All terms originated by myself. NFY stands for 'not found yet' – but part of a series.

Deity Bowls (Male – Shiva,
  Chenrezig, Manjusri,
  Kuntazangpo, Maitreya, etc.)
Deity Bowls (Female – Tara,
  Durga, Kali, Saraswati, etc.)
Vairocana Buddha Bowl (Dhyani
  Buddhas)
Amitabha Buddha Bowl
Ratnasambhava Buddha Bowl
Akshobhya Buddha Bowl
Amogasiddhi Buddha Bowl
Master Bowl – Morya (Ray 1)
  Dhyani Chohan (NFY)
Master K.H. (Ray 2)
The Venetian Master (Ray 3) NFY
Master Serapis Bey (Ray 4)
Master Hilarion (Ray 5) NFY
Master Jesus (Ray 6)
Master R (Ray 7)

Mahachohan (NFY)
Sanat Kumara
Buddha Bowl
Alignment Bowl (Antakharana)
Radiation of the Light Bowl
Root Chakra Bowl (also to do
  with the qualities within their
  sound)
Sacral Chakra Bowl
Solar Plexus Chakra Bowl
Hrit Padma Chakra Bowl
Heart Chakra Bowl
Higher Heart (a.k.a. Thymus
  Chakra) Chakra Bowl
Third Eye Chakra Bowl
Soma Chakra Bowl
Bindu Chakra Bowl
Guru Chakra Bowl
Crown Chakra Bowl

Personal Planets: Sun Bowl
Moon
Mercury
Venus
Social Planets: Mars
Jupiter
Saturn
Trans-Saturnian Planets: Uranus
Neptune
Pluto
Zodiac Bowls (12) Aries (NFY)
Taurus
Gemini (NFY)
Cancer (NFY)
Leo
Virgo
Libra
Scorpio
Sagittarius
Capricorn (NFY)
Aquarius (NFY)
Pisces (NFY)
Arachne (thirteenth sign of the
* Lunar Zodiac. NFY)*
Angel Bowl
Healing Angel Bowl
Archangel Bowl (or Fixed Stars –
* Michael – Aldebaran)*
Archangel Bowl (Gabriel) NFY
Archangel Bowl (Raphael –
* Regulus)*
Archangel Bowl (Haniel) NFY
Archangel Bowl (Samael) NFY
Archangel Bowl (Zadkiel) NFY
Archangel Bowl (Cassiel – or
* Jophiel) NFY*
Aura Healing Bowl (auric re-
* alignment)*
Colour Ray Bowl – Red Ray Bowl
Pink Ray Bowl
Orange Ray Bowl
Yellow Ray Bowl
Green Ray Bowl

Blue Ray Bowl
Indigo Ray Bowl
Amethyst Ray Bowl
Violet Ray Bowl
Purple Ray Bowl
Silver Ray
Gold Ray
Pearl Ray
White Light Ray
Multi-Ray Bowl – Two or more
  colours
Shamanic Journey Bowl
Initiation Bowl
Samadhi Bowl – state of samadhi
  is induced
Flowing Water Bowls – Jumping
* Bowls (Water)*
Windhorse Bowls – Jumping
* Bowls (Air)*
Fiery Worlds Bowls – Jumping
* Bowls (Fire)*
Oracle Bowl – including Jumping
  Bowls
'Far Memory' Bowl – effect of
* sound induces this experience*
'Out-of-body' Bowl – effect of
* sound induces this experience*
Trance Bowl – effect of sound
* induces this experience*
Ceremonial Bowl – used during
* specific ceremonies, e.g. Guru*
* Purnima*
Balancing Bowl – effect of sound
* induces this experience L/R*
* hemispheres*
Meditation Bowl – Visualizations
* (particular to the bowl)*
Meditation Bowl – Breathing
* (various)*
Meditation Bowl – Shi-ne
* (Tranquil Abiding)*
Meditation Bowl – Nada Yoga
Meditation Bowl – Deep Listening

*Meditation Bowl – Vac (four
  differentiated partials – found in
  Manipuri Lingam bowls)*
*Meditation Bowl – Gnana Yoga
  (Self-enquiry)*
Meditation Bowl – Sky Gazing
Meditation Bowl – Trekchod
*Meditation Bowl – Nothingness
  (*for exercises working with spirit
  mediumship)
Meditation Bowl – Voidness
Meditation Bowl – Impermanence
*Meditation Bowl – Formlessness
  (as in section 2)*
Meditation Bowl – Mindfulness
Meditation Bowl – Divine Light
Meditation Bowl – Star Light
Meditation Bowl – Yab-Yum
*Meditation Bowl – Nirvanic
  consciousness*
Wisdom Bowl – to overcome
  the rational mind and resolve
  conflict using the higher mind
Purification Bowl
Crystal-cleansing Bowl

Healing Ray Bowl
*Projection of Healing Enfoldment
  Bowl*
Relaxation Bowl
Quiet Mind Bowl
Courage Bowl
Humility Bowl
Joy Bowl
Peace Bowl
Patience Bowl
Accepting Impermanence Bowl
Acceptance/Surrender Bowl
Indomitable Bowl
Invincible Bowl
Resolute Bowl.
Hungry Ghosts Bowl
Dedication Bowl
Invocation Bowl
Mystical Bowl
Shambhala Bowl
Alchemical Bowl
Ritual Bowl (no writing)
*Psychic/Paranormal/Alchemical
  Bowl*

The observations I have made have arisen from direct perception
with no preconceived ideas regarding the specific bowls. This
list has not arisen from brainstorming, or imagination, nor has
it been derived intellectually, but rather from observations of
bowls that I own or have handled i.e. experienced (via checking
the 'stories' of bowls from the collections of others). In the case
of archangels, I own the two for the equinoxes but don't have the
two others but I can speculate that these could exist. This is also
the case with bowls for colour rays or zodiac signs etc where I
have several but not the entire range.

However, I feel that I must include a word of warning to the
wise. If any seller tells you (or if it is so-called in a label underneath
alongside the price, etc,) that the bowl you are interested in is a
'*Master Bowl*', a '*Chakra Bowl*', a '*Planet Bowl*' an '*Archangel
Bowl*', or any bowl above listed – ignore it. If a bowl is stated to

have come from regions or countries such as Assam, Manipur, China, Japan, Bengal, etc., this may be true – these are fairly regular designs and shapes – but any claims to subtle energies e.g. *planet bowl, chakra bowl,* etc., are highly unlikely to mean much because the ability to divine such a thing is rare. If you are happy to work with a supposed bowl energy that has been characterized using a mechanistic model defined by its frequency (i.e., a note close to a piano note or a frequency derived from mathematical applications of planetary orbits, etc., e.g. Cousto) then fine, that is your choice although I'd not recommend it. I work intuitively and suggest you always follow your own conscience in this field.

Many of these bowl names have been originated by myself (those in italics and all in the supersensible section) while alternative names might exist, given by other people involved with bowls (e.g., Stem Bowls, Pedestal Bowls, or Naga Bowls for my *Chalice Bowls*) and other terms might yet exist but I've not found them. Only very recently in the past forty plus years of my experience have sellers provided names to identify specific shapes or designs.

Appendix C: Dhyani Buddhas

Dhyani Budda	Akshobhya	Ratnasambhava	Amitabha	Amogasiddhi	Vairocana
Element	Water	Earth	Fire	Air	Space
Meaning of Name	Unshakeable One	Source of Preciousness	Infinite Light	One Who Accomplishes What is Meaningful	On Who Comletely Manifests
Buddha Family	Vajra	Ratna	Padma	Karma	Buddha
Symbol	Vajra	Jewel	Lotus	Double Vajra	Wheel
Wisdom	Mirror-like Wisdom	Wisdom of Equanimity	Discriminating Wisdom	All-Accomplishing Wisdom	Wisdom of Emptiness
Negative Expression	Jealousy	Ignorance	Greed	Pride	Anger
Direction	East	South	West	North	Centre
Sense	hearing	smell	sight	touch	taste
Emotions	anger	joy	sympathy	fear	grief
Five Elements (Pulses)	Water	Earth	Fire	Wood	Metal
Mudra	earth-touching	giving	meditation	fear-dispelling	dharmacakra

Table of the Dhyani Buddhas

Notes

Please refer to 'Recommended Reading' for full details of books mentioned if an abbreviated form is given in the notes.

Chapter 1, Himalayan Singing Bowls (p. 11)

[1] Henry Wolff and Nancy Hennings, with Drew Gladstone. 'Tibetan Bells' (Island Records HELP3, 1972); 'Tibetan Bells II' (Celestial Harmonies 13005-2, 1978) and 'Tibetan Bells III' (Celestial Harmonies 13027-2, 1988). Mickey Hart, Henry Wolff & Nancy Hennings, 'Yamantaka' (Celestial Harmonies 13003-2. 1991 CD Reissue - Bonus Tracks). Henry Wolff & Nancy Hennings. 'The Bells of Sh'ang Sh'ung' (Celestial Harmonies 13037-2. 1991)

[2] Alain Presencer. 'The Singing Bowls of Tibet' (Saydisc SDL326,1981).

[3] Mitch Nur. Interview from 1999 between *Dimensions* Magazine and Mitch Nur. Available on his website www.9ways.

[4] Tom Kenyon, 'The Gandarva Experience' (S.E.E. Publishing Co., T801-CD. 1996)

[5] Suren Shrestha, HOW TO HEAL WITH SINGING BOWLS, p. 15.

[6] Mitchell L. Gaynor, M.D., SOUNDS OF HEALING, p. 111

[7] Taken from Percival Price, BELLS AND MAN, p. 26

[8] Hui-Li, compiler: THE LIFE OF HUAN-TSANG, translated under the auspices of the Shan Shih Buddhist Institute (Peking, 1959), p. 102

Chapter 2, Bells in Ancient China (p. 38)

[1] Taken from Eric Hatch, THE LITTLE BOOK OF BELLS (Hawthorn Books, Inc. 1964), p. 25

[2] Taken from John Camp, IN PRAISE OF BELLS: THE FOLKLORE AND TRADITIONS OF BRITISH BELLS (London, Robert Hale, 1988), Chapter 6: 'Magic Bells'; Satis N. Coleman, BELLS: THEIR HISTORY, LEGENDS, MAKING AND USES (Rand McNally & Company. 1928), Chapter VI: 'Celtic Bell Lore'.

[3] Taken from Satis N. Coleman, BELLS: THEIR HISTORY, p. 51.

[4] Satis N. Coleman, BELLS: THEIR HISTORY, p. 295

[5] 'The Imperial Bells of China' (Fortuna Records,17075-2 (1990); 'Unique Music of Great Antiquity' (China Record Corporation, CCD-89/28 (1997); 'Tan Dun Symphony' 1997 (SK 63368). 'Awakening the Bells' on BBC TV, 1997; 'Bells Tolling Chu', two programmes on 'Centre Stage' on China's CNNTV channel, featuring the Hubei Provincial Music and Dance Theatre, and BBC Radio 3 programme featuring an interview with Sin-yan Shen, 'Acoustics of Ancient Chinese Bells' (1992).

[6] Percival Price, BELLS AND MAN, p. 9

[7]Y. H. Yum, 'Study on Korean Bell' (Acad. Korean studies, Seoul, 1988)

[8]From J. S. Gale, A HISTORY OF THE KOREAN PEOPLE, quoted in Evelyn McCune, THE ARTS OF KOREA (Rutland and Tokyo, 1962), p. 100

[9]Percival Price, BELLS AND MAN, p. 43

Chapter 3, Tibet (p. 54)

[1]Nicholas Roerich, HIMALAYAS: ABODE OF LIGHT. Nalanda Publications, 1947, p. 13

[2]Dirk Gillabel, SINGING BOWLS, p. 15

[3]Alexandra David-Neel, MAGIC AND MYSTERY IN TIBET, p. 210

[4]Norma Levine, BLESSING POWER OF THE BUDDHAS, pp. 100-1

[5]Philip Rawson, SACRED TIBET. (Thames & Hudson, 1991), p. 80

[6]H.H. Dalai Lama, 'The Gyuto Monks: Freedom Chants from the Roof of the World' (Notes for the booklet with RYKODISC RCD20113, 1989)

[7]Buddhist Monks of Maitri Vihar Monastery. 'Tibetan Mantras and Chants: Sounds of the World' (SOW 90179); Ven. Karma Tashi, 'Tibetan Singing Bowls' (Tibetan Music Center, 1999. TMC-CD-02); the Venerable Choesang, 'The Medicine of Sound: Tibetan Healing with Singing Bowls and Chants' (Paradise Music, PMCD0032, 2006)

[8]Dirk Gillabel, SINGING BOWLS, pp. 9, 17

[9]John Vincent Bellezza, ZHANG ZHUNG FOUNDATIONS OF CIVILIZATION IN TIBET: A HISTORICAL AND ETHNOARCHAEOLOGICAL STUDY OF THE MONUMENTS, ROCK ART, TEXTS, AND ORAL TRADITION OF THE ANCIENT TIBETAN UPLAND. Verlag der Osterreichischen Akademie der Wissenschaften, 2008), p. 206

[10]Nicholas Roerich, HIMALAYAS: ABODE OF LIGHT, pp. 52-53

[11]Nicholas Roerich, HIMALAYAS: ABODE OF LIGHT, pp. 130-131

[12]White Eagle, SPIRITUAL UNFOLDMENT: THE FOURTH BOOK (1944), p. 37

[13]Frank Perry, 'Deep Peace'. (Mountain Bell Music. BELCD 001, 1980)

[14]Eva Rudy Jansen, SINGING BOWLS, p. 5

[15]On Dirk Gillabel's website (http://www.soul-guidance.com/houseofthesun/soosbio.htm), and taken from the book JOSKA SOOS, IK GENEES NIET, IK HERSTEL DE HARMONIE, written by Robert Hartzman, published by Karnak, Amsterdam, 1985

[16]Alexandra David-Neel, TIBETAN JOURNEY (1912; now published by Book Faith India, 1992), p. 184

[17]Alexandra David-Neel, TIBETAN JOURNEY, pp. 186-7

[18]Christoph Baumer, TIBET'S ANCEINT RELIGION, BON, p. 78

Chapter 5, Drilbu (p. 96)

[1]Colin McPhee, MUSIC IN BALI (1966)

[2]Manly Palmer Hall, 'Ritual Instruments of Northern Buddhism' in PRS Journal, Spring 1971, pp. 46-7

Chapter 6, The World of Singing Bowls (p. 103)

[1]Nicholas Roerich, HIMALAYAS: ABODE OF LIGHT, pp. 21-2

[2]Ted Andrews, SACRED SOUNDS, p. 158.

[3]JEHM Films, 'The Yogis of Tibet: a film for posterity' (2002) FILM DVD.

[4]Alvin Lucier, 'Septet for Three Winds, Four Strings and Pure Wave Oscillator' (Lovely Music Ltd. LCD 1018, 1990)

[5]White Eagle, SPIRITUAL UNFOLDMENT: THE THIRD BOOK (1944), p. 37

[6]Omraam Mikhael Aïvanhov, THOUGHT OF THE DAY (Duddleswell, Uckfiield, Sussex, Editions Prosveta S.A.), 25 May 2009

[7]La Monte Young and Marian Zazeela, 'The Tamburas of Pandit Pran Nath' (Just Dreams JD 001, recorded 1982, released on CD in limited edition, 1999)

[8]Wavanal software is available from www.hibberts.co.uk/wavanal.htm

Chapter 7, Yin–Yang (p. 125)

[1]Omraam Mikhael Aïvanhov, 'The Key to the Problems of Existence', in COMPLETE WORKS, Volume 11 (Editions Prosveta, 2003), p. 31

Chapter 8, Mallets and Wands (p. 133)

[1]Frank Perry, 'Tibetan Singing Bowls', Volume 3: 'Ancient Tibetan Initiation Bowls' (Mountain Bell Music, 2001. BELCD 012)

[2]Frank Perry, 'Tibetan Singing Bowls', Volume 1: 'The Healing Bowls of Tibet' (Mountain Bell Music, 1998. BELCD 006)

Chapter 10, Techniques (p. 160)

[1]Frank Perry, 'Tibetan Singing Bowls', Volume 2: 'Path to Shambhala'. (Mountain Bell Music, 2000. BELCD 010)

[2]Jenny Dent, A COMPANION TO THE QUIET MIND: A PERSONAL JOURNEY IN THE LIGHT OF WHITE EAGLE'S TEACHING. Liss, Hampshire, White Eagle Publishing Trust, 1993

[3]Frank Perry, 'Tibetan Singing Bowls', Volume 3: 'Ancient Tibetan Initiation Bowls' (Mountain Bell Music, 2001. BELCD 012)

[4]Frank Perry, 'Tibetan Singing Bowls', Volume 1: 'The Healing Bowls of Tibet' (Mountain Bell Music, 1998. BELCD 006)

[5]Frank Perry, 'Tibetan Singing Bowls', Volume 13. 'Tibetan Peace: Freedom to Follow their True Path (Mountain Bell Music, 2007. BELCD 024)

[6]Frank Perry, 'Tibetan Singing Bowls', Volume 2: 'Path to Shambhala'. (Mountain Bell Music, 2000. BELCD 010)

[7]The Overtone Choir, 'Sound and Light' (1998).

[8]Frank Perry, 'Tibetan Singing Bowls', Volume 2: 'Path to Shambhala'. (Mountain Bell Music, 2000. BELCD 010)

[9]Frank Perry, 'Tibetan Singing Bowls', Volume 7. 'Himalayan Studies, #2). (Mountain Bell Music. 2005 BELCD 017)

[10]Frank Perry, 'Tibetan Singing Bowls', Volume 3: 'Ancient Tibetan Initiation Bowls' (Mountain Bell Music, 2001. BELCD 012)

[11]Frank Perry, 'Tibetan Singing Bowls', Volume 1: 'The Healing Bowls of Tibet' (Mountain Bell Music, 1998. BELCD 006)

[12]Frank Perry, 'Tibetan Singing Bowls', Volume 13. 'Tibetan Peace: Freedom to Follow their True Path (Mountain Bell Music, 2007. BELCD 024)

[13]Frank Perry, 'Tibetan Singing Bowls', Volume 2: 'Path to Shambhala'. (Mountain Bell Music, 2000. BELCD 010)

[14]Frank Perry, 'Tibetan Singing Bowls', Volume 7. 'Himalayan Studies, #2). (Mountain Bell Music. 2005 BELCD 017)

[15]Frank Perry, 'Tibetan Singing Bowls', Volume 7. 'Himalayan Studies, #2). (Mountain Bell Music. 2005 BELCD 017)

[16]Frank Perry, 'Tibetan Singing Bowls', Volume 3: 'Ancient Tibetan Initiation Bowls' (Mountain Bell Music, 2001. BELCD 012)

[17]Frank Perry, 'Tibetan Singing Bowls', Volume 3: 'Ancient Tibetan Initiation Bowls' (Mountain Bell Music, 2001. BELCD 012)

Chapter 11, Struck and Stroked Bowls (p. 195)

[1]Nicholas Roerich, HIMALAYAS: ABODE OF LIGHT, pp. 26-7, 29

[2]H. P. Blavatsky, THE VOICE OF THE SILENCE, p. 41 (#79)

[3]Thomas D. Rossing, SCIENCE OF PERCUSSION INSTRUMENTS, p. 186

[4]Nicholas Roerich. Several hundred paintings, including this one, may be viewed on the New York-based website – www.roerich.org

Chapter 12, Bowl Stories (p. 221)

[1]Yellow Hat Productions, Inc.: 'Jesus in India'. Film/DVD (2008)

[2]Guru R.H.H. TALK DOES NOT COOK THE RICE, p. 55

[3]Rudolf Steiner, INITIATION AND ITS RESULTS, p. 23

[4]Rudolf Steiner, INITIATION AND ITS RESULTS, p. 7

[5]Frank Perry, 'New Atlantis' (Celestial Harmonies 14007-2. 1983)

[6]'Spirit of Tibet: the Life and World of Dilgo Khyentse Rinpoche (Beckmann BD131 1998), and 'Brilliant Moon: Glimpses of Dilgo Khyentse Rinpoche' (Axiom Films. AXM640 2010)

[7]Frank Perry, 'Deep Peace'. (Mountain Bell Music. BELCD 001, 1980)

Chapter 13, Teachings from the Bowls (p. 252)

[1]Omraam Mikhael Aïvanhov, THOUGHT OF THE DAY (Duddleswell, Uckfiield, Sussex, Editions Prosveta S.A.) 1 February, 2009)

[2]Lama Anagarika Govinda, PSYCHO-COSMIC SYMBOLISM, p. 38.

[3]Nicholas Roerich, REALM OF LIGHT, p. 212.

[4]Nicholas Roerich, SHAMBHALA, p. 148.

[5]Nicholas Roerich, REALM OF LIGHT, p. 56.

[6]Ngakpa Chogyam, WEARING THE BODY OF VISIONS (Aro Books, 1995), p. 49.

Chapter 14, Elemental Bowls (p. 281)

[1]Geoffrey Hodson, THE KINGDOM OF THE GODS

[2]Dirk Gillabel website: Joska Soos sound & light paintings (http://www.soul-guidance.com/houseofthesun/soosother.htm & http://www.soulguidance.com/houseofthesun/soosentities.htm)

[3]Tenzin Wangyal Rinpoche, HEALING WITH FORM, ENERGY AND LIGHT, p. 74

[4]Tenzin Wangyal Rinpoche, HEALING WITH FORM, ENERGY AND LIGHT, p. 72

[5]Tenzin Wangyal Rinpoche, HEALING WITH FORM, ENERGY AND LIGHT, p. 73

[6]Tenzin Wangyal Rinpoche, HEALING WITH FORM, ENERGY AND LIGHT, p. 73
[7]Tenzin Wangyal Rinpoche, HEALING WITH FORM, ENERGY AND LIGHT, p. 73
[8]Frank Perry, 'Tibetan Singing Bowls', Volume 3: 'Ancient Tibetan Initiation Bowls' (Mountain Bell Music, 2001, BELCD 012) Track 3: 'Within the Space of Silence'
[9]Ngakpa Chogyam, RAINBOW OF LIBERATED ENERGY
[10]Tenzin Wangyal Rinpoche, HEALING WITH FORM, ENERGY AND LIGHT

Chapter 15, Sound Made Visible (p. 295)

[1]Paul Devereux, STONE AGE SOUNDTRACKS, pp. 89-92
[2]Bruce L. Cathie, 'The Bridge to Infinity: 371244' (Alternative Science) (post 1997) 139–46
[3]White Eagle, SPIRITUAL UNFOLDMENT: THE THIRD BOOK (1944), p. 87
[4]Swami Sivananda, MUSIC AS YOGA, pp. 39-41.
[5]John Stuart Reid, EGYPTIAN SONICS, p. 15
[6]John Stuart Reid, EGYPTIAN SONICS, p. 21
[7]Theodore Levine with Valentina Suzukei, WHERE RIVERS AND MOUNTAINS SING, pp. 175-6

Chapter 16, Partials Exercises (p. 317)

[1]Omraam Mikhael Aïvanhov, ORAL TEACHINGS (Duddleswell: Prosveta)
[2]White Eagle, INITIATIONS ON THE PATH OF THE SOUL
[3]Christopher Hansard, THE TIBETAN ART OF LIVING: WISE BODY, WISE MIND, WISE LIFE. Hodder & Stoughton, 2001, p. 28
[4]Swami Sri Yukteswar, THE HOLY SCIENCE, pp. 7-20; Paramahansa Yogananda, AUTOBIOGRAPHY OF A YOGI, p. 174; Richard Poor, DWAPARA YUGA AND YOGANANDA
[5]Dane Rudhyar: see Recommended Reading
[6]White Eagle, INITIATIONS ON THE PATH OF THE SOUL: see Recommended Reading
[7]Rudolf Steiner, INITIATION AND ITS RESULTS, p. 23
[8]Paramahansa Yogananda, THE SECOND COMING OF CHRIST: THE RESURRECTION OF THE CHRIST WITHIN YOU. A REVELATORY COMMENTARY ON THE ORIGINAL TEACHINGS OF JESUS, Volume I (Self-Realization Fellowship, 2000), p 187
[9]T. Subba Row, THE TWELVE SIGNS OF THE ZODIAC
[10]Dale S. Wright, THE SIX PERFECTIONS
[11]Rudolf Steiner, INITIATION AND ITS RESULTS, p. 7
[12]Lama Surya Das, BUDDHA IS AS BUDDHA DOES
[13]Alice A. Bailey, THE LABOURS OF HERCULES

Chapter 17, Nada Yoga (p. 370)

[1]Paramahansa Yogananda, THE SECOND COMING OF CHRIST: THE RESURRECTION OF THE CHRIST WITHIN YOU. A REVELATORY COMMENTARY ON THE ORIGINAL TEACHINGS OF JESUS, Volume II (Self-Realization Fellowship, 2000), pp. 989-90
[2]Guru R.H.H. TALK DOES NOT COOK THE RICE, Series 2, p. 119
[3]Hazrat Inayat Khan, THE SUFI MESSAGE OF HAZRAT INAYAT KHAN, p. 61.
[4]H. P. Blavatsky, THE VOICE OF THE SILENCE, pp. 28-30

[5]Shri Brahmananda Sarasvati (Ramamurti S. Mishra M.D), NADA YOGA: THE SCIENCE, PSYCHOLOGY AND PHILOSOPHY OF ANAHATA NADA YOGA' Monroe, CT: Baba Bhagavandas Publishing Trust. 'Classifications of Nada'. Third Edition 2007, pp. 31-3

[6]Swami Sivananda, KUNDALINI YOGA, p. 175

[7]Swami Sivananda, KUNDALINI YOGA, p. 176.

[8]Swami Yogeshwaranand Saraswati, SCIENCE OF DIVINE SOUND, p. 58

[9]Dane Rudhyar, THE PLANETARIZATION OF CONSCIOUSNESS, p. 78

[10]Pauline Oliveros, DEEP LISTENING, p. 22

[11]Georg Feuerstein, TANTRA: THE PATH OF ECSTASY. Boston: Shambhala Publications, Inc., p. 189–90

[12]David Frawley (Pandit Vamadeva Shastri), MANTRA YOGA AND PRIMORDIAL SOUND – SECRETS OF SEED (BIJA) MANTRAS. Lotus Press. 2010, p. 55.

[13]H. P. Blavatsky, THE VOICE OF THE SILENCE, p. 226

[14]Helena Petrovna Blavatsky (TPH 1900), p. 425

[15]Helena Petrovna Blavatsky (TPH 1900), p. 360

Chapter 18, Mantra (p. 402)

[1]White Eagle, 'Serenity and Health: The Way Lies Open': address by White Eagle on August 4th 1968, reprinted in *Stella Polaris*, vol. xliii (1943), p. 168

[2]Sri Aurobindo, THE FUTURE POETRY (SABCL, vol. 9), p. 369.

Chapter 19, Planet Bowls (p. 417)

[1]John Mead, SOUND PERECPTIONS, p. 21

[2]Dane Rudhyar: see Recommended Reading

[3]C. W. Leadbeater and Annie Besant, see Recommended Reading

[4]Geoffrey Hodson, MUSIC FORMS

[5]Geoffrey Hodson, CLAIRVOYANT INVESTIGATIONS

[6]Sri Shyamji Bhatnagar and David Isaacs, Ph.D. MICROCHAKRAS, p. 59

[7]Harish Johari, CHAKRAS: ENERGY CENTRES OF TRANSFORMATION, p. 47

[8]Thomas Ashley-Farrand, CHAKRAS MANTRAS, Appendix, p. 255

Chapter 20, More on the Chakras (p. 440)

[1]Thomas Ashley-Farrand, CHAKRA MANTRAS, Appendix, p. 255-9

[2]Shyam Sundar Goswami, LAYAYOGA, p.182

[3]Mircea Eliade, YOGA, IMMORTALITY, AND FREEDOM, p. 128

[4]Omraam Mikhael Aïvanhov, MAN'S SUBTLE BODIES AND CENTRES, pp. 151-2

[5]Omraam Mikhael Aïvanhov, MAN'S SUBTLE BODIES AND CENTRES, p. 138

[6]Omraam Mikhael Aïvanhov, MAN'S SUBTLE BODIES AND CENTRES, p. 139

Glossary

Avalokitesvara translates as 'the one who looks out onto the world with eyes of compassion'. In Tibetan he is named Chenrezig and is the patron deity of that country and H. H. the Dalai Lama is considered to be an embodiment of this great being. Chenrezig in female form is White Tara and Green Tara (Gwanyin or Kuan Yin in China and Kwannon in Japan).

Agni Yoga. The yoga of Fire, said to be the yoga for our current time. The fire of spirit gradually transforms the personality. From the book AGNI YOGA (1929): 'The most precise name will be Agni Yoga. It is precisely the element of fire which gives to this Yoga of self-sacrifice its name'. *Agni yoga* is also a blend of *karma yoga* (action performed for its own sake with no attachment to the fruits of the action), *bhakti yoga* (the way of the heart, of the devotee along the Path of Love for the Beloved), and also *raja yoga* (the yoga of meditation, leading to *samadhi* – ecstatic union with the divine). The pan-yoga nature of *agni yoga* is rooted in the teaching of *kalachakra* (the wheel of time), a teaching which constructively unites many domains of spiritual knowledge and is ascribed to the various lords of *shambhala*. *Kalachakra* is a Tantra found in Tibetan Buddhism and periodically offered to thousands of people by H. H. the Dalai Lama. See also p. 69, reference Nicholas and Helena Roerich.

Anti-node: an acoustic term given to those areas of a plate or string, or tube, etc, that vibrate and are most active when sounding.

Bhajans: any type of devotional song. Including songs based upon poems by spiritually-minded poets such as Kabir, Mirabai, Tulsidas, etc., or else the teachings of saints or episodes from scriptures or descriptions of the gods all serve the purposes of *bhajan*.

Bhakti Yoga: the spiritual approach to God that stresses all-surrendering love as the principal means of communion with God.

Bianzhong: a set of ancient Chinese orchestral tuned bells.

Bindu is most often depicted as a dot and is the term used to describe this spiritual origination of all things. There is also a chakra in the head named the *bindu chakra*.

Bodies of Man. In occultism it is taught that we each possess a Physical, Etheric, Astral, Mental, Buddhic and Nirvanic body. As our physical body permits us to function upon the physical plane so too our astral body provides a vehicle for experience on the astral plane; our mental body upon the mental plane, and so on.

Bon: the pre-Buddhist localized ensemble of faiths existing in Tibet that coalesced into the spiritual path of this name. The Bonpo don't follow Shakyamuni Buddha but have their own Buddha, Tonpa Shenrab Miwoche.

Bon-po: followers of the Bon Path.

Buddhist Sects. The four main sects in Tibetan Buddhism are the Nyingma, Kagyupa, Sakya, and Gelugpa.

Chenrezig – see Avolakitesvara.

Chladni: Ernst E.F. Chladni (1756-1827) is credited as being the founder of modern acoustics with the invention of the Chladni Plate. This is a flat plate of metal clamped in position and then, with some substance sprinkled across its surface, bowed to produce sound with each harmonic from the plate producing a repeatable geometric pattern. These patterns are based upon the nodes and anti-nodes within the plate.

Cymatics. A name given by Hans Jenny to his work investigating the making of sound visible based upon the Chladni Plate. As with Chladni material is sprinkled upon the plate which when sounded creates geometric figures arising from those areas of the plate that are not vibrating (nodes).

Daoism. One of the three great traditions of China, sometimes spelt Taoism. It is generally linked to the philosophy of Lao Tse, around 600 CE. It is largely a mystical Way of nature.

Dharma. Eternal principles of righteousness that uphold all creation; man's inherent duty to live in harmony with these principles.

Dhyani Buddhas. Five exist and there are details in Appendix C. These are meditation buddhas representing a fivefold meditation process, used also as aids for transformation within ourselves of the five elements to which they are linked. Sometimes a sixth is mentioned, considered to be over and above these five.

Dhyani Chohan. This term is used in the Alice A. Bailey teachings for those Masters at the Head of each of the Seven Rays within the White Lodge (also the Hierarchy, the White Brotherhood) under whom are all other Masters on their ray plus adepts, initiates, disciples, neophytes, etc.

Drilbu. The name given to the Tibetan ritual handbell, called *ghanta* in India and *rei* in Japan.

Dzogchen – Given as the highest level of attainment within the Nyingma tradition of Tibetan Buddhism and also in Bon. It denotes instant enlightenment, otherwise spoken of as 'no process' or as 'immediate process'. For further definition see p. 258.

Equal Tempered Tuning. In this system all of the twelve semitones are tuned to divide up the octave equally. This is primarily for instruments of Fixed

Pitch. An instrument (such as the piano) is tuned in order to play in all of the keys. This is the standard method of tuning so that all instruments are similarly tuned to the piano in order that they all play in tune.

Hinayana Buddhism. Originally translated the 'Individual Vehicle' but usually translated as the 'Lesser Vehicle' where liberation of oneself from the unreality of this samsaric world is sought after. *Hinayana* concerns itself with what are considered as being the verified words of the Lord Buddha. The first vehicle to unfold, it was a monastic or individual vehicle, so-called because it provided institutional, doctrinal, and contemplative methods for individuals to liberate themselves from egocentric delusion.

Jataka Tales: a compilation of stories about the lives of Buddha.

Jnana Yoga (pronounced 'gyana'). The path to union with God through transmutation of the discriminative power of the intellect into the omniscient wisdom of the soul.

Just Intonation: the oldest form of tuning one of our musical keys derived from the ratios found within the harmonic series. There are many varieties, one being Pythagorean tuning – after Pythagoras himself (around 600 BCE) An instrument would have to be retuned in order to play in any one of our twenty-four keys. 'Fixed pitch' instruments, such as the piano, proved especially cumbersome with this tuning.

Karma Yoga. The path to God through non-attached action and service. By selfless service, by giving the fruits of one's actions to God, and by seeing God as the sole Doer, the devotee becomes free of the ego and experiences God.

Kirtans. A form of chanting found in the *bhakti* (devotional) traditions, where one sings praises to the god/goddess. It is performed in a call-and-response style.

Lotus Sutra: is a revered Sutra of Mahayana Buddhism, otherwise entitled *Sutra of the Lotus of the Wonderful Law*.

Mahayana Buddhism. Originally translated 'Universal Vehicle', it is often translated today as 'Greater Vehicle', for it is based upon the Bodhisattva ideal of self-sacrifice. The Bodhisattva renounces *nirvana,* vowing to remain with humanity until all are ready to enter this celestial state. This form of Buddhism is prevalent in countries such as Tibet, China, Japan, etc. It was the second development in Buddhism.

Mandala: two-dimensional depiction originally in the medium of coloured sands of the palace of a deity from the Tibetan Buddhist pantheon. These typically combine the circle, square, and triangles in their main forms. Used in religious ceremonies designed to allow the central being (the particular deity) to come among their earthly worshippers.

Mantra Yoga. Divine communion attained through devotional concentrated repetition of root-word sounds that have a spiritually beneficial vibratory potency.

Meditation. Generally this refers to interiorised concentration with the objective of perceiving or otherwise experiencing God.

Microtones. Generally taken to mean the notes-within-the-notes of our Western music, 'micro' signifying smaller than a semitone – and providing divisions of the musical scale into a total larger than the twelve of our Diatonic scale (for instance, the twenty-four tones of the octave known as quarter tones) – meaning that often these other notes lie inbetween our usual twelve and may not include any of those twelve.

Nadi: the channels along which the pranic energy flows throughout the body.

Nine Ways: the Nine Vehicles of Bon are parallel to the Nine Ways of the Nyingmapa tradition, in which the teachings are sub-divided into nine vehicles. According to this classification, the doctrines of the Dzogchen meditation system are considered the ultimate and highest vehicle.

Node. In our case, areas of a plate or string that do not vibrate when a sound is produced.

OM: a sacred word in Hinduism and Buddhism also spelt AUM.

Om mani padme hum – The most famous mantra of Tibet, usually translated as 'OM the Jewel in the Lotus.'

Partials. Musical sounds when produced generate other sounds that are progressively higher in pitch than the starting (fundamental) note. 'Partials' is a term used for these in the context of bells, where the pitch is irregular and the terms 'harmonics' or 'overtones' are better reserved for the regular intervals tuned instruments produce.

Prana: the energy current that sustains the human body, called *qi or chi* in Chinese acupuncture.

Rinpoche : meaning 'precious jewel', the title signifies one who has reached a certain level of attainment within the Tibetan Buddhist traditions.

Samadhi: the highest state of meditative consciousness, whereby the meditator is completely absorbed in oneness with God, the Supreme or the Nameless (Void).

Samsara refers to the realm of illusion or to the delusion of our everyday consciousness and attachment to ego. The impermanence of this world is contrasted to the transcendant awareness of *nirvana*.

Self is capitalized in the text to denote the *atman,* otherwise known as the God Self or Higher Self and to distinguish it from the ego or the ordinary self or everyday personality.

Shamanism: a form of spiritual practice that involves travelling to the inner worlds and often going into trance.

Shambhala: the place that the Masters of the White Lodge (a.k.a. the White Brotherhood, Spiritual Hierarchy) are said to inhabit. In Tibetan Buddhist tradition *shambhala* is a mystical kingdom hidden somewhere beyond the snow peaks of the Himalaya. It is mentioned in various ancient texts including the *kalachakra* and the ancient texts of the Zhang Zhung culture which pre-dated Buddhism in Western Tibet. The Bon scriptures speak of a closely-related land called *olmolungring*. As with many concepts in Vajrayana Buddhism, the idea of *shambhala* is said to have 'outer', 'inner' and 'secret' meanings. The outer meaning understands *shambhala* to exist as a physical place, although only individuals with the appropriate *karma* can reach it and experience it as such. There are various ideas about where this society is located, but it is often placed in central Asia, north of Tibet.

Sutra: a book of teaching from the Lord Buddha. The Sutric path is the slowest with no short cuts but a steady safe progression.

Tai-Chi symbol: the Chinese symbol of the union of *yin* and *yang*.

Tantra is a faster spiritual path than Sutra, and often spoken of as self-liberation.

Thanka, thangka: a kind of painting (most often upon silk or cloth) depicting a central deity or spiritual figure and around this either the main human representatives, or spiritual school/tradition, or accompanying deities, or events from their life. It is for use in meditation or rituals.

Theosophical Society. Founded in 1875 by H. P. Blavatsky and Colonel Olcott, it is famous for bringing the ancient wisdom teachings to the West (including the several bodies of man) from the Trans-Himalayan Occult brotherhood. The brotherhood of man is one of its founding principles.

The Seven Rays arise from teachings given by 'the Tibetan' (the Master D. K.) through Alice A. Bailey, but also appeared in earlier Theosophical publications. It is said that within the Trans-Himalayan Occult Brotherhood D. K. is the Master most knowledgeable on the subject of the seven rays.

Ting-sha: small Tibetan cymbals usually in a pair tied together with a piece of cord. Also known as ting-shaws, ding-sha, Ting-shag and Nagani Bells.

Triratna: the 'Three Jewels' of Buddhism, namely the Buddha (an 'Awakened One', full of compassion), *dharma* (his teaching and truth) and sangha (the community who have joined the 'family' and been given a new name – monk, nun, or lay men or women).

Tunings. Ways of dividing up the octave. Our tuning system is based upon twelve notes to the octave, which can be tuned to Just Intonation or Well-Tempered or (now) Equal-Tempered tunings. Different musical styles, from various regions, will have a number of tunings for their stringed instruments to play. In practice, this means that the musical intervals vary. Seven of these twelve notes are used to make a musical key signature. There exists also Pentatonic scales (five to the octave).

Vajrayana or Tantrayana Buddhism: the third form of Buddhism and the one most involved with the Tantric teachings that came from India to Tibet. It is a magical vehicle, also called the Diamond, Thunderbolt (*vajra*), and technology (Tantra) vehicle. Rapid progress along the path towards the *bodhisattva* ideal is the aim of this school.

Wand: the name I use for the piece of wood used when stroking the bowl to produce a continuous sound.

Well-Tempered Tuning: a system of tuning our diatonic scale that arose around the time of J. S. Bach. All tuning systems are dependent upon mathematical formulae. The primary purpose of this tuning system was to avoid the problems caused by changing musical key on 'fixed pitch' instruments, e.g. the piano. It is considered to be not as perfect in this endeavour as our current Equal-Tempered tuning system.

Yab-Yum: most usually depicts a god with their consort in sexual union – either in sculpture or in a *thanka*.

Yuga: Hindu term denoting a cycle or sub-period of creation, outlined in ancient texts and relating to the Equinoctial Cycle of around 24,000 years, which occurs within the much longer universal cycle in the ancient texts from India. There are four *yuga*, known as *satya yuga* (or Gold Age), *kali yuga* (Dark Age), *dwapara yuga* (Bronze Age) and *treta yuga* (Silver Age), which are further understood to follow an ascending and descending process. These yugas are not of the same equal length of time and there is a debate about their extent (see p. 322).

Zhang-Zhung. Otherwise transliterated as 'Sh'ang Sh'ung'. An ancient site in the Garuda Valley where the ancient Bon lived together in a cave complex. Various travellers have found this ancient centre. The kingdom was conquered by the Tibetan monarchy in the eighth century CE. It included what is today western Tibet from Khyung-lung Dngul-mkhar to Dongra Khyung-rdzong in the East to Tsang in the South and to Kashmir in the West.

Recommended Reading

Aïvanhov, Omraam Mikhael, MAN'S SUBTLE BODIES AND CENTRES. Duddleswell, Sussex, Editions Prosveta, 1987

—, CREATION, ARTISTIC AND SPIRITUAL. Editions Prosveta, 1987

—, MAN'S TWO NATURES, HUMAN AND DIVINE. Editions Prosveta, 1985

Andrews, Ted. SACRED SOUNDS: TRANSFORMATION THROUGH MUSIC AND WORD. Llewellyn Publications, 1992

Anrias, David. THROUGH THE EYES OF THE MASTERS: MEDITATIONS AND PORTRAITS. Routledge & Kegan Paul Ltd. 1969

Arnsby-Jones, George. THE JOURNEY OF SOUNDING FIRE. Arthur H. Stockwell, Ltd. 1956

Arya, Pandit Usharbudh. MANTRA AND MEDITATION. Himalayan International Institute of Yoga Science & Philosophy of the USA. 1981

Ashley-Farrand, Thomas. CHAKRA MANTRAS: LIBERATE YOUR SPIRITUAL GENIUS THROUGH CHANTING. Weiser Books. 2006

—, MANTRA MEDITATION: CHANGE YOUR KARMA WITH THE POWER OF SACRED SOUND. Sounds True, Inc. 2004

Atmananda, Swami. THE FOUR YOGAS: THE FOUR PATHS TO SPIRITUAL ENLIGHTENMENT (in the words of ancient Rishis). Bharatiya Vidya Bhavan. 1991

Author of *The Initiate*, by. THE ADEPT OF GALILEE: A STORY AND AN ARGUMENT. George Routledge & Sons Ltd. 1920

Avalon, Arthur. THE SERPENT POWER kunda press. 1900

Bailey, Alice A. THE LABOURS OF HERCULES. Lucis Publishing Company. 1974

Baschet, Francois. LES SCULPTURES SONORES: THE SOUND SCULPTURES OF BERNARD AND FRANCOIS BASCHET. Sound World. 1999

Baumer, Christoph. TIBET'S ANCIENT RELIGION, BON. Orchid Press. 2002

Beaulieu, John. MUSIC AND SOUND IN THE HEALING ARTS. Station Hill Press, Inc. 1987

Beer, Robert. TIBETAN TING-SHA: SACRED SOUND FOR SPIRITUAL GROWTH. Connections Book Publishing. 2004

Bellezza, John, Vincent. ZHANG ZHUNG (Foundations of Civilization in Tibet. A Historical and Ethnoarchaeological Study of the Monuments, Rock Art, Texts, and Oral Tradition of the Ancient Tibetan Upland.) Verlag der Osterreichischen Akademie der Wissenschaften. 2008

Bernard, Patrick. MUSIC AS YOGA: DISCOVER THE HEALING POWER OF SOUND. Mandala Publishing. 2004

Bhatnagar, Sri Shyamji, and Isaacs,

David, Ph.D. MICROCHAKRAS: INNERTUNING FOR PSYCHOLOGICAL WELL-BEING. Inner Traditions. 2009

Blavatsky, H.P. THE VOICE OF THE SILENCE. Theosophical Publishing House. 1971

Blofeld, John. MANTRAS: SACRED WORDS OF POWER. Unwin Paperbacks. 1977

—, THE TANTRIC MYSTICISM OF TIBET: A PRACTICAL GUIDE TO THE THEORY, PURPOSE, AND THE TECHNIQUES OF TANTRIC MEDITATION. Arkana, 1992

Brahmananda, Swami. WISDOM TEACHINGS FROM THE MANDUKYA UPANISHAD. The Divine Life Society. 2005

Bromage, Bernard. TIBETAN YOGA. The Aquarian Press. 1979

Campbell, Don. MUSIC PHYSICIAN FOR TIMES TO COME: AN ANTHOLOGY. Quest Books, Theosophical Publishing House. 1991

Campbell, Joseph. THE INNER REACHES OF OUTER SPACE: METAPHOR AS MYTH AND AS RELIGION. Harper & Row Publishers. 1988

—, MYTHS OF LIGHT: EASTERN METAPHORS OF THE ETERNAL. New World Library. 2003

Chogyam, Ngakpa. RAINBOW OF LIBERATED ENERGY: WORKING WITH EMOTIONS THROUGH THE COLOUR AND ELEMENT SYMBOLISM OF TIBETAN TANTRA, Element Books, 1986

Chogyam, Ngakpa with Khandro Dechen. SPECTRUM OF ECSTASY: EMBRACING THE FIVE WISDOM EMOTIONS OF VAJRAYANA BUDDHISM. Shambhala Publications, Inc. 2003

Conroy, Ellen. THE FOUR GREAT INITIATIONS. Rider & Co. 1928

Cooper, Lyz. SOUNDING THE MIND OF GOD. THERAPEUTIC SOUND FOR SELF-HEALING AND TRANSFORMATION. Hampshire, U.K.: O Books, 2009

Cousto, Hans, THE COSMIC OCTAVE. ORIGIN OF HARMONY: PLANETS, TONES, COLORS – THE POWER OF INHERENT VIBRATIONS. Liferhythm, 1987

D'Angelo, James. SEED SOUNDS FOR TUNING THE CHAKRAS: VOWELS, CONSONANTS AND SYLLABLES FOR SPIRITUAL TRANSFORMATION. Destiny Books. 2012

Danielou, Alain. THE RAGAS OF NORTHERN INDIAN MUSIC. Munshiram Manoharlal Publishers Pvt. Ltd. 2010

Das, Lama Surya. BUDDHA IS AS BUDDHA DOES: THE TEN ORIGINAL PRACTICES FOR ENLIGHTENED LIVING. HarperCollins. 2007

David-Neel, Alexandra. MAGIC AND MYSTERY IN TIBET. Unwin. 1984

Dennis, Lynnclaire. Jytte Brender McNair. Louis H. Kauffman (Ed). THE MEREON MATRIX: UNITY, PERSPECTIVE AND PARADOX. Elsevier. 2013

Devereux, Paul. STONE AGE SOUNDTRACKS: THE ACOUSTIC ARCHAEOLOGY OF ANCIENT SITES. (Companion to Channel Four's 'Secrets of the Dead: Sounds from the Stone Age' TV programme). Vega. 2001

Dey, Suresh Chandra. THE QUEST FOR MUSIC DIVINE. Ashish Publishing House, 1990

Duffin, Ross W. HOW EQUAL TEMPERAMENT RUINED HARMONY (AND WHY

YOU SHOULD CARE). W. W. Norton & Company Ltd. 2007

Emoto, Masaru. MESSAGES FROM WATER. Hado, Kyokusha. 2003

Eagle, White. SPIRITUAL UNFOLDMENT II: THE MINISTRY OF ANGELS AND THE INVISIBLE WORLD OF NATURE. Liss, White Eagle Publishing Trust. 1969

—, SPIRITUAL UNFOLDMENT: THE FOURTH BOOK. London, White Eagle Lodge, 1944

—, WISDOM FROM WHITE EAGLE. Liss, White Eagle Publishing Trust. 1974

—, WALKING WITH THE ANGELS: A PATH OF SERVICE. Liss, White Eagle Publishing Trust. 1998

—, INITIATIONS ON THE PATH OF THE SOUL. Liss, The White Eagle Publishing Trust. Rev. 2007

—, WHITE EAGLE'S LITTLE BOOK OF ANGELS. Liss, White Eagle Publishing Trust. 2010

—, CHAKRAS, AURAS, SUBTLE BODIES. Liss, The White Eagle Publishing Trust. 2013

Eliade, Mircea. YOGA, IMMORTALITY AND FREEDOM. Princeton University Press, 2009

Falkenhausen, Lothar Von. SUSPENDED MUSIC: CHIME-BELLS IN THE CULTURE OF BRONZE AGE CHINA. University of California Press. 1993

Frawley, Dr David. MANTRA YOGA AND PRIMAL SOUND: SECRETS OF SEED (BIJA) MANTRAS. Lotus Press. 2010

Fyzee-Rahamin, Atiya Begum. THE MUSIC OF INDIA. Kessinger. No date.

Garbett, Sir Colin. THE RINGING RADIANCE. Shri K.L. Khanna. 1972

Gardner, Kay. SOUNDING THE INNER LANDSCAPE. Caduceus Publications, Stonington, Maine. 1990

Gaynor, Mitchell L. SOUNDS OF HEALING: A PHYSICIAN REVEALS THE THERAPEUTIC POWER OF SOUND, VOICE AND MUSIC. Broadway Books, New York 1999

Gillabel, Dirk. SINGING BOWLS: A GUIDE TO HEALING THROUGH SOUND. Woodstock, NY, U.S.A. 2001

Goldman, Jonathan. HEALING SOUNDS: THE POWER OF HARMONICS. Element Books Limited. 1992

Goodall, Howard. BIG BANGS: THE STORY OF FIVE DISCOVERIES THAT CHANGED MUSICAL HISTORY. Vintage Books. 2001

Goswami, Shyam Sundar. LAYAYOGA: THE DEFINITIVE GUIDE TO THE CHAKRAS AND KUNDALINI. Inner Traditions. Rochester, Vt. 1999

Govinda, Lama Anagarika. FOUNDATIONS OF TIBETAN MYSTICISM. Rider & Co., 1960

—, PSYCHO-COSMIC SYMBOLISM OF THE BUDDHIST STUPA. Dharma Publishing. 1976

—, CREATIVE MEDITATION AND MULTI-DIMENSIONAL CONSCIOUSNESS. Unwin (Mandala). 1977

Gray, Rain. TIBETAN SINGING BOWLS: A HISTORICAL PERSPECTIVE. Lama Thupten Lobsang Leche as interviewed by Rain Gray. In the Light Publishers. 1989. Available via his website:- http://www.bodhisattva.com/history_singing_bowl.htm.

Gustafson, Eric, A. THE RINGING SOUND: AN INTRODUCTION TO THE SOUND CURRENT (The Key to Enlightenment Ringing in Your

Soul). Conscious Living Press. 2000

Hall, Manly Palmer. THE NOBLE EIGHTFOLD PATH. Philosophical Research Society, Inc. 1964

—, 'Ritual Instruments of Northern Buddhism', in volume 30, no. 4 of the *Philosophical Research Society Journal* (Spring 1971)

Hamilton, James. FARADAY: THE LIFE. Harper Collins. 2009

Heindel, Max. THE MUSICAL SCALE AND THE SCHEME OF EVOLUTION. Rosicrucian Fellowship. 1972

Heline, Corinne. MUSIC: THE KEY-NOTE OF HUMAN EVOLUTION. New Age Press, Inc. 1965

Heline, Theodore.THE ARCHETYPE UNVEILED: A STUDY OF THE SOUND PATTERNS FORMED BY THE CREATIVE WORD. New Age Press. 1965

Hess, Peter. SINGING BOWLS FOR HEALTH AND INNER HARMONY THROUGH SOUND MASAGE. Verlag Peter Hess. 2008

Hodson, Geoffrey. THE KINGDOM OF THE GODS. Theosophical Publishing House. 1972

—, THE BROTHERHOOD OF ANGELS AND OF MEN. Theosophical Publishing House. 1973

—, MUSIC FORMS. Theosophical Publishing House. 1976

Hodson, Geoffrey. THE SEVEN HUMAN TEMPERAMENTS. Theosophical Publishing House. 1973

—, ANGELS AND THE NEW RACE. Theosophical Publishing House. 1971

—, CLAIRVOYANT INVESTIGATIONS. Theosophical Publishing House. 1984

Hodgson, Joan. ASTROLOGY, THE SACRED SCIENCE. White Eagle Publishing Trust. 1978

—, (as Cooke, Joan). WISDOM IN THE STARS. White Eagle Publishing Trust. 1959

Jansen, Eva Rudy. SINGING BOWLS: A PRACTICAL HANDBOOK OF INSTRUCTION AND USE. Binkey Kok Publications, Haarlem, NL, 1990

— & Dick de Ruiter. SINGING BOWL HANDBOOK: SINGING BOWLS, TINGSHAWS, BHELL, DORJE. Binkey Kok 2008

Jenny, Hans. CYMATICS Basilius Press. 1974

—, CYMATICS II Basilius Press. 1974

—, CYMATICS Macromedia 2000

Johari, Harish. TOOLS FOR TANTRA. Destiny Books. 1986

—, CHAKRAS: ENERGY CENTRES OF TRANSFORMATION. Destiny Books. 1987

Johnson, Russell & Kerry Moran. KAILAS: ON PILGRIMAGE TO THE SACRED MOUNTAIN OF TIBET. Thames & Hudson. 1989

Khan, Hazrat Inayat, THE SUFI MESSAGE OF HAZRAT INAYAT KHAN, VOLUME XI. (The Mysticism of Sound, Music, The Power of the Word, Cosmic Language). London, Barrie & Jenkins, 1962, 1973.

—, THE MUSIC OF LIFE: THE INNER NATURE AND EFFECTS OF SOUND. Omega Publications. 1983, 2005.

Kenyon, Tom. BRAIN STATES. United States Publishing. 1994

Keyes, Laurel Elizabeth, with Don Campbell. TONING THE CREATIVE AND HEALING POWER OF THE VOICE. DeVorss Publications Camarillo,

California. 2008 (New edition with CD).

Lauterwasser, Alexander. WATER SOUND IMAGES. Macromedia Publishing , 2006

Leadbeater, C. W. THE CHAKRAS: A MONOGRAPH. Theosophical Publishing House. 1971

— & Besant, Annie. THOUGHT FORMS, Theosophical Publishing House (1925 onwards). 1901

Levine, Norma. BLESSING POWER OF BUDDHAS: SACRED OBJECTS, SECRET LANDS. Vajra Publications, second edition, 2008

Levine, Theodore with Valentina Suskei. WHERE RIVERS AND MOUNTAINS SING: SOUND, MUSIC, AND NOMADISM IN TUVA AND BEYOND. Indiana University Press, Bloomington & Indianapolis. 2006

Lewis, Robert C. THE SACRED WORD AND ITS CREATIVE OVERTONES: RELATING RELIGION AND SCIENCE THROUGH MUSIC. Oceanside, CA, Rosicrucian Fellowship, 1986

Leo, Alan. SYMBOLISM AND ASTROLOGY. L. N. Fowler & Co.

Lyddon, Andrew. WORKING WITH SINGING BOWLS: A SACRED JOURNEY. London: Polair Publishing, 2007

Mead, J. SOUND PERCEPTIONS, BOWL DIMENSIONS AND SHAMANS. Published privately, 1997

Michael, Salim. THE WAY OF INNER VIGILANCE. PATH TO THE INNER LIGHT AND THE REALIZATION OF ONE'S DIVINE NATURE. Signet Press. 1983

Mookerji, Ajit & Khanna Madhu. THE TANTRIC WAY: ART, SCIENCE, RITUAL. Thames & Hudson. 1993

Motoyama, Hiroshi. AWAKENING OF THE CHAKRAS AND EMANCIPATION. Human Science Press. 2003

Murray, Muz. SHARING THE QUEST. Element Books. 1986

Oliveros, Pauline. DEEP LISTENING: A COMPOSER'S SOUND PRACTICE. Deep Listening Publications. 2005

Paul, Russill. THE YOGA OF SOUND. HEALING AND ENLIGHTENMENT THROUGH THE SACRED PRACTICE OF MANTRA. New World Library. 2004

Poor, Richard. DWAPARA YUGA AND YOGANANDA: BLUEPRINT FOR A NEW AGE, 307 DWAPARA. 2007

Power, Richard, THE LOST TEACHINGS OF LAMA GOVINDA: LIVING WISDOM FROM A MODERN TIBETAN MASTER. New Age Books. 2007

Price, Percival. BELLS AND MAN. Oxford University Press. 1983

Rama, Swami. OM, THE ETERNAL WITNESS: SECRETS OF THE MANDUKYA UPANISHAD. Himalayan Institute Hospital Trust. 2007

Rawson, Philip. SACRED TIBET. Thames & Hudson. 1991

Reid, John Stuart. EGYPTIAN SONICS: A PRELIMINARY INVESTIGATION CONCERNING THE HYPOTHESIS THAT THE ANCIENT EGYPTIANS HAD DEVELOPED A SONIC SCIENCE BY THE FOURTH DYNASTY, 2520 BCE. Sonic Age Ltd. 2001

R.H.H, Guru. TALK DOES NOT COOK THE RICE: A COMMENTARY ON THE TEACHING OF AGNI YOGA. Samuel Weiser, Inc. 1982

—, TALK DOES NOT COOK THE RICE: A COMMENTARY ON THE TEACHING OF AGNI YOGA, series 2. Samuel Weiser. 1985

Rinpoche, Chogyam Trungpa. SE-
CRET BEYOND THOUGHT: THE FIVE
CHAKRAS AND THE FOUR KARMAS.
Vajradhatu Publications. 2008

Rinpoche, Tenzin Wangyal. HEAL-
ING WITH FORM, ENERGY AND LIGHT:
THE FIVE ELEMENTS IN TIBETAN SHA-
MANISM, TANTRA, AND DZOGCHEN.
Snow Lion Publications. 2002

—, THE FIVE ELEMENTS IN DZOGCHEN.
Ligmincha Institute. 2000

—, THE FIVE ELEMENTS IN TIBETAN
SHAMANISM AND TANTRA. Ligmincha Institute, second edn., 2003

—, TIBETAN SOUND HEALING: SEVEN
GUIDED PRACTICES FOR CLEARING
OBSTACLES, ACCESSING POSITIVE
QUALITIES, AND UNCOVERING YOUR
INHERENT WISDOM. Sounds True,
Inc. 2006

—, TIBETAN YOGAS OF BODY, SPEECH,
AND MIND. Snow Lion Publications. 2011

—, AWAKENING THE SACRED BODY:
TIBETAN YOGAS OF BREATH AND
MOVEMENT. Hay House, 2011

—, AWAKENING THE LUMINOUS MIND.
TIBETAN MEDITATION FOR INNER
PEACE AND JOY. Hay House, 2012

—, WONDERS OF THE NATURAL MIND:
THE ESSENCE OF DZOGCHEN IN THE
NATIVE BON TRADITION OF TIBET.
Station Hill Press. 1993

Rockwell, Irini. THE FIVE WISDOM
ENERGIES: A BUDDHIST WAY OF UN-
DERSTANDING PERSONALITIES, EMO-
TIONS, AND RELATIONSHIPS. Shamb-
hala Publications Inc. 2002

Roerich, Nicholas. REALM OF LIGHT.
Roerich Museum Press. 1931

—, SHAMBHALA. Nicholas Roerich
Museum. 1985

—, HIMALAYAS: ABODE OF LIGHT. Nalanda Publications, 1947

Rossing, Thomas D. SCIENCE OF
PERCUSSION INSTRUMENTS. World
Scientific. 2001

Row, T Subba. THE TWELVE SIGNS OF
THE ZODIAC. Wizards Bookshelf.
1977

Rudhyar, Dane. THE PLANETARIZA-
TION OF CONSCIOUSNESS. Servire/
Wassanaar. 1970

—, AN ASTROLOGICAL MANDALA: THE
CYCLE OF TRANSFORMATIONS AND
ITS 360 SYMBOLIC PHASES: A REINTER-
PRETATION OF THE SABIAN SYMBOLS,
PRESENTING THEM AS A CONTEMPO-
RARY AMERICAN I CHING. Random
House New York. 1973

—, THE MAGIC OF TONE AND THE ART
OF MUSIC. Shambhala Publishers.
1982

—, PATHS TO THE FIRE. Hermes Press,
Inc. 1978

—, CULTURE, CRISIS AND CREATIVITY.
Theosophical Publishing House.
1977

—, THE REBIRTH OF HINDU MUSIC.
Samuel Weiser, Inc. 1979

—, ART AS RELEASE OF POWER. Hamsa
Publications. 1930

Ruiter, Dick de. YOGA AND SOUND:
PRACTICAL NADA YOGA, THEORY
AND PRACTICE, WITH UNIQUE TRIAD
AND CHAKRA TONES FOR A MAGICAL
EFFECT. Binkey Kok Publications.
Havelte, Netherlands. 2005

Ruland, Heiner. EXPANDING TONAL
AWARENESS: A MUSICAL EXPLORATION
OF THE EVOLUTION OF CONSCIOUS-
NESS, GUIDED BY THE MONOCHORD.
Rudolf Steiner Press. 1992

Sanders, C.W. THE INNER VOICE.

Radha Soami Satsang Beas. Ninth edition, 1991

Sarasvati, Shri Brahmananda. DIRECT EXPERIENCE OF 'I-AM': APARAKSHANUBHUTTI BY SHRI SHANKARACHARYA. George Leone Publishing Centre. 1988

—, MANDUKYA UPANISHAD. George Leone Publishing Centre. 1990

—, THE SCIENCE, PSYCHOLOGY AND PHILOSOPHY OF ANAHATA NADA YOGA. Baba Bhagavandas Publishing Trust, Monroe NY 10950, USA. Rev. edn, 2007

Saraswati, Swami Pratyagatmananda. JAPASUTRAM: THE SCIENCE OF CREATIVE SOUND. Parampara. Rev. edn., 2007

Saraswati, Swami Satyananda. DHYANA YANTRAS: TOOLS FOR MEDITATION. Yoga Publications Trust. 2006

Saraswati, Swami Yogeshwaranand ji Maharaji. SCIENCE OF DIVINE SOUND: A TREATISE ON HIGHER YOGA. Yog Niketan Trust, 1984

Saraydarian, Torkom. THE CREATIVE SOUND: SACRED MUSIC, DANCE AND SONG. T.S.G. Publishing Foundation, Inc. 1999

—, TALKS ON AGNI, VOL. I. Aquarian Edcucational Group. 1987

Scott, Cyril. MUSIC: ITS SECRET INFLUENCE THROUGHOUT THE AGES. Samuel Weiser, Inc. 1969

Shrestha, Suren. HOW TO HEAL WITH SINGING BOWLS: TRADITIONAL TIBETAN HEALING METHODS. First Sentient Publications. 2009

Simmer-Brown, Judith. DAKINI'S WARM BREATH: THE FEMININE PRINCIPLE IN TIBETAN BUDDHISM. Shambhala Publishing Inc. 2001

Sivananda, Swami. MEDITATION ON OM AND THE MANDUKYA UPANISHAD. Divine Life Society. 1941

—, JAPA YOGA: A COMPREHENSIVE TREATISE ON MANTRA-SASTRA. Divine Life Society. 2005

—, MUSIC AS YOGA. Divine Life Society. 2007

—, TANTRA YOGA, NADA YOGA AND KRIYA YOGA. Divine Life Society. 1994

—, KUNDALINI YOGA. Divine Life Society. 2011

So, Jenny F. (editor) MUSIC IN THE AGE OF CONFUCIUS. Freer Gallery of Art & Arthur M. Sackler Gallery, Washington, DC

Steiner, Rudolf. INITIATION AND ITS RESULTS: A SEQUEL TO 'THE WAY OF INITIATION'. London, Theosophical Publishing Society. 1910

—, THE ARTS AND THEIR MISSION. Anthroposophic Press, 1964

—, THE FOUR TEMPERAMENTS. Anthroposophic Press, Inc. Second edn, revised, 1968

—, ART IN THE LIGHT OF MYSTERY WISDOM. Rudolf Steiner Press, London, 1970

—, EGYPTIAN MYTHS AND MYSTERIES. Anthroposophic Press, 1971

—, THE INNER NATURE OF MUSIC AND THE EXPERIENCE OF TONE. Anthroposophic Press, 1983

Sumedho, Ajahn. THE SOUND OF SILENCE. English Sanskrit Trust, Ltd. 2007

Tigunait, Pandit Rajmani. THE POWER OF MANTRA AND THE MYSTERY OF INITIATION. Himalayan International Institute of Yoga. 1996

Tucci, Giuseppe. THE THEORY AND PRACTICE OF THE MANDALA, WITH SPECIAL REFERENCE TO THE MODERN PSYCHOLOGY OF THE SUBCONSCIOUS. Rider & Company. 1971

Twelfth Khentin Tai Situpa, The. TILOPA: SOME GLIMPSES INTO HIS LIFE. Dzalendara Publications. 1988

Tyndall, John. SOUND. Longmans, Green, & Co. 1893

Van Dyke, Deborah. TRAVELLING THE SACRED SOUND CURRENT: KEYS FOR CONSCIOUS EVOLUTION. Sound Current Music. 2001

Vessantara. THE VAJRA AND BELL. Windhorse Publications. 2001

Watts-Hughes, Margaret. THE EIDO-PHONE VOICE FIGURES: GEOMETRICAL AND NATURAL FORMS PRODUCED BY VIBRATIONS OF THE HUMAN VOICE. Christian Herald Co., 1904

—, 'Visible Sound', in *The Century Magazine*, May 1891 (pp. 37-40)

Wilson, Burt. THE THIRD THEORY: CREATION ACCORDING TO THE ANCIENT WISDOM. Paloria Press, 2000

Wood, Ernest. THE SEVEN RAYS. Theosophical Publishing House. 1972

—, RAJA YOGA: THE OCCULT TRAINING OF THE HINDUS. Theosophical Publishing House.

Woodroffe, Sir John. SHAKTI AND SHAKTA. NuVision Publications, LLC. 1918. (2007)

—, THE SERPENT POWER, 1970

Wright, Dale S. THE SIX PERFECTIONS: BUDDHISM AND THE CULTIVATION OF CHARACTER. Oxford University Press, 2009

Yogananda, Paramahansa. AUTOBIOGRAPHY OF A YOGI. Los Angeles: Self-Realization Fellowship. Tenth edn, 1969

Yukteswar, Swami Sri. THE HOLY SCIENCE. Los Angeles: Self-Realization Fellowship, 1990

Index

List of Exercises

POLAIR PUBLISHING

The publishers of this book specialize in subjects such as astrology, meditation, self-help, alternative therapies, tai chi, and yoga. For a full list, see our website **www.polairpublishing.co.uk**, or for a printed catalogue, write to us at P. O. Box 34886, London W8 6YR or email info@polairpublishing.co.uk.

CENTAURY FOR VIRGO, ROCK ROSE FOR PISCES by Debbie Sellwood is a complete home reference of the many repertoires of flower essnces, arranged for prescription by their astrological sign. ISBN 978-1-905398-13-3

THE SHAKESPEARE ENIGMA by Peter Dawkins tackles the simple question, 'Who was Shakespeare?' and shows that, whoever he was, the dramatist of the plays was most unlikely to have been the actor from Stratford-upon-Avon. There is a wealth of contemporary focus in this penetrating study of the plays and their milieu. ISBN 978-0-9545389-4-1

THE POLAIR ILLUSTRATED YOGA DICTIONARY. Janita Stenhouse. Nearly 1500 Sanskrit terms explained for students and teachers. 160pp. ISBN 978-1-905389-17-1

YOUR YOGA BIRTHGUIDE Unique combination of a yoga teacher and a midwife writing together to help your or your students through childbirth with a profound growth in consciousness. By Jenny Beeken and Sally Townsend. 160pp, ISBN 978-1-905389-19-5

YOUR YOGA BODYMAP FOR VITALITY. Acclaimed yoga teacher Jenny Beeken puts the emphasis firmly on the body, joint by joint and limb by limb. Get to know your body better, whether you are active in sport or recovering from illness, or just seeking a more 'whole' lifestyle. This is yoga for everyone. Drawings, stop-action photographs and clear, precise instructions make this one of the most helpful yoga books around. ISBN 978-0-9545389-1-0

POLAIR GUIDES SERIES
The volumes of the Polair Guides series cover all sorts of mind/body/spirit issues briefly and clearly. Each book is illustrated. Titles so far include:

MAKING COMPLEMENTARY THERAPIES WORK FOR YOU Gaye Mack
     ISBN 978-1-905398-007-2
INCENSE Jennie Harding ISBN 978-0-9545389-7-2
CREATIVITY AND THE SIX SENSES Jennie Harding ISBN 978-1-905398-05-8
DON'T HOLD YOUR BREATH Jenny Beeken ISBN 978-0-9545389-9-6
IF I CHANGE, SO CAN THE WORLD Paula Pluck ISBN 978-1-905398-06-5
WHY MEDITATION WORKS James Baltzell ISBN 978-1-905398-08-9
MORNING YOGA, EVENING YOGA Janita Stenhouse
     ISBN 978-1-905398-09-6
ANCIENT WISDOM: FOLLOWING THE YOGA OF THE HEART Jenny
     Beeken ISBN 978-1-905398-11-9
ESSENTIAL OILS AND MEDITATION Kathleen Pepper
     ISBN 978-1-905398-12-6

POLAIR PERSONAL GROWTH

THE MEDITATION LIFESTYLE: GOING BEYOND THE PRACTICE
COLUM HAYWARD
To live entirely in the moment is one of the most wonderfully subversive things you can do, and this vibrant book tells you how! Meditation is sometimes understood as a spiritual 'high', but in fact it brings strength and richness to every minute of every day. With this awareness of each gorgeous moment, a new you develops – gentle, appreciative, sensitive to others, full of inner fire, strong before the winds and waves of life – and creates a non-violent warrior for truth. Meditation is a real form of experience and a skill, and its regular practice can change everyone's life. THE MEDITATION LIFESTYLE offers tips for regular meditators, commentary on the benefits of meditation, and above all details of how to change your life – in a moment! 144pp, 178 x 111mm, line illustrations. ISBN 978-1-905398-26-3

IN A NEW LIGHT
ANNA HAYWARD

Beneath a veil of your fears there is a you that at first you will only half recognize. It's a happier, brighter, more confident you, obscured by the defences that have built up and the doubts that conceal the self in all its magnificence. In this remarkable book, Anna carefully helps you to unveil the veil, reveal the real and BE the self you truly ARE! 192pp, 198 x 129 mm, ISBN 978-1-905398-25-6

NOW WE'RE COPING
CHRIS SANGSTER
A sound healer like Frank Perry, Chris Sangster offers coping strategies for when life gets really tough - including sound healing. It's based on mindfulness techniques but offers really practical guidance alongside some deep and comforting philosophy. ISBN 978-1-905398-30-0

HAND IN HAND WITH ANGELS by Kathleen Pepper. A yoga teacher shows you how to contact and work with angels. Large format, 176pp. ISBN 978-1-905389-21-8

MEDITATION IS... written and illustrated by Bodel Rikys, who tells you how to meditate ... through pictures that themselves bring the serene smile. ISBN 978-1-905398-14-0

IGNITING SOUL FIRE : SPIRITUAL DIMENSIONS OF THE BACH FLOWER REMEDIES. Author Gaye Mack shows that the impact of Dr Bach's famous flower essences goes deeper than has ever been demonstrated. Gaye extracts the hidden formula, which is linked both to the chakras and to the signs of the zodiac. ISBN 0-978-0-9545389-2-7

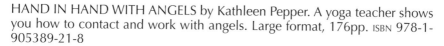

www.polairpublishing.co.uk

WORKING WITH SINGING BOWLS

ANDREW LYDDON

Polair Publishing's other title on singing bowls is a practical introduction to the subject. Learn the basics: how to buy a bowl, how to play it, keep it clearn - and begin to use it as part of a spiritual quest. Andrew learnt his craft from Frank Perry and has much helpful advice to offer. It is a book that enables every individual find contentment and self-realization through the power of sound. 'Polair Guides' series, ISBN 978-1-905398-10-2

POLAIR'S 'THE VIEW' SERIES

THE CATHAR VIEW:
THE MYSTERIOUS LEGACY OF MONTSEGUR.
The latest title in the VIEW series brings together over twenty sympathetic takes from well-known names on the extraordinary Cathars of the thirteenth century and the special secret they carried. A multifaceted approach. 288pp, 234 x156 mm, ISBN 978-1-905398-28-7

THE VIEW BEYOND:
SIR FRANCIS BACON: ALCHEMY, SCIENCE, MYSTERY
The extraordinary story of Bacon's influence on science today as well as the esoteric stature of the man who might have been Shakespeare. Was he, indeed one of those we call a Master? 20 contributors including Mark Rylance, Peter Dawkins, Ervin Laszlo, Rose Elliot. 'Shows that Francis Bacon's project for the advancement of knowledge included an esoteric understanding that goes far beyond the current materialistic scientific worldview. In doing so, it provides the essential missing dimension for a cultural renaissance emerging from Western civilization.' David Lorimer, Scientific and Medical Network. 288pp, 234 x156 mm, ISBN 978-1-905398-22-5

THE VIEW:
FROM CONAN DOYLE TO 'CONVERSATIONS WITH GOD'.
Twenty-nine influential thinkers including Neale Donald Walsch, Ervin Laszlo, Peter Russell and Dorothy Maclean offer their personal 'vital message' for the future of human kind in a time of change. Beginswith the legacy of Sir Arthur Conan Doyle's Spiritualism and published for his birth anniversary. Subjects range from spirituality to 'new' business. 288pp, 234 x156 mm, ISBN 978-1- 905398-18-8

www.polairpublishing.co.uk